Sun® Certified System Administrator for Solaris™ 10 Study Guide

(Exams CX-310-200 and CX-310-202)

Paul Sanghera

McGraw-Hill is an independent entity from Sun Microsystems, Inc. and is not affiliated with Sun Microsystems, Inc. in any manner. This publication and CD m be used in assisting students to prepare for the Sun Certified Solaris Administra Exam. Neither Sun Microsystems nor McGraw-Hill warrants that use of this publication and CD will ensure passing the relevant exam. Sun, Sun Microsysten and the Sun Logo are trademarks or registered trademarks of Sun Microsystem Inc. in the United States and other countries. Solaris and all Solaris-based marks trademarks or registered trademarks of Sun Microsystems, Inc. in the United States and other countries.

McGraw-Hill/Osborne
New York Chicago San Francisco Lisbon London Madrid
Mexico City Milan New Delhi San Juan Seoul Singapore Sydney Toronto

McGraw-Hill/Osborne
2100 Powell Street, 10th Floor
Emeryville, California 94608
U.S.A.

To arrange bulk purchase discounts for sales promotions, premiums, or fund-raisers, please contact **McGraw-Hill**/Osborne at the above address.

Sun® Certified System Administrator for Solaris™ 10 Study Guide (Exams CX-310-200 and CX-310-202)

Copyright © 2006 by The McGraw-Hill Companies. All rights reserved. Printed in the United States of America. Except as permitted under the Copyright Act of 1976, no part of this publication may be reproduced or distributed in any form or by any means, or stored in a database or retrieval system, without the prior written permission of publisher, with the exception that the program listings may be entered, stored, and executed in a computer system, but they may not be reproduced for publication.

1234567890 DOC DOC 0198765

Book p/n 0-07-222960-8 and CD p/n 0-07-222961-6
parts of
ISBN 0-07-222959-4

Acquisitions Editor
Tim Green

Production Coordinator
Katherine Bishop

Production Manager
Jody McKenzie

Acquisitions Coordinator
Jennifer Housh

Technical Editor
Nalneesh Gaur

Copy Editor
Harlan James

Proofreader
Shelly Gerger

Indexer
Randi Dubnick

Composition
G&S Book Services

Illustration
G&S Book Services

Series Design
Roberta Steel and Peter Hancik

Cover Series Design
Peter Grame

This book was composed with Adobe® InDesign®.

Information has been obtained by **McGraw-Hill**/Osborne from sources believed to be reliable. However, because of the possibility of human or mechanical error by our sources, **McGraw-Hill**/Osborne, or others, **McGraw-Hill**/Osborne does not guarantee the accuracy, adequacy, or completeness of any information and is not responsible for any errors or omissions or the results obtained from the use of such information.

To my son, Adam Sanghera, the thinking man
Who can walk the sky and talk the land
To venture to a beach for a crab grab
And play with the waves under sea's command
To command the music to enable my eyes
To see the universe in a grain of sand

About the Author

Dr. Paul Sanghera, SCSA, Project+, Linux+, Network+, SCJP, SCBCD, CNA, is a technologist, educator, and entrepreneur based in Silicon Valley, California. With a Ph.D. in physics from Carleton University, and a master's in computer science from Cornell University, Paul is an expert in TCP/IP networking, Java Technologies, and distributed systems. He has more than 15 years' experience working with the UNIX system environment, which includes working at world-class research laboratories, such as CERN and the Wilson Nuclear Synchrotron Laboratory at Cornell University, and in the computer industry. He has taught courses on a wide spectrum of operating systems—Solaris, Linux, and all flavors of Windows from Windows 95 to Windows 2003—at various educational institutions, including San Jose State University and Brooks College.

Paul has worked as a senior software engineer at Novell, and Netscape, and has contributed to technologies such as NDS and Netscape Communicator. As a senior software engineer and an engineering manager, he has been on the ground floor of several successful startups such as WebOrder and mp3.com.

The author and co-author of about 150 research papers published in American and European research journals, Paul has made professional presentations by invitation at several international conferences. He has also authored the *Sun Certified Business Component Developers Exam Study Kit.*

About the Technical Editor

Nalneesh Gaur has 12 years of professional experience in information technology and consulting. He has published numerous articles on information security for journals such as *Information Security Magazine*, *The ISSA Journal*, *Sys-Admin*, *The Linux Journal*, *Inside Solaris*, among others. Nalneesh is the technical editor for several Solaris books published by McGraw-Hill/Osborne. He also speaks on the topic of Internet fraud at various security conferences. Nalneesh has a master's degree in civil engineering from the University of Oklahoma. He holds the SUN Enterprise Certified Engineer, CISSP, and ISSAP certifications.

CONTENTS AT A GLANCE

CONTENTS

ACKNOWLEDGMENTS

As they say (well, if they don't any more, they should), first things first. Let me begin by thanking Scott Rogers for not ignoring my first email to him, which finally led to this writing project. My sincere thanks to both Scott Rogers and Timothy Green for offering me the wonderful opportunity to write this book. With two thumbs up, thanks to all the incredibly hard-working folks at Osborne: Tim Green, Jessica Wilson, and Jennifer Housh, for their team spirit and professionalism, which made this project a smooth ride.

I am thankful to Nalneesh Gaur, the technical editor of this book, for doing an excellent job in reviewing each chapter and offering valuable feedback. It is my pleasure to acknowledge the hard work of the production team at G&S Book Services, in particular, Katherine Bishop, the production coordinator, and Harlan James, the copy editor.

In some ways, writing this book is an expression of the technologist and educator inside me. I thank my fellow technologists who guided me at various places during my journey in the computer industry from Novell to Dream Logic: Chuck Castleton at Novell, Delon Dotson at Netscape and MP3.com, Kate Peterson at Weborder, and Dr. John Serri at Dream Logic. I also thank my colleagues and seniors in the field of education for helping me in so many ways to become a better educator: Dr. Gerald Pauler, Brooks College; Professor David Hayes, San Jose State University; Professor Michael Burke, San Jose State University; and Dr. John Serri, University of Phoenix.

Friends always lend a helping hand, in many visible and invisible ways, in almost anything important we do in our lives. Without them, the world would be a very boring and uncreative place. Here are a few I would like to mention: Stanley Huang, Patrick Smith, Kulwinder, Major Bhupinder Singh Daler, Ruth Gordon, Srilatha Moturi, Baldev Khullar, and the Kandola family (Gurmail and Sukhwinder).

Last, but not least, my appreciation (along with my heart) goes to my wife Renee for not getting irritated with my using the living room as the author room to write this book.

INTRODUCTION

I think, therefore I am.

—René Descartes

The primary purpose of this book is to help you pass the Sun Certified System Administrator for Solaris 10 Exams CX-310-200 and CX-310-202. Since the book has a laser-sharp focus on the exam objectives, expert system administrators who want to pass the exam can use this book to ensure that they do not miss any objective. Yet, it is not an exam cram book. The chapters and the sections within each chapter are presented in a logical learning sequence: every new chapter builds upon knowledge acquired in previous chapters, and there is no hopping from topic to topic. The concepts and topics, both simple and complex, are clearly explained. This facilitates stepwise learning and prevents confusion, making this book useful also for beginners who want to get up to speed quickly to get certified, even if they are new to system administration. Furthermore, Chapter 1 bridges the gap for beginners, and experts can choose to skip it. Regardless if you are a beginner or an expert, you will find yourself returning to this book as a handy reference even after you have taken and passed the exam.

In This Book

This book tells the story of Solaris system administration in a cohesive, concise, yet comprehensive fashion. Although it's not an exam cram, each section of each chapter is directly associated with a specific exam objective clearly spelled out in the beginning, and each chapter ends with two exam-focused features: Two-Minute Drill and Inside the Exam.

At the time of this book's publication, all the exam objectives were final and posted on the Sun Web site and the final exams had been released. Sun announced its commitment to measuring real-world skills. This book is designed with that premise in mind: The author has practical experience in the field, using the Solaris operating environment in hands-on situations, and has followed the development of the product since early beta versions. Furthermore, the author has contributed to the development of the exam by participating in the blueprint survey phase of the exam development.

The exam assumes that you have a minimum of 6 to 12 months of experience as a system administrator and that you have an in-depth knowledge of basic UNIX and

Solaris OS commands. Therefore, it is essential that you work with the operating environment to gain and enhance your proficiency. Toward that end, this book includes practical step-by-step exercises in each chapter that are designed to give you hands-on experience as well as guide you in learning the Solaris 10 operating environment itself, and not just learning *about* it.

Part I of the book covers the CX-310-200 exam, which is a prerequisite for the CX-310-202 exam covered in Part II of the book.

Typographical Conventions

Following are the typographical conventions used in presenting the commands in this book:

- A word in angle brackets < > represents a variable part of a construct. You must provide its value.
- Square brackets around a construct means the construct is an option, for example, `cd [dir]`.
- A vertical bar between constructs mean the constructs are alternatives.
- A word in bold is the command name.
- Italics are used to emphasize special terms.

On the CD-ROM

The CD-ROM contains the MasterExam that provides you with a simulation of the actual exam. For more information on the CD-ROM, please see the Appendix.

In Every Chapter

We've created a set of chapter components that call your attention to important items, reinforce important points, and provide helpful exam-taking hints. Take a look at what you'll find in every chapter:

- Every chapter begins with the **Certification Objectives**—what you will need to know in order to pass the section on the exam dealing with the chapter topic. The objective headings are based on the official exam objectives spelled out within the chapter, so you'll always know which objective you are working on!
- **Exam Watch** notes call attention to information about, and potential pitfalls in, the exam. These helpful hints are written by authors who have taken the exams and received their certification—who better to tell you what to worry about? They know what you're about to go through!

- **Exercises** are interspersed throughout the chapters. These are step-by-step exercises that allow you to get the hands-on experience you need in order to pass the exam. They help you master skills that are likely to be an area of focus on the exam. Don't just read through the exercises; they are hands-on practice that you should be comfortable completing. Learning by doing is an effective way to increase your competency with a product.

- **On the Job** notes describe the issues that come up most often in real-world settings. They provide a valuable perspective on certification-and product-related topics. They point out common mistakes and address questions that have arisen from on-the-job discussions and experience.
- **Scenario and Solutions** sections lay out potential problems and solutions in a quick-to-read format.

SCENARIO & SOLUTION	
Which command would you issue to enable the rlogin service whose PMRI name is `network/login/rlogin`?	`svcadm enable network/login:rlogin`
Now, how will you disable this service?	`svcadm disable network/login:rlogin`

- The **Certification Summary** provides you the big unified picture while reviewing the salient concepts in the chapter.

- The **Two-Minute Drill** at the end of every chapter is a checklist of the main points of the chapter. It can be used for last-minute review.
- **Inside the Exam** at the end of every chapter highlights the important points in the chapter from the perspective of the exam: the stuff that you must comprehend, the stuff that you should watch out for because it might not fit with your common sense or with the ordinary order of things, and the stuff that you should memorize for the exam.

- The **Self Test** has a two-prong purpose: to help you test your knowledge about the material presented in the chapter and to help you evaluate your ability to answer the exam questions based on the exam objectives covered in the chapter. By taking the Self Test after completing each chapter, you'll reinforce what you've learned from that chapter while becoming familiar with the structure of the exam questions. The answers to these questions, as well as explanations of the answers, can be found at the end of each chapter.

Last-Minute Preparations

Once you've finished working through this book, set aside some time to do a thorough review before the exam. You might want to return to the book several times and make use of all the methods it offers for reviewing the material:

1. *Re-read all the Two-Minute Drills* or have someone quiz you.
2. *Re-read all the Inside the Exam* sections or have someone quiz you. You can also use the drills and Inside the Exam sections as a way to do a quick prep before the exam. You might want to make some flash cards out of 3 × 5 index cards that have the Two-Minute Drill and Inside the Exam material on them.
3. *Re-read all the Exam Watch and On the Job notes*. Remember that these notes emphasize the important points from the exam viewpoint.
4. *Review all the S&S sections* for quick problem solving.
5. *Re-take the Self Tests*. Taking the tests right after you've read the chapter is a good idea, because the questions help reinforce what you've just learned. However, it's an even better idea to go back later and do all the questions in the book in one sitting. Pretend that you're taking the live exam. When you go through the questions the first time, you should mark your answers on a separate piece of paper. That way, you can run through the questions as many times as you need until you feel comfortable with the material.
6. *Complete the exercises*. Did you do the exercises when you read through each chapter? If not, do them now! These exercises are designed to cover exam topics, and there's no better way to get to know this material than by practicing. Be sure you understand why you are performing each step in each exercise. If there is something you are not clear on, re-read that section in the chapter.

Taking the Exam

Sun offers the following three certifications for Solaris OS:

1. Sun Certified System Administrator for the Solaris Operating System.
2. Sun Certified Network Administrator for the Solaris Operating System.
3. Sun Certified Security Administrator for the Solaris Operating System.

This book prepares you for the Sun Certified System Administrator certification, which is also a prerequisite for taking the exam for the Sun Certified Network Administrator certification. To get the certification, you must pass both exams:

CX-310-200 and CX-310-202. The details about these exams are listed in the following table:

Exam Detail	CX-310-200	CX-310-202
Prerequisite	None	CX-310-200
Exam type	Multiple choice, including drag and drop	Multiple choice, including drag and drop
Total number of questions	59	61
Pass score	61%	62%
Maximum time allowed	90 minutes	90 minutes
Price (may vary by country, and also if you have discount coupons)	$150.00	$150.00

The question types are multiple choice and may include drag and drop. In most of the questions, you are asked to select the correct answers out of multiple answers presented for a question. The number of correct answers is given. Pay attention to the **Exhibit** button if it appears in a question. You click it to get the required information for the question. An exhibit usually contains a command, the output from a command, or both. The question, in this case, will test your understanding of the command and the output. While preparing for the exam, it is important to become familiar with the options (at least the most commonly used options) and output of a each command included in the exam objectives.

For the latest information on the exam, you can visit the following Web site: http://www.suned.sun.com.

Following are the main steps in the process of taking the exam:

1. First, you should purchase an exam voucher from your local Sun Education Services Office. You can also purchase the voucher online by going to http://suned.sun.com/US/certification/register/index.html.
2. The exams are conducted by Prometric all across the world, and you need to schedule your exam with them. After you have purchased the exam voucher, contact an authorized Prometric Testing Center near you. You can get the information regarding this from the Web site http://www.prometric.com.
3. Reach the testing center 15 minutes before the test start time, and be prepared to show two forms of ID, one of which must be a photo ID.

4. After you finish the test, the computer screen will display the exam result, that is, if you have passed or not. You will also receive a printed copy of the detailed results.
5. Within a month or so after you pass the second exam, you will receive your certificate from SUN in the mail.

Best wishes for the exams; go get 'em!

Exam Readiness Checklist

Exam CX-310-200

Exam Objective	Chapter #
1.1 Explain the Solaris 10 OS installation and upgrade options for CD / DVD, including how to provide Minimal Installations for SPARC, x64, and x86-based systems. 1.2 Perform an OS installation from CD / DVD for SPARC, x64, and x86- based systems.	2
2.1 Explain the Solaris 10 OS directory hierarchy, including root subdirectories, file components, and file types, and create and remove hard and symbolic links.	4
2.2 Explain disk architecture including the UFS file system capabilities and naming conventions for devices for SPARC, x64, and x86-based systems. 2.3 Use the prtconf and format commands to list devices, explain critical issues of the /etc/path_to_inst file, and reconfigure devices by performing a reconfiguration boot or using the devfsadm command for SPARC, x64, and x86-based systems. 2.4 Given a scenario, partition a disk correctly using the appropriate files, commands, and options, and manage disk labels using SMI and EFI labels as they relate to disk sets.	5
2.5 Explain the Solaris 10 OS file system, including disk-based, distributed, devfs, and memory file systems related to SMF, and create a new UFS file system using options for <1Tbyte and > 1Tbyte file systems. 2.6 Given a scenario, check and resolve Solaris 10 OS file system inconsistencies using fsck, and monitor file system usage using the command line (df, du, and quot commands).	4
2.7 Perform mounts and unmounts on a Solaris 10 OS file system, and use volume management to access mounted diskettes and CD-ROMs, restrict access, troubleshoot volume management problems, and explain access methods without volume management.	5
2.8 Perform Solaris 10 OS package administration using command-line interface commands and manage software patches for the Solaris OS, including preparing for patch administration and installing and removing patches using the patchadd and patchrm commands.	2
3.1 Given a scenario, explain boot PROM fundamentals, including OpenBoot Architecture Standard, boot PROM, NVRAM, POST, Abort Sequence, and displaying POST to serial port for SPARC. 3.2 Given a scenario, explain the BIOS settings for booting, abort sequence, and displaying POST, including BIOS configuration for x64 and x86-based system. 3.3 Execute basic boot PROM commands for a SPARC system. 3.4 Use the Xorg configuration files or kdmconfig utility to configure the keyboard, display, and mouse devices for an x64 and x86 based system. 3.5 Perform system boot and shutdown procedures, including identifying the system's boot device, creating and removing custom device aliases, viewing and changing NVRAM parameters, and interrupting an unresponsive system. 3.6 Explain the Service Management Facility and the phases of the boot process. 3.7 Use SMF or legacy commands and scripts to control both the boot and shutdown procedures.	3

Exam Readiness Checklist

Exam CX-310-200

Exam Objective	Chapter #
4.1 Explain and perform Solaris 10 OS user administration, and manage user accounts and initialization files.	6
4.2 Monitor system access by using appropriate commands. 4.3 Perform system security by switching users on a system, and by becoming root and monitoring su attempts. 4.4 Control system security through restricting ftp access and using /etc/hosts.equiv and $HOME/ .rhosts files, and SSH fundamentals. 4.5 Restrict access to data in files through the use of group membership, ownership, and special file permissions.	7
5.1 Configure and administer Solaris 10 OS print services, including client and server configuration, starting and stopping the LP print service, specifying a destination printer, and using the LP print service. 5.2 Control system processes by viewing the processes, clearing frozen processes, and scheduling automatic one-time and recurring execution of commands using the command line	8
6.1 Given a scenario, develop a strategy for scheduled backups, and backup an unmounted file system using the appropriate commands. 6.2 Perform Solaris 10 OS file system restores using the appropriate commands, including restoring a regular file system, the /usr file system, the /(root) file system, and performing interactive and incremental restores for SPARC, x64, and x86 based systems. 6.3 Backup a mounted file system by creating a UFS snapshot and performing a backup of the snapshot file. 6.4 Restore data from a UFS snapshot and delete the UFS snapshot.	9

Exam Readiness Checklist

Exam CX-310-202

Exam Objective	Chapter #
1.1 Control and monitor network interfaces including MAC addresses, IP addresses, network packets, and configure the IPv4 interfaces at boot time. 1.2 Explain the client-server model and enable/disable server processes.	10
2.1 Explain virtual memory concepts and given a scenario, configure, and manage swap space. 2.2 Manage crash dumps and core file behaviors. 2.3 Explain NFS fundamentals, and configure and manage the NFS server and client including daemons, files, and commands. 2.4 Troubleshoot various NFS errors. 2.5 Explain and manage AutoFS and use automount maps (master, direct, and indirect) to configure automounting.	12
3.1 Analyze and explain RAID (0,1,5) and SVM concepts (logical volumes, soft partitions, state databases, hot spares, and hot spare pools). 3.2 Create the state database, build a mirror, and unmirror the root file system.	13

Exam Readiness Checklist

Exam CX-310-202

Exam Objective	Chapter #
4.1 Configure role-based access control (RBAC) including assigning rights profiles, roles, and authorizations to users. 4.2 Analyze RBAC configuration file summaries and manage RBAC using the command line. 4.3 Explain syslog function fundamentals, and configure and manage the /etc/syslog.conf file and syslog messaging.	14
5.1 Explain naming services (DNS, NIS, NIS+, and LDAP) and the naming service switch file (database sources, status codes, and actions). 5.2 Configure, stop and start the Name Service Cache Daemon (nscd) and retrieve naming service information using the getent command. 5.3 Configure naming service clients during install, configure the DNS client, and set up the LDAP client (client authentication, client profiles, proxy accounts, and LDAP configurations) after installation. 5.4 Explain NIS and NIS security including NIS namespace information, domains, processes, securenets, and password.adjunct. 5.5 Configure the NIS domain: build and update NIS maps, manage the NIS master and slave server, configure the NIS client, and troubleshoot NIS for server and client failure messages.	11
6.1 Explain consolidation issues, features of Solaris zones, and decipher between the different zone concepts including zone types, daemons, networking, command scope, and given a scenario, create a Solaris zone. 6.2 Given a zone configuration scenario, identify zone components and zonecfg resource parameters, allocate file system space, use the zonecfg command, describe the interactive configuration of a zone, and view the zone configuration file. 6.3 Given a scenario, use the zoneadm command to view, install, boot, halt, reboot, and delete a zone. 6.4 Explain custom JumpStart configuration including the boot, identification, configuration, and installation services. 6.5 Configure a JumpStart including implementing a JumpStart server, editing the sysidcfg, rules and profile files, and establishing JumpStart software alternatives (setup, establishing alternatives, troubleshooting, and resolving problems). 6.6 Explain flash, create and manipulate the flash archive, and use it for installation. 6.7 Given a PXE installation scenario, identify requirements and install methods, configure both the install and DHCP server, and boot the x86 client.	15

Part I

Sun Certified System Administrator Examination for Solaris 10 Study Guide, Exam CX-310-200

CHAPTERS

1

UNIX Operating System: Mind the Gap

LEARNING OBJECTIVES

- Understanding the Operating System
- Evolution of the UNIX Operating System
- Understanding the System Concepts
- Understanding the UNIX Commands and File Organization
- Breaking the Ice with Your Solaris Machine

Sun Certified System Administrator for the Solaris 10 Operating System. Sounds great, I want this certification. But by the way, what do they mean by Solaris 10 Operating System?

If this sounds like you, welcome to this chapter. Otherwise, you can quickly browse through this chapter, or if you are already familiar with UNIX, you can skip this chapter altogether. In other words, this chapter is meant for folks who are relatively new to the UNIX world and want to come up to speed quickly to fill the gap before they start this journey toward their Solaris System Administration certification. If you have bought this book, you cannot possibly be a perfect stranger to an operating system. When you work on any computer, you actually interact with the operating system such as Windows, Mac, Linux, or Solaris.

So the central question in this chapter to think about is: what is Solaris, and how do we use it? In search of an answer to this question, we will explore three thought streams: what is an operating system (OS), how is Solaris OS related to UNIX, and how do you interact with Solaris?

Understanding the Operating System

Your computer is made of hardware and software components. Some examples of the hardware components include the central processor unit (CPU), which processes the instructions coded in a software program; the physical memory, which stores the instructions and data of a currently running program; and a hard disk, which stores the programs that are not currently running. You can look at a computer as a processor. It takes some input data from the user, processes it, and produces results in terms of output data. You use some input device to feed the input data to the computer, and the computer uses some output device to display the results or the output data. Examples of input and output (I/O) devices connected to a computer include monitor, keyboard, disk, and printer.

Applications (the software programs that do something useful for users) such as the Netscape browser and Microsoft Word are examples of software components. Without applications computers would be of little use for their users. The applications (software components) need hardware components to run. For example, an application needs the CPU to process the instructions, as well as memory and a hard disk to store instructions and data. The relationship between computer applications and the computer hardware gives rise to the following three issues:

- Each application requires access to resources such as CPU and I/O devices. The access must be managed.

- The resources themselves must be managed.
- If multiple applications are running concurrently, they may try to access a resource at the same time. Who would break the tie?

These issues apply to all applications. Therefore, it is not efficient to handle them separately within each application, which is possible in principle but would be a duplication of efforts. Consequently, these issues are handled for all applications in one software system called the operating system. As shown in Figure 1-1, all the applications access the computer resources through the operating system. This is a very high level view: each layer may have sublayers.

An operating system performs the following types of functions:

- *Control program.* The operating system is a control program that controls the I/O devices and the execution of the user's programs (and applications) to ensure the correct operation of the computer. For example, if two programs are trying to access the hard disk at the same time, the OS would decide in which order they would have access, and it manages the usage of the CPU by multiple programs executing concurrently.
- *Resource manager.* The operating system also works as a resource manager. It allocates the hardware and software resources needed by a running program. CPU, I/O devices, and files are some examples of resources.
- *Mediator.* The operating system acts as a mediator (agent) between the users (or applications) and the computer hardware.

So, the operating system is a software system that controls and manages computer resources and acts as an agent between the user and the computer hardware, as well

FIGURE 1-1

Relationship among applications, operating system, and computer hardware

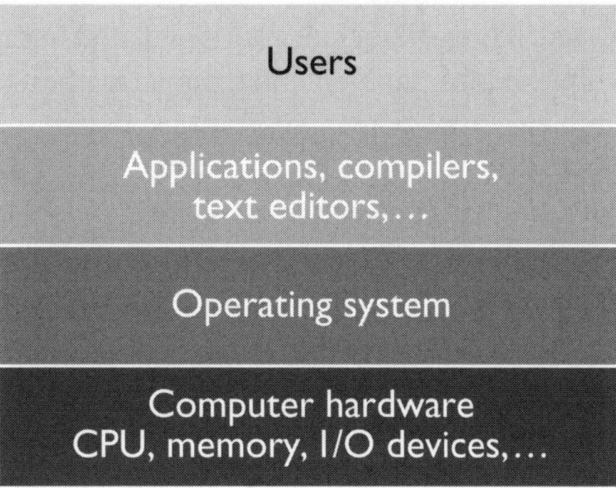

as between the applications and the computer hardware. There are a number of operating systems available in the market—for example, Windows, which is a family of operating systems from Microsoft, and UNIX, which is a family of UNIX-based operating systems, such as Linux and Solaris, from multiple vendors. If you know the history of UNIX, you will know not only that UNIX was the first operating system but that it has also been a trail blazer in the field of operating systems for providing state of the art features. Other operating systems such as Windows have adopted the features first proposed by and implemented in UNIX.

Evolution of the UNIX Operating System

Solaris is a flavor of UNIX—that is, it is one of many members of a family of operating systems called UNIX. As a Solaris system administrator, you need to understand the history of UNIX—its origin, how it evolved, and where it is now. The most important point to remember in exploring the history of UNIX is that UNIX is not an operating system that was built by one company with a wonderful marketing department.

So, repeat: UNIX, pronounced as *yoo-niks*, is not the name of one operating system; it refers to a family of operating systems.

A Brief History of UNIX

The roots of UNIX lie in Comprehensive Time Sharing System (CTSS) developed by F. Corbato at MIT in the early 1960s. Continuing along the principles of CTSS, a multiuser and multitasking system was designed under the Multiplexed Information and Computing Service (MULTICS) project started by General Electric and AT&T Bell Labs. Because the project fell behind schedule, AT&T pulled out in 1969, but the work of building a system along these lines continued, and during the early 1970s a system called Uniplexed Information and Computing Service (UNICS) was developed at Bell Labs in New Jersey. Some important events in the history of UNIX subsequent to these early developments are listed in Table 1-1.

UNIX is the oldest operating system that pioneered several OS concepts used by other operating systems such as Microsoft DOS and Microsoft Windows. Originally, Bell Labs distributed UNIX along with the source code so that anybody could modify and customize the OS to meet specific needs. This gave rise to several flavors of UNIX, some of which are listed in Table 1-2 along with the hardware architectures they support.

TABLE 1-1

Some events in the history of UNIX

Year	UNIX Event
1969	Emergence of UNIX at AT&T Bell Labs for a Digital PDP minicomputer as an alternative to GE's multiuser mainframe running MIT's Multics.
1970–1972	System refinement and many new features added. Confined to AT&T sites in New Jersey. Demand for UNIX started growing. AT&T, reluctant to go into business outside its arena of telephony and telegraphy, gave away UNIX to universities and research sites for a nominal fee with no support and no bug fixes. This gave birth to the UNIX community.
1973	Sixteen UNIX installations by February.
1974	First UNIX users meeting at Columbia University's College of Physicians and Surgeons in May 1974, attended by 24 people from 12 institutions.
1975	Second UNIX users meeting attended by 40 people from 20 institutions
1978	First Berkeley Software Distribution (BSD) version released.
1982	SUN Microsystems Inc. released first UNIX workstation based on the BSD flavor of UNIX.
1983	BSD 4.2 included TCP/IP implementation. AT&T releases UNIX System V.
1989	SPARCstation 1 introduced.

Accordingly, when people say "UNIX," they are really referring to the common functionality of a family of operating systems—that is, multiple flavors of UNIX.

A high-level view of a general architecture of the UNIX OS is presented in Figure 1-2. The heart of the OS is the kernel that contains the programs to manage and control resources. It's the kernel that interfaces with the computer hardware. The

TABLE 1-2

Examples of UNIX flavors

UNIX Flavor	Vendor	Chip Architecture
Solaris	Sun Microsystems	SPARC, x86
HP-UX	Hewlett-Packard	IA-64, and HP PA-RISC
Irix	Silicon Graphics	MIPS
AIX	IBM	PowerPC
UNIXWare	SCO/Caldera	Xeon, Pentium, x86
Linux	Freeware	Alpha, SPARC, Power PC, and Intel

FIGURE 1-2

Structure of UNIX

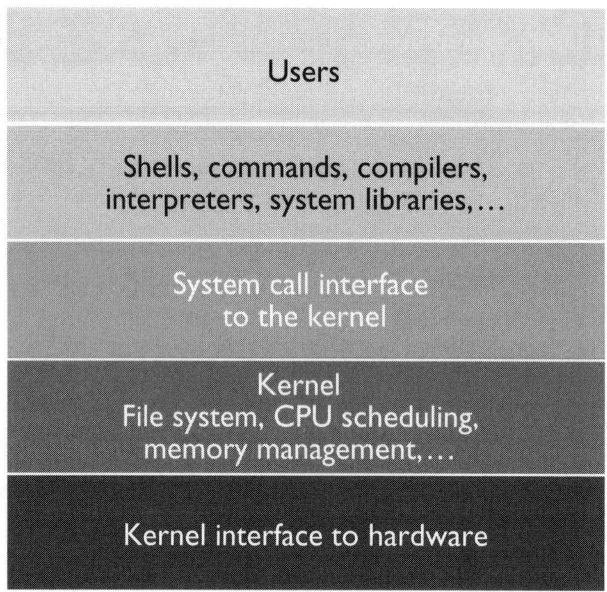

users (or the applications) communicate with the kernel through a software program called the shell. The shell interprets the commands from the user for the kernel.

Some important characteristics of UNIX with their advantages and disadvantages are listed in Table 1-3.

These days, other operating systems such as Windows also offer support for network protocols, multiple processes, and multiple users, but UNIX has been the trail blazer in these areas. The underlying philosophy of UNIX may be outlined as follows:

- *Modularity (independence).* UNIX is composed of small, independent components (referred to as programs, utilities, or tools). Every component is designed to do one thing well. This makes UNIX very modular and efficient.
- *Interrelation (interconnection).* The components are designed to be able to connect to each other. For example, the output of one component may become input into another component. This makes UNIX very powerful.
- *Evolution (innovation).* UNIX is designed to facilitate building new components. This keeps UNIX evolving and multiplying.

This book is about Solaris which is the current name of a flavor of UNIX that became the reason for founding a company called SUN (Stanford University Network) Microsystems, and it still remains one of its two flagship product lines, the other being Java.

TABLE 1-3 Characteristics of UNIX

UNIX Characteristics	Advantages	Disadvantages
UNIX is built from small components; each component does one job and does it well.	Simplicity. Freedom to combine these components to create new and powerful tools	Makes it difficult to get a unified grasp of the entire system.
Support for virtually all network protocols.	Makes UNIX the premier networking system.	Too sophisticated for a common user.
Many flavors of UNIX.	Multiple vendors, competition, more choices for customers.	Confusing because of lack of a unified system.
Wide variety of software available for UNIX.	Increases usability.	System becomes bigger in size and more complex. Troubleshooting becomes more involving.
Open standard, open source.	Freedom to innovate. Makes the system better on a regular basis.	More varieties, less commercial/customer support.
UNIX supports running multiple tasks and processes at the same time. Not only multiple user programs, but also some programs in the background running all the time.	Makes the system efficient and powerful.	Makes the system more cumbersome for most users. Troubleshooting becomes more involving.
Support for multiple users. Multiple users can log on to the same machine and do their work.	Enhances efficiency and usability.	Makes the system more cumbersome for most users. Troubleshooting becomes more involving.

A Brief History of Solaris

Except for the recent rise in the popularity of Linux, no other flavor of UNIX has been as popular as Solaris from SUN Microsystems, founded in February 1982 by Bill Joy (among others), who was previously involved in the development of BSD 4.1. It was the improved version of BSD 4.1 that was released by SUN as SunOS in 1983.

In the early 1980s, AT&T saw a future in UNIX; it released System III in 1983, followed by System V. From there on, for a long time, the evolution of UNIX was for the most part carried on by the interaction between BSD and System V. In 1984, AT&T released System V release 2, followed by release 3 in 1987. In 1988, AT&T

shocked the UNIX community by purchasing a percentage of Sun Microsystems. This triggered efforts for merging the distribution of BSD and System V. In 1990, AT&T released System V release 4, which was a merger of System V and BSD. So, SunOS 5.x, released in 1992, was based on System V release 4 and as a result was significantly different from SunOS 4.x, which was based entirely on BSD. At this time, AT&T once again exited the UNIX world (it was a distraction for the company from its focus on telecommunications hardware) by selling its UNIX Software Lab to Novell; Novell eventually sold its UNIX (UNIXware) to Santa Cruz Operation in 1995.

SunOS 5.x, based on System 5, was also referred to as Solaris. The rest of the Solaris releases are listed in Table 1-4.

The ability to create new flavors of UNIX offers the freedom to innovate, but it can also cause confusion and incompatibilities. So, to keep some coherence within the multiplicity of flavors, some open standards were needed.

The UNIX Unification: POSIX Standards

The problems posed by variations among several flavors of UNIX motivated efforts to developing standards for UNIX. A standard called Portable Operating System Interface (POSIX) was developed by the Institute of Electrical and Electronics Engineers (IEEE) and the American National Standards Institute (ANSI). The goal of this standard is to define a standard operating system that functions as UNIX.

In fact, POSIX is a set of standards. Each standard defines a particular aspect of the standard operating system. For example, POSIX.1 defines the standard for an application interface that the OS would provide, whereas POSIX.2 defines the command interface—that is, the shell.

TABLE 1-4 History of Solaris releases

Year	Solaris Release
1992	Solaris (also called SunOS 5.x. Based on System 5.)
1994	Solaris 2.4
1995	Solaris 2.5
1997	Solaris 2.6
1998	Solaris 7
2000	Solaris 8
2002	Solaris 9
2004	Solaris 10

In this age of the Internet (the information age), you hardly ever work on an isolated computer; instead, you work on (or interact with) a system. For example, when you send an email to your friend, you are using the largest system of connected computers on the planet, called the Internet. A system could be as small as your machine with various components, and as large as the Internet. So, it's very important that you understand the system concepts.

Understanding the System Concepts

A system is a combination of independent but related elements functioning together as a unified whole in order to accomplish a set of specific tasks. The term *system* has Greek and Latin roots and means combination. An element of a system may be a system in itself and is called a subsystem of the system. For example, a country is a system of citizens, cities, and states, and a city is a subsystem of its country. An operating system is another example of a system, and a file system is a subsystem that the operating system manages. Your Solaris system machine is a part of a network system that may contain client and server machines. In the following list we define some general and some UNIX-related system concepts that are referred to throughout this book:

- *Machine*. Machine is a very generic term used for any standalone computer or a computer connected to the network.
- *Host*. A host is a machine connected to a network and having a network (e.g., IP) address.
- *Workstation*. The term *workstation* refers to a machine that has its own storage, CPU, and memory to run the applications. This term originally developed as an alternative to dummy terminals during the era of mainframe computers. The dummy terminals did not have their own resources (storage, memory, and CPU power) to run applications on their own. So, generally speaking, a workstation can be a client or a server. However, vendors such as Microsoft and Sun use the term workstation in a more specific sense which is different from what is described here.
- *Client*. A client is a machine connected to the network, running a program that makes a request for a service. For example, when you are browsing the web, your machine is acting as a client, and the web browser application (e.g., Netscape or Internet Explorer) is the client program running on your machine. Obviously, a client must have a network address.

- *Server*. A server is a machine connected to the network, running a program that accepts and serves the requests made by the client machines on the network. A machine connected to the network that is running a web server is an example of a server.
- *Process*. A process is a program being executed on the machine, whereas a program is an executable file residing on a disk. In other words, a process is an executing instance of a program, which has a unique numeric identifier called *process ID*.
- *Daemon*. A daemon is a process that often runs continuously as long as the system is up. The daemons are often started when the system is booted, and they terminate when the system is shut down. It is said that the daemons run in the background, meaning that there is no controlling terminal window for a daemon. It runs independent of a terminal or a login session. The term daemon is derived from the Greek mythology where it means an intermediary between the gods and mankind. This is an accurate description of daemons in UNIX in the sense that UNIX provides services through daemons, which act as the intermediary between services and users.
- *Kernel*. An operating system has a core, which consists of the defining programs for that operating system, and some utilities around it that can use the core. The core of an operating system is called the kernel. Programs (or utilities) interact with the kernel through system calls.
- *Shell*. A shell is a wrapper around the kernel; it protects the kernel from the user. In other words, it's a program that lets a user interact with the kernel. When a user issues a command, the command goes to the shell; the shell gets the information from the kernel and provides it to the user. So, the user interacts with the kernel through the shell. The user can put multiple commands and their logic in a file called a shell script, written according to the rules of that shell. That shell script can be executed like any other program. UNIX and Solaris support a number of shells such as C shell, Korn shell, and Bourne shell. When a user logs on to the system, a shell is activated that the user interacts with during the login session.
- *Commands and utilities*. A command is an instruction that a user writes at a prompt in a terminal window in order to accomplish a task—for example, to see the list of files in a directory. A utility is a program that does something useful for a user and is not part of the kernel. A command accomplishes the task by executing a program. For that reason, commands are sometimes also called utilities. In other words, there are a number of programs other than kernel and

shell that are part of UNIX. These programs can be run as commands in a shell. The shell interprets the command for the kernel.

- *Multiuser and mutitasking*. In the primitive days of computing, a computer could support only one user running one application at a time. However, UNIX has been a multiuser and multitasking operating system, which means it allows multiple users to log on to a machine at the same time and multiple applications to be run on the same machine concurrently, sharing resources such as CPU, memory, and file systems. Currently, most operating systems (even Windows) support multitasking and multiusers, but UNIX was the pioneer in this arena, as in many other areas of the operating systems.
- *Distributed system*. A distributed computer system is a collection of autonomous computers networked together that collaborate to accomplish a common task. The Internet is the largest distributed system that supports services such as the World Wide Web and email.
- *Fault tolerance*. A distributed system is called fault tolerant if it keeps working even if one or more of its components should fail. (The capability of a system to keep functioning when one or more of its components fails is called fault tolerance.) One common method to implement fault tolerance is through redundancy. That means there are multiple components capable of offering the given functionality; when one component fails, the other component takes over to provide the functionality of the failed component. Consequently, the user does not experience the failure.

An operating system manages resources for the users, and one of those resources is the file system. Users interact with the file system through the operating system. There are two ways to interact with the operating system: GUI and command line. Although substantial work has been done on the GUI front, UNIX traditionally has been a command-based operating system. As a system administrator, you must become familiar with the UNIX commands and know how to use those commands to interact with the file system.

Understanding the UNIX Commands and File Organization

The UNIX commands and the file systems get a fair coverage in this book. To make use of that coverage, you must understand the basic command structure and the general organization of files on a UNIX system.

The UNIX Command Structure

A command is the text that you type after the command prompt on the command console. Issuing a command involves typing the command on the command prompt and pressing RETURN on the computer keyboard. A command has a structure. It is, in general, composed of the following elements:

- *Name*. The name of the command specifies the action to be performed. This is the name of a program that would be executed when you issue the command. The name is always the first element of a command.
- *Option*. This is a command modifier in the sense that it specifies the way in which the action (specified by the command name) would be performed. There may be more than one option in a command. Options usually begin with a hyphen (-). In the OS literature, options are also called switches. Options generally follow the name.
- *Argument*. Arguments usually specify the target of the action. For example, if the command instructs to display the content of a directory, the argument would be the name of the directory whose content is to be displayed. Arguments often follow options in the command. Arguments are also called parameters in the literature.

Following is the syntax of a UNIX command:

```
$ <commandName> [<options>] [<arguments>]
```

The symbol `$` specifies the prompt and is already there on the console. The `<options>` specifies a list of options, and the `<arguments>` specifies a list of arguments. The square brackets around `<options>` and `<arguments>` indicate that these elements are optional. For example, the following command displays the names of the files in the directory named `mydir` in the long format.

```
ls -l mydir
```

The command name `ls` specifies that a list of files should be displayed, the option `-l` specifies that the display should be in the long format, and the argument `mydir` specifies the name of the directory whose files should be displayed. If the directory name is not specified, the current directory is assumed by default. You type `ls -l` mydir after the prompt and press RETURN. The command is issued. The important basic points about UNIX commands are summarized below:

- In a command:
  - There must be a space between any two elements.
  - There must not be any space within the same element.
- The name of a command is a required element. The other two elements are often optional. If not given, their default values are used.
- UNIX commands are case sensitive.

When a command is issued, it executes a program that interacts with the kernel through a shell to do its job, as shown in Figure 1-3.

on the job

Solaris provides both the options GUI and the command console for the user to interact with the OS.

You use the commands to interact with the operating system to perform various tasks. Quite a few of those tasks involve browsing through the files on your system. The files on a UNIX (and therefore Solaris) system are organized into a directory tree, so you should become quite comfortable with the concepts related to the directory tree.

FIGURE 1-3

Relationship among the commands, shells, and kernel

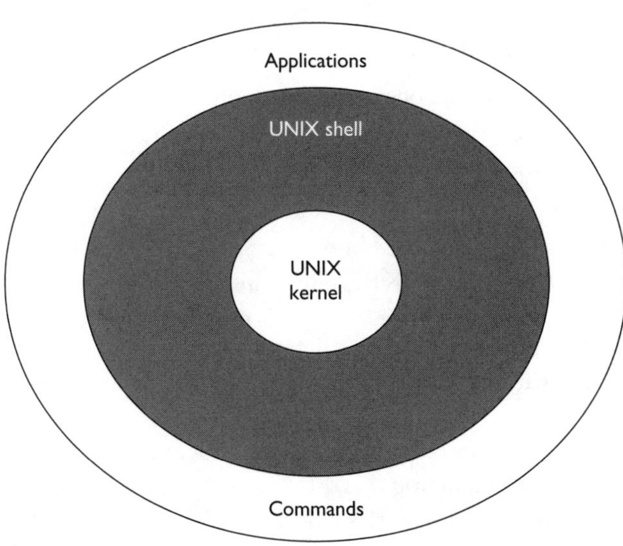

Understanding the Directory Tree

One important task of an operating system is to manage files. The UNIX operating system keeps the files in a hierarchy called the *directory tree*. You can use a number of commands to manage files in the directory. Before you do that, you should be familiar with the following concepts related to the directory tree:

- *File*. A file is the smallest container of data. In other words, the digital (computer) data is stored in files. Each file has a name. In UNIX, the file names are case sensitive. For example, `myfile` and `myFile` are the names of two different files. File in UNIX is a very general concept. The files are of the following types:
  - *Regular file*. Such a file contains data. The text files, binary files, and programs are examples of regular files.
  - *Special file*. I/O devices are also treated as files in UNIX.
  - *Links*. A link is a mechanism to allow several file names to refer to the same file on the disk.
  - *Directory*. This is a binary file containing the list of other files; it may include other directories as well. Files are organized into directories. Any file exists in some directory, which is a UNIX equivalent of folder in the Windows OS.
- *Storage device*. The files are stored on a storage device such as a hard disk, a floppy disk, a CD-ROM, or a tape.
- *File system*. The way an operating system organizes files on the storage device is called a file system. The operating system uses a file system to store, locate, and retrieve the data in a convenient and efficient fashion. The file system is maintained on a storage device.
- *Directory*. Files are organized into directories. Any given file exists in some directory. Directory is a UNIX equivalent of folder in the Windows OS.

During OS installation, a file system is created. The layout of the file system is in the form of a hierarchical tree with the root directory (/) as the root of the tree. This hierarchy is called (inverted) directory tree with root (/) at the top. Part of the hierarchy created during installation is shown in Figure 1-4. The root directory (/) contains subdirectories including `bin`, `etc`, `export`, and `home`. These subdirectories may contain their own subdirectories, and so on. A file exists inside a directory (or a subdirectory).

When you log into your system, you are put into your home directory as a starting point. From there on you can move around in the directory tree, described as follows:

- *You are here*. When you are browsing the directory tree from the command console, there is a concept of being in a directory called current directory. It is important to know in which directory you currently are. This directory would work as a default directory for some commands. If your command prompt does not indicate where you are, you can find out by issuing the command:

  ```
  pwd
  ```

- *Path*. The path is the address of a file or a directory on the directory tree. No two files in a directory tree may have the same path. The path contains a series of names of directories separated by a forward slash (/) and ending in the name of the directory or the file being addressed. For example, a file `passwd` in the directory `etc` in the directory tree shown in Figure 1-4 may be addressed as: `/etc/passwd`. The path indicates that the file `passwd` exists inside the directory `etc`, and the directory `etc` exists inside the root directory `/`. A path may be absolute or relative.
  - *Absolute path*. The path that starts from the root directory is called the absolute path. Each file or directory may have only one absolute path. For example, the absolute path for the directory password is `/etc/password`, as shown in Figure 1-4. A directory or a file may be accessed from anywhere on the tree using its absolute path. The absolute path always starts with /.

FIGURE 1-4 A very small part of the directory hierarchy created during Solaris installation (the directory `jkerry` is a fictitious directory name that you can create inside the `home` directory; it's not part of the directories automatically created)

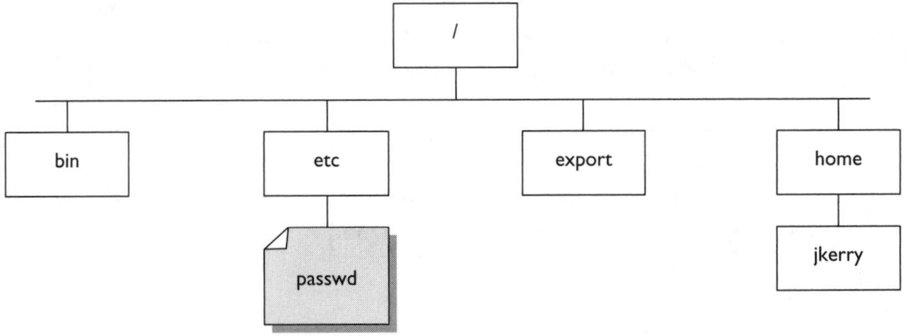

- *Relative path*. The path that starts from the current directory (where you currently are on the command prompt) is called the relative path. The relative path of a file depends on where you are trying to access it. For example, if you are in the root directory (/), the relative path to home is home, and to jkerry is home/jkerry. The double dots (..) take you one level up in the tree. For example, the relative path to the passwd file from the jkerry directory is ../../etc/passwd. The relative path never starts with /.

The absolute path of a file or a directory always starts with a forward slash (/), and a relative path never starts with the forward slash.

Now that you understand the basic command structure and the concepts related to the directory tree, you can roll up your sleeves to engage in some hands-on experience with your Solaris machine.

Breaking the Ice with Your Solaris Machine

In this section, you will try some commands to break the ice with your Solaris machine. We are assuming that you have installed Solaris on your machine following the instructions given in Chapter 2 or that you have access to a machine that has Solaris installed on it.

In order to use the Solaris system, you need to log into it.

Logging In and Logging Out

A standard login session (or work session) is the interval starting with the time you log in to the system and ending with the time you log out. The multiuser environment of Solaris requires that you type in your login name and password as your identification each time you want to log into the system. So you, the system administrator, need to create a login name and a password in order to enable a user to use the system.

Before you log in to the system, your screen should display the following:

```
<hostname> console login:
```

Type in the login name at the prompt and press RETURN. For example, assume the hostname of your machine is dem, and your login name is *jkerry; you would type jkerry at the prompt:*

```
dem console login: jkerry
```

When you press RETURN, the system requests your password as follows:

```
dem console login: jkerry
Password:
```

Type in your password at the prompt and press RETURN. Note that, as a security feature, the system does not display your password on the screen as you type it.

on the job

The key referred to as RETURN in this book may be labeled ENTER on some keyboards, and vice versa.

When you initially log in to the system, you actually log into a shell that is automatically started for you. Your command prompt will indicate the shell, and this shell is called your *login shell*. The Bourne shell is the default shell, but it can be changed. The availability of some commands or programs may depend upon the login shell you are using.

When you have finished, you are done with your session and are ready to exit the system. You can log out by typing exit on the command prompt:

```
exit
```

When you press RETURN, the system once again displays the login prompt:

```
<hostname> console login:
```

The appearance of the login prompt indicates that you have successfully logged out and the system is ready for a user to log in.

Now that you know how to log in and log out of the system, you can try a few commands after logging in.

Getting Started with Issuing Commands

When you log into your machine, you will be put into your home directory, which is the directory created when your account was created. You can, if you are a typical user, create directories and files under your home directory. That is, your directory tree starts from your home directory. A command prompt will appear that will depend on the shell that was started when you logged in, as shown in Table 1-5. Of course, these prompts are by default and can be changed by the system administrator—that is, you.

TABLE 1-5 Command prompts displayed by different shells for an ordinary user and a superuser

Shell User	C	Bourne, Korn
Ordinary user	<machineName>%	$
Superuser	<machineName>#	#

In this section, we will assume that you are logged into the Bourne shell, and hence your command prompt is `$`. When you see this command prompt, it means the system is waiting for a command from you. Issuing a command means typing the command at the command prompt and pressing RETURN. The command is not issued until you press RETURN. This means you can retype (or correct) your command before pressing RETURN. Let's try a few commands.

Find out in which directory you are by issuing the following command:

```
$ pwd
```

Remember, you do not type `$`; that is a prompt already displayed. It will display the absolute path of the directory in which you are, such as:

```
/home/jkerry
```

You can issue the following command to find out the time on the system:

```
$ date
```

The output of this command will look like the following:

```
Fri Jul 08 11:25:34 PST 2005
$
```

Try the following command now:

```
$ Date
```

The output will look like the following:

```
Date: Command not found.
$
```

This tells you that commands (and file names) in UNIX (and hence in Solaris) are case sensitive. Most commands in Solaris are in lowercase. To see the list of content (names of files and subdirectories) in the /etc directory, issue the following command:

```
$ ls /etc
```

Here you used the absolute path to the directory etc. Assuming you are in your home directory, directly under the /home directory you can issue the following command by using the relative path to the /etc directory:

```
$ ls ../../etc
```

This will obviously generate the same output as the `ls /etc` command. To display the whole directory tree underneath the etc directory, issue the following command:

```
$ ls -aR /etc
```

This will recursively display the whole subtree of directories underneath /etc with the directory names and file names. You can use the `cd` command to change the directory:

```
$ cd <targetDirectory>
```

The argument `<targetDirectory>` specifies the relative or the absolute path of the directory to which you want to go. The `cd` command without any argument takes you to your home directory. You can see a list of commands recently issued on this terminal by issuing the following command:

```
$ history
```

It will display an output that looks like this:

```
1 pwd
2 date
3 ls /etc
4 ls ../../etc
5 ls -aR /etc
6 history
```

Here are some useful tips about the commands:

- You can issue more than one independent command in one command line by separating them from each other with a semicolon (;), such as:

  ```
  $ date; pwd
  ```

- To repeat the last command, just issue the following command:

  ```
  $ !!
  ```

- To repeat any previous command, just issue it by its history number. For example, the following will reissue the command with history number 3:

  ```
  $ !3
  ```

You can find the history number by issuing the `history` command. Let's try some advanced commands now. Create a file named `test.txt` by issuing the following command:

```
$ touch test.txt
```

It will create an empty file with name `test.txt`. You can verify that the file is created by issuing the `ls` command. Now you can write the output of an `ls` command into the `test.txt` file by issuing the following command:

```
$ ls /etc > test.txt
```

This is called redirecting the output, and the symbol > is called the redirection operator. You can verify that the `test.txt` file does have the output of the `ls` command by issuing the following command:

```
$ more test.txt
```

This will display the content of the file one page at a time, and you can push the space bar to display the next page. You can also direct the output of a command as an input to another command. This is called piping. As an example consider the following:

```
$ ls -l /etc | grep test
```

This will pipe the output of `ls -l` command into the `grep` command, which will display only those lines of the output that contain the string test. The vertical bar (|) is called the pipe operator or pipe symbol.

Another very useful command, the `wc` command, can be used to count the characters, words, or lines in a file. The command has the following syntax:

```
$ wc [-c] [-C] [-lw] [-m] [<filename>]
```

The argument `fileName` specifies the name of the file under analysis. The options are described here:

- **-c.** Count the bytes.
- **-C.** Count characters.
- **-l.** Count lines.
- **-m.** Same as `-C`.
- **-w.** Count words delimited by white space or new line character.

If no options are specified, `-lwc` is assumed as default. If you want to count only the unique lines (ignore the duplicates) in a file, issue the following command:

```
$ uniq -u <filename> | wc -l
```

The `uniq -u` command generates the list of unique lines and pipes it as an input into the `wc` command, which counts the number of lines and displays the number.

To count the number of files in a directory, you can issue the following command:

```
$ ls -l | wc -l
```

The `ls -l` will produce one line for each file, and the `wc -l` command will give you the line counts; hence, you have the count for the number of files in the directory.

There will be situations when you will need help regarding commands, such as when you know the name of a command but you are not sure how to use it. In this case use the `man` command, which will display the so-called man (manual) pages for the command. For example, if you want to know about the `ls` command, issue the following `man` command:

```
$ man ls
```

However, be patient. It takes a while to get used to the man pages; they may look cumbersome and sound confusing to a beginner.

The three most important takeaways from this chapter are the following:

- An operating system is a software system that controls and manages the computer resources and acts as an agent between the user and the computer hardware, and between the applications and the computer hardware.
- Solaris is an operating system that is one member of a family of operating systems called UNIX.
- You interact with any UNIX operating system, including Solaris, through a shell that interprets your commands for the kernel, which is the core of the operating system.

SUMMARY

An operating system is a software system that manages computer resources such as files and CPU, and acts as an agent between a computer user and the computer hardware. Solaris 10 from SUN is the latest version of an operating system that is a member of a family of operating systems called UNIX. Although substantial progress has been made on the GUI front, the UNIX operating system has largely been a command-based operating system. It's important for a UNIX system administrator to be proficient in using commands. When you log into a UNIX operating system such as Solaris, a shell is started. This is a software system that will interpret the commands from you for the kernel—the core of the operating system. The files in a UNIX operating system are organized into a directory tree, and when you log into the system, you are put into your home directory, which is created at the time your account was created.

An operating system is a software system that must be installed on your computer before it can start helping you to use the machine. In the next chapter, we show you how to install the Solaris 10 flavor of UNIX operating system.

2

Installing Solaris 10 Software

CERTIFICATION OBJECTIVES

As you learned in the previous chapter, your computer is composed of hardware and software: software applications run on the software system called the operating system, which in turn runs on the computer hardware. To build a Solaris 10 system, you need to install Solaris 10 OS on a compatible hardware machine and then install the applications that your system will be running. The applications in the Sun Solaris world are distributed in the form of so-called *packages*. Sometimes, in between the two releases of an OS, a problem needs to be fixed or a new feature needs to be added to keep the system up to date. This is accomplished through the use of what are called *patches*.

So, the central question to think about in this chapter is: how to install Solaris software and keep your system up to date? In search of an answer, we will explore three thought streams: installing Solaris 10 OS, installing and uninstalling packages, and installing and uninstalling patches.

CERTIFICATION OBJECTIVE 2.01

Installation Requirements and Options

Exam Objective 1.1: *Explain the Solaris 10 OS installation and upgrade options for CD / DVD, including how to provide Minimal Installations for SPARC, x64, and x86-based systems.*

You can install Solaris 10 from scratch, called initial installation, or you can upgrade Solaris 7 or higher version to Solaris 10. There is a wide spectrum of installation methods available. We will discuss basic installation methods in this chapter, and some advanced methods in Chapter 15.

Before installing Solaris 10, you must make sure that the hardware on which you are planning to install Solaris is compatible with it.

Hardware Compatibility

As you learned in Chapter 1, an operating system controls the computer hardware—that is, it runs on top of hardware architecture. Solaris 10 OS supports the SPARC and x86 families of processor architectures: UltraSPARC, SPARC64, IA-32, and AMD64.

To be more specific, the following SPARC systems are supported:

- *For workstation systems:*
  - Sun Blade <n>, where <n> stands for 100, 150, 1000, 1500, 2000, or 2500.
  - Ultra <n>, where <n> stands for 2, 5, 10, 30, 60, 80, or 450.
- *For workgroup (entry level) servers:*
  - Sun Fire <x>, where <x> stands for V100, V120, V210, V240, V250, 280R, V440, V480, V490, V880, V890, B100s, or B10n.
  - Sun Enterprise <n>, where <n> stands for 2, Ultra 5S, Ultra 10S, 250, 450, 220R, or 420 R.
- *For midrange servers:*
  - Sun Fire <x>, where <x> stands for V1280, 3800, 4800, 4810, 6800, E2900, E4900, or E6900.
  - Sun Enterprise <n>, where <n> stands for 3000, 4000, 5000, 6000, 3500, 4500, 5500, or 6500.
- *For high-end servers:*
  - Sun Fire <x>, where <x> stands for E20K, E25K, 12K, or 15K.
  - Sun Enterprise <n>, where <n> stands for 10000.
- *Netra Servers.*

All these SPARC systems are 64-bit, but they support both 64-bit and 32-bit applications. Also note that none of these platforms requires any special installation or upgrade instructions for Solaris 10—that is, you can just follow the general procedure described in this chapter.

Although Solaris was originally designed to run on SPARC hardware, the PC hardware support has been improving gradually. This makes perfect business sense, because PC hardware is cheaper than the SPARC hardware and has a larger customer base. Solaris 10 supports the PC hardware that in this book is referred to by the *term x86* which includes the Intel 32-bit family of microprocessors and compatible 64-bit and 32-bit microprocessors from Advanced Micro Devices (AMD).

exam watch

For the exam, you do not need to remember all the numbers associated with the SPARC systems. They are given here just to give you a feel for the varieties of options available for the hardware systems ranging from workstations to servers.

To find detailed information about hardware support for SPARC and x86-based systems, you can check out the hardware compatibility lists at the following SUN web site:

```
http://www.sun.com/bigadmin/hcl
```

The minimum hardware requirements for installing Solaris 10 are listed in Table 2-1.

Once you make sure that your machine meets the hardware requirements, you need to determine which installation method to use.

Installation/Upgrade Options and Requirements

There is a wide spectrum of installation options (methods) available to install Solaris 10 or to upgrade to it. These options let you choose the installation media such as CD or DVD, the installation environment such as standalone system or network installation, the installation programs such as text or GUI installer, and so on. In order to avoid confusion, remember that not all the installation methods are independent of each other; you will see a lot of overlap between these methods in the sense that you may be using a combination of more than one "method" to complete your installation. If the machine on which you want to install Solaris 10 already has a Solaris system installed on it, you can choose one of the following two kinds of installation:

- *Initial installation*. If your machine does not have any OS installed on it, obviously you will choose this method. If your machine does have a previous

TABLE 2-1 Hardware requirements for Solaris 10 installation

Item	Requirement
Platform	Various platforms based on SPARC or x86 systems
Memory for installation or upgrade	Minimum: 64MB Recommended: 256MB For GUI-based installation: 384 MB or higher
SWAP area (the hard disk space used as memory)	Default: 512MB. You may need to customize it as discussed in Chapter 12.
Processor	SPARC: 200 MHz or faster. x86: 120 MHz or faster. Hardware support for floating points is required.
Disk space	Minimum: 12GB

version of OS installed on it, this method will overwrite the disk with the Solaris 10 OS. However, if you want to save the local modifications that you made after the previous installation, you can back up the local modifications before the Solaris 10 installation and then restore them after the installation. For initial installation, you can use any of the installation methods discussed in this section.

- *Upgrade*. If your machine already has Solaris 7, Solaris 8, or Solaris 9 installed, you can choose to upgrade the existing system to Solaris 10. There are two upgrade methods available: standard upgrade, which maintains as many existing parameter settings as possible, and live upgrade, which makes a copy of the existing system and performs a standard upgrade on the copy while maintaining the original installation as well. The advantage of the live upgrade is that if the new installation fails, you can switch to the old installation with a simple reboot. It enables you to keep your existing system running while you upgrade to Solaris 10, hence the name *live upgrade*.

Remember the installation methods listed in Table 2-2 and under which condition each of these methods should be used.

Once you have decided between initial installation and upgrade, some other installation options (methods) are available. Which installation method you should use depends on your need—for example, how many systems are you going to install and whether you want to save the current configuration, and so on. The various methods are listed in Table 2-2.

In this chapter, we will describe one system installation using Solaris installation program from CD or DVD. In Chapter 15, we will explore more advanced methods such as Custom JumpStart, Solaris Flash archives, and Solaris Zones.

When you use the Solaris installation program, you have the option to install in one of the following two modes:

- *Text installer mode*. The Solaris text installer enables you to install interactively by typing information in a terminal or a console window. You can run the text installer either in a desktop session with a window environment or in a console session. In addition to keyboard and monitor, the text installer will require a local DVD or CD-ROM drive or a network connection. You can run the Solaris installation text installer remotely by using the `tip` command.

TABLE 2-2 Different installation methods

Installation Task	Installation Method
Install one system interactively (locally).	Use the Solaris installation program from CD-ROM or DVD.
Install one system over the local area network.	Use the Solaris installation program over the local area network—network-based installation.
Automatic installation of multiple systems based on profiles created by the system administrator that contain the installation requirements.	Use Custom JumpStart.
Replicate the same software and configuration on multiple systems.	Use Solaris flash archive.
Install multiple systems over the wide area network (or Internet).	Use WAN boot.
Upgrade a system while it's running.	Use Solaris live upgrade.
Create isolated application environments on the same machine after original Solaris OS installation.	Use Solaris zones.

- *Graphical user interface (GUI) mode.* The Solaris GUI installer enables you to interact with the installation program by using graphic elements such as windows, pull-down menus, buttons, scrollbars, and icons. In addition to keyboard, monitor, and video adapter, the GUI installer requires a local DVD or CD-ROM drive, or a network connection. The minimum memory requirement for GUI installation is 384 MB.

If there is enough memory, the GUI option is presented by default, which you can override with the `nowin` or `text boot` option. Strictly speaking, as shown in Table 2-3, there are three display options available for installation depending on the range of available memory.

If you choose the `nowin` boot option or install remotely through the `tip` command, you are using the console-based text option. If you choose the `text boot` option and have enough memory, you will be installing with the console-based windows option.

TABLE 2-3 Different display options

Memory	Display Option
64–127MB	Console-based text only
128–383MB	Console-based windows—no other graphics
384MB or greater	GUI-based: windows, pull-down menus, buttons, scroll bars, and icons

Before you begin installing the Solaris software (starting with the OS), you need to know how the Solaris software distribution is arranged, and that involves understanding some software terms and concepts.

Solaris Software Terminology

When you install Solaris 10 on your machine, you install one flavor of Solaris from several available flavors depending on your needs. In Solaris terminology, this flavor is called a software group, which contains software clusters and packages. These terms are described in the following list:

- *Package*. Sun and its third-party vendors deliver software products in the form of components called packages. A package is the smallest installable modular unit of Solaris software. In other words, a package is a collection of software—that is, a set of files and directories grouped into a single entity for modular installation and functionality. For example, SUNWadmap is the name of the package that contains the software used to perform system administration, and SUNWapchr contains the root components of the Apache HTTP server.
- *Cluster*. A cluster is a logical collection of packages (software modules) that are related to each other by their functionality.
- *Software group*. A software group is a grouping of software packages and clusters. During initial installation, you select a software group to install based on the functions you want your system to perform. For an upgrade, you upgrade the software group installed on your system. Remember that in order to manage the disk space, you can add or remove individual software packages from the software group that you select.
- *Patch*. Generally speaking, a patch is a software component that offers a small upgrade to an existing system such as an additional feature, a bug fix, a driver

for a hardware device, or a solution to address issues such as security or stability problems. A narrower definition of a patch is that it is a collection of files and directories that replaces or updates existing files and directories that are preventing proper execution of the existing software. Patches are issued to address problems between two releases of a product.

As shown in Table 2-4, the disk space requirement to install Solaris 10 depends on the software group that you choose to install.

TABLE 2-4 Disk space requirements for installing different Solaris software groups

Software Group	Description	Required Disk Space
Reduced Network Support Software Group	Contains the packages that provide the minimum support required to boot and run a Solaris system with limited network service support. This group provides a multiuser text-based console and system administration utilities and enables the system to recognize network interfaces. However, it does not activate the network services.	2.0GB
Core System Support Software Group	Contains the packages that provide the minimum support required to boot and run a networked Solaris system.	2.0GB
End User Solaris Software Group	Contains the packages that provide the minimum support required to boot and run a networked Solaris system and the Common Desktop Environment (CDE).	5.0GB
Developer Software Group	Contains the packages for the End User Solaris Software Group plus additional support for software development which includes libraries, man pages, and programming tools. Compilers are not included.	6.0GB
Entire Solaris Software Group	Contains the packages for the Developer Solaris Software Group and additional software to support the server functionality.	6.5GB
Entire Solaris Software Group plus Original Equipment Manufacturer (OEM) support	Contains the packages for the Entire Solaris Software Group plus additional hardware drivers, including drivers for hardware that may not be on the system at the installation time.	6.7GB

Note that there is an overlap between the functionality of different software groups as shown in Figure 2-1. For example, the core group includes the functionality of the reduced network support group, the entire group includes the functionality of all the groups except OEM.

on the job

The name for a Sun package always begins with the prefix `SUNW` such as in `SUNWaccr`, `SUNWadmap`, and `SUNWcsu`. However, the name of a third-party package usually begins with a prefix that identifies the company in some way, such as the company's stock symbol.

When you install Solaris, you install a Solaris software group that contains packages and clusters. It's time to explore how the installation is performed.

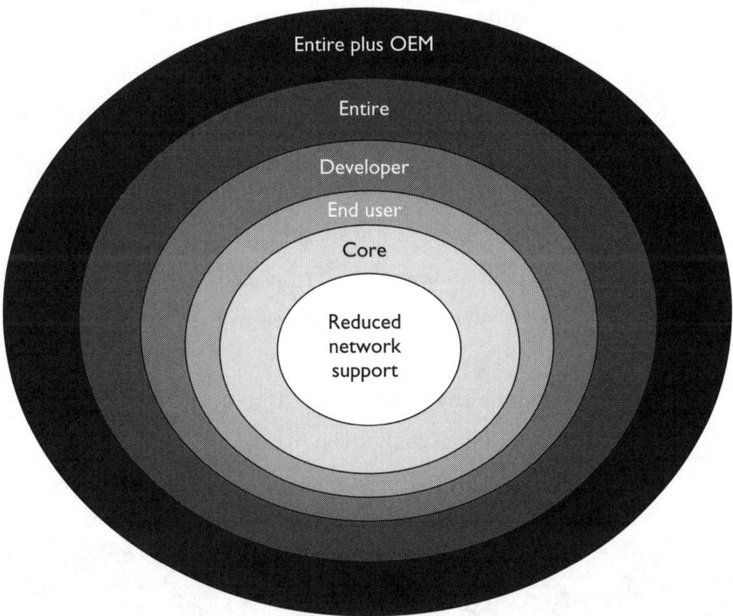

FIGURE 2-1 Different software groups. Each group includes the functionality of the inner groups

CERTIFICATION OBJECTIVE 2.02

Performing Installation

Exam Objective 1.2: *Perform an OS installation from CD/DVD for SPARC-, x64-, and x86-based systems.*

In this section, we will explain how to install or upgrade Solaris 10 on SPARC- or x86-based machines interactively by using the Solaris installation program from the installation CD or DVD. Before you start installation, obviously, you will make sure you have the installation CD or DVD appropriate for the machine on which you are going to install it, as shown in Table 2-5. The language CD is used in case the installation program prompts you for it to support languages for specific geographic regions.

The other pre-installation requirement checks you should perform are the following:

- Make sure your machine meets the hardware requirements described in the previous section.
- Make sure your machine has one of the following media:
  - CD-ROM drive for an installation from CD
  - DVD drive for an installation from DVD
- For a system that will not be connected to the network, keep the following information ready:
  - The hostname that you will assign to the system you are installing
  - Language and locales that you plan to use for the system
  - The root password you are going to use for the root account

TABLE 2-5 The required installation media and software

Installation Media Platform	CD	DVD
SPARC	Solaris 10 Software CDs. Solaris 10 Languages for SPARC Platforms CD.	Solaris 10 Operating System for SPARC Platforms DVD.
x86	Solaris 10 Software CDs. Solaris 10 Languages for x86 Platforms CD.	Solaris 10 Operating System for x86 Platforms DVD.

- For a system that will be connected to a network, gather the following information:
    - The hostname that you plan to assign to the system you are installing
    - Language and locales that you plan to use for the system
    - The IP address for the machine
    - The subnet mask for the network
    - Domain name
    - The type of name services to be used such as DNS, NIS, or NIS+
    - The hostname and IP address of the name server
    - The root password you are going to assign to the root account

If you want to preserve any existing data or applications, you should back up the system. The backups and restores are covered in Chapter 9. Once you have checked all the installation requirements, and gathered the required information, you are ready to install.

Installing or Upgrading on a SPARC Machine

In order to install (or upgrade) Solaris 10 on a standalone SPARC machine by using the installation CD or DVD, use the following procedure:

1. Insert the installation media into the drive:
    a. If you are installing from the CD, insert the Solaris 10 Software for SPARC Platforms 1 CD into the CD-ROM drive.
    b. If you are installing from the DVD, insert the Solaris 10 Operating System for SPARC Platforms DVD into the DVD drive.
2. Boot the system:
    a. If the system is new—that is, nothing is installed on it, turn on the system.
    b. If you want to install a system that is currently running, shut down the system to reboot from the CD-ROM (or DVD) drive. For example, bring the system to the `boot` command prompt `ok` by issuing an `init` or `halt` command. The end result of this step is the `ok` prompt; see Chapter 3 if you need help.

3. Start the Solaris installation program by booting from the CD or DVD:
   a. If you want to use the Solaris installation GUI, boot from the local CD or DVD by issuing the following command at the `ok` prompt:

      ```
      ok boot cdrom
      ```

   b. If you want to use the text installer in a desktop session, boot from the local CD or DVD by issuing the following command at the `ok` prompt:

      ```
      ok boot cdrom -text
      ```

      The `-text` option is used to override the default GUI installer with the text installer in a desktop session.

   c. If you want to use the text installer in a console session, boot from the local CD or DVD by issuing the following command at the `ok` prompt:

      ```
      ok boot cdrom -nowin
      ```

   The `-nowin` option is used to override the default GUI installer with the text installer in a console session.

   After you issue one of these `boot` commands, the installation program starts; it prompts you to select a language to use during the installation. To tell the installation program to move to the next step, you typically click Next in a GUI and perform a similar action in the text installer. Here, we are going to use the GUI terminology when it comes to saying continue or move to next step. If you are using the text installer, just follow the instruction on the monitor about what to do to continue.
4. Select the language you want to use during the installation, and press ENTER. After a few seconds, the Solaris Installation Program Welcome message appears.
5. Click Next to begin the installation. If you are prompted, answer the system configuration questions about such matters as hostname, IP address, and so on. Use the information that you gathered earlier in this chapter.

   After you get through the configuration questions, the Welcome to Solaris dialog box is displayed.
6. Select whether you want to reboot the system automatically and whether you want to automatically eject the disc, and click Next. The Specify Media screen appears.

7. Specify the media you are using to install and click Next.
8. Select whether you want to perform an initial installation or an upgrade and click Next. If you choose to upgrade the existing system, the Solaris installation program will determine whether the system can be upgraded. For example, to be able to upgrade, it must have an existing Solaris root (/) file system. After detecting the necessary conditions, the installation program will upgrade the system.
9. Select the type of installation that you want to perform, as shown in the following:
   a. Select Default Install if you want to install the Entire Solaris Software Group and the Sun Java™ Enterprise System software. This is a good choice if you are a beginner and your machine has enough disk space.
   b. Select Custom Install if you want to perform the following tasks and you know how to do it:
      1. Install a specific software group
      2. Install specific software packages
      3. Install a specific locale
      4. Customize the disk layout

   Click Next.
10. Answer any additional configuration questions, if you are prompted. Once you have provided the required information, the Ready to Install screen is displayed.
11. Click Install Now to install the Solaris software including the OS, and follow the instructions on the screen.

When the installation program finishes installing the Solaris software, the system will reboot automatically or it will prompt you to reboot manually. If you chose to install additional products, you would be prompted to insert the CD or DVD for those products. If you were performing an initial installation, the installation is complete, and you can move on to the next step. If, on the other hand, you were upgrading an existing system, you might need to make corrections to some local modifications that were not preserved:

- Review the contents of the `/a/var/sadm/system/data/upgrade_cleanup` file to determine whether you need to make any correction to the local modifications that the Solaris installation program could not preserve.

- Make corrections to any local modifications that were not preserved.

12. If you did not select the automatic reboot option earlier, reboot the system by issuing the following command:

```
# reboot
```

Note that the text installer will not prompt you to select a default or custom installation. Instead, you will be provided the text installer screens with default values. Accept those values for default installation, or edit the values to customize the installation.

If you are planning to install Solaris on a PC (x86 machine), follow the installation steps presented in the next section.

Installing or Upgrading on an x86 Machine

Just as on a SPARC machine, you can choose to install or upgrade the Solaris OS on an x86 machine by using the Solaris installation program from the installation CD or DVD. Note that the machine's BIOS must support booting from a CD or DVD. You may need to manually set your BIOS to boot from a DVD or CD. See your machine's hardware documentation for more information on how to set the BIOS. The installation procedure is described here:

1. Insert the CD or DVD into appropriate drive:
   a. If you plan to boot from the CD drive, insert the Solaris 10 Software -1 CD into the drive.
   b. If you plan to install from the DVD drive, insert the Solaris 10 Operating System DVD into the drive.
   c. If you plan to install from the diskette drive, insert the Solaris 10 Device Configuration Assistant diskette into the system's diskette drive.
2. Boot the system by shutting it down, turning it off, and then turning it back on. If you need to manually set the BIOS to boot from CD or DVD, press the appropriate key sequence to interrupt the system boot process. After modifying the boot priority in the BIOS, exit the BIOS to return to the installation program.

After executing the memory test and hardware detection, the screen refreshes, and the Solaris Booting System screen is displayed.

3. Decide whether you want to modify the device settings. You may need to do this if you want to perform any of the following tasks:
   - Install device drivers or Install Time Updates (ITUs). Check your hardware documentation to see whether you need any ITUs or additional drivers.
   - Disable Advanced Configuration and Power Interface (ACPI).
   - Set up a serial console.
   - Reset the default boot device.

   If you need to modify device settings with the Solaris Device Configuration Assistant (DCA), press ESC. Note that you must press ESC within five seconds to interrupt the installation in order to get the DCA screen displayed. To modify the device settings, follow the instructions on the DCA screens. Subsequently, the Solaris installation program checks the default boot disk for the requirements to install or upgrade the system. If the installation program cannot detect the required system configuration, the program prompts you for any missing information. When the check is complete, the installation selection screen is displayed.

4. Select an installation type. The installation selection screen displays the following options; Select the type of installation that you want to perform:
   a. Solaris Interactive
   b. Custom JumpStart
   c. Solaris Interactive Text (Desktop session)
   d. Solaris Interactive Text (Console session)

   Enter the number of your choice (for example, 4 for the text console session) followed by ENTER. Solaris Interactive (with GUI) is the default that will be started if you wait for more than 30 seconds. After you make your selection, the system configures the devices and interfaces and searches for configuration files. After a few seconds, the Solaris Installation Program screen is displayed.

5. On the Solaris Installation Program screen, press F2 to Continue. Now, there are two possible scenarios to proceed with:
   - If the installation program detects the types of display, keyboard, and mouse on your system, the Select a Language screen is displayed, and you can go to step 7.

- If, on the other hand, the installation program does not detect the types of display, keyboard, and mouse on your system, the Introduction screen from the `kdmconfig` is displayed. In this case, go to step 6.

6. Choose one of the following two ways to go from here:
   - If you want to install the Solaris OS with the GUI, configure your system to use the keyboard, display, and mouse, by following the instructions on the screen.
   - If you want to do the text installation, press F4 to bypass the steps related to GUI and go directly to step 7.

   We are now at Select the Language screen.

7. Select the language you plan to use during the installation and press ENTER. Within seconds, the Solaris Installation Program Welcome screen is displayed.
8. Click Next to begin the installation. If you are prompted, answer the remaining system configuration questions. Use the information that you gathered as described previously.

   After you get through the configuration questions, the Welcome to Solaris dialog box is displayed.

9. Select whether you want to reboot the system automatically and automatically eject the disc and click Next. The Specify Media screen appears.
10. Specify the media you are using to install and click Next.
11. Select whether you want to perform an initial installation or an upgrade and click Next. If you choose to upgrade the existing system, the Solaris installation program will determine whether the system can be upgraded. For example, to be able to upgrade it must have an existing Solaris root (/) file system. After detecting the necessary conditions, the installation program upgrades the system.
12. Select the type of installation that you want to perform, as shown here:
    - Select Default Install if you want to install the entire Solaris Software Group and the Sun Java™ Enterprise System software. This is a good choice if you are a beginner and your machine has enough disk space.

- Select Custom Install if you want to perform the following tasks and you know how to do it:
  a. Install a specific software group
  b. Install specific software packages
  c. Install a specific locale
  d. Customize the disk layout

We discuss software groups and packages later in this chapter.
Click Next.

13. Answer any additional configuration questions, if you are prompted. Once you have provided the required information, the Ready to Install screen is displayed.
14. Click Install Now to install the Solaris software including the OS, and follow the instructions on the screen.

    When the installation program finishes installing the Solaris software, the system will reboot automatically or prompt you to reboot manually. If you chose to install additional products, you would be prompted to insert the CD or DVD for those products. If you were performing an initial installation, the installation would complete and you could move on to the next step. If, on the other hand, you were upgrading an existing system, you might need to make corrections to some local modifications that were not preserved, which are discussed as follows:

    - Review the contents of the `/a/var/sadm/system/data/upgrade_cleanup` file to determine whether you need to make any correction to the local modifications that the Solaris installation program could not preserve.
    - Make corrections to any local modifications that were not preserved.

15. If you did not select the automatic reboot option earlier, reboot the system by issuing the following command:

```
# reboot
```

After the installation is complete, you can find the installation logs saved in the `/var/sadm/system/logs` and `/var/sadm/install/logs` directories.

After you have installed a software group, you can add packages to it, and you can remove packages from it. You can also apply patches to the installed system.

CERTIFICATION OBJECTIVE 2.03

Working with Packages and Patches

Exam Objective 2.8: *Perform Solaris 10 OS package administration using command-line interface commands and manage software patches for the Solaris OS, including preparing for patch administration and installing and removing patches using the patchadd and patchrm commands.*

Installing and removing software products, an essential part of software management, is one of many responsibilities of a system administrator. Sun and its third-party vendors deliver software products in the form of components called *packages*. Furthermore, between the two releases of the OS, you also need to deal with patches, which present either new features or fixes to existing problems.

Performing Package Administration

The application software for Solaris OS is delivered in units called packages. A package is a set of files and directories in a defined format. The package format conforms to the application binary interface (ABI), which is a supplement to the System V Interface Definition. An ABI describes the low-level interface between an application program and the operating system, between an application and its libraries, or between different parts of the application. An ABI is like an Application Programming Interface (API): an API defines the interface between the application source code and libraries, thereby enabling the same source code to compile on any system supporting that API. Similarly, an ABI allows compiled object code to function without changes or the need to recompile on all systems using compatible ABIs.

Building a software product in units of one or more packages makes it easier to transfer it to a medium, to mass produce it, and to install and manage it. To build a package, an application developer must provide the following package components:

- Required components:
  - Package objects. These are the files and directories of the application software.
  - Control files. These are the information files and installation scripts. Only two control files, which are the information files, are required: the `pkginfo` and `prototype` files.
- Optional components:
  - Optional information files
  - Installation scripts

The Solaris OS provides a set of utilities (commands) that can interpret the package format (ABI) to perform tasks such as installing a package, verifying a package installation, and removing a package. The commonly used commands to manage packages are listed in Table 2-6.

Making a package work on your system requires more than simply copying it to your system; you need to install it. Installing and uninstalling packages are the two most important tasks involved in package management.

Installing a Package

To install a package, you can use the `pkgadd` command, which uncompresses the files in the package, copies them from the installation media to a local system's disk, and does other necessary things. Note that the package files are delivered in package

TABLE 2-6 Some commands for package management

Command	Description
`pkgask`	Used to save the responses (to the questions that will be asked by the `pkgadd` command from the user) in a file that can later be used by a `pkgadd` command instead of user needing to type the responses.
`pkgadd`	Adds (installs) a software package.
`pkgchk`	Checks a package installation.
`pkginfo`	Lists the package information.
`pkgparam`	Displays the parameter values for a software package.
`pkgrm`	Removes a software package.
`pkgtrans`	Translates a package from one format to another.

format and are unusable in the form they are delivered. Therefore, the pkgadd command interprets the control files of the software package and then uncompresses them and installs the product files onto the system's local disk. The pkgadd command has the following syntax:

```
pkgadd [-n] [-a <admin>] [-d <device>] [-G] [-r <response>]
[-R <rootPath>] [<source>] [<instances>]
```

The options and arguments are described here:

- **-a <admin>.** This indicates to use the installation administration file specified by <admin> instead of the default file. If the full path is not specified, the file is first looked for in the current working directory; if not found there, it is then looked for in the /var/sadm/install/admin directory.
- **-d <device>.** This indicates that the package to be installed should be copied from the device specified by <device>, which could be a full path name to a directory or the identifier for a tape, floppy disk, or removable disk such as /var/tmp or /floppy/<floppy_name>. The <device> can also specify a device alias or a datastream created by the pkgtrans command.
- **-G.** This instructs the user to add the package only to the current zone. Zones are described in Chapter 15.
- **-n.** This specifies the installation mode to be non-interactive, and the list of the installed files is not displayed. The default mode is interactive.
- **-r <response>.** This specifies the full path to the file that contains the responses from the previous pkgask command. These responses can be used by the pkgadd command instead of requiring the user to type the responses.
- **-R <rootPath>.** This specifies the full path to the directory to be used as the root for installation.
- **<source>.** This is an alternative to the -d <device> option; it is to specify the source of the packages to be installed.
- **<instances>.** This lists the package instances to be installed. By default, the command searches for the instances on the source and presents the list for you to select the instances for installation. Think of an instance of a package as a working copy of the package.

on the job

An instance of a package is created by opening the package; it contains a working copy of all the private data of the package. Opening a package allocates memory for the instance's data and sets the data to the initial values stored in the package. The package instance exists until it is terminated by closing the package, which frees the memory used to hold the package data. Multiple instances, which can exist simultaneously, can be created from the same package.

On occasion you may just want to copy the packages to the system for a possible installation at a later time. You can do this by using the `pkgadd` command with the spool option that follows:

```
pkgadd -d <deviceName> -s <spoolDir> <pkgid>
```

This form of the command copies the packages from the device specified by `<deviceName>` to the directory specified by `<spoolDir>`. The argument `<pkgid>` specifies a space-delimited list of packages that need to be copied; the default is to copy all the packages from the specified device.

on the job

If the `-d <device>` option is not specified, the `pkgadd` command looks for the packages in the spool directory `/var/spool/pkg`.

Once you've installed a package, you need to verify the accuracy of the installation.

Checking a Package

You can use the `pkgchk` command to check the accuracy of installed files, including the integrity of directory structures and files in a package. You can also use this command to display the information about the package files. The detected discrepancies are written to the standard error device along with a detailed explanation of the problem. The syntax for the `pkhchk` command is as follows:

```
pkgchk [-a|-c] -l] [-p <pathName>[-v] <pkgid>
```

The options are described here:

- **`-a|c`.** The `-a` option means check the file attributes only and not the file contents, whereas the `-c` option means check the file contents only and not the file attributes. The default is to check both the file attributes and the file contents.

- **-l.** This option specifies to list the information about the files contained in the package.
- **-p <pathName>.** This option specifies to limit the check to the files whose path names are given in a comma or white space-delimited list specified by <pathName>.
- **-v.** This option specifies the verbose mode.
- **<pkgid>.** This option specifies the space-delimited list of packages. By default, all the installed packages on the system are checked.

You can also use the pkgchk command with the -d <device> option to check the content of the packages that have not yet been installed but were spooled on the device specified by <device>, which could be a directory, tape, or floppy disk.

Now that you know how the pkgchk command works, here are some practical scenarios and their solutions.

SCENARIO & SOLUTION	
You want to check the content of an installed package SUNWbash.	Issue the command pkgchk -c SUNWbash.
You want to check the file attributes of an installed package SUNWPython.	Issue the command pkgchk -a SUNWPython.
You want to check the software packages that have not yet been installed but were spooled in the /var/install/packages directory.	Issue the command pkgchk -d /var/install/packages.

At times you may just want some information about packages; you can get that by using the pkginfo command.

Retrieving Information about Packages

You can use the pkginfo command to retrieve information about software packages that are installed on the system or about the packages that reside on a particular device such as a directory or a tape. Without options (that is, by default), the pkginfo command displays the primary category, package instance, and the names of all completely and partially installed packages — one line per package. The command has the following syntax:

```
pkginfo [-i|-p] [-l |-q|-x] [-c <category>] [<instances>]
```

The options are described here:

- **-i|-p.** The -i option means display information only about the fully installed packages, whereas the -p option means display information only about the partially installed packages.
- **-l|-q|-x.** The -l option specifies the long display format, the -q option specifies do not display any information (used by programs), and the -x option specifies an extracted listing of package information.
- **-c <category>.** This option only displays packages whose category is included in the list specified by <category>. The category is a package attribute whose value is defined in the pkginfo file of the package.

You can also use the pkginfo command with the -d <device> option to get the information about the packages that have not yet been installed but were spooled on a device specified by <device>, which could be a directory, tape, or floppy disk.

On occasion, you may want to remove a package from your system, and you can do that by using the pkgrm command.

Removing a Package

You can use the pkgrm command to remove a completely or partially installed package from the system. If the command finds a dependency of another package on the package under removal, an action defined in the admin file is taken. The default mode for the command is interactive, which means that the prompt messages are displayed to allow you to confirm the actions to be taken. However, while issuing the command, you can override the default interactive mode with the non-interactive mode by using the -n option. Also, by default, the pkgrm command deletes all the files that compose the package except those shared by other packages.

The pkgrm command has the following syntax:

```
pkgrm [-a <admin>] [-A] [-n] [<pkgid>]
```

The operand `<pkgid>` specifies the space-delimited list of packages that will be removed. The default is to remove all the available packages. The options are described here:

- **`-a <admin>.`** This option indicates to use the installation administration file specified by `<admin>` instead of the default file. If the full path is not specified, the file is first looked for in the current working directory; if not found there, it is then looked for in the `/var/sadm/install/admin` directory.
- **`-A.`** This option instructs to remove all the files of the package including those shared by other packages.
- **`-n.`** This option specifies the non-interactive mode; the default is the interactive mode.

You already know that you can spool (store) packages without installing them by using the `pkgadd` command. Accordingly, you can remove the spooled packages by using the `pkgrm` command as follows:

```
pkgrm -s <spoolDir>
```

The argument `<spoolDir>` specifies the full path to the spool directory from which the packages are to be removed. The default spool directory is `/var/sadm/pkg`.

on the Job

Use the same kind of tool to uninstall a software package as you used to install it. For example, if you used SUN GUI to install a software package, use the GUI to uninstall it and not the command. Also never uninstall a package manually by using the `rm` command on its files. It will create inconsistencies and can damage the other installed packages.

The application packages are independent modules of software offering additional functionality, and their task does not include modifying the existing files on the system. The software components (special packages) that may update or replace the existing files are called patches. In addition to managing the packages, you will also need to manage patches.

Performing Patch Administration

A *patch* is a collection of files and directories that may replace or update existing files and directories that are preventing proper execution of the existing software. A patch is identified by its unique *patch ID*, which is an alphanumeric string that consists of a patch base code and a number that represents the patch revision number; both separated by a hyphen (e.g., 108528-10). You can get Solaris patches from the following web site:

```
http://sunsolve.sun.com
```

If the patches you downloaded are in a compressed format, you will need to use the `unzip` or the `tar` command to uncompress them before installing them. You do not have to install each available patch. The strategy for updating software (applying patches) recommended by Sun includes these practices:

- Analyze the need to apply patches (or update your software) based on risk, cost, availability, and timing.
- Minimize change to your environment whenever possible.
- Address Sun Alert notifications and other critical issues as soon as possible.
- Make other changes to your environment only to address known problems.
- Keep your environment as current as appropriate for your business and application needs.

You can install and uninstall the patches on your system by using the `patchadd` and `patchrm` commands, respectively.

Managing Patches with the `patchadd` Command

You can use the `patchadd` command to install patches and to find out which patches are already installed on your system. You can use this command only on Solaris 2.x or higher version. Remember that to apply a patch means to install it, and the files to be patched refer to the already installed files that are being modified or replaced as a result of installing the patch. The `patchadd` command used to apply (install) a patch has the following syntax:

```
patchadd [-d] [-G] [-u] [-B <backoutDir>] <source> [<destination>]
```

The options and operands are described here:

- **`-d`.** Do not back up the files to be patched (changed or removed due to patch installation). When this option is used, the patch cannot be removed once it has been added. The default is to save (back up) the copy of all files being updated as a result of patch installation so that the patch can be removed if necessary.

- **-G.** Adds patches to the packages in the current zone only. Zones are discussed in Chapter 15.
- **-u.** Turns off file validation. That means that the patch is installed even if some of the files to be patched have been modified since their original installation.
- **-B <backoutDir>.** Saves the backout data to a directory whose full path is specified by `<backoutDir>`. The backout data is the data created when a patch is applied to enable the system to return to its previous state if the patch is removed—that is, backed out.
- **<source>.** Specifies the source from which to retrieve the patch, such as a directory and a patch id.
- **<destination>.** Specifies the destination to which the patch is to be applied. The default destination is the current system.

The following form of the `patchadd` command can be used to find out which patches are currently installed:

```
patchadd -p <destination>
```

Now that you know how to use the `patchadd` command to manage patches, here are some practical scenarios and their solutions.

SCENARIO & SOLUTION	
Obtain information about all the patches that have already been applied on your system.	Issue the command `patchadd -p`.
Find out if a particular patch with the base number 113029 has been applied on your system.	Use `patchadd -p | grep 113029`.
Install a patch with patch id 105754-03 from the `/var/sadm/spool` directory on the current standalone system.	Use `patchadd /var/sadm/spool/105754-03`.
Verify that the patch has been installed.	Use `patchadd -p | 105754`.

While you install a patch, the `patchadd` command logs information into the following file:

```
/var/sadm/patch/<patch-ID>/log
```

Note that the `patchadd` command cannot apply a patch under the following conditions:

- The package is not fully installed on the system.
- The architecture of the patch package differs from the architecture of the system on which it is being installed.
- The version of the patch package does not match the version of the corresponding installed package.
- A patch with the same base code and a higher revision number has already been applied.
- A patch that makes this patch obsolete has already been applied.
- The patch to be applied is incompatible with a patch that has already been applied to the system. Each installed patch keeps this information in its `pkginfo` file.
- The patch to be applied depends on another patch that has not yet been applied.

on the job

In the process of installing a patch, the `pkgadd` command is called to apply the patch packages from the patch directory to a local system's disk. However, do not use the `pkgadd` command directly to install a patch; use the `patchadd` command instead.

You can issue the following command to get the revision information about the patches installed on your system:

```
showrev -p
```

In general, the `showrev` command is meant for displaying the machine, software revision, and patch revision information. If issued without any argument and option, this command displays the system revision information in general, including hardware provider, hostname, hostid, domain, release, kernel architecture and version, and application architecture.

Clearly, installing a patch is more involved than installing a package, because when you install a patch you might be updating or overwriting some existing files. Consequently, there are issues of saving those files and restoring them if you need to uninstall the patch at a later time.

Removing Patches

You can remove (uninstall) a patch and restore the previously saved files by using the `patchrm` command. This command can be used only on Solaris 2.x or higher versions. The command has the following syntax:

```
patchrm [-f] [-G] -B <backoutDir>] <patchID>
```

The operand `<patchID>` specifies the patch ID such as 105754-03. The options are described here:

- **`-f`.** Forces the patch removal even if the patch was superseded by another patch.
- **`-G`.** Removes the patch from the packages in the current zone only. Zones are discussed in Chapter 15.
- **`-B <backoutDir>`.** Specifies the backout directory for a patch to be removed so that the saved files could be restored. This option is needed only if the backout data has been moved from the directory where it was saved during the execution of the `patchadd` command.

For example, the following command removes a patch with patch ID `105975-03` from a standalone system:

```
patchrm 105975-03
```

As a security feature, a package can include a digital signature. The valid digital signature of a package ensures that the package has not been modified since the signature was applied to it. Because the digital signature can be verified before the package is added to your system, using signed packages is a secure method of downloading or adding packages. A signed package is identical to an unsigned package, except for the digital signature. The same holds true for the patches.

The three most important takeaways from this chapter are as follows:

- Solaris installation software offers several installation methods to address different situations under which the installation will be performed. Solaris can be installed on both SPARC and x86-based hardware systems.

- When you install Solaris, you install a software group that consists of software packages and clusters. Applications in the Solaris world are distributed in the form of packages that you can add to an installed Solaris system.
- You can also add patches that are released between the two releases of the OS to an installed system to fix existing problems or to add new features to keep the system current.

CERTIFICATION SUMMARY

You can install Solaris 10 from scratch (called initial installation), or you can upgrade your Solaris 7 (or higher version) system to Solaris 10. Depending on your need and environment, there are various installation methods available such as installing from CD-ROM or DVD, network-based installation, custom JumpStart, Solaris flash archives, WAN boot, Solaris live upgrade, and Solaris zones. The minimum memory requirement for Solaris installation is 64 MB for the text installer and 384 MB for the GUI installer.

When you install Solaris, you install a software group that determines the functionality of the system. There are six software groups available: reduced network support, core system support, end user support, developer support, entire support, and entire plus OEM support. A software group consists of clusters and packages. A cluster consists of packages, and a package is a modular software unit that consists of directories and files. After you install a software group, you can install more packages to it, and you can uninstall packages from it by using the `pkgadd` and `pkgrm` commands respectively. You can verify the package installation by using the `pkgchk` command and get information about packages by using the `pkginfo` command.

Between any two software releases, patches are provided to correct an existing problem or to introduce a new feature. You can install and uninstall the patches by using the `patchadd` and `patchrm` commands, respectively. The revision information about all the installed patches on the system can be obtained by using the `showrev -p` command.

Before you make your system available for other users and start administering it, you need to know how to boot the system and how to shut it down properly under different conditions. We discuss these topics in the next chapter.

INSIDE THE EXAM

Comprehend

- If there is enough memory (a minimum of 384 MB), the GUI installation is offered by default and can be overridden with the `nowin` or `text boot` option.
- When you use the `pkgadd` command with the `-s` option to spool the packages, the packages are only stored to the specified directory but are not actually installed.
- In order to be able to back out of a patch installation (i.e., to bring the system back to the state in which it was before the patch installation), you must not use the `-d` option with the patch add command and must not remove the backout files in the backout directory that are created during the patch installation.

Look Out

- By default, the `pkgrm` command removes all the files associated with the package except those files that are also associated with another package. You can use the `-A` option to remove even those files shared by other packages without any confirmation.
- Even though the `pkgadd` command is used in the process of installing a patch, do not use the pkgadd command directly to install a patch; instead, use the `patchadd` command.
- The `-d` option instructs the `patchadd` command *not* to save copies of the files being updated or replaced by this patch installation.

Memorize

- You can upgrade the existing Solaris System to Solaris 10 only if the existing system has the version number 7 or higher; otherwise, you have to use the initial installation.
- The minimum memory requirement for text-based installation is 64 MB and for GUI-based installation is 384 MB.
- The default installation spool directory is `/var/spool/pkg`.

✓ TWO-MINUTE DRILL

Installation Requirements and Options

- ❑ Solaris 10 supports SPARC-based and x86-based platforms.
- ❑ Various installation methods are available to support several installation circumstances, such as local or remote installation, installation of single or multiple systems, upgrade or installation from scratch, and installation in which the current configuration is maintained.
- ❑ Three installation display options are available: console-based text only; console-based windows; and GUI with windows, pull-down menus, scroll bars, buttons, and icons.
- ❑ When you install Solaris, you install one of the six available software groups: reduced network support, core system support, end user support, developer support, entire support, and entire plus OEM support.

Performing Installation

- ❑ You can install Solaris 10 on a SPARC machine from the installation CD or DVD.
- ❑ You can install it on an x86 machine from the installation CD, DVD, or diskette.
- ❑ For an installation on an x86 machine, you must make sure that the BIOS supports booting from CD or DVD, and you must make the appropriate BIOS boot setting when the machine is turned on.

Working with Packages and Patches

- ❑ You can use the `pkginfo` command to find out which packages are already installed on the system.
- ❑ You can use the `pkgadd` command to install a software package on the system, or to spool (store) the packages on a device such as a directory or a tape.
- ❑ You can use the `pkgchk` command to check the accuracy of the installed packages or to check the spooled packages.

- You can use the `pkgrm` command to uninstall the installed packages or to remove the spooled packages.
- You can use the `patchadd` command to find out which patches are already installed on the system and to install new patches.
- You can use the `patchrm` command to uninstall a patch and to restore the previously saved files during the installation of this patch.
- You can use the `showrev -p` command to get the revision information about all the patches installed on the system.

SELF TEST

The following questions will help you measure your understanding of the material presented in this chapter. Read all the choices carefully because there might be more than one correct answer. Choose all correct answers for each question.

1. You need to install Solaris 10 on a workstation which will be used mostly for software development. Which of the following software group you will choose to install?

   A. Reduced network support software group

   B. Core system support software group

   C. End user Solaris software group

   D. Entire Solaris software group

   E. Developer software group

2. What is the minimum amount of RAM your machine requires before you could install Solaris 10 on it?

   A. 64MB

   B. 256MB

   C. 384MB

   D. 32MB

3. Which of the following are not the names for the software groups in Solaris 10?

   A. Core system support plus OEM software group

   B. End user Solaris software group

   C. Entire development software group

   D. Entire Solaris software group plus OEM

4. Which of the following are the valid methods for installing Solaris 10?

   A. WAN boot

   B. Network cloning

   C. Live upgrade

   D. UUCP (UNIX to UNIX copy protocol)

   E. Interactive

5. The `pkgchk` command can be used for which of the following tasks?

   A. To check whether the data in the package files is corrupted

   B. To check the content of the packages that have not yet been installed

   C. To verify the installation of a package

   D. To check a package out of the spool directory in order to control the version number by tracking changes.

6. Which of the following commands can be used to uninstall a package?

   A. `pkgrm`

   B. `rm -r`

   C. `uninstall`

   D. `patchrm`

7. Which of the following statements is not true about patches?

   A. The `patchadd` command creates a backup of the files to be patched.

   B. If you don't want to create a backup of the files to be patched, use the patchadd command with the `-n` option.

   C. The `patchrm` command attempts to restore the previously saved files.

   D. The `patchadd` command can be used to find out which patches are currently installed on the system.

8. Which of the following conditions will prevent the patchadd command from installing a patch?

   A. The patch version is not the latest version.

   B. A patch with the same base code but higher revision number is already installed.

   C. The patch that is being installed depends on another patch which has not yet been installed.

   D. An already installed patch has made this patch obsolete.

9. Which of the following commands can you use to verify that a package has been correctly installed?

   A. `pkginfo`

   B. `pkgask`

C. `pkgcheck`

D. `pkgchk`

10. You need to put a package on your organization's web site and make it available for downloads. The package is currently not in the format in which you want to put it on the site. Which of the following commands would you use to convert the package into the right format?

    A. `pkgformat`

    B. `pkgmake`

    C. `pkgtrans`

    D. `pkgadd`

SELF TEST ANSWERS

1. ☑ **E**. The developer software group contains the packages for the end user Solaris software group plus additional support for software development.
☒ **A**, **B**, and **C** are incorrect because these groups do not include development tools. **D** is incorrect because this group contains software for the server functionality that is unnecessary for this workstation.

2. ☑ **A**. The minimum RAM requirement for installing or upgrading to Solaris 10 is 64MB.
☒ **B** is incorrect because 256MB is the recommended RAM, not the minimum required; **C** is incorrect because 384MB is required only if you want to use installation GUI; and **D** is incorrect because 32MB is less than the minimum required.

3. ☑ **B** and **D**. The six software groups in Solaris 10 are: reduced network support software group, core system support software group, end user Solaris software group, developer Solaris software group, entire Solaris software group, and entire plus OEM support.
☒ **A** is incorrect because core system support is a software group, while core system support plus OEM is not. **C** is incorrect because the name for a software group is the developer software group and not the entire developer software group.

4. ☑ **A**, **C**, and **E**. The WAN boot method is used to install Solaris over a wide area network (or Internet), the live upgrade method is used to upgrade the system to Solaris 10 while it's running, and certainly you can install Solaris 10 interactively by using the text installer or the GUI.
☒ **B and D** are incorrect because you cannot install Solaris by using network cloning or UUCP.

5. ☑ **B** and **C**. The `pkgchk` command can be used to verify the installation of a package and also to get the information about the packages in the spool directory.
☒ **A** is incorrect because the purpose of the `pkgchk` command is not to detect the errors in the data of the package files. **D** is incorrect because `pkgchk` is not a version control utility.

6. ☑ **A**. The `pkgrm` command is used to uninstall (remove) packages.
☒ **B** is incorrect because you should never use the `rm -r` command to uninstall a package; uninstalling the package is not identical with just removing the package files. **C** is incorrect because there is no uninstall file to uninstall the packages, and **D** is incorrect because the `patchrm` command is used to uninstall the patches and not the packages.

7. ☑ **B**. It is the `-d` option and not the `-n` option used with the `patchadd` command that will instruct not to back up the files to be patched.
   ☒ **A, C,** and **D** are incorrect answers because they are the correct statements.

8. ☑ **B, C,** and **D**. A patch will not be installed if it is being made obsolete by an already installed patch, if it has the same base code but lower revision code than an already installed patch or if it depends on a patch that has not yet been installed.
   ☒ **A** is incorrect because the patch to be installed does not have to be the latest version.

9. ☑ **D**. The `pkgchk` command can be used to check the accuracy of the installed packages and also to check the content of the spooled packages.
   ☒ **A** is incorrect because the `pkginfo` command is used to list the package information and not to check the accuracy of the package installation. **B** is incorrect because the `pkgask` command is used to save the responses from the user for the `pkgadd` command in a file. **C** is incorrect because the correct command is `pkgchk`, not `pkgcheck`.

10. ☑ **C**. The `pkgtrans` command is used to convert a package from one format to another.
    ☒ **A** and **B** are incorrect because `pkgformat` and `pkgmake` are not commands in Solaris 10. **D** is incorrect because the `pkgadd` command is used either to install or to spool packages and not to transform their formats.

3

Performing System Boot and Shutdown

CERTIFICATION OBJECTIVES

Once installed, the Solaris operating system is designed to run continuously so that its resources and services are available to users on a 24 × 7 basis. On occasion, however, you will need to shut down the system and reboot it for such reasons as system configuration changes, scheduled maintenance procedures, or anticipated power outages. Consequently, you need to be familiar with system boot and shutdown procedures. The system boot process is controlled by the boot configuration variables and the system is shutdown by bringing it down to a level where the power can be turned off. At any given time the system is running in a state called the *run level* defined by the services running on the system. In Solaris 10, most of the services are managed by the Service Management Facility (SMF).

So, the core question to think about in this chapter is: how to manage the system boot and shutdown? In search of an answer to this question, we will explore three thought streams: the boot and shutdown processes, the boot configuration variables, and the relationship of SMF to the run levels.

CERTIFICATION OBJECTIVE 3.01

Understanding the Solaris Boot Process

Exam Objective 3.1: *Given a scenario, explain boot PROM fundamentals, including OpenBoot Architecture Standard, boot PROM, NVRAM, POST, Abort Sequence, and displaying POST to serial port for SPARC.*
Exam Objective 3.3: *Execute basic boot PROM commands for a SPARC system.*

The term *booting* has its origin in the phrase "pull yourself up by your bootstraps." The physical memory of your computer does not keep the program instructions or data when the system is shutdown. When you just start up your Solaris machine, there is no operating system running on it. The CPU wakes up, and there is nothing for it in the RAM; therefore, it starts by taking instructions from a chip that has the instructions burned in. In other words, each SPARC-based system has a programmable read-only memory (PROM) chip that contains a program called the OpenBoot PROM *monitor*. The monitor controls the operation of the system before the Solaris kernel is loaded into the memory.

When a system is turned on, the monitor runs a quick self test to check the hardware and memory on the system, called power-on self test (POST). If no errors are found, the system continues the boot process.

The Basic Boot Process

The boot process takes the machine from the point at which the machine is turned on to the point at which the operating system (Solaris in this case) takes over the machine. To understand the boot process, it is important to clearly understand the terms that are explained in the following text.

The Basic Terms

The basic terms involved in the boot process are described here:

- *OpenBoot PROM chip*. This is a programmable read-only memory (PROM) chip based on the OpenBoot architecture standard. It contains a program called OpenBoot PROM Monitor. Such programs, stored in read-only memory (ROM) or PROM, are also called firmware.
- *OpenBoot PROM monitor*. The most important job of OpenBoot firmware (OpenBoot PROM monitor) is to boot the system, which is the process of checking the hardware devices and loading and starting the operating system. The boot process is governed by a number of configuration variables that are stored in NVRAM.
- *NVRAM*. Non-Volatile Random Access Memory (NVRAM) is a chip that stores the system configuration variables whose values determine the startup machine configuration. If you modify the variable values, the modifications will survive across system shutdowns and reboots (or across power cycles). That is why it's called non-volatile. The variables it stores, called NVRAM configuration variables, control the boot process.
- *OpenBoot configuration variables*. These are the variables that govern the boot process. They are also called NVRAM configuration variables.
- *eeprom*. This is the utility that Solaris offers to change the values of the OpenBoot configuration variables.
- *Power cycle*. The power cycle of a machine consists of powering on the machine, booting it, working on it, shutting it down, and turning the power off. The data in RAM does not persist across power cycles.

Now that you can distinguish these terms related to the boot process from each other, let's take a look at the boot process itself.

The Boot Phases

The different phases of the boot process on SPARC-based systems are described here:

- *Boot PROM phase.* The PROM displays the system identification information and then runs power-on self test (POST), which is a diagnostics routine that scans the system to verify the installed hardware and memory. POST runs diagnostics on hardware devices and builds a device tree, which is a data structure describing the devices attached to the system. After the completion of POST, the PROM loads the primary boot program bootblk.
- *Boot programs phase.* The bootblk program loaded by PROM finds the secondary boot program ufsboot located in the UFS file system on the default boot device and loads it into the memory.
- *Kernel initialization phase.* The ufsboot program loads the kernel into the memory. The kernel initializes itself and uses the ufsboot program to locate and load OS modules to control the system. A module is a piece of software with a specific functionality, such as interfacing with a particular hardware device. After loading enough modules to mount the root (/) file system, the kernel unmaps the ufsboot program and continues gaining control of the system. At the end of the kernel initialization phase, the kernel starts the `/sbin/init` process.
- *The init phase.* The init phase starts when, after initializing itself, the kernel starts the `/sbin/init` process, which in turn starts `/lib/svc/bin/svc.startd` to start the system services to do the following:
  - Check and mount file systems.
  - Configure network and devices.
  - Start various processes and perform tasks related to system maintenance.

The `svc.startd` process also executes run control (rc) scripts for backward compatibility. The steps in the boot process are illustrated in Figure 3-1.

You might ask: how can I control the boot process? The boot process is controlled by the boot configuration variables. If the value of the `auto-boot?` variable is false,

FIGURE 3-1 Steps in the boot process

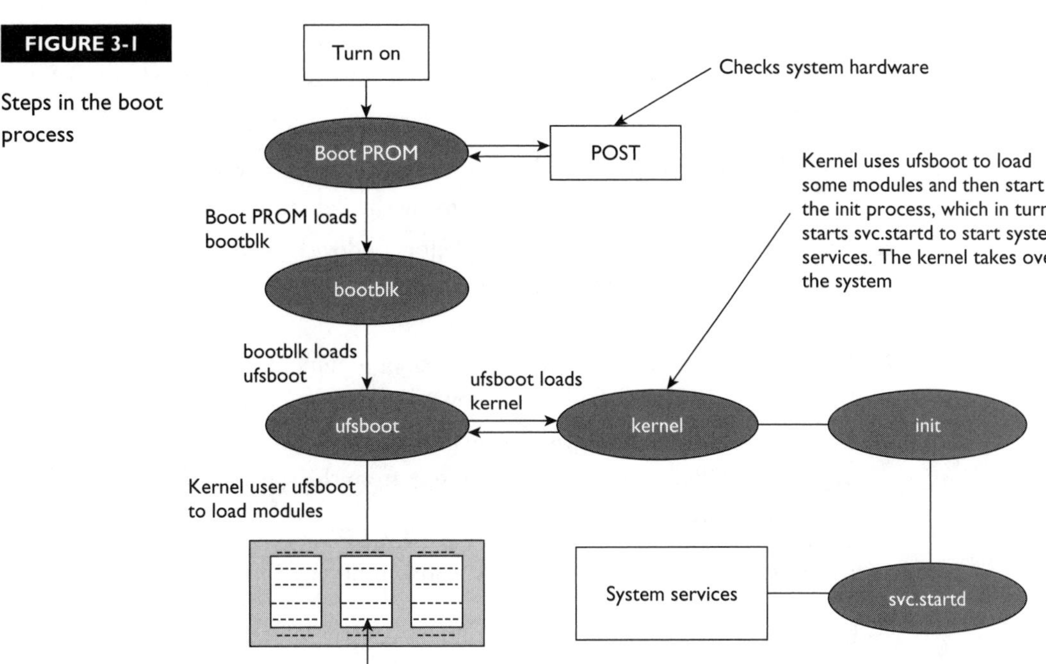

the system will display the Boot PROM prompt: `ok`. On this prompt you can issue various Boot PROM commands.

Basic Boot PROM Commands

When the system is turned on or reset, it first runs POST, and then one of the following two things can happen:

- The system will automatically reboot if the value of the configuration variable `auto-boot?` is true, the value of the `boot-command` variable is boot, and OpenBoot is not in diagnostic mode. In order to boot, the system will automatically load, and executes the program and its arguments specified by the `boot-file` variable from the device described by the `boot-device` variable.
- If the configuration variable `auto-boot?` is false, the system may stop at the OpenBoot user interface without booting the system and will display the `ok` prompt.

You can issue the Boot PROM commands at the `ok` prompt. One obvious command is the `boot` command to boot the system, which you can use in one of the following ways:

- Issue the `boot` command without any arguments if you want to boot the system from the default boot device using the default boot arguments.
- Issue the `boot` command with an explicit boot device as an argument if you want to boot the system from the specified boot device using the default boot arguments.
- Issue the `boot` command with explicit boot arguments if you want to boot the system from the default device by using the specified arguments.
- Issue the `boot` command with an explicit boot device and with explicit arguments if you want to boot the system from the specified device with the specified arguments.

The general syntax of the `boot` command is shown here:

```
boot [<device>] [<arguments>]
```

Arguments and options are described here:

- **`<device>`.** Specifies the full path or the alias for the boot device. The typical values are:
  - **`cdrom`** for CD-ROM drive
  - **`disk`** for hard disk
  - **`floppy`** for 3.5 inch diskette drive
  - **`net`** for network
  - **`tape`** for SCSI tape
- **`<arguments>`.** Specify the arguments for the `boot` command such as the name of the file that contains the program that will be started as a result of the command. The name is relative to the selected device and partition. If this argument is not specified, the boot program uses the value of the NVRAM parameter: `boot-file`.

In addition to the `boot` command there are other administrative and diagnostic commands that you can issue at the Boot PROM prompt: `ok`. The commonly used OpenBoot PROM commands issued from the `ok` prompt are described in Table 3-1.

TABLE 3-1 Commonly used OpenBoot PROM commands (do not type `ok`; it's a command prompt)

Command	Description	Example
ok `banner`	Displays current power-on banner.	`-h`
ok `boot [<arguments>] [<options>]`	Boots the system.	**ok** `boot` Boots with default options.
ok `.enet-addr`	Displays current Ethernet address of the machine.	—
ok `.version`	Displays the version of the Boot PROM.	—
ok `eject <media>`	Ejects the media.	**ok** `eject floppy` **ok** `eject cdrom` **ok** `eject tape`
ok `help [<category>]` **ok** `help [<command>]`	The `help` command without arguments displays a list of command categories, and, with a category as an argument, displays help for all the commands in that category.	**ok** `help dump` Displays help for the `dump` command.
ok `password`	Sets the security password.	—
ok `printenv`	Displays a table showing the boot configuration variable names, their current values, and default values.	—
ok `reset-all`	Resets the system. It's equivalent to performing a power cycle.	—
ok `set-default <varName>`	Sets the value of the specified variable to its default value.	**ok** `set-default auto-boot?`
ok `setenv <varName> <value>`	Sets the value of a boot configuration variable.	**ok** `auto-boot? false`
ok `show-devs`	Displays the list of all the devices in the OpenBoot device tree.	—
ok `test <device>`	Tests the specified device. No message displayed means test succeeded.	**ok** `test floppy` **ok** `test cdrom` **ok** `test /memory` **ok** `test tape`

You can issue the PROM commands either from the console (most commonly) or from the serial terminal attached to the ttya or ttyb port on a Solaris machine. Table 3-2 presents some useful emergency commands related to booting.

You can use the `Stop-A` command to get the Boot PROM command prompt from the running system. You can also use this command to reboot a hung system, as shown

TABLE 3-2 Emergency commands from keyboard (<key1>-<key2> means hold down both keys at the same time)

Command Hold down the key or keys during power-on sequence	Effect
`Stop`	Bypass POST.
`Stop-A`	Abort.
`Stop-D`	Enter diagnostic mode. Enter this command if your system bypasses POST by default and you don't want it to.
`Stop-N`	Reset NVRAM content to default values.

in the following exercise. If you only want to allow the Stop-A key combination to work during the boot sequence and you don't want it to work when the system is up and running, uncomment the following line in the `/etc/default/kbd` file:

```
KEYBOARD_ABORT = disable
```

EXERCISE 3-1

Rebooting the Hung System

In order to reboot the hung system and force a crash dump, perform the following steps. This procedure will work even if the system is not hung.

1. Press the stop key sequence for your system. The specific stop key sequence depends on your keyboard type. For example, it could be Stop-A or L1-A. On terminals, press the Break key. The system will go to the PROM phase and display the `ok` prompt.
2. Synchronize the file systems and write the crash dump.

```
> n
ok sync
```

   After the crash dump has been written to disk, the system will continue to reboot.

3. Verify that the system boots to run level 3. The login prompt is displayed when the boot process has finished successfully.

```
<login prompt>:
```

4. Login as root, and issue the following command to force a crash dump:

```
halt -d
```

5. At the ok prompt, issue the boot command to boot the system:

```
ok boot
```

In this exercise, the sync command actually returns control to the OS, which performs the data-saving operation. This is important because the system may have frozen (crashed) without saving the data that was supposed to be saved to the disk.

When a system is booted, a certain number of services are started at the end of the boot process. Which services are started depends on the run level to which the system boots.

Understanding Run Levels

A run level denoted by a digit or a letter represents the state of a system. The Solaris system always runs in one of a set of well-defined run levels. Run levels are also referred to as *init states* because they are maintained by the init process. The Solaris system has eight run levels described in Table 3-3. The default run level is specified in the /etc/inittab file by the initdefault entry, and its value in the default version of the file is 3. However, note that this value will be used by the init process only if the milestone property has not been specified for the SMF facility svc.startd; otherwise, the default run level specified by the milestone property will be used.

You can determine the run level in which your system is currently running by issuing the following command:

```
who -r
```

The output will look like the following:

```
run-level 3 Jul 04 11:15 3 2 1
```

The parts of this sample output are described here:

- *run-level 3*. The current run level of the system.
- *Jul 04 11:15*. Time of last run level change.

TABLE 3-3 Solaris run levels

Run Level	Init State	Purpose
0	Power-down	Shut down the operating system so that it will be safe to turn off the power to the machine.
S or s	Single-user	Run the system in a single-user mode with some file systems mounted and accessible.
1	Single-user administrative	Run the system in a single-user administrative mode with all available file systems accessible but user logins disabled.
2	Multiuser	Run the system in multiuser mode. Multiple users can log in, all file systems are accessible, but the NFS daemon is not running.
3	Multiuser with NFS	Run the system in the standard mode: normal operations allowed, NFS used to share resources. Default run level.
4	Alternative multiuser	Unused by default, but you can define it according to your needs.
5	Power-down	Same as run level 0; in addition it will automatically turn off the power if the hardware supports that.
6	Reboot	Shut down the system to run level 0 and then reboot it to the default run level specified in the `inittab` file.

- *3*. Current run level of the system, same as column one.
- *2*. Number of times the system has been at this run level since the last reboot.
- *1*. The previous run level.

Different run levels are distinguished from each other by the services or the processes running on the system. When you boot the system or change the run level with the `init` (or the `shutdown`) command, the `init` daemon starts processes by reading information from the `/etc/inittab` file. This file contains two important pieces of information for the `init` process: which processes to use to start monitor and restart if they terminate, and what to do if the system enters a new run level. The default `inittab` file installed with Solaris 10 looks like the following:

```
ap::sysinit:/sbin/autopush -f /etc/iu.ap
sp::sysinit:/sbin/soconfig -f /etc/sock2path
smf::sysinit:/lib/svc/bin/svc.startd >/dev/msglog 2<>/dev/msglog
p3:s1234:powerfail:/usr/sbin/shutdown -y -i5 -g0 >/dev/msglog 2<>/dev/...
```

An entry in the inititab file has the following general syntax:

```
id>:<runState>:<action>:<command>
```

The colon (:) separated fields are described here:

- **`<id>.`** Specifies one to four characters long id used to uniquely identify the entry.
- **`<runState>.`** Specifies a list of run levels for which this entry will be processed. If this field is left blank, then the entry is assumed to be valid for all run levels from 0 through 6.
- **`<action>.`** Specifies a keyword to tell `init` how to treat the process specified in this entry. Some of the valid keywords for this field include:
  - **`boot.`** The entry will be processed only when the `init` process reads it at boot-time. The `init` will start the specified process, will not wait for its termination, and will not restart it if it dies.
  - **`once.`** If the process specified in the entry is currently running (exists), do nothing and continue scanning the `inittab` file. If the process does not already exist, start the process, do not wait for its termination, and do not restart the process when it dies.
  - **`respawn.`** If the process specified in the entry is currently running (exists), do nothing and continue scanning the `inittab` file. If the process does not already exist, start the process, do not wait for its termination, and restart the process when it dies.
  - **`wait.`** Start the process and wait for its termination before proceeding further. This will be done only once when the system enters the specified run level, and all the subsequent readings of the `inittab` file during the time the system is in the same run level will ignore this entry.
  - **`powerfail.`** Execute the specified process only if init receives the power fail signal: SIGPWR.
  - **`sysinit.`** Execute the specified process before displaying the login prompt. Start the process and wait for its completion before proceeding further. This entry is used only to initialize the devices.
- **`<command>.`** Specifies a command to execute a process.

The* `initdefault` *entry is ignored in Solaris 10 if the milestone property for the* `svc.startd` *facility has been specified to be used as the default run level. You can use the "*`svcadm milestone -d`*" for the functionality similar to modifying the* `initdefault` *entry in previous versions of Solaris.

As an example, the fields of an entry in the `/etc/inittab` file are described in Figure 3-2.

The Solaris system normally runs in run level 3. Following is the list of things that happen when the system is brought to run level 3:

1. The `init` process is started, which reads the `/etc/default/init` file to set any environment variables. By default, only the `TIMEZONE` variable is set.
2. The `init` process reads the `inittab` file and does the following:
   - Executes any process entries that have `sysinit` in the `<action>` field so that any special initializations can take place before users log in.
   - Passes the startup activities to the `svc.startd` daemon.
   - The `init` process initiates the core components of the service management facility, `svc.configd` and `svc.startd`, and restarts these components if they fail.

Each run level <n> has a corresponding run control script `/sbin/rc<n>`: `/sbin/rc0` for run level 0, `/sbin/rc1` for run level 1, and so on. When the system enters a run level <n>, the `init` process runs the corresponding `/sbin/rc<n>` script, which in turn executes the files in the `/etc/rc<n>.d` directory, which are actually links to files in the `/etc/init.d` directory. This is illustrated in Figure 3-3.

FIGURE 3-2

Fields of an entry in the `/etc/inittab` file

Id: uniquely identifies this entry

Execute the process specified in this entry only when the init process receives a power fail signal: SIGPWR

p3:s1234:powerfail:/usr/sbin/shutdown –y –i5 –g0> /dev/msglog

This entry is to be processed for run levels s, 1, 2, 3, and 4

The command to be executed

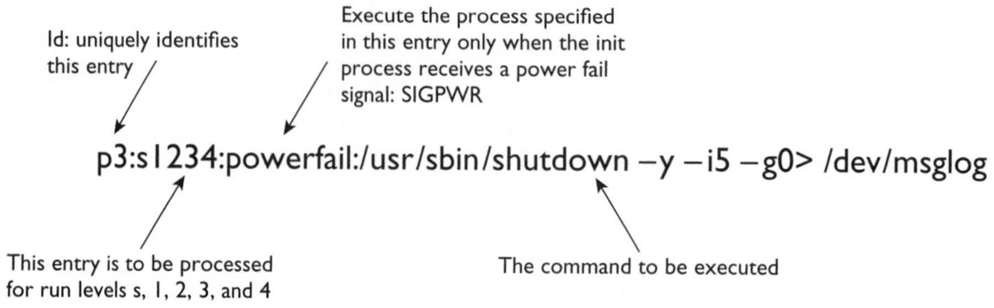

FIGURE 3-3 Relationship between run levels and run control scripts

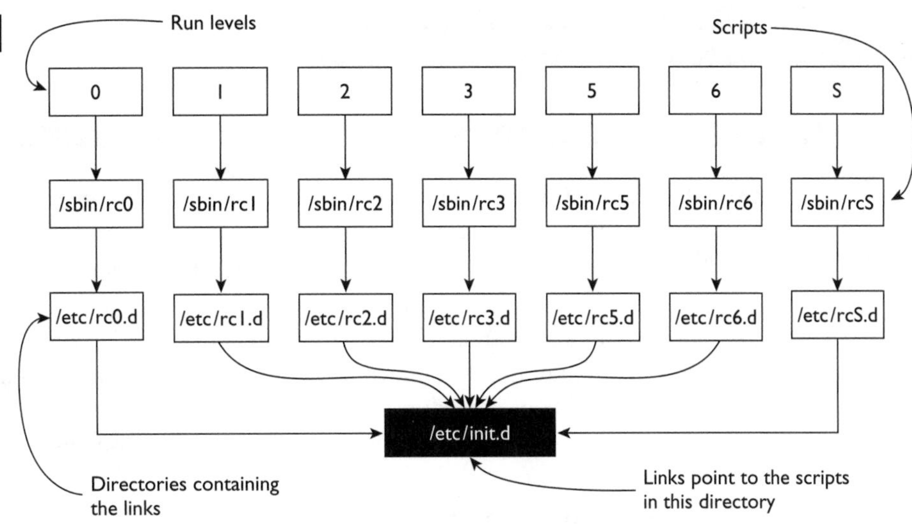

The /etc/rc<n>.d scripts are always run in ASCII sort order. The scripts have names of the form:

```
[K|S][0-9][0-9]*
```

For example, K03samba and S47pppd are two files (actually the links to the files in the /etc/init.d directory) in the /etc/rc2.d directory.

Files that begin with K are run to terminate (kill) a system service, whereas files that begin with S are run to start a system service.

on the job

If you want to add a run control script to start or stop a service, copy the script into the /etc/init.d directory and create links in the appropriate rc<n>.d directory corresponding to the run level where you want the service to start or stop.

You can use the init command or the svcadm command to initiate a transition of the system from current run level to another run level. The init command takes a run level as an argument. For example, the following command will transition the system from the current run level to run level 2:

```
init 2
```

Now you have an overall view of the boot process, and shutting down the system is just changing its run level to 0 or 5. However, as a system administrator, you can have more control over the boot and shutdown procedures that we discuss next.

CERTIFICATION OBJECTIVE 3.02

Performing Boot and Shutdown Procedures

Exam Objective 3.5: *Perform system boot and shutdown procedures, including identifying the system's boot device, creating and removing custom device aliases, viewing and changing NVRAM parameters, and interrupting an unresponsive system.*

The Solaris operating system is designed to run continuously, but there will be situations that will require shutdown and reboot. Consequently, you need to know the shutdown and boot procedures and how to control them by using appropriate commands and by setting the appropriate configuration variables.

Performing System Shutdown

You would shut down a Solaris system only when some system administration task or an emergency situation requires it, such as adding or removing hardware or preparing for an anticipated power outage. Shutting down the system means bringing it down to a run level where it is safe to turn off the power. Guess which command is used to shut down the system. Yes, you are right, it is the `shutdown` command. Because shutting down a running system is equivalent to changing its run level, the `init` command will work as well. When you shut down a system, remember the following:

- Obviously, you need the privileges of a superuser to shut down the system by using the proper commands (that is, to shut down the system gracefully).
- The commands that can be used for shutting down the system are `init` and `shutdown`.
- You should use the `shutdown` command to shut down a server. That is because with this command logged-in, users and systems that have mounted resources from the server are notified before the server is actually shut down.

Both the `shutdown` and `init` commands take a run level as an argument. The appropriate run level to use for a system shutdown depend on the situation. Different run levels to be used for different situations are listed in Table 3-4.

The procedure for shutting down the system by using the `shutdown` command is described here step by step:

1. Become a superuser.

TABLE 3-4 Different ways of shutting down a system under different situations

Reason for System Shutdown	Action
To turn off system power due to an anticipated power outage.	Shut down to run level 0 where it is safe to turn off the power, or shut down to run level 5 where the power will be turned off automatically if the hardware supports this feature.
Changed kernel parameters in the `/etc/system` file.	Shut down to run level 6 (reboot).
To perform tasks related to file system maintenance.	Shut down to single-user mode: run level S or 1, according to your need.
To reboot the system by using the kernel debugger (kmdb) in case the debugger can't be loaded at runtime.	Shut down to run level 6.

2. Issue the following command to determine whether users are logged in to the system:

```
Who
```

The command will display the list of all users logged on to the system. You may want to broadcast a message with the `shutdown` command to alert the users.

3. Issue the `shutdown` command which has the following syntax:

```
/usr/sbin/shutdown [-y] [-g <gracePeriod>] [-i <initState>] [<message>]
```

The options are described here:

- **`-y`.** Pre-answers the confirmation questions so that the command continues without asking for your intervention.
- **`-g <gracePeriod>`.** Specifies the number of seconds before the shutdown begins. The default value is 60.
- **`-i <initState>`.** Specifies the run level to which the system will be shut down. Default is the single-user level: S.
- **`<message>`.** Specifies the message to be appended to the standard warning message that will be sent out. If the `<message>` contains multiple words, it should be enclosed in single or double quotes. For example:

```
shutdown -i 0 -g 120 "!!!! Power Outage Time Approaching!!!"
```

TABLE 3-5 Prompts for different run levels

Specified Run Level	System Prompt: SPARC	System Prompt: x86
Single-user level: S	#	#
Power-down level: 0	`ok` `>`	Press any key to reboot
Multiuser level: 3	<loginPrompt>	<loginPrompt>

If you used the `-y` option in the command, you will not be prompted to confirm.

4. If you are asked for confirmation, type `y`.

```
Do you want to continue? (y or n): y
```

5. Use Table 3-5 to verify that the system is at the run level that you specified in the `shutdown` command.
6. If you brought the system to single-user mode, press CTRL-D to proceed with normal startup after you are finished with the system administration tasks. This will bring the system to default run level.

There are several commands available to shut down the system; these commands are summarized in Table 3-6.

TABLE 3-6 Different commands for shutting down the system under different situations

Command	Description	When to Use
`init`	Kills all active processes and synchronizes the file systems before changing to the target run level (0 or 5).	Recommended for standalone systems when users will not be affected.
`halt` `poweroff`	Synchronizes the file systems and stops the processor.	Not recommended, because it does not shut down all the processes. Not a clean shutdown, should be used only in an emergency.
`reboot`	Synchronizes the file systems and initiates a multiuser reboot.	The `init` command is the preferred command.
`shutdown`	Calls the init program to shut down the system; the default target run level is S.	Recommended for servers, because users are notified before the shutdown.

Now that you have learned about the run levels and the system shutdown procedures, here are some practical scenarios and their solutions.

SCENARIO & SOLUTION	
You want to bring your server down for an anticipated power outage, and you want a clean shutdown with a 5-minute warning to the users.	Issue the `shutdown` command as follows: `shutdown -i5 -g300 -y "System going down in 5 minutes."`
You have changed the kernel parameters on your server and want to apply the new values. What command will you issue?	Reboot the system, for example: `shutdown -i6 -y`
You want to shut down your standalone system.	init 0
You want to shut down a system immediately in an emergency.	Issue one of the following commands: `halt` `poweroff`

After you shut down a system, at some point you will need to boot it.

Performing System Boot

The boot process was discussed in detail previously in this chapter. After a system has been shut down, it is booted as described here:

- By using the `boot` command on the boot PROM prompt if the system is on the SPARC machine. If the value of the `auto-boot?` variable is true, the system will be booted automatically. We discuss further on in this chapter how to find out the values of this and other variables.
- By using the `boot` command at the Primary Boot Subsystem menu if the system is on the x86 machine.

It is possible to reboot a system by turning the power off and then back on. However, use this method only in emergency situations when there is no graceful alternative. Note that this method is likely to cause file system damage because system services and processes are being terminated abruptly.

You can also boot a system from the network in the following cases:

- When the system is installed.
- If the system does not boot from the local disk or if the system is a diskless client.

Different methods for booting under different situations are listed in Table 3-7. As you know by now, the first step in the booting process is to check the hardware devices. These devices have complicated names, and you can create aliases for them.

Creating and Removing Device Aliases

OpenBoot directly deals with the hardware devices in the system. Each device is identified by its full path, which includes the type of the device and where it is located. The device path can be represented by a short name called a device alias. You can create a temporary device alias with the `devalias` command or a permanent device alias with the `nvalias` command.

The `devalias` command issued without any arguments displays all the device aliases on the system:

```
devalias
```

TABLE 3-7 Different methods for booting under different situations

Reason for Reboot	Appropriate Boot Option
System power turned off, for example, due to anticipated power outage.	Turn the system power back on.
Changed the kernel parameters in the `/etc/system` file.	Reboot the system to run level 3.
Performed administrative tasks in single-user run level.	Press CTRL-D to transition the system back to run level 3.
Hardware added to or removed from the system.	Turn the power back on after the hardware addition or removal task is complete.
To recover from a hung system and force a crash dump.	Recovery boot: use `Stop-A` and `halt -d`. Take a look at the exercise in a previous section.

To display the device path name corresponding to an alias, issue the following command:

```
devalias <alias>
```

The `<alias>` argument specifies the alias for which you want to know the device path. To create an alias specified by `<alias>` for a device path specified by `<devicePath>`, issue the following command:

```
devalias <alias> <devicePath>
```

If the device path specified by `<devicePath>` already has an alias, it is overwritten with the new alias. The aliases created by the `devalias` command are temporary and are lost when the system is reset or power-cycled.

To create permanent aliases that persist across power cycles, you can use the `nvalias` command which has the following syntax:

```
nvalias <alias> <devicePath>
```

The argument `<alias>` specifies the alias, and the argument `<devicePath>` specifies the device path for which the alias is being created. An alias created by the `nvalias` command will persist along system shutdowns (power-cycles) until the `nvrunalias` command is used, which has the following syntax:

```
nvrunalias <alias>
```

This will delete the alias specified by the `<alias>` argument.

The boot process is controlled by the configuration variables stored in the NVRAM chip, and therefore these variables are also called NVRAM parameters.

Working with NVRAM Parameters

The system configuration variables are stored in NVRAM and therefore are also called NVRAM parameters. These variables determine the startup configuration for the system as well as some related communication characteristics. If you make changes to these variables, the changes will persist across power cycles because they are stored in non-volatile memory.

Commonly used NVRAM parameters are described in Table 3-8.

The values of the NVRAM configuration variables can be viewed and changed by using the commands listed in Table 3-9. Remember that these commands are issued at the OpenBoot PROM prompt: `ok`.

TABLE 3-8 A list of NVRAM parameters, also called openboot configuration variables

Parameter Name	Description	Default Value
`auto-boot?`	If true, boot automatically after power-on or reset, else display the open boot prompt: `ok`, after power-on or reset.	true
`boot-command`	Execute this command if `auto-boot?` is true.	boot
`boot-device`	The device from which the system boots.	disk or net
`boot-file`	Arguments passed to the boot program.	Empty string
`diag-device`	Diagnostic boot source device.	net
`diag-file`	Arguments passed to the boot program in diagnostic mode.	Empty string
`diag-switch?`	If true, run in diagnostic mode, else not.	false
`fcode-debug`	If true, include name fields for plugin device FCodes.	false
`input-device`	Console input device such as keyboard, ttya, or ttyyb.	keyboard
`nvramrc`	The NVRAMRC content.	Empty
`oem-banner`	Customized oem banner.	Empty string
`oem-banner?`	If true, use customized oem-banner specified by oem-banner.	false
`oem-logo`	Customized oem logo displayed in hexadecimal.	No default
`oem-logo?`	If true, display customized oem logo specified by oem-logo.	false
`output-device`	Console output device such as screen, ttya, or ttyb.	screen
`screen-#columns`	Number of columns on the screen: number of characters per line.	80
`screen-#rows`	Number of on-screen rows (lines).	34
`security-#badlogins`	Number of incorrect security password attempts.	No default
`security-mode`	Firmware security level: none, command, or full.	None
`security-password`	Firmware security password. It's never displayed, for good.	No default
`use-nvramc?`	If true, execute commands in NVRAMRC during system startup, else not.	false

For example, the `printenv` command will generate an output like the one shown here:

```
ok printenv
Variable Name Value Default Value
oem-logo
```

TABLE 3-9 Commands to view and change the values of the NVRAM parameters

Command	Description
printenv	Displays the current variables and their values.
printenv <var>	Displays the current value of the variable specified by <var>.
set-defaults	Sets the values of all the variables to the factory default.
set-default <var>	Sets the value of the variable specified by <var> to its factory default.
setenv <var> <value>	Sets the value of the variable specified by <var> to the value specified by <value>.

```
oem-logo? false false
oem-banner? False false
output-device ttya screen
input-device ttya keyboard
```

The following command will display the current default boot device for the system:

```
ok printenv boot-device
```

To change the boot device, you can issue the following command:

```
ok setenv boot-device <value>
```

The `<value>` parameter specifies the default device from which to boot such as disk or net.

Many variable changes do not take effect during the current power cycle. The new values will certainly be used during the next power cycle or after a system reset.

You can also use the `eeprom` command from the OS command line to display or change the boot configuration variables. For example, the following command will display the values of the boot configuration variables:

```
/usr/sbin/eeprom
```

Any user can use this command, but only the superuser can use the command to change the values of a variable by using the following syntax of the command:

```
eeprom <parameter>=<value>
```

For example the following command will set the value of the auto-boot? variable to false:

```
eeprom auto-boot?=false
```

You can find out the OpenBoot PROM revision on your system by issuing the following command:

```
prtconf -V
```

Although the read-only memory used to boot a SPARC machine is called PROM, the read-only memory to boot an x86 (PC) machine is called BIOS, which we explore next.

CERTIFICATION OBJECTIVE 3.03

Understanding BIOS Settings and Configuration

Exam Objective 3.2: *Given a scenario, explain the BIOS settings for booting, abort sequence, and displaying POST, including BIOS configuration for x64 and x86-based system.*

Like SPARC machines, x86 (PC) machines go through a booting process before the Solaris operating system takes control of the machine. The read-only memory that contains the boot instructions is called the Basic Input/Output System (BIOS) in an x86 machine as opposed to Boot PROM in a SPARC machine. The functions of the BIOS include controlling installed peripheral devices such as keyboard and mouse and to providing I/O services via software interrupts.

The phases of the boot process on an x86 machine are described here:

- *BIOS.* When the system is turned on, the BIOS runs the self-test diagnostics program for the system's hardware and memory. If problems are found, the error messages are displayed with recovery options. If no errors are found, the BIOS boot program is started automatically, and it attempts to find and load what is called the master boot record (MBR), mboot, from the first sector in the boot device. An error is displayed if the `mboot` file does not exist.

- *Boot programs*. The mboot program loads the Solaris boot program called pboot, which in turn loads the primary boot program, bootblk, whose purpose is to load the secondary boot program located in the UFS file system. If there are more than one bootable partitions on the system, the bootblk reads the fdisk table to determine the default boot partition. It builds and displays a menu of available partitions and gives you 30 seconds to select an alternative partition to boot from. The primary boot program—bootblk—starts the secondary boot program boot.bin or ufsboot in the root file system, which in turn starts a command interpreter that executes the `/etc/bootrc` script. This script presents a menu of choices for booting the system, and you have 5 seconds to specify a boot option or to start the boot interpreter. The default choice is to load the kernel.
- *Kernel initialization*. After the kernel has been loaded, it initializes itself and uses the secondary boot program boot.bin (or ufsboot) to load system modules. When the kernel loads enough modules to mount the root (/) file system, it unmaps the secondary boot program and continues taking over the system. It creates a user process and starts the `/sbin/init` process, which then starts other processes by reading the `/etc/inittab` file.
- *init*. In Solaris 10, the `init` process starts `/lib/svc/bin/svc.startd`, which in turn starts system services to perform the following tasks:
  - Check and mount file systems
  - Configure network and devices
  - Start various processes and perform system maintenance tasks

The `svc.startd` daemon also executes the run control (rc) scripts for backward compatibility. During the booting process, you have some control over the way in which the system is booted. Two menus are displayed for you: the Boot Solaris menu and the Current Boot Parameters menu.

The Boot Solaris menu allows you to select the device from which to boot the Solaris OS. At this point, you can also perform some optional tasks such as viewing and editing `autoboot` and property settings. Once you select a boot device and choose Continue, the Solaris kernel begins to boot. The menu looks like the following:

```
Boot Solaris
Select one of the identified devices to boot the Solaris kernel and
choose Continue.
To perform optional features, such as modifying the autoboot and property
settings, choose Boot Tasks.
An asterisk (*) indicates the current default boot device.
> To make a selection use the arrow keys, and press Enter to mark it [X].
[X] DISK: (*) Target 0:QUANTUM FIREBALL1280A
on Bus Mastering IDE controller on Board PCI at Dev 7, Func 1
[ ] DISK: Target 1:ST5660A
on Bus Mastering IDE controller on Board PCI at Dev 7, Func 1
[ ] DISK: Target 0:Maxtor 9 0680D4
on Bus Mastering IDE controller on Board PCI at Dev 7, Func 1
[ ] CD : Target 1:TOSHIBA CD-ROM XM-5602B 1546
on Bus Mastering IDE controller on Board PCI at Dev 7, Func 1
F2_Continue F3_Back F4_Boot Tasks F6_Help
```

The second menu that you are offered is the current boot parameter menu, which looks like the following:

```
<<< Current Boot Parameters >>>
Boot path: /pci@0,0/pci-ide@7,1/ide@0/cmdk@0,0:a
Boot args:
Type b [file-name] [boot-flags] <ENTER> to boot with options
or i <ENTER> to enter boot interpreter
or <ENTER> to boot with defaults
<<< timeout in 5 seconds >>>
Select (b)oot or (i)nterpreter:
```

The following file contains the `eeprom` variables used to set up the boot environment on an x86 machine:

```
/boot/solaris/bootenv.rc
```

All directories and files needed to boot an x86-based system are contained in the `/boot` directory.

In addition to BIOS configurations, there may be situations in which you will need to configure (or reconfigure) some devices such as keyboard, display, and mouse.

CERTIFICATION OBJECTIVE 3.04

Configuring Devices

Exam Objective 3.4: *Use the Xorg configuration files or kdmconfig utility to configure the keyboard, display, and mouse devices for an x64 and x86-based system.*

You can use the `kdmconfig` command to configure or unconfigure keyboard, display, and mouse devices for OpenWindows and internationalization. This command can be used for any of the following tasks:

- To configure or unconfigure the `/etc/openwin/server/etc/OWconfig` file with the keyboard, display, and mouse information that is relevant to a client's machine on x86-based systems.
- To set up the *display*, *pointer*, and *keyboard* entries in the `/etc/bootparams` file on a server machine. The information that you enter is stored in the `/etc/bootparams` file, which contains one entry per client. The entry for a client contains the client's name and the values for the boot parameters for that client. Diskless clients, while booting, retrieve this information by issuing requests to the server running the `rpc.bootparamd`.
- To set up the monitor, *keyboard*, *display*, and *pointer* keywords in a system identification configuration (`sysidcfg`) file. When a diskless client boots for the first time, or a system installs over the network, the booting software tries to obtain the configuration information about the system, such as the system's root password or name service, first from a `sysidcfg` file and then from the name service databases.

The `kdmconfig` command has the following syntax:

```
kdmconfig [-fv] [-s <hostname>]-c | -t | -u | -d <filename>
```

The command will display screens for you to enter the information. The options are described here:

- **`-c`.** Execute the program in the configuration mode used to create or update the `/etc/openwin/server/etc/OWconfig` file. It then displays the screens for you to enter the information.

- **-d <filename>.** This option is used to create a system configuration identification file that will be used when a diskless client boots for the first time or when you install a system over the network. It is used to avoid prompts for the user and provide a totally hands-off booting process. This command displays the same screens as `-c` option. The argument `<filename>` specifies the system identification configuration filename under which the information will be saved.
- **-f.** Forces screen mode; no network probing will be performed. This option can be used when you want to debug the client's configuration environment.
- **-s <hostname>.** This option is used to set up configuration information on this machine for the diskless clients.
- **-t.** Run the command in test mode.
- **-u.** Unconfigure the system.
- **-v.** Enable verbose mode.

If you issue the `kdmconfig` command without any options, it will edit the configuration information from the `OWconfig` file—that is, it will run like `-c` option.

You can also use the following commands to reconfigure the system:

```
/usr/X11/bin/xorgconfig
/usr/X11/bin/Xorg -configure
```

As mentioned previously, the services at the init phase of the boot process are started by the SMF facility `svc.startd`. Nevertheless, the `/etc/rc<n>.d` continues to be started as well, for backward compatibility reasons.

CERTIFICATION OBJECTIVE 3.05

Service Management Facility and Run Levels

Exam Objective 3.6: *Explain the Service Management Facility and the phases of the boot process.*

Exam Objective 3.7: *Use SMF or legacy commands and scripts to control both the boot and shutdown procedures.*

Solaris 10 offers Service Management Facility (SMF) to provide an infrastructure that augments the traditional UNIX startup scripts, init run levels, and configuration files. In the init phase, the unit process starts the `svc.startd` process, which is an SMF process, and it starts the system services.

Although many standard Solaris services are now managed by SMF, the scripts placed in the `/etc/rc<n>.d` directories continue to be executed when a run level transition occurs. Even though most of these scripts from the previous Solaris releases have been removed as a result of moving to SMF, the ability to continue running the remaining scripts allows for third-party applications and services to be added without the need to convert the services to use SMF.

There is another reason to keep the run-script infrastructure intact for now: the need to make the `/etc/inittab` and `/etc/inetd.conf` files available for packages to amend with post install scripts, called legacy-run services. You can use the `inetconv` command to convert these services to the SMF, which will add these services to the service configuration repository (the place where SMF maintains the configuration information). After a service has been converted to SMF, it will not need to make modifications to the `/etc/inittab` and `/etc/inetd.conf` files, and it will obviously not use the `/etc/rc<n>.d` scripts.

SMF offers the `svcadm` command to administer the SMF services. This command can also be used to change the run level of a system by selecting what is called a milestone at which to run. The `svcadm` command to change the run level has the following syntax:

```
/usr/sbin/svcadm [-v] milestone [-d] <milestone_FMRI>
```

If you do not use the `-d` option, this command will transition the system to the run level specified by `<milestone_FMRI>`. If you use the `-d` option, it will make the run level specified by the `<milestone_FMRI>` as the default run level for the system at boot time. The relationship between the values of `<milestone_FMRI>` and run levels is shown in Table 3-10.

TABLE 3-10 Relationship between the init run levels and the SMF milestones

Run Level	`<milestone_FMRI>`
S	milestone/single-user:default
2	milestone/multi-user:default
3	milestone/multi-user-server:default

The Fault Management Resource Identifier (FMRI) is a string that is used to identify a particular resource for which Solaris can perform automated fault management. You will learn more about SMF further on in this book. For example, the following command restricts the running services to a single-user mode:

```
# svcadm milestone milestone/single-user
```

The following command restores all the running services:

```
svcadm milestone all
```

Therefore, you can use the `init` command or the `svcadm` command to initiate a run-level transition. As an alternative to the `initdefault` entry in the `inititab` file, the following command will make run level 3 as the default run level:

```
svcadm milestone -d milestone/multi-user-server
```

The default milestone defined by the `initdefault` entry in the `inittab` file is not recognized in Solaris 10.

The three most important takeaways from this chapter are the following:

- A number of programs are executed in the boot process in this order: POST to check the hardware and memory, the boot programs bootblk and ufsboot, kernel, init, and svc.startd. Shutting down a system means changing its run level to a level (0 or 5) from which it is safe to turn off the power.
- The boot configuration variables can be managed with a number of commands issued at the Boot PROM command prompt `ok`, such as `setenv` command to set the value of a variable. You can also change the values of these variables at the OS command line by using the `eeprom` command.
- In Solaris 10, most of the services are managed by the Service Management Facility (SMF), but the run control scripts are still executed to provide backward compatibility. Do not count on the `initdefault` entry in the `inittab` file; instead use the `svcadm` command to set (or change) the default run level of the system.

CERTIFICATION SUMMARY

There will be situations in which you will need to shut down the Solaris system and reboot it—for example, scheduled maintenance procedures or an anticipated power outage. The system boot is controlled by the boot configuration variables. If the value of the `auto-boot?` variable is true, the system will boot automatically by using the default values; otherwise the Boot PROM command prompt `ok` will be displayed. You can manage the boot configuration variables by using a number of commands at this prompt, such as `printenv` to display the current values of the variables and `setenv` command to change the value of a variable. You can also use the `eeprom` command to change the values of the variables at the OS command line.

At the end of the boot process the system enters the default run level determined by the milestone property of the SMF service: `svc.startd`. If this property is set, the `initdefault` entry in the `inittab` file is ignored in Solaris 10. You can change the default run level of the system by using the `svcadm` command. A run level determines which services will be running on the system. You can change the run level of a running system by using the `init` command or the `svcadm` command. Shutting down the system means changing its run level to a level from which it is safe to turn off the power. Although most of the services in Solaris 10 are managed by SMF, the run control scripts are still executed for compatibility and to support legacy services.

Everything in UNIX (and hence in Solaris) is represented by files, and files are one of the most important resources supported by an operating system. In the next chapter, you will explore how to manage file systems in Solaris.

INSIDE THE EXAM

Comprehend

- The values of the configuration variables stored in the NVRAM chip persist across the power cycles.
- In Solaris 10, you should use the SMF command `svcadm` with the milestone as the argument to change (or set) the default run level.
- You can use either the `svcadm` or the `init` command to change the run level of a system.

Look Out

- In Solaris 10, the `initdefault` entry in the `/etc/inittab` file is used for the default run level only if the milestone property for the `svc.startd` facility has not been defined.
- Both the `init 0` and `init 5` commands will shut down the system, but `init 5` will also attempt to turn off the power if the hardware supports it.
- To display and change the NVRAM parameters, the `eeprom` command is used from the OS command line, whereas the `setenv` and `printenv` commands are used at the Boot PROM prompt `ok`.

Memorize

- You push the `Stop-A` keys to recover form a hung system. The `Stop-D` keys are used to force the POST execution if your system bypasses it by default.
- The `halt -d` command is used to force a crash dump.
- The `devalias` command is used to create a device alias that will not persist across power cycles, and the `nvalias` command is used to create a device alias that will persist across power cycles.
- The `kdmconfig` command can be used to configure or unconfigure the `/etc/openwin/server/etc/OWconfig` file with the keyboard, display, and mouse information relevant to a client's machine on x86-based systems.

TWO-MINUTE DRILL

Understanding the Solaris Boot Process

- ❑ When the system is first turned on, the OpenBoot PROM runs the power-on self test (POST) to check the hardware and the memory.
- ❑ The phases of the boot process are Boot PROM, boot programs, kernel initialization, and the init, in the order given.
- ❑ During the boot process, programs run in this order: POST, bootblk, ufsboot, kernel, and init.

Performing Boot and Shutdown Procedures

- ❑ After POST, the Boot PROM command prompt `ok` is displayed if the `auto-boot?` variable is false; otherwise the system boots by using default values.
- ❑ At the `ok` prompt, you can issue the `boot` command and some other commands such as `test <device>` to test a device.
- ❑ The `setenv` command at the `ok` prompt is used to set the values of the NVRAM parameters, while the `printenv` command is used to display the values of the NVRAM parameters.

Understanding BIOS Settings and Configuration

- ❑ Solaris always runs in one of the available run levels, which are represented by integers and letters: 0 to 6, and S (for single user).
- ❑ The default run level is defined by the `initdefault` entry in the `/etc/inittab` file. However, in Solaris 10 the `initdefault` entry is used only if the milestone property for the `svc.startd` facility has not been defined, which is preferably used as the default run level.
- ❑ Most of the services in Solaris 10 are managed by the Service Management Facility (SMF), but the run control (rc) scripts are started for backward compatibility.
- ❑ You can use the `init` or the `svcadm` command to change the run levels, and the `init` or the `shutdown` command to shut down the system.

Configuring Devices

- NVRAM parameters are the Boot configuration variables stored in the NVRAM chip.
- You can use the `printenv` and `setenv` commands at the Boot prompt `ok` to display and change the NVRAM parameters, respectively, and you can use the `eeprom` command at the OS command line to do the same thing.
- The `set-defaults` command at the `ok` prompt set the value of the NVRAM parameters to the factory default.
- The `devalias` command is used to create a device alias that will not persist across power cycles, and the `nvalias` command is used to create a device alias that will persist across power cycles.

Service Management Facility and Run Levels

- The `svcadm` command to change the run level has the syntax:

```
svcadm milestone <milestone_FMRI>
```

- The `svcadm` command to change the default run level has the syntax:

```
svcadm milestone -d <milestone_FMRI>
```

SELF TEST

The following questions will help you measure your understanding of the material presented in this chapter. Read all the choices carefully because there might be more than one correct answer. Choose all correct answers for each question.

1. The system configuration variables that determine the startup system configuration are stored in which of the following?

   A. OpenBoot PROM

   B. NVRAM

   C. Boot device

   D. File in the `/etc` directory

2. Which tasks are performed during the Boot PROM phase of the system startup?

   A. Kernel initialization

   B. Loading ufsboot

   C. Loading bootblk

   D. Executing power-on self test (POST)

3. Which order of tasks best describes the boot process on a SPARC machine?

   A. Executing POST, loading bootblk, loading ufsboot, executing init, starting svc.startd

   B. Executing POST, loading bootblk, loading ufsboot, starting svc.startd, executing init

   C. Executing POST, loading ufsboot, loading bootblk, executing init, starting svc.startd

   D. Loading bootblk, executing POST, loading ufsboot, executing init, starting svc.startd

4. Your Solaris system is hung? Which of the following actions should you take?

   A. Shut the power down

   B. Push Stop-A

   C. Push Stop-D

   D. Push Stop-N

5. Which sequence represents the phases of the boot process on an x86 machine in the correct order?

   A. Boot PROM, Boot Programs, Kernel Initialization, init

   B. Boot PROM, BIOS, Boot Programs, Kernel Initialization, init

C. Boot PROM, BIOS, Boot Programs, Kernel Initialization, init

D. BIOS, Boot Programs, Kernel Initialization, init

6. Which of the following programs is responsible for starting svc.startd?

   A. svcadm

   B. svcs

   C. init

   D. ufsboot

7. In Solaris 10 what would you do to change the default run level of the system, assuming that the milestone property is set in svc.startd?

   A. Change the value of the `initdefault` entry in the `inittab` file.

   B. Use the `svcadm` command with `-d` option.

   C. Use the `init` command.

   D. Use the `initdefault` command.

8. Which command would you use to change the value of an OpenBoot configuration variable at the OpenBoot PROM command prompt `ok`?

   A. `eeprom`

   B. `setvar`

   C. `set`

   D. `setenv`

9. Which of the following commands creates a device alias that will persist across power cycles?

   A. `devalias`

   B. `nvalias`

   C. `setenv`

   D. `dev-alias`

10. Which of the following commands can be used to change the run level of the Solaris system?

   A. `init`

   B. `shutdown`

   C. `halt`

   D. `run-level`

11. When the SPARC system is being turned on, you push the STOP-D key combination. What is the effect of you action?

    A. It puts the firmware in the diagnostic mode.

    B. It resets the NVRAM parameters to their default values.

    C. It displays a GUI for you so that you can reset the NVRAM parameters.

    D. It resets the NVRAM parameters to their factory default values.

12. Which of the following are the boot phases of an x86-based system?

    A. BIOS loads the MBR program mboot.

    B. The mboot program runs POST.

    C. The mboot program loads the Solaris boot program, pboot.

    D. The pboot program starts ufsboot.

13. Consider the following command and output at OpenBoot prompt:

    ```
    >ok setenv auto-boot? false
    auto-boot? = false
    ```

    What is the effect of this command on the system?

    A. The syntax for the command is incorrect because the name of the variable is `auto-boot` and not `auto-boot?`. So there will be no effect.

    B. The next time you turn the system on, it will not boot until you set the `auto-boot?` variable back to true.

    C. The next time you turn the system on, it will boot into single-user mode.

    D. The next time you turn the system on, it will display the OpenBoot prompt `ok` and you will need to give the `boot` command to boot it.

SELF TEST ANSWERS

1. ☑ **B**. The boot configuration variables are stored in the non-volatile random access memory (NVRAM) chip.
   ☒ **A** is incorrect because OpenBoot PROM contains the OpenBoot PROM monitor program and not the boot configuration variables. **C** is incorrect because a boot configuration variable determines which boot device to use, and **D** is incorrect because the system must be booted before it has access to the `/etc` directory.

2. ☑ **C** and **D**. The two main tasks of the Boot PROM phase are to execute POST followed by loading the primary boot program bootblk.
   ☒ **A** is incorrect because Kernel Initialization is done in the kernel initialization phase, and **B** is incorrect because ufsboot is loaded in the Boot Programs phase.

3. ☑ **A**. When you turn the machine on, first the Power- On Self Test (POST) is run; then the primary boot program bootblk is loaded, which in turn loads the secondary boot program ufsboot. The ufsboot program loads the kernel, which starts the `init` process; then the `init` process starts the SMF utility `svc.startd`.
   ☒ **B** is incorrect because the `init` process starts the `svc.startd`, so it has to be started before `svc.startd`. **C** is incorrect because bootblk is the primary boot program and must be started before the secondary boot program ufsboot. **D** is incorrect because POST is the first program that is run when the machine is turned on.

4. ☑ **B**. Pushing the Stop-A combination will eventually take you to the `ok` prompt, where you can issue command if you want to synchronize the file system and then boot.
   ☒ **A** is incorrect because shutting the power down is likely to damage the file system. Never do this unless there is an emergency and you have no other choice. **C** is incorrect because pushing Stop-D is used during startup to put the system into diagnostic mode—that is, to force POST to run, if POST was bypassed by default. D is incorrect because Stop-N is used to reset the NVRAM content to default values.

5. ☑ **D**. The phases of the boot process on an x86 machine are BIOS, Boot Programs, Kernel Initialization, and init.
   ☒ **A**, **B**, and **C** are incorrect because Boot PROM does not exist in an x86 machine.

6. ☑ **C**. The kernel starts the init program and the init program starts the SMF utility svc.startd.
   ☒ **A** is incorrect because the `svcadm` command is used to administer the SMF services such as to disable or enable them. **B** is incorrect because the `svcs` command is used to find the status of services. **D** is incorrect because `ufsboot` starts the kernel and not the `svc.startd`.

7. ☑ **B**. The `svcadm` command with `-d` option will change the default run level in Solaris 10.
   ☒ **A** is incorrect because the `initdefault` entry is not used in Solaris 10 if the milestone property is set for `svc.startd`. **C** is incorrect because the `init` command can be used to change the run level but not to change the default run level. **D** is incorrect because there is no such command as `initdefault`.

8. ☑ **D**. The `setenv` command is used to change the value of a boot configuration variable at the OpenBoot PROM command prompt `ok`.
   ☒ **A** is incorrect because the `eeprom` command is used to change the value of a boot configuration variable at the OS command line and not at the OpenBoot prompt.
   B and **C** are incorrect because there are no `set` and `setvar` commands at the `ok` prompt to change the value of a boot configuration variable.

9. ☑ **B**. A device alias created with the `nvalias` command will persist across power cycles.
   ☒ **A** is incorrect because a device alias created with the `devalias` command will not persist across power cycles. **C** is incorrect because the `setenv` command is used to change the value of a boot configuration variable. **D** is incorrect because there is no such command as `dev-alias`.

10. ☑ **A**, **B**, and **C**. Any of these commands (`init`, `shutdown`, and `halt`) will change the run level of the system.
    ☒ **D** is incorrect because there is no such command as `run-level`.

11. ☑ **A**. Pushing the Stop-D key combination at startup of a SPARC system will put the system into diagnostic mode. It is useful to force the POST to run, if the POST was bypassed by default.
    ☒ **B** is incorrect because you need to push the Stop-N key combination to set the NVRAM parameters to their default values. **C** is incorrect because no key press will give you the GUI to reset the NVRAM parameters. **D** is incorrect because there is no key combination that you can push to reset the NVRAM parameters to their factory defaults.

12. ☑ **A** and **C**. BIOS loads the master boot record program, mboot, which loads pboot.
    ☒ **B** is incorrect because POST is run by BIOS, and **D** is incorrect because the secondary boot program ufsboot is started by the primary boot program bootblk, which is started by the Solaris boot program pboot.

13. ☑ **D**. The `auto-boot?` parameter is a boolean whose value determines whether or not the system will be automatically booted when it is turned on.

    ☒ **A** is incorrect because the name `auto-boot?` is the correct name for this parameter.
    B is incorrect because even if the `auto-boot?` is false, you can boot the system by issuing the `boot` command at the `ok` prompt. **C** is incorrect because the `auto-boot?` parameter does not determine the run level of the system.

4

Managing File Systems

CERTIFICATION OBJECTIVES

4.01	Exploring the Solaris Directory Hierarchy	✓	Two-Minute Drill
4.02	Understanding Solaris File Systems	Q&A	Self Test
4.03	Managing File System Inconsistencies and Disk Space		

Files are an important resource supported by an operating system. The way an operating system organizes files on a medium is called a file system. One of your tasks as a Solaris system administrator will be managing the file systems supported by Solaris. There are a number of file system types reflecting the media (e.g., disk or memory) on which the files can be stored and the various ways of accessing the stored files (e.g., locally or remotely over a network). Once the data has been stored in files, it is important to keep the data consistent. Therefore, handling file system inconsistencies is one of the important tasks that we will explore in this chapter. The disk spaces that hold most of the data systems need to be managed, and you will see that Solaris offers commands to manage disk space usage at various levels of detail. To avoid exposing the files directly to the users, you can create links to the files that look like and work exactly like files from a user's perspectives. In addition, we will explore link management.

The central issue to think about in this chapter is: how are the file systems managed on a Solaris 10 system? To understand this we will explore three thought streams: understanding file systems and dealing with their inconsistencies, managing disk space usage, and managing links to avoid direct exposure of files to users.

CERTIFICATION OBJECTIVE 4.01

Exploring the Solaris Directory Hierarchy

Exam Objective 2.1: *Explain the Solaris 10 OS directory hierarchy, including root subdirectories, file components, and file types, and create and remove hard and symbolic links.*

As in other operating systems, the files on Solaris are grouped into a directory, and the directories are organized into a hierarchy. A directory (called folder in the Windows operating systems) may contain files and other directories, called subdirectories. In Solaris, however, directories are just a special kind of file.

In this section we explore the Solaris Directory Hierarchy, beginning with the concept of a file.

File: The Atom of the Solaris World

As in Java, it is said that everything is object; in Solaris everything is file. File is the basic unit, the atom, in Solaris. Everything is treated as a file. Here are a few examples:

- *Commands.* These are the executable files.
- *Devices.* All devices on the system, such as disk drive, printer, or terminal, are

treated as files by the system—that is, the system communicates with them through files.

- *Directories*. The directories are special files that contain other files.
- *Documents*. These are the regular files such as text file or a computer program containing the source code.

A file occupies the space on disk in units of what is called a *block*. The blocks are measured in two sizes: physical block size, which is the size of the smallest block that the disk controller can read or write, and logical block size, which is the size of the block that UNIX (Solaris in our case) uses to read or write files. The physical block size and the logical block size may not be the same.

A file has a name that is a link to the file, and the user accesses the file by its name. The name is stored inside a directory. All the other information about a file is stored in a data structure called *inode*. An inode, which is 128KB in size and is stored in the cylinder information block, contains the following information about the file:

- The type of the file—regular, block special, character special, directory, FIFO named pipe, socket, symbolic link, or other inode
- The file modes (i.e., the read, write, and execute permissions)
- The number of hard links to the file
- The group ID to which the file belongs
- The user ID of the user that owns the file
- The number of bytes in the file
- An array of addresses for 15 disk blocks
- The date and time the file was last accessed
- The date and time the file was last modified
- The date and time the file was created

Note that the first 12 (0 to 11) of the 15 disk-block addresses point directly to the blocks that store the file content. In other words, the first 12 elements of the address array point directly to the logical blocks in which the file content is stored. If the file is larger than 12 logical blocks, the additional (up to 3) addresses point to indirect blocks that contain the addresses of direct blocks. The physical block size is usually 512 bytes, and the logical block size is set (by default) to the page size of the system, which is 8KB for a UFS file system, the default file system for Solaris.

Because each file needs an inode, the number of inodes on a file system determines the maximum number of files that can be created on the system.

The maximum number of inodes you can create depends on the size of the file system. For example, you can create one inode for each 2KB of disk space for a file system of size up to 1GB. That means 1GB/2KB = 500,000 files can be created at maximum on a file system of 1GB size. For larger file systems, the number of bytes needed on the disk per inode increases, as shown in Table 4-1.

Files in Solaris are grouped into directories, and the directories are organized into a directory hierarchy, which we explore next.

Directory Hierarchy in Solaris

Just as in any other OS, files in Solaris are organized into directories, and directories are organized into a hierarchy called a directory tree, which is an inverted tree with the root directory (symbolized by /) on the top, which contains other directories. The root directories and several other directories underneath it are created when you install Solaris. You must be familiar with the following directories underneath the root:

- **`/bin`.** Symbolic link to the `/usr/bin` directory.
- **`/dev`.** Contains logical device names (defined in the next chapter) for the devices.
- **`/devices`.** Device-related files controlled by the file system: devfs.
- **`/lib`.** Contains shared libraries such as SMF executables.
- **`/etc`.** Administrative and configuration files.
- **`/export`.** You can define it according to your needs, but commonly used to hold user home directories.
- **`/home`.** This is the default mount point for user home directories.

TABLE 4-1 Number of bytes per inode with varying disk size

File System Size (GB)	Number of Bytes per Inode (KB)
0–1	2
1–2	4
2–3	6
3–1000	8
>1000	1024

- **/mnt.** Default mount point used to temporarily mount file systems.
- **/sbin.** Contains system administration commands and utilities. Used during booting when `/usr//bin` has not yet been mounted.
- **/tmp.** Contains temporary files that are deleted when the system is rebooted.
- **/usr.** UNIX System Resources. Holds OS commands and programs.

Of course you can create your own directories and files in the already existing tree.

The user refers to the files and directories by their names. It can be advantageous not to expose the real names of some directories and files to users. Instead create something that points to the file, and if that pointer is deleted, the actual file is not (hence the advantage). These pointers are called links, which we discuss next.

Managing Hard and Symbolic Links

A link is a file that points to another file. There are two kinds of links available in Solaris: hard links and symbolic links. A hard link is a pointer to a file that is indistinguishable from the original file. That is, any changes to a file are effective regardless of the name used to refer to the file—the link name or the original file name. Furthermore, a hard link can point only to a file, not to a directory. In addition, a hard link cannot span file systems; that is, the link and the file must be on the same file system because both have the same inode number.

A symbolic link, on the other hand, is an indirect pointer to a file—that is, its directory entry contains the name of the file to which it points. Furthermore, it may span file systems and point to either a directory or a file.

Creating Hard and Symbolic Links

To create a symbolic link or a hard link, you use the same command name, `ln`, which has the following syntax:

```
ln [-fns] <source> [<target>]
```

In this command, `<source>` is the original file and `<target>` is the link that will be created and linked to the `<source>`. The options for the command are listed here:

- **-f** (force). Link the file without questioning the user.

watch ***Hard link is the default output of the `ln` command—that is, if you issue the `ln` command without the `-s` option, a hard link will be created.***

TABLE 4-2 Comparison of hard and soft links

Characteristic	Hard Link	Soft Link
Existence of original file	You cannot create a hard link to a file that does not exist.	You can create a symbolic link to a file that does not exist.
File systems	A hard link cannot span file systems—that is, the link and the file it points to have to be in the same file system.	A soft link can span file systems.
Kind of original file	A hard link can only point to a file that is not a directory.	A soft link can point to a file or a directory.
I-node	A hard link has the same inode number as the file it points to.	A soft link has a different inode from the file it points to.

- **-n.** If the `<target>` is an existing file, do not overwrite the content of the file. The `-f` option overrides this option.
- **-s.** Create a symbolic link. The default is a hard link.

The hard links and symbolic links are compared in Table 4-2.

Removing Hard and Symbolic Links

To remove a file, all hard links that point to it must be removed, including the name by which it was originally created. Only after removing the file itself and all of its hard links, will the inode associated with the file be released.

In both cases, hard and soft links, if you remove the original file, the link will still exist. A link can be removed just as can a file:

```
rm <linkName>
```

When you delete a file, the clean thing to do is: delete all the symbolic links pointing to it.

Remember that you can (but should not) delete a file without deleting the symbolic links. However, you cannot delete the file (its content) unless you delete all the hard links pointing to it.

The directory tree in Solaris appears as one uniform file system to an ordinary user, who can assume that it is true for all practical purposes. However, you, the system administrator, must know that the tree is made of several file systems. Next, we explore the file systems supported by Solaris.

CERTIFICATION OBJECTIVE 4.02

Understanding Solaris File Systems

Exam Objective 2.5: *Explain the Solaris 10 OS file system, including disk-based, distributed, devfs, and memory file systems related to SMF, and create a new UFS file system using options for <1Tbyte and >1Tbyte file systems.*

A file system is a structure of directories that an operating system uses to store and organize files. The Solaris directory tree, although it looks like one file system, consists of several file systems connected to the tree, which is called mounting a file system. You will learn more about mounting in the next chapter. When we refer to a file system, we may mean any of the following:

- A specific type of file system, such as a disk-based file system or a distributed file system, which we will discuss in this section
- The entire directory tree on the system, beginning with the root (/) directory
- A subtree that is mounted to a point in the main directory tree
- The data structure of a storage medium, such as a disk

The Solaris operating system uses the virtual file system (VFS) architecture, which enables the kernel to handle basic file operations such as reading, writing, and listing files within a specific file system. A user can work issuing the same commands across the file systems—that is, the user does not have to know which specific file system is being used, hence the name virtual file system. In addition to the VFS, Solaris can also use the memory-based virtual file systems, which we discuss further on in this section.

There are several types of file systems supported by Solaris. Let's begin our exploration with disk-based file systems.

Disk-Based File Systems

Disk-based file systems reside on, well, disks: hard disks, diskettes, and CD-ROMs. Solaris supports the following disk-based file systems:

- *High Sierra file system (HSFS).* High Sierra is the first file system for CD-ROMs. Its official standard version is ISO9660 with the Rock Ridge extensions, which provide all the UFS features and file types except the write and the hard links features. It is a read-only file system.
- *PC file system (PCFS).* The personal computer file system is used to gain read and write access to disks formatted for the disk operating system (DOS) running on the PCs.
- *Universal disk format (UDF).* The universal disk format file system is used to store information on digital versatile disk or digital video disk (DVD).
- *UNIX file system (UFS).* The UNIX file system, based on the traditional UNIX file system known as the BSD fast file system, is the default for Solaris. We will explore this file system further on in this chapter.

exam watch

Note the general association of a file system with the specific media device: HSFS with CD-ROM, PCFS with diskette, UDF with DVD, and UFS with hard disk. However, these associations are not hard and fast; you can also create UFS on CD-ROMs and diskettes.

A disk-based file system can be accessed by logging on to the machine to which the disk is attached. (Everything is connected these days.) So, how can we access files across systems over the network, or the Internet, which is just a big network? Solaris has the answer to this question using the distributed file systems, which we explore next.

Distributed File Systems

The distributed file systems, also called network-based file systems, are used to store data that can be accessed across systems over a network. For example, the files could be stored on a Solaris system called a server and can be accessed from other Solaris systems over the network. Solaris 10 supports version 4 of the network file system (NFS), which improves security by integrating file access, file locking, and mount protocols into a single unified protocol. We explore NFS in further detail in Chapter 11.

So far, we have considered file systems that reside on a disk—that is, the permanent storage medium. One can imagine storing files in a volatile storage medium—that is, memory. There are file systems that do exactly that, and those files systems are called memory-based file systems, which we discuss next.

Memory-Based File Systems

Memory-based file systems use the physical memory rather than the disk and hence are also called virtual file systems or pseudo file systems. Note, however, that some virtual file systems may make use of disk space. For example, a cache file system uses a local disk for cache, and a temporary file system may use a disk for swap space. In general, virtual file systems provide access to special kernel information and facilities. Virtual file systems supported by Solaris are listed here:

- *Cache file system (CacheFS).* The cache file system uses the local disk drives to cache the data from slow file systems such as CD-ROM drives or network file systems. This helps improve system performance.
- *Loopback file system (LOFS).* Let's assume that for some reason you want to make a file system available under an alternative path name. For example, you want to call the root (/) directory `/tmp/newroot`. Solaris lets you do that by creating a new virtual file system called loopback file system, which will make the entire root (/) file system (in this example) appear as if it were duplicated under `/tmp/newroot`. In this example, all the files in the root file system could be accessed by using a path name that begins with either a / (forward slash) or `/tmp/newroot`.
- *Process file system (PROCFS)*. The process file system is used to contain a list of active processes on the Solaris system by their process ID numbers, in the `/proc` directory. This information in the `/proc` directory is used by commands such as `ps`. Other tools such as debuggers can access the address space of the processes by making system calls. The PROCFS resides in memory.
- *Temporary file system (TEMPFS).* When programs are executed, files are created and manipulated that may involve significant reads and writes. The temporary file system is designed to improve the performance of these programs

by using the local memory (and not the disk) for reads and writes. TEMPFS is the default file system for the `/tmp` directory on Solaris. As a result, the files in the `/tmp` directory are deleted when the file system is unmounted, or when the Solaris system is rebooted or shutdown. You can, however, move these file elsewhere (just like any other file) if you want to save them.

- *Other virtual file systems*. There are other virtual file systems that do not require administration. Some of them are listed here:
  - *FIFOFS*. First in first out file system. Contains named pipe files that are used to give processes access to data.
  - *MNTFS*. Contains information about the mounted file systems.
  - *SWAPFS*. This file system is used by the kernel for swapping.

The files in the `/proc` directory are used by the system to maintain the active processes on the system; do not delete these files. Even if you want to kill a process, deleting a file in the `/proc` directory is not going to do it. Furthermore, remember that these files take no disk space.

As you now know, everything in Solaris is a file. Solaris treats devices as files too, and those files are managed by the device file system (devfs), which we discuss next.

Device File System (devfs)

The device file system (devfs) manages devices in Solaris 10 and is mounted to the mount point/devices. Therefore, the content in the `/devices` directory is controlled by the devfs, and the files in the `/dev` directory are symbolic links to the files in the `/devices` directory. This way, you can continue to access all devices through entries in the `/dev` directory.

However, the `/devices` directory contains files only for the currently accessible devices on the system and dynamically represents the current state of these devices without requiring any system administration. Note the following two features:

- When a driver is loaded and attached to a device instance, a file is created in the `/devices` directory. A symbolic link is created in the `/dev` directory and attached to the file in the devices directory. Unused device entries are detached.

- The devfs improves the system performance because only those device entries that are needed to boot the system are attached. New entries are attached as new devices are accessed.

on the job

The files under the `/devices` directory are entirely controlled by the devfs, and you cannot change that. Also, the `/devices` namespace cannot be unmounted.

Although Solaris supports several file systems discussed in this section, the default file system for Solaris is called UNIX file system (UFS). Most of the time you will be creating a UFS as opposed to any other file system. Let's now explore creating UFS file systems.

Creating UFS File Systems

UNIX file system (UFS) is a disk-based file system, which is a default for Solaris. As a system administrator, you will spend a considerable amount of your time with this system. UFS offers the following features:

- *Extended Fundamental Types (EFTs).* Provides a 32-bit user ID (UID), a group ID (GID), and device numbers.
- *Large file systems.* This file system can be up to 1 terabyte in size, and the largest file size on a 32-bit system can be about 2 gigabytes.
- *Logging.* Offers logging that is enabled by default in Solaris 10. This feature can be very useful for auditing, troubleshooting, and security purposes.
- *Multiterabyte file systems.* Solaris 10 provides support for mutiterabyte file systems on machines that run a 64-bit Solaris kernel. In the previous versions, the support was limited to approximately 1 terabyte for both 32-bit and 64-bit kernels. You can create a UFS up to 16 terabytes in size with an individual file size of up to 1 terabyte.
- *State flags.* Indicate the state of the file system such as active, clean, or stable. We explore the state flags further on in this chapter.

on the job

In Solaris 10, logging is enabled by default for all UFS file systems unless there is insufficient file system space for the log.

A multiple number of UFSs are created on your system disk during the installation of Solaris. These default Solaris file systems are organized in a hierarchy with the root (/) file system at the top; they are described in Table 4-3.

TABLE 4-3 Default file systems created during Solaris installation

File System	Type	Description
/ (root)	UFS	Contains directory and files critical for system operations: kernel, device drivers, and programs to boot the system. Contains mount point directories for other (local and remote) file systems.
/etc/mnttab	MNTFS	Provides read-only access to the table of mounted file systems; only for the local system.
/export/home or /home	NFS, UFS	Mount point for user home directories.
/lib	NFS, UFS	Provides mount point for directories that contains shared libraries such as Service Management Facility (SMF) executable files.
/opt	NFS, UFS	Provides optional mount point, usually for third-party software.
/proc	PROCFS	Contains a list of active processes on the system by their ID numbers.
/system/contract	CTFS	Provides a virtual file system that contains the contract information.
/system/object	OBJFS	Used by debuggers to access the information about kernel symbols without accessing the kernel directly.
/tmp	TMPFS	Contains temporary non-system files that will be deleted when the system is rebooted.
/usr	UFS	Contains system files and directories that all users share.
/var	UFS	Contains system files and directories that will likely grow, such as system logs.
/var/run	TMPFS	Contains temporary system files that will be deleted when the system is rebooted.

Make sure you understand what kind of files each file system shown in Table 4-2 contains.

Note the following additional points about these file systems:

- Owing to their content, the root (/) and `/usr` file systems are required to run the Solaris system on your machine, as they contain the system commands and programs.
- You will notice that some of the commands in the `/usr` file system (such as mount) are also included in the root file system because they will be needed during boot or in the single-user mode, when the `/usr` file system has not been mounted yet.
- There are two temporary file systems: `/tmp` for non-system files, probably created by programs that are running, and `/var/run` for the system files.

In addition to the file systems created during installation, you can create new UFSs. Before creating a UFS on the disk, you may need to perform the following tasks:

- Format the disk and divide it into slices, if that has not already been done.
- In case you are re-creating an existing UFS file system, unmount it.
- Find out the device name of the slice that will contain the file system.
- Make a backup of the disk as a protection against loss of data. Backups are discussed in Chapter 9.

EXERCISE 4-1

Creating a UFS File System

1. Become superuser.
2. Issue the following command:

```
# newfs /dev/rdsk/<deviceName>
```

3. The system asks for confirmation. Make sure you have specified the correct `<deviceName>`. If you specify the wrong device, you will end up erasing the data from that device.

4. Verify your newly created system with the following command:

```
# fsck /dev/rdsk/<deviceName>
```

5. Mount your newly created file system.

Files, and hence file systems, hold data, and the operations are made on the data: addition, deletion, and modification. During these operations, or for other reasons, inconsistencies can occur, which we explore next.

CERTIFICATION OBJECTIVE 4.03

Managing File System Inconsistencies and Disk Space

Exam Objective 2.6: *Given a scenario, check and resolve Solaris 10 OS file system inconsistencies using fsck, and monitor file system usage using the command line (df, du, and quot commands).*

File system data consistency is important to ensure that the content of the file system is always available. To ensure consistency, file systems must be checked periodically. When you boot a system, a consistency check on the file systems is automatically performed. However, you can also perform the file system consistency check, when needed, after the system has been booted. In order to facilitate the consistency check, Solaris offers the `fsck` utility. In this section, we explore where the inconsistencies come from, how to detect them, and how to repair them using the `fsck` command.

on the Job

If the `fsck` command finds the files and directories that are allocated but unreferenced (that is, some inodes are allocated to files but not attached to any directory), it names them by their inode numbers and places them in the `lost+found` directory. If the `lost+found` directory did not exist, the `fsck` command would create it.

Understanding File System Inconsistencies

The information about files is stored in inodes, and the data is stored in blocks. The UFS file system uses a set of tables to keep track of used inodes and available blocks. Inconsistencies will arise, for example, if these tables are not properly synchronized with the data on disk. This condition can arise as a result of an abrupt termination of the operating system. The reasons for inconsistencies are listed here:

- A software error in the kernel
- Turning off the system without the proper shutdown procedure (e.g., accidentally unplugging the system), or through a power failure
- Defective hardware, such as problems with the disk

Solaris offers the `fsck` command, which can be used to find the inconsistencies and repair them. How does `fsck` know that a file system needs to be checked for inconsistencies? It uses a flag, called the *state flag*, to make this determination. The *state flag* for a file system is recorded in the superblock (discussed in the next chapter). The possible values of the state flag are described in Table 4-4.

The `fsck` utility makes multiple passes on a file system as listed here:

- *Phase 1*. Checks blocks and sizes.
- *Phase 2*. Checks path names.

TABLE 4-4 Possible values of a file system state flag

State Flag Value	Description
FSACTIVE	Mounted file system has modified data in memory. Data would be lost if power to the system were interrupted.
FSBAD	The file system contains inconsistent data.
FSCLEAN	The file system was unmounted cleanly and doesn't need to be checked for consistency.
FSLOG	Logging is enabled for this file system.
FSSTABLE	The file system contains consistent data (i.e., no data would be lost if the power to the system were interrupted). There's no need to run `fsck` before mounting.

- *Phase 3*. Checks connectivity.
- *Phase 4*. Checks reference counts.
- *Phase 5*. Checks cylinder groups.

Unmount a file system before you run the `fsck` command on it. This way you will ensure that you don't add any inconsistencies during the `fsck` repair.

A file system must be inactive when you use `fsck` to repair it. Otherwise, the file system changes that were waiting to be written to the system and the changes that occur during the repair might cause the file system to be corrupted.

Now that you know about the inconsistencies, let's see how to use the `fsck` command to detect and fix them.

Using the `fsck` Command

The syntax for the `fsck` command is presented here:

```
fsck [<options>] [<rawDevice>]
```

The `<rawDevice>` is the device interface in `/dev/rdsk`. If no `<rawDevice>` is specified, `fsck` looks into the `/etc/vfstab` file, which lists the file systems. The file systems represented by the entries in the `/etc/vfstab` with the following two properties will be checked:

- The value of the `fsckdev` field is a character-special device.
- The value of the `fsckpass` field is a non-zero numeral.

The `/etc/vfstab` file is discussed in detail in Chapter 12.

The options for the `fsck` command are as follows:

- **`-F <FSType>`.** Limit the check to the file systems specified by `<FSType>`.
- **`-m`.** Check but do not repair—useful for checking whether the file system is suitable for mounting.
- **`-n | -N`.** Assume a "no" response to all questions that will be asked during the `fsck` run.
- **`-y | -Y`.** Assume a "yes" response to all questions that will be asked during the `fsck` run.

EXERCISE 4-2

Checking a File System Manually

1. Become superuser (e.g., login as root).
2. Unmount a local file system, say `/export/home`.
3. Use the `fsck` command by specifying the mount point directory or the `/dev/dsk/<deviceName` as an argument to the command. If you provide no argument, all the file systems with `fsck` pass field greater than 0 in the `/etc/vfstab` file will be checked.
4. Messages about the inconsistencies will be displayed.
5. The `fsck` command may not be able to fix all errors in one run. If necessary, you can run the `fsck` command again—for example, if you see a message that looks like the following:

```
FILE SYSTEM STATE NOT SET TO OKAY or FILE SYSTEM MODIFIED
```

6. Mount the repaired file system.
7. Move the files in the `lost+found` directories to where they belong with their proper names (you will rename them to their original names). The files and directories that you cannot identify should eventually be removed to save space.

After you create the file systems, make sure the data on them stays consistent. You need to monitor how these file systems are using the disks on which they reside. We explore this system administration task next.

Monitoring Disk Space Usage

Monitoring disk space usage is an important administrative task, not only to ensure proper usage of disk space but also to ensure correct functioning of the system. For example, think of the situation when the disk is full and, as a result, the running programs have no space to store their data. The Solaris system allows you to get reports on disk space usage at different levels. You can use commands to determine disk usage by file systems, files, and users.

Using the `df` Command

Solaris offers the `df` command to monitor disk space usage at file system level. To be specific, the `df` command can be used to determine the following:

- The amount of disk space occupied by currently mounted or unmounted file systems
- The total amount of used and available space
- The fraction of the file system's total capacity that has been used

The file system is specified by referring to the device, or a file, or a directory on the file system. The following is the syntax for the `df` command:

```
df [-F <FSType>] [<options>] [<fileSystem>]
```

The options are described here:

- **`-a.`** Report on all file systems.
- **`-b.`** Print the total number of kilobytes free.
- **`-F <FSType>.`** Display disk usage information on the file systems with the specified file system type.
- **`<fileSystem>.`** Display disk usage information on the file system specified by referring to a device, file, or directory.
- **`-k.`** Display disk usage information in kilobytes.
- **`-t <type>.`** Display the total number of blocks along with blocks used for each mounted file systems.

The output for the `df` command looks like the following:

```
Filesystem kbytes used avail capacity Mounted on
senate:/ 7450 4715 1985 70% /
senate:/usr 42280 35295 2756 93% /usr
```

The headings in the output are self-explanatory. The column after the output represents total space size allocated to the file system, while the second and third columns specify used and available space.

on the job

Note in the example that the amount of space in the file system (kbytes) is greater than the sum of the used and available space, because the system reserves a fraction of the space to ensure that its file system allocation

routines work well. You can adjust the reserved amount, which is typically about 10 percent, by using the `tunefs` command.

Suppose that with the `df` command you determine disk usage at the file system level. Further suppose that you want to go into more detail and determine disk usage by directories. In that case, you will need the `du` command, which we explore next.

Using the `du` Command

The `du` command is used to get the report on disk usage at the directory and file level. You can use the `du` command to determine the following:

- Total space allocated to a directory
- Total space allocated to a directory subtree
- Total space allocated to a non-directory file—that is, a file that is not a directory

The syntax for the `du` command is presented here:

```
du [<options>] [<file>]
```

The operand `<file>` can be a directory or a non-directory file. If `<file>` is not specified, the command is run on the current directory. The reported disk space size allocated to a directory is the sum total of space allocated to the whole subtree of files and directories with the specified directory as the root. The options are listed here:

- **`-a`.** In addition to the default output, display the size of each non-directory file in the subtree of the specified directory.
- **`-h`.** Display the output in a human-readable format. All the subdirectories in the target subtree with the full path name and disk usage information are listed.
- **`-k`.** Display the file sizes in kilobytes rather than blocks (512 bytes), which is the default. All the subdirectories in the target subtree with the full path name and disk usage information are listed.
- **`-s`.** Display only the total sum for the specified file/directory.

Now that you know how to get reports on disk usage at file system level and to go down to the directories and files level, you can become more ambitious and ask: how can I find out disk usage by user? Well, Solaris has an answer for you, and the answer is the `quot` command, which we explore next.

Using the quot Command

There will be times when you want to know how much space is being used by each user on a given file system. The quot command is used to get the report on disk usage by user name. The syntax for the quot command is as follows:

```
quot [<options>] [<fileSystem>]
```

The <fileSystem> specifies the mount point for the file system(s) to be checked. The options are listed here:

- **-a.** Report on all mounted file systems.
- **-f.** Display the output in three columns representing user name, total number of blocks, and total number of files owned by the user.
- **-v.** In addition to the default output, display the number of blocks not accessed during the past 30, 60, and 90 days.

The quot command displays the disk space in kilobytes, and you can use it as superuser.

The three most important takeaways from this chapter are the following:

- Several file systems are created during Solaris installation, and these file systems are organized into an inverted hierarchy tree with the root (/) file system at the top. The consistency of these file systems is checked and maintained using the fsck command.
- Most of the file systems reside on disk, and Solaris offers commands to monitor disk space usage at different levels of detail: df at file system level, du at file level, and quot at user level.
- You can avoid direct exposure of the files to users by creating links, which come in two types: hard links and symbolic links.

CERTIFICATION SUMMARY

Everything in Solaris is a file—for example, a regular file, a directory, a link, a command, and a device. Information about a file is contained inside a data structure called an inode. The maximum number of inodes you can create on a file system determines the maximum number of files that can be created and depends on the file system size. The files are grouped into a directory, and the directories in turn are organized into an inverted hierarchy tree with root (/) at the top.

Files can be stored on a permanent storage medium (the disk) or in a volatile storage medium (the memory); the corresponding file systems are called disk-based file systems and memory-based file systems. Files can be stored in such a way that they can be accessed across systems over a network. The file systems that support this access are called distributed or network-based file systems. File system inconsistencies are detected and fixed by using the `fsck` command, which is automatically run during booting. If you run the `fsck` command manually, make sure you unmount the file system before running `fsck` on it.

Solaris offers commands to monitor disk space usage at different levels of detail: `df` at the file system level, `du` at the file level, and `quot` at the user level. If you do not want your users to access a file or a directory directly, create links that point to these files or directories. A hard link can point only to a file and not to a directory, and only to a file existing on the same file system where the link itself is. A symbolic link, in contrast, can point to a file or a directory and can span across file systems. Furthermore, you cannot create a hard link for a non-existent file, whereas you can create a symbolic link for it. Links can be removed with the same `rm` command that is used to remove files.

Most of the file systems that you will manage as a system administrator reside on a disk, and the disk must be managed as well. Therefore, in the next chapter we will explore disk management.

INSIDE THE EXAM

Comprehend

- Only the connected devices have entries in the `/devices` directory, and the `/dev` directory contains symbolic links to these entries (files).
- Unmount a file system before running the `fsck` command on it, in order to avoid generating inconsistencies during the repair.
- A hard link cannot point to a file across the file systems because the file and the link must have the same inode.

Look Out

- The `fsck` is used not only to check the file system inconsistencies but to repair them.
- Deleting a file in the `/proc` directory does not kill the corresponding process.
- Files in the `/tmp` and `/var/run` directories are deleted when the system is rebooted.
- The command `ln` creates a hard link by default if you do not give the option `-s` for creating the symbolic link.

Memorize

- Logging is enabled by default in Solaris 10 UFS.
- You can create a multiterabyte UFS in Solaris 10 with a size of up to 16 terabytes and a maximum file size of up to about 1 terabyte.
- A hard link can only point to a file, whereas a symbolic link can point to either a file or a directory.
- The `/tmp` directory contains temporary non-system files, whereas the /var/run directory contains the temporary system file.

TWO-MINUTE DRILL

Exploring the Solaris Directory Hierarchy

- ❑ Everything in Solaris is a file: regular files, directories, commands, links, devices, etc.
- ❑ Information about a file is contained inside a data structure called inode.
- ❑ The maximum number of files that you can create on a system depends on the maximum number of inodes that you can create, which in turn depends on the size of the file system.

Understanding Solaris File Systems

- ❑ The general associations of disk-based file systems to the storage media are as follows: HSFS is created on a CD-ROM, PCFS on a diskette, UDF on a DVD, and UFS on a hard disk.
- ❑ Solaris 10 supports network file system (NFS) version 4.
- ❑ Solaris supports the following memory-based file systems: cache file system, loopback file system, process file system, and temporary file system.
- ❑ The `/proc` directory contains information about the active processes on the system.
- ❑ The devices on Solaris 10 are managed by device file system (devfs), which is mounted to `/devices`.
- ❑ UNIX file system (UFS) is the default file system for Solaris.

Managing File System Inconsistencies and Disk Space

- ❑ File system inconsistencies arise when the system is shut down improperly or from hardware errors, such as disk errors.
- ❑ The inconsistencies can be checked and repaired by using the `fsck` command.
- ❑ The `fsck` runs automatically during the system bootup but can be executed manually any time after the system is up and running.
- ❑ You must unmount a file system before running `fsck` on it.

- The `df` command is used to get a report on disk usage by the file systems.
- The `du` command is used to get a report on disk usage by directories and files.
- The `quot` command is used to get a report on disk usage by users.
- The links are created with the following command:

```
ln [-fs] <source> [<target>]
```

- The hard link is created by default, whereas the symbolic link is created with the `-s` option.
- The links are removed with the following command:

```
rm [<linkName>]
```

- A file can be removed without removing its symbolic link, but all of its hard links must be removed. Unless the last hard link is removed, the file content will still exist.

SELF TEST

The following questions will help you measure your understanding of the material presented in this chapter. Read all the choices carefully because there might be more than one correct answer. Choose all correct answers for each question.

1. Which of the following commands are used to obtain disk space information? (Choose all that apply.)

   A. `df`

   B. `du`

   C. `quot`

   D. `ls`

   E. `ds`

2. Which of the following file systems are (memory-based) virtual file systems? (Choose all that apply.)

   A. NFS

   B. CacheFS

   C. ProceFS

   D. UFS

   E. TEMPFS

   F. UDF

3. Which of the following directories on Solaris 10 contain the files related to the physical devices?

   A. `/drivers`

   B. `/dev`

   C. `/devices`

   D. `/etc`

   E. `/drv`

4. Which of the following directories on Solaris 10 contain the configuration files? (Choose all that apply.)

   A. `/drivers`

   B. `/mnt`

C. `/export`

D. `/etc`

E. `/bin`

5. Which of the following types of links can span across the file systems? (Choose all that apply.)

   A. Symbolic links

   B. Hard links

   C. Loop links

   D. Directory links

6. Which of the following commands can you use on a mounted file system? (Choose all that apply.)

   A. `fsck`

   B. `ls`

   C. `quot`

   D. `du`

7. The files under the `/devices` directory are controlled by which file system?

   A. MNTFS

   B. devicefs

   C. devfs

   D. HSFS

8. Which of the following statements are not true? (Choose all that apply.)

   A. A hard link can only point to a file that is not a directory.

   B. A hard link has a different inode number from that of the file that it points to.

   C. You cannot create a hard link to a file that does not exist.

   D. You cannot create a symbolic link to a file that does not exist.

9. You want to find out how each user on a file system is using disk space? Which of the following commands can you use? (Choose all that apply.)

   A. `df`

   B. `du`

   C. `quot`

   D. `ls`

10. What can be the maximum size of a large UFS file system?

    A. 1 terabyte

    B. 1 gigabyte

    C. 10 terabytes

    D. 2 gigabytes

11. You have just installed Solaris 10 on your system. Underneath which directory can you locate the SMF components?

    A. `/smf`

    B. `/etc`

    C. `/lib`

    D. `/bin`

12. There have been problems in mounting the `/var` file system? You reboot the system into a single-user mode and issue the `fsck` command on `/var`. The system reports an allocated but unreferenced file, and you say yes when asked whether the file should be reconnected. After the system has been booted, in which directory can you find this reconnected file?

    A. `/lost+found`

    B. `/unreferenced`

    C. `/var/tmp/lost+found`

    D. `/var/lost+found`

    E. `/tmp`

SELF TEST ANSWERS

1. ☑ **A**, **B**, and **C**. The `df` command is used to get a report on disk usage by the file systems, the `du` command to get a report on disk usage by directories and files, and the `quot` command to get a report on disk usage by users.
   ☒ **D** is incorrect because the `ls` command displays information about files and not about the disk space. **E** is incorrect because there is no such command as `ds` to display disk space information.

2. ☑ **B**, **C**, and **E**. The file systems CacheFS, ProcFS, and TEMPFS are memory-based virtual file systems.
   ☒ **A** is incorrect because NFS is a network file system that resides on a disk and is accessible from systems across the network. **D** is incorrect because the UNIX file system, the default file system for Solaris, is a disk-based system. **F** is incorrect because universal disk format is used to store information on DVDs.

3. ☑ **B** and **C**. Device-related files are in the `/devices` directories, and links to those files are in the `/dev` directory.
   ☒ **A** and **E** are incorrect because there are no such directories as `/drivers` and `/drv`. **D** is incorrect because the `/etc` directory contains configuration files and not device files.

4. ☑ **D**. The `/etc` directory contains administrative and configuration files.
   ☒ **A** is incorrect because there is no such directory as `/devices`. **B** is incorrect because the `/mnt` directory is the default mount point for fault systems. **C** is incorrect because the `/export` directory is used for creating home directories. **E** is incorrect because the `/bin` directory contains links to standard system commands.

5. ☑ **A**. Symbolic links span across the file systems.
   ☒ **B** is incorrect because hard links can point only to the files on the same file system. **C** and **D** are incorrect because there are no such links.

6. ☑ **B**, **C**, and **D**. The `ls` command is used to obtain information about files, and the `quot` and `du` commands are used to obtain disk space information.
   ☒ **A** is incorrect because the `fsck` command is used only while the file system is unmounted; otherwise you could create data inconsistencies.

7. ☑ **C**. The files in the `/devices` directory represent the physical devices and are entirely controlled by the devfs file system
   ☒ **A** is incorrect because the MNTFS is a virtual file system that contains information about the mounted file systems. **B** is incorrect because there is no such file system as `devicefs`. **D** is incorrect because HSFS is the file system that is used to write on the CD-ROMs.

8. ☑ **B** and **D**. All the hard links that point to a file share the inode with the file. You can create symbolic links to a file that does not yet exist.
   ☒ **A** and **C** are incorrect because both are true statements.

9. ☑ **C**. The `quot` command drills down the disk usage by user name.
   ☒ **A** is incorrect because the `df` command is used to get information about disk space usage by file system. **B** is incorrect because the `du` command is used to determine the disk space allocated to files and directories. **D** is incorrect because the `ls` command is used to get information about files, not about disk usage.

10. ☑ **A**. The maximum size of a large file system is 1 terabyte.
    ☒ **B**, **C**, and **D** are incorrect because they do not represent the maximum size of a large file system, which is 1 terabyte.

11. ☑ **C**. The shared libraries including the SMF components are in the directories underneath `/lib`.
    ☒ **A** is incorrect because there is no automatically created `/smf` directory in Solaris 10. **B** is incorrect because the `/etc` directory contains mostly the configuration files, and **D** is incorrect because `/bin` is a symbolic link to the directory `/usr/bin`.

12. ☑ **D**. The `fsck` command places the unreferenced files in the `lost+found` directory at the top of the file system on which the command is run.
    ☒ **A** and **C** are incorrect because the `fsck` command places the unreferenced files in the `lost+found` directory at the top of the file system on which the command is run, and **B** is incorrect because no directory named `/unreferenced` is automatically created during Solaris installation.

5

Managing Disks

CERTIFICATION OBJECTIVES

- 5.01 Understanding Disk Architecture
- 5.02 Partitioning a Disk
- 5.03 Listing and Reconfiguring Devices
- 5.04 Mounting and Unmounting File Systems
- ✓ Two-Minute Drill
- Q&A Self Test

The operating system itself is installed on a hard disk. Additional disks can be added to serve data, support more users, or offer reliability by replicating data. Therefore, every Solaris system you will work with will have one or more hard disks to support data. On occasion, you may be required to add a new disk to the system and partition the disk into slices to enable you to create the file systems on the slices. Once the file systems have been created, you can make them available to users by mounting them to the directory tree.

The central question to think about in this chapter is: how do you present the file systems to the users on a disk? In search of an answer, we will explore three thought streams: configuring devices attached to the Solaris system, partitioning disks, and mounting (and unmounting) the file systems. In other words, here is the story in a nutshell that we are going to explore in this chapter: You add a disk to the system, partition the disk into slices, and mount (attach) the file systems on the slices to the directory tree so that users may use them.

CERTIFICATION OBJECTIVE 5.01

Understanding Disk Architecture

Exam Objective 2.2: *Explain disk architecture including the UFS file system capabilities and naming conventions for devices for SPARC, x64, and x86-based systems.*

In addition to the operating system, the persistent data largely reside on hard disks. Therefore, a hard disk is an important device on your Solaris system that you will be managing as a system administrator. It is important to understand the disk architecture, which includes the disk geometry and naming conventions for the disks.

Understanding a Disk's Geometry

To understand how data, organized into file systems, reside on a disk and how disk management is performed, you need to understand the geometry of a disk and how it works. The basic unit of a hard disk is a platter made of a material, such as aluminum or glass, on which data can be stored by creating magnetic patterns. The geometry of such a platter is shown in Figure 5-1.

FIGURE 5-1 A disk platter with tracks and sectors

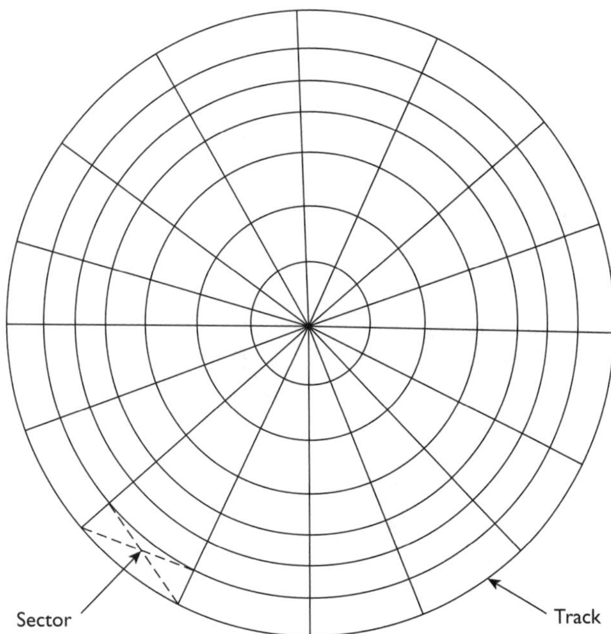

As shown in Figure 5-2, a disk drive may consist of a stack of several platters that spin together. Different elements of a disk are described here:

- *Track*. A platter is divided into concentric circles called tracks.
- *Sector*. The smallest storable unit on a track is called a sector. The storage capacity of a sector is typically 512 bytes.
- *Cylinder*. A cylinder consists of a set of tracks with the same radius, one from each platter from the stack. For example, if each platter has 300 tracks, there will be three 300 cylinders on the disk. Assuming the disk has three platters, each cylinder will consist of three tracks if only one side of the platter is used.
- *Disk controller*. The disk controller consists of a chip and its circuitry, which instructs the read/write head to move across the platter to read or write data.
- *Disk label*. The disk label is the first disk sector that contains information about disk geometry and partitions. We will discuss disk labels and partitions further on in this chapter.

FIGURE 5-2

A disk with tracks, sectors, and cylinders

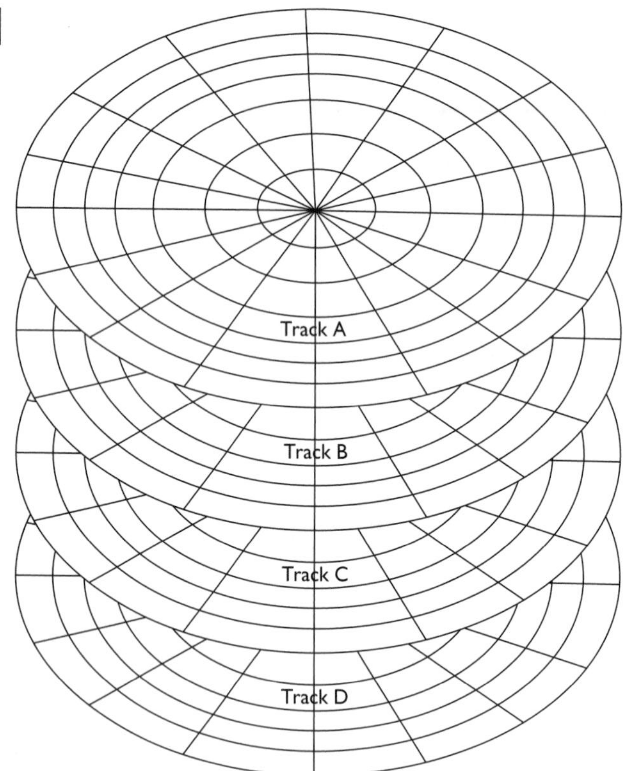

Track A + Track B + Track C + Track D = One cylinder

The read/write heads move across the disk surfaces inward or outward to get to the right cylinder, and the disk spins on a spindle to get to the right sector.

The operating system stores the data in files, which are made up of one or more blocks. Therefore, the data is transferred to and from disks in units of blocks. A file block may occupy one or more sectors. The UNIX file system (UFS) uses the following kinds of blocks:

- *Boot block*. Contains the information for booting the system.
- *Superblock*. Contains information about the file system.
- *Inode*. Contains information about one file in the file system.
- *Data block*. Contains the data for a file.

In order to work with disks, you will need to refer to them by their names. To understand the disk names, you will need to understand the device-naming conventions defined in Solaris, which we explore next.

Understanding Naming Conventions for Devices

The devices—including disks—in Solaris are referenced by their names, called device names. There are three kinds of device names in Solaris that we discuss in this section. When a device is first added to the system, a name with a full path in the device hierarchy tree is created, and this name is called the *physical device name*. However, the kernel and the system administrators refer to the devices by convenient names called *instance names* and *logical device names*, respectively.

Physical Device Names

A physical device name represents the device name with full path in the device information hierarchy tree. This name for a device is created when the device is first added to the system; the corresponding device files are created in the `/devices` directory and are controlled by the devfs file system.

You can display the physical device names by using any of the following commands:

- **`dmesg`**. The basic function is to look into the system buffer for recently printed diagnostic messages and print them on the standard output.
- **`format`**. Basically a disk partition and maintenance utility.
- **`prtconf`**. A utility to print system configuration.
- **`sysdef`**. A utility that outputs the system definition.

Note that `dmesgd` has been made obsolete by `syslogd` to maintain the system error log. The kernel, however, uses the abbreviated names for these devices, called instance names, which we discuss next.

Instance Names

An instance name is the kernel abbreviated name for a device, and the kernel has them for all possible devices on the system. For example, sd0 and sd1 are the instance names of two disk devices. The mapping between the instance names and the physical device name is contained in the following file:

```
/etc/path_to_inst
```

You can display the instance names by using the following commands:

- dmesg
- prtconf
- sysdef

Remember, however, that of these commands, only the `dmesg` command displays the mapping between the physical device names and the instance names. Of course, you can see the mapping by displaying the content of the `/etc/path_to_inst` file as well—for example, by issuing the following command:

```
less /etc/path_to_inst
```

Although the kernel uses the instance names to refer to the device, you, the system administrator, use the logical names, which we explore next.

Logical Device Names

When a device is first added to the system, a logical device name is created in addition to the physical device name. Logical device files live in the `/dev` directory whereas the physical device files live in the `/devices` directory. Just like instance names, the logical device names point to the physical device names. You, the system administrator, will use the logical device names to refer to the devices in various system commands.

There is a slight difference between the structure of a logical name on a SPARC-based system and on an x86-based system, as is discussed next.

Logical Device Names on SPARC-Based Systems The structure of a logical device name on a SPARC-based system is shown in Figure 5-3. We describe here the different components of the name:

- *Device directory*. This refers to the top directory for the devices—that is `/dev`.

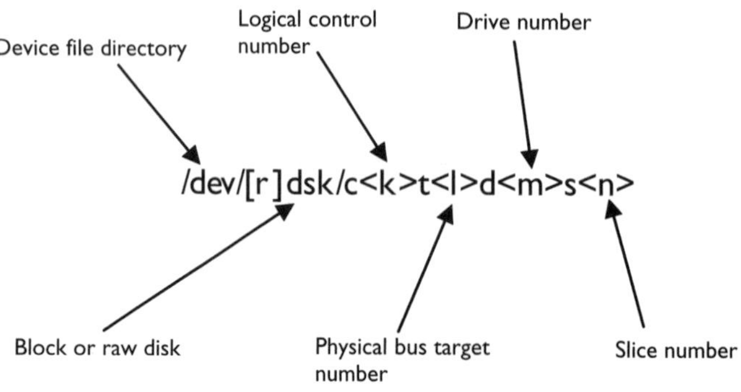

FIGURE 5-3 The structure of a logical device name for a device on a SPARC-based system

- *Block or raw disk.* This refers to the `rdsk` subdirectory for raw device interface that transfers data one character at a time, and the `dsk` subdirectory for block device interface that transfers data in buffers.
- *Logical controller number.* This refers to the disk controller number. The system assigns a number to each controller in the order it was discovered. If there is only one controller, this number is usually 0.
- *Physical bus target number.* This is the disk number that the controller uses to address each disk individually. Each disk under a controller has a unique target number.
- *Drive number.* This is the logical unit number of the disk. For single disks the number is always 0, but in a group of disks (e.g., in SCSI disk arrays), this number uniquely identifies a disk in the group.
- *Slice number.* This number uniquely identifies a slice (partition) on a disk. We will discuss slices (partitions) further on in this chapter.

Logical controller numbers are assigned automatically during system initialization. The numbers are strictly logical, and are assigned in the order the controller is discovered. For example the controller discovered first may be numbered 1, and the controller discovered second may be named 2, and so on.

Note that disk drives have entries under both `/dev/dsk` and `/dev/rdsk` directories. An entry in `/dev/rdsk` refers to a raw device. In this case the data is transferred to and from the device one character at a time, and it bypasses the system's I/O buffers. A raw device is used only for small data transfers. In contrast, an entry in the `/dev/dsk` directory refers to a block (or buffered) device, and the system in this case uses I/O buffers to speed up the data transfer.

As Table 5-1 shows, some commands require the specific interface type (blocked or raw) to use in referring to a device in the command. For example, you must use the raw interface type in the `fsck` command as shown here:

```
fsck /dev/rdsk/c0t0d0s0
```

There are two kinds of controller—direct controllers and bus-oriented controllers. Direct controllers, such as an IDE controller, access the disk directly, whereas a bus-oriented controller, such as a SCSI controller, accesses the disk through the bus. SPARC-based systems use the same scheme, the bus-oriented logical name scheme discussed in this section for both kinds of controllers. For direct controllers, the physical bus target number is usually set to 0.

TABLE 5-1 Device interface types required by some commonly used commands

Command Name	Device Interface Type	Example of Use
df	Block	df /dev/dsk/c0t0d0s0
fsck	Raw	fsck /dev/rdsk/c0t0d0s0
mount	Block	mount /dev/dsk/c1t0d0s7 /home
newfs	Raw	newfs /dev/rdsk/c0t3d0s6
prtvtoc	Raw	prtvtoc /dev/rdsk/c0t0d0s3

exam watch

The SPARC-based systems always use the same logical device name scheme for both direct and bus-oriented controllers, whereas x86-based systems use different schemes for direct controllers and bus-oriented controllers.

Disk devices with direct controllers and bus-oriented controllers are named differently on x86 systems, which we explore next.

Logical Device Names on x86-Based Systems On x86-based systems, the logical names for disk devices with bus-oriented controllers, such as SCSI controllers, are determined following the same scheme as in SPARC-based systems. However, the structure of a logical name for a disk device with direct controllers, such as an IDE controller, is slightly different, as is shown in Figure 5-4. Note that this figure is identical to Figure 5-3 except that the bus target number element is missing.

Now that you know how to format a disk and how it is named by the system, see the next page for some practical scenarios and their solutions.

In this section, we have explored how the disk platters are divided into different elements and how to name a disk device. Dividing the disk into tracks and sectors is called *low-level formatting*. Once a disk has gone through low-level formatting, it is ready for partitioning, which is a process of grouping cylinders together into a slice on which a file system will reside.

FIGURE 5-4 Structure of a logical device name for a disk with a direct controller, such as an IDE controller, on an x86-based system

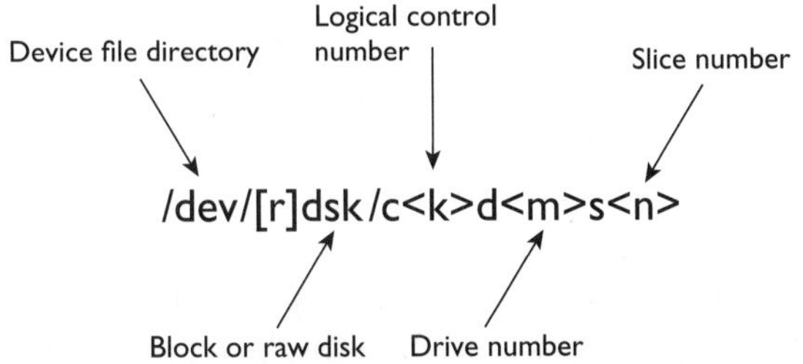

SCENARIO & SOLUTION	
How would you refer to the third partition on a disk connected to a SPARC-based Solaris system with bus target number 0, logical unit number 0, and controller number 2?	`c2t0d0s3`
How would you refer to this slice in the `fsck` command?	`/dev/rdsk/c2t0d0s3`
How would you refer to this slice in the `mount` command?	`/dev/dsk/c2t0d0s3`

CERTIFICATION OBJECTIVE 5.02

Partitioning a Disk

Exam Objective 2.4: *Given a scenario, partition a disk correctly using the appropriate files, commands, and options, and manage disk labels using SMI and EFI labels as they relate to disk sets.*

A disk can, and often does, hold a number of file systems. Each file system occupies its own space on the disk, called a slice or a partition. In this section, we will explore what partitions are, how the partition information is stored on the disk, and how a disk is actually partitioned.

Understanding Partitions

As you already know from the previous chapter, a file lives inside a file system. Each file system, in turn, resides in a specific part of the disk called a slice, or a partition. In other words, a slice (or a partition) is a group of cylinders of the disk set aside for use by a specific file system.

You might be wondering, is it a slice or a partition? As you noticed in the previous section, the logical device name still uses "s" in it to refer to a slice on the disk. Slices were called partitions in Solaris 4.x, and as you see in the exam objectives for Solaris 10, they are called partitions as well. In this book, we will be using these two terms interchangeably. Having said that, no confusion is permitted on this issue.

The location of a disk slice is defined by two elements: an offset that specifies the distance from cylinder 0 to mark the beginning of the slice, and a size in cylinders to mark the end of the slice. Usually, the administrator provides the first cylinder and the last cylinder while using a utility to partition a disk. In order to manage slices effectively, remember the following rules about them:

- Each disk slice can hold only one file system.
- Each file system can reside only on one slice (i.e., a file system cannot span multiple slices).
- A slice cannot span multiple disks.
- Once you have created a file system on a slice, its size cannot be changed without destroying it—that is, repartitioning it.

Table 5-2 presents a comparison between disk slices on SPARC and x86 systems. On an x86 system, a disk can be divided into 10 fdisk partitions numbered 0 to 9, an fdisk partition being a slice of the disk reserved for a specific OS. Table 5-3 describes the slices that may be found on a Solaris system.

TABLE 5-2

Differences between the disk slices on SPARC and x86 systems

Feature	SPARC	x86
Multiple booting	Entire disk is dedicated to Solaris OS.	You can divide the disk into fdisk partitions, one partition per OS.
Volume Table of Contents (VTOC) disk	Disk is divided into 8 slices numbered 0 to 7.	Disk is divided into 10 slices numbered 0 to 9.
Extensible Firmware Interface (EFI) disk.	Disk is divided into 7 slices numbered 0 to 6.	Disk is divided into 7 slices numbered 0 to 6.

TABLE 5-3 File systems on disk slices

Slice	File System	Content
0	/ (root)	Files and directories that make up the OS.
1	swap	Provides space on the disk to be used as virtual memory.
2	—	In a disk with a VTOC label, this is reserved for referring to the entire disk, and its size should not be changed. In a disk with an EFI label, you can use it as you wish.
3	For example: /export	Optional slice; you can use it based on your site's need.
4	—	Optional slice; you can use it based on your site's need.
5	For example: /opt	Optional slice; you can use it based on your site's need.
6	/usr	System-related commands, programs, and library routines.
7	Standalone system: /home Server: /export/home	Files created by individual users.
8	—	VTOC: NA On EFI: reserved slice created by default; do not modify it or delete it. It is similar to slice 9 on VTOC.
9	For x86 only	VTOC: Known as alternate sector slice; reserved for alternate disk blocks. EFI: NA.

In a VTOC disk, slice 2 is reserved for referring to the entire disk, while in an EFI disk, you can use it to meet your needs. Furthermore, you cannot boot a system using a disk with an EFI label.

Once you partition a disk, you need to make this information available to the operating system, and you do that by labeling the disk, which we explore next.

Labeling the Disk

A disk label is the information about the disk's controller, geometry, and slices. A special area is set aside on each disk to store this information. The process of storing the slice information into this area is called disk labeling. You store this information after you create slices, and if you fail to do so, the OS will have no way to find out about the slices. An important component of a disk label is called a *partition table*, which identifies each slice, its boundaries by cylinders, and its size.

In order to provide support for multiterabyte disks, Solaris offers the Extensible Firmware Interface (EFI) disk label for both 64-bit and 32-bit Solaris kernels. The EFI label differs from the VTOC label in the following ways:

- It provides support for disks greater than one terabyte in size.
- It provides seven slices numbered from 0 to 6, all of them being usable—that is, slice 2 is just another slice.
- A slice cannot overlap with the label or with another slice. That means the first slice will start at sector 34, because the size of the EFI label is typically 34 sectors.
- The unit for reporting sizes is a block.
- The EFI label does not contain any cylinder, head, or sector information.
- The information that was stored in the last two cylinders of the disk is stored in slice 8 of an EFI disk.
- If you use the format utility to change the partition sizes, the unassigned partition tag will be assigned to partitions with size equal to zero. The format utility assigns, by default, the `/usr` tag to any slice with a size greater than zero. Although you can reassign the partition tags by using the partition change menu, you cannot change a partition with non-zero size to the unassigned tag.
- The `/etc/format.dat` file contains the list of predefined partition tables that can be used by the format utility.

> **exam watch**
> ***Sector 0 on a VTOC disk is reserved for storing the label, and the first 34 sectors of an EFI disk are used for the label. Therefore, you cannot include these sectors in the slices.***

Let's explore how the disks are actually partitioned.

Performing Disk Partition

When you install the Solaris system, disk drives are partitioned and labeled by the Solaris installation utility. After the system has been installed, you can use the format utility to perform low-level formatting, partitioning, and labeling on additional disks, along with many other tasks. You will mostly be using the format utility just to partition a disk, because the low-level formatting on the disk usually has already been performed. To partition a disk, you will perform the following steps:

- Determine which slices are needed.
- Determine the size of each slice.
- Partition the disk by using the format utility.
- Label the disk with the new partition information.
- Create the file system for each partition.

The easiest way to partition a disk is to select the partition option provided by the `format` command, and then select the `modify` option from the `partition` menu. The `modify` command helps you in two ways:

- It allows you to create partitions by specifying the size of each partition without having to keep track of the cylinder boundaries.
- The `modify` command also keeps track of any disk space that remains in the free hog slice.

The free hog slice is a temporary slice that automatically expands and shrinks to accommodate the unused disk space during slice-resizing operations. The format utility is used by issuing the `format` command, which has the following syntax:

```
format [<options>] <deviceNames>
```

The `<deviceNames>` is a list of raw disk logical device names such as `/dev/rdsk/c<k>t<l>d<m>s<n>`. Following are some typical options for the `format` command:

- **`-d <deviceName>`**. The logical device name from the list specified by `<deviceNames>`; this disk will become the current disk for the utility to work on. You do not need this option if `<deviceNames>` contain only one disk name.
- **`-f <commandFile>`**. Take input to the format command from the file specified by `<commandFile>`, not from the standard input.
- **`-l <logFile>`**. Create a log of your format session and save it in the file whose name is specified by `<logFile>`.
- **`-m`**. Enable more detailed error messages. This option is useful when you are getting an error message and want to probe deeper.

- **`-M`**. Enable diagnostic messages in addition to everything that `-m` option does.
- **`-s`**. Suppress all the output.

When you issue the `format` command, it displays a long menu that includes the tasks listed in Table 5-4.

The IDE disks have low-level formatting already performed on them by the manufacturer. You may, however, need to perform low-level formatting on the SCSI disks before you can partition them. You can do this by selecting the `format` option from the format command menu.

on the job

When you are running the format utility, do not select the system, otherwise you will delete the OS and lose the data on the disk.

From time to time you will need to know which devices are connected to the system or which devices the system recognizes. Furthermore, when the system is up

TABLE 5-4 Main tasks that you can perform by using the format utility

Task	Description
analyze	Perform surface analysis on the disk.
current	Display the information about the current disk: device name, path name to the disk device, and disk geometry.
defect	Display defect list. Supported only for SCSI devices.
disk	Select a disk to format.
fdisk	Run the `fdisk` utility to create an fdisk partition on an x86 system.
format	Do the low-level formatting on SCSI disks. IDE disks are preformatted by their manufacturers.
inquiry	Display the product name, vendor name, and revision level of the current disk.
label	Write label to the current disk.
partition	Create and modify slices.
repair	Repair a specific sector on a disk.
save	Save new disk and slice information.
type	Select and define the disk type.
verify	Display labels.
volname	Assign an 8-character volume name to the disk.

and running you will want it to recognize a newly added device. Now, let's explore how to list devices on a Solaris system and how to reconfigure the devices.

CERTIFICATION OBJECTIVE 5.03

Listing and Reconfiguring Devices

***Exam Objective 2.3**: Use the prtconf and format commands to list devices, explain critical issues of the /etc/path_to_inst file, and reconfigure devices by performing a reconfiguration boot or using the devfsadm command for SPARC, x64, and x86-based systems.*

As a system administrator, you will need to know the list of devices that the system recognizes. While the system is up and running, you may need to add a new device to the system and configure it. We explore these issues in this section.

Listing Devices

The commands listed in Table 5-5 display the information about system and device configuration, and their output includes the device names.

TABLE 5-5 Commands that generate the output that includes a list of devices

Command	Displays
`dmesg`	A list of devices attached to the system since last reboot along with system diagnostic messages.
`format`	The product name, vendor name, and revision level of the current disk, if the inquiry option of the format menu is selected.
`prtconf`	System configuration information that includes total amount of memory and the device configuration information from the system's device hierarchy.
`sysdef`	Device configuration information that includes loadable modules, pseudo devices, selected kernel parameters, and system hardware.

The `prtconf` command displays the system configuration information including the device configuration information, and its syntax is as follows:

```
/usr/sbin/prtconf [<options>] [<devPath>]
```

If `<devPath>` is specified, the command will display information only about this device. Some common options for both SPARC and x86 are listed here:

- **-a**. Display all the ancestor nodes of the device specified by `<devPath>` up to the root node of the device tree.
- **-c**. Display the device subtree whose root is the device specified by `<devPath>`.
- **-v**. Verbose mode.
- **-V**. Display version information about PROM (for SPARC) or booting system (for x86).
- **-x**. Report whether the firmware on this system is 64-bit ready.

Note that the `prtconf` command offers a great deal of flexibility. You can get information about just one device or about a subtree of devices. If you issue the command without any option or argument, it will display information about all the devices attached to the system. For example, on a SPARC-based system the `prtconf` command will generate an output like the following:

```
# prtconf
System Configuration: Sun Microsystems sun4u
Memory size: 512 Megabytes
System Peripherals (Software Nodes):
SUNW,Sun-Blade-1000
scsi_vhci, instance #0
packages (driver not attached)
SUNW,builtin-drivers (driver not attached)
deblocker (driver not attached)
disk-label (driver not attached)
terminal-emulator (driver not attached)
obp-tftp (driver not attached)
dropins (driver not attached)
kbd-translator (driver not attached)
ufs-file-system (driver not attached)
chosen (driver not attached)
openprom (driver not attached)
client-services (driver not attached)
```

```
options, instance #0
aliases (driver not attached)
memory (driver not attached)
virtual-memory (driver not attached)
SUNW,UltraSPARC-III, instance #0
memory-controller, instance #0
SUNW,UltraSPARC-III, instance #1
memory-controller, instance #1
pci, instance #0
ebus, instance #0
```

The output is truncated.

on the job

The "driver not attached" message displayed by the `prtconf` command does not necessarily mean that the driver is not available for this device; it means that the driver is not currently attached to the device instance because the device is not in use. The driver is loaded automatically when a device is accessed, and unloaded when the device is no longer in use.

You can use a number of commands such as `dmesg`, `prtconf`, and `sysdef` to get information about devices attached to the system. The `dmesg` command displays the mapping between the physical device names and the instance names. Of course, you can see the mapping by displaying the content of the `/etc/path_to_inst` file as well—for example, by issuing the following command:

```
less /etc/path_to_inst
```

However, take extra precautions while handling the `path_to_inst` file, because the system uses this file in a very important way.

Issues with the `path_to_inst` File

As you already know from a previous section, the instance names, which are the abbreviations used by the kernel for referring to the devices, are mapped to physical device names in the `/etc/path_to_inst` file. Once an instance name has been assigned to a device, the system records the mapping in the `/etc/path_to_inst` file in order to stay consistent across reboots.

The system counts on this file to find the root, usr, and swap devices; it cannot start up without it. In other words, do not remove the `/etc/path_to_inst` file and make changes to it unless you've thought through those changes. In general, you will not need to make changes to this file, because the file is maintained by the system.

If due to a problem with the `/etc/path_to_inst` file you cannot start the system from the startup disk, remember that the CD-ROM still has the `/etc/path_to_inst` file. You can perform the following steps:

- Start up from the CD-ROM by using the `boot -sw cdrom` at the OpenBoot prompt.
- Mount the root file system from the startup disk on `/a`.
- Copy the `/etc/path_to_inst` contained on the CD-ROM to `/a/etc/path_to_inst` on the startup disk.
- Start with the startup disk.

Now you know how to find information about the devices currently attached to the system. What if you add a new device when the system is up and running? What would you need to do so that the system can recognize the newly added device? Let's explore this issue next.

EXERCISE 5-1

Displaying Information on Devices Attached to the Solaris System

1. Determine the mapping between the instance names and the physical device names by issuing the following command:

   ```
   dmesg
   ```

2. If the output is too long and it quickly rolls over, you can browse the output by issuing the command in the following way:

   ```
   demesg | more
   ```

   Browse the output page by page by pressing the space bar.
3. Determine the mapping between the instance device names and the physical device names from the output. The mapping entries for the devices will be similar to the following:

   ```
   simba0 is /pci@1f,0/pci@1,1
   ```

4. Now, use the `prtconf` command to see how much memory is installed on your Solaris system:

   ```
   prtconf | grep Memory
   ```

   The output will look like the following:

   ```
   Memory size: 128 Megabytes
   ```

Reconfiguring Devices

In the earlier versions of Solaris, you had to reboot the system in order to recognize the devices newly added to the system. The `devfsadm` command eliminates the need for reboot in order to discover new devices.

The `devfsadm` command manages the device files in the `/dev` and `/devices` directories. This command, by default, attempts to load all drivers in the system and attach to all possible device instances. Subsequently, `devfsadm` creates the device files in the `/devices` directory and also creates links in the `/dev` directory that point to the files in the `/devices` directory. Furthermore, the `devfsadm` command maintains another device-related file, the `/etc/path_to_inst` file. The syntax for this command is as follows:

```
/usr/sbin/devfsadm [<options>]
```

Some common options are described here:

- **`-c <deviceClass>`**. Restrict operation to devices of the class specified by `<deviceClass>` with acceptable values: disk, tape, port, audio, and pseudo.
- **`-C`**. Cleanup mode. Cleanup dangling `/dev` links.
- **`-i <driverName>`**. Load only the driver specified by `<driverName>`, and configure the devices only for this driver.
- **`-n`**. Do not attempt to load drivers or add new nodes to the device tree.
- **`-s`**. Suppress reporting any changes to `/dev`.
- **`-v`**. Display changes to `/dev` in verbose mode. Use this option if you need more information for troubleshooting purpose.

If you want to specify more than one class of device, you will need to repeat the `-c` option as shown here:

```
devfsadm -c disk -c audio
```

You format and partition a disk so that the file systems can reside in partitions. After creating a file system in a partition, you make it available to users by mounting it, which we explore next.

CERTIFICATION OBJECTIVE 5.04

Mounting and Unmounting a File System

***Exam Objective 2.7**: Perform mounts and unmounts on a Solaris 10 OS file system, and use volume management to access mounted diskettes and CD-ROMs, restrict access, troubleshoot volume management problems, and explain access methods without volume management.*

To the user, all the file systems on a Solaris system appear to be one unified directory tree with its root (/) directory at the top. When you create a file system on a disk, you attach it to the tree at some point underneath root (/), and this process is called mounting the file system. The different ways of mounting file systems are as follows:

- If a file system is used infrequently, you can mount it by issuing a mount command from the command line.
- You can make entries for the frequently used file systems in the `/etc/vfstab` file, and these file systems will be mounted automatically when the system is booted.
- You can use the `AutoFS` utility, which automatically mounts the file system when it's accessed and unmounts it when the user moves to another directory.

When a Solaris system is booted, it automatically mounts the file systems listed in the virtual file system table (`vfstab`) file.

Automatic Mounting with /etc/vfstab

During the boot procedure, when the system enters the multiuser mode, the `mountall` command, which mounts the file systems specified in the `/etc/vfstab` file, is executed.

The kernel mounts the root (/), `/usr`, and `/var` file systems before the `mountall` command is executed; the command mounts the file systems listed in the `/etc/vfstab` file with the value of the `mount at boot` field equal to yes.

The fields of an entry in the `/etc/vfstab` file are described here:

- **`Device to mount`**. This field identifies the block device name (e.g., `/dev/dsk/c0t0d0s0`) corresponding to the file system being mounted or a directory name for a virtual file system.
- **`Device to fsck`**. This field identifies the raw device name (e.g., `/dev/rdsk/c0t0d0s0`) that will be used by the `fsck` command for the file system. Use a hyphen (-) if this field is not applicable—for example, in the case of a read-only file system or a network-based file system.
- **`Mount point`**. This field identifies where on the directory tree the file system is to be mounted—for example, `/usr`.
- **`FS type`**. This field identifies the type of the file system.
- **`fsck pass`**. This field specifies the pass number for the `fsck` command to indicate how to check the file system:
  - A value of hyphen (-) means the file system is not checked.
  - A value of zero means the file system is not checked if it is a UFS file system, otherwise it's checked.
  - A value of greater than zero means the file system is checked.
- *Mount at boot*. Specifies whether the file system will be mounted automatically by the `mountall` command during the system boot; the values for this field are yes and no. The value of this field should be set to no for

the root (/), /usr, and var/ file systems, as well as for the virtual file systems such as /proc and /dev/fd.

- *Mount options*. A list of comma-separated options, with no spaces, which are used for mounting the file system. Use a hyphen (-) to indicate no option.

In an entry in the /etc/vfstab file, you must specify the value for each field. To specify that there is no value, type a hyphen (-), not a white space; otherwise, the system may not boot successfully.

Once the Solaris system has been booted, you may still need to mount a file system to the existing directory tree. You can do that manually, as is discussed in the next section.

Manual Mounting and Unmounting

As a system administrator, you will need to mount new file systems to a directory tree that is already up and running. The new file systems may be on a hard drive or on a medium such as a floppy or a CD-ROM. In order to mount and unmount file systems manually, you can use the commands described in Table 5-6.

***Note that the commands to unmount the file systems are* umount *and* umountall*, and not* unmount *and* unmountall.**

The umount and umountall commands do not unmount a file system that is busy (except when you use the -f option). A file system is

TABLE 5-6 Commands for mounting and unmounting file systems

Command	Description
mount	Used to mount a file system as well as remote resources.
umount	Used to unmount a mounted file system or a remote resource.
mountall	Used to mount all file systems that are specified in the /etc/vfstab file. This command runs automatically when the system enters the multiuser mode.
umountall	Used to unmount all file systems specified in the /etc/vfstab file.

considered busy if a user is accessing a file in the file system, a file in the file system is open, or the file system is being shared.

The `mountall` command is executed automatically during bootup when the system enters the multiuser mode, and it mounts all the file systems specified in the `/etc/vfstab` file with the value of the `mount at boot` field set equal to `yes`. To mount an individual file system after the system is up and running, you can use the `mount` command, which has the following syntax:

```
mount [<options>] [-o <specificOptions>] <mountDevice> <mountPoint>
```

`<mountDevice>` is the name of the device that contains the file system that needs to be mounted, and `<mountPoint>` is the name of an existing directory in the directory tree. If the directory has content, it will be hidden until the file system is unmounted. The options specified by <options> are described as follows:

- **-F <FSType>**. Specify the type of the file system that will be mounted.
- **-m**. Mount the file system without making an entry in the `/etc/mnttab` file.
- **-p**. Print. Display the list of the mounted file systems in the `/etc/vfstab` format. It must be the only option specified.
- **-r**. Mount the file system read only.
- **-v**. Verbose. Display the list of the mounted file systems in verbose format. It must be the only option specified.

The `<specificOptions>` are the file system–specific options described in Table 5-7.

TABLE 5-7 Operands to be used with the -o option of the mount command

Option	Description	Default
`devices | nodevices`	Allow (or disallow) the opening of device-special files.	devices
`exec | noexec`	Allow (or disallow) the execution of programs in the file system.	exec
`ro | rw`	Read-only (or read/write) permissions.	rw
`setuid | nosetuid`	Allow (or disallow) executing setuid and setgid.	setuid

The /etc/mnttab file is managed by the MNTFS file system, and it provides a read-only access to the list of file systems currently mounted on the local system.

You can unmount a mounted file system by using the umount command, which has the following syntax:

```
umount <mountPoint>
```

The <mountPoint> may specify either the directory name where the file system is mounted or the device name for the file system. You can use the -f option to force the file system to unmount even if it is busy. But be warned that use of this option can cause open files to lose data.

EXERCISE 5-2

Mounting a CD-ROM, Browsing Its Content, and Unmounting It

Make the access readable only. Assume the CD-ROM is attached as a slave to the primary IDE channel, and the file system you want to access is of type hsfs and it resides on slice 0.

1. Insert the CD-ROM into the CD-ROM drive.
2. Mount the CD-ROM by issuing the following command:

   ```
   # mount -F hsfs -o ro /dev/dsk/c0t1d0s0 /cdrom
   ```

3. You can browse the subtree starting with /cdrom by using the ls command—for example:

   ```
   # ls -l /cdrom
   ```

4. Unmount the CD-ROM by issuing the following command:

   ```
   # umount /cdrom
   ```

5. Eject the CD by issuing the following command:

   ```
   # eject cdrom
   ```

Instead of manually mounting the removable medium, such as a CD-ROM or a diskette, you can use volume management to accomplish this task.

Accessing Removable Media with Volume Management

As with manual mounting, you can use volume management to access the removable media. Accessing the media with volume management (the volume management) will be easier and you will not even need superuser privileges to do that. Table 5-8 shows how to access removable media that is being managed by volume management.

Volume management (`vold`), by default, manages all removable media devices. Occasionally, you will need to manage the media manually without using volume management. In that case, stop the `vold` daemon, use the media manually, and start the `vold` daemon when you want to. You can use the following commands to stop and start volume management:

```
/etc/init.d/volmgt stop
/etc/init.d/volmgt start
```

The most important takeaways from this chapter are the three most important tasks to perform before a user can use the file systems on a disk:

- You add the disk to the system, and the system assigns it a device name that reflects its full path in the device tree. The system itself refers to the disk with

TABLE 5-8 Accessing data on removable media managed by volume management

Removable Media	Action	Directory in Which to Find the Files
Diskette	Insert the diskette and issue the command: `volcheck`.	`/floppy`
Removable hard disk	Insert the removable hard disk and issue the command: `volcheck`.	`/rmdisk/jaz0` or `/rmdisk/zip0`
CD-ROM	Insert the CD. You may have to wait for a few seconds.	`/cdrom/<volName>`
DVD	Insert the DVD. You may have to wait for a few seconds.	`/dvd/<volName>`

an abbreviated name called instance name, which is mapped to the physical device name in the `/etc/path_to_inst` file.

- You partition the disk by referring to it with its logical device name, which also points to its physical device name.
- You create the file system on a disk partition and make it available by mounting it to the existing directory tree by using the `mount` command.

CERTIFICATION SUMMARY

Persistent data on a system is stored mostly on hard disks. The smallest storage unit on a disk is a sector, which typically has a capacity of 512 bytes. The disks have three kinds of names, which are automatically assigned to them when they are added to the system: the physical device name in the device information hierarchy, instance names used by the kernel, and the logical name used by the system administrator. SPARC-based systems use the same logical name scheme for disks with direct controllers (e.g., IDE) and disks with bus-oriented controllers (e.g., SCSI), whereas x86-based systems use different logical name schemes for these two kinds of disks.

Before a file system can reside on a disk, the disk must be divided into slices, and the process is called partitioning. Each file system resides on its own slice. You can perform partitioning by using the `format` command. Partition information is stored in the disk area called the disk label. Solaris 10 offers Extensible Firmware Interface (EFI) labels to support disks with storage capacities of multiterabytes. If you add a new device to a Solaris 10 system admin, you do not need to reboot the system; just use the `devfsadm` command to have the system configure it and recognize it.

After a file system has been created on a disk slice, it must be mounted—that is, connected to the directory tree, in order to make it available for users. When the Solaris system is booted, it automatically mounts the file systems listed in the `/etc/vfstab` file with the `mount on boot` field set to yes. Once the system is booted, you can mount the new file systems and unmount them based on your needs by using the `mount` and `umount` commands, respectively.

Before users can use the file systems, they will be required to have accounts on the Solaris system. It will be one of your responsibilities as a system administrator to create and manage the user accounts. We explore this subject in the next chapter.

INSIDE THE EXAM

Comprehend

- Sector 0 on a VTOC disk is reserved for storing the label, and the first 34 sectors of an EFI disk are used for the label. Therefore, you cannot include these sectors in the slices.
- In Solaris 10, you do not need to reboot the system in order to recognize the newly added devices; just use the `devfsadm` command.

Look Out

- SPARC-based systems use the same logical device name scheme for disks with direct controllers and bus-oriented controllers, but x86-based systems use different schemes for these two kinds of disks.
- You cannot change the slice size after creating a file system on it without destroying it — that is, repartitioning it.
- In a VTOC disk, slice 2 is reserved for referring to the entire disk, whereas in an EFI disk, you can use it to meet your needs.
- You provide a raw device name (`/dev/rdsk`), not a blocked device name (`dev/dsk`), in the `format` command.

Memorize

- Each disk slice can hold only one file system, and each file system can reside only on one slice.
- Know all the options available in the format utility and what they do.
- The procedures to boot the system are stored in the boot block.
- In order to specify a no value for any field of an entry in the `/etc/vfstab`, type a hyphen (-), because a white space is not a valid value and may cause boot problems.
- You cannot edit the `/etc/mnttab` file.

TWO-MINUTE DRILL

Understanding Disk Architecture

- A disk consists of multiple platters, each of them divided into concentric circles called tracks. A set of tracks, one from each platter, at an equal distance from the center is called a cylinder.
- A track is divided into sectors, and a sector has a typical capacity of 512 bytes. A file consists of blocks, and a block may occupy one or more sectors on the disk.
- A physical device name represents the full path name for a device in the device information hierarchy; it is created when the device is connected for the first time to the system.
- An instance name is an abbreviated name for a device that the kernel uses to refer to the device.
- A logical device name is the name for a device that the system administrator uses in system commands.

Partitioning a Disk

- Each disk slice can hold only one slice, and vice versa.
- A slice cannot span multiple disks.
- You cannot change the size of a slice after creating a file system on it without re-partitioning.
- In a VTOC disk, slice 2 is reserved for referring to the entire disk, whereas in an EFI disk, you can use it to meet your needs.
- The disks are partitioned by using the partition option from the menu provided by the format utility.

Listing and Reconfiguring Devices

- You can use the `prtconf` and `sysdef` command to find out the device configuration information including the list of devices that can also be found with the `demesg` command.
- The `/etc/path_to_inst` file is maintained by the system and is used at the startup time. Do not remove it, and if you have to edit it, be careful in making changes.

- The devfsadm command by default loads all the drivers, but it can also be used to configure only the newly added devices so that you don't have to reboot the system.

Mounting and Unmounting a File System

- The mountall command is automatically executed when the system enters the multiuser mode, and it mounts all the file systems specified in the /etc/vfstab file.
- The /etc/mnttab file is a read-only file and contains a table of all the file systems currently mounted on the local system.
- You can mount an individual file system from the command line by using the mount command and unmount it by using the umount command.

SELF TEST

The following questions will help you measure your understanding of the material presented in this chapter. Read all the choices carefully because there might be more than one correct answer. Choose all correct answers for each question.

1. The `/etc/path_to_inst file` maps the instance device names to which of the following? (Choose all that apply.)

   A. Physical devices

   B. Logical device names

   C. Physical device names

   D. Pseudo device names

2. Which of the following would refer to the slice number 0 of a disk with a direct IDE controller on an x86-based system with logical controller number 0 and drive number 0?

   A. `/dev/rdsk/c0d0s3`

   B. `/dev/rdsk/c0t0d0s3`

   C. `/dev/rdsk/s3d0c0`

   D. `/dev/rdsk/s3t0d0c0`

3. Which of the following would refer to the slice number 0 of a disk with a direct IDE controller on a SPARC-based system with logical controller number 0 and drive number 0?

   A. `/dev/rdsk/c0d0s3`

   B. `/dev/rdsk/c0t0d0s3`

   C. `/dev/rdsk/s3d0c0`

   D. `/dev/rdsk/s3t0d0c0`

4. Which of the following contains the procedures that are used to boot the system?

   A. Inode

   B. Disk label

   C. Boot block

   D. Superblock

5. Which of the following actions would you take so that your Solaris 10 system will recognize the newly added device?

   A. Reboot the system.

   B. Execute the `prtconf` command.

   C. Edit the `/etc/path_to_inst` file.

   D. Execute the `devfsadm` command.

6. If you want to see which file systems are currently mounted, which of the following files would you look into?

   A. `/etc/path_to_inst`

   B. `/etc/mnttab`

   C. `/etc/mounttab`

   D. `/etc/vfstab`

   E. `/var/adm/syslog`

7. Which of the following mounted file systems will be unmounted as a result of executing the `mountall` command when the system is up and running? (Choose all that apply.)

   A. `/home`

   B. `/usr`

   C. `/var`

   D. `/misc`

   E. `/`

8. You mounted a floppy to your Solaris system by issuing the following command:

   ```
   mount -F pcfs /dev/diskette /floppy
   ```

   Which of the following commands will unmount the floppy? (Choose all that apply.)

   A. `umount /floppy`

   B. `unmount /floppy`

   C. `umount /dev/diskette`

   D. `umount pcfs`

9. Which of the following are valid Solaris 10 commands?

   A. `mount /dev/rdsk/c0t0d0s0 /proj`

   B. `mount /dev/dsk/c0t0d0s0 /proj`

   C. `fsck /dev/dsk/c0t0d0s0`

   D. `fsck /dev/rdsk/c0t0d0s0`

10. Which of the following commands allow you to see the mapping between the instance device names and physical device names?

    A. `dmesg | more`

    B. `less /etc/path_to_inst`

    C. `prtconf`

    D. `sysdef`

11. You were having difficulties accessing a CD-ROM, so you decided to manually mount the CD-ROM. Assume the file system on the CD-ROM is `hsfs` and it resides on slice 1 of the CD-ROM. Further assume that the CD-ROM is attached as the slave device to the primary IDE channel. After stopping the volume management (vold), which of the following commands would you issue to mount the CD-ROM?

    A. `mount -F hsfs -o ro /cdrom`

    B. `mount -F hsfs /dev/dsk/c0t1d0s0 /cdrom`

    C. `mount -F hsfs /dev/dsk/c0t1d0s0`

    D. `mount -o ro /dev/dsk/c0t1d0s0 /cdrom`

SELF TEST ANSWERS

1. ☑ **C.** The mapping between the instance names and the physical device name is contained in the `/etc/path_to_inst` file.
   ☒ **A** is incorrect because it is the physical device names and not the physical devices that are mapped. **B** and **D** are incorrect because instance names are not mapped to logical device names, and there is no such name for a disk as pseudo device name.

2. ☑ **A**. The bus target number is not used to name the disks with direct controllers on x86-based systems.
   ☒ **B** is incorrect because it uses the bus target number in the logical name for disk with direct controller on an x86-based system. **C** and **D** are incorrect for the same reason; furthermore, the order of different elements of the name is not correct.

3. ☑ **B**. The bus target number is used to name the disks with direct controllers on x86-based systems.
   ☒ **A** is incorrect because the bus target number is missing. **C** and **D** are incorrect because the order of different elements of the name is not correct.

4. ☑ **C**. The procedures to boot the system are stored in the superblock.
   ☒ **A** is incorrect because an inode contains information about a file, not about booting. **B** is incorrect because the disk label contains the information about the disk geometry and partitions not about booting. **D** is incorrect because a superblock contains information about a file system, not about booting.

5. ☑ **D**. The `devfsadm` command with the `-i <driverName>` option will load the driver for the device and configure it without rebooting the system.
   ☒ **A** is incorrect because Solaris 10 offers the `devfsadm` command that you can use to recognize the newly added device without rebooting the system. **B** is incorrect because the `prtconf` command is used to display the system configuration. **C** is incorrect because it is recommended that you do not edit the `/etc/path_to_inst` file unless you have to.

6. ☑ **B**. When a file system is mounted, its entry is automatically made by the system into the `mnttab` file, which is a read-only file.
   ☒ **A** is incorrect because the `/etc/path_to_inst` file contains the mapping between the instant device names and the physical device names. **C** is incorrect because the correct file is spelled `mnttab`, not `mounttab`. **D** is incorrect because the `/etc/vfstab` file only specifies which file systems should be mounted at bootup time. **E** is incorrect because the `/var/adm/syslog` file is used to keep the log of the system messages.

7. ☑ **A** and **D**. The `umountall` command unmounts all the mounted file systems except root (/), `/dev/fd`, `/proc`, `/usr`, `/var`, `var/adm`, and `/var/run`.
☒ **B**, **C**, and **E** are incorrect because the `umountall` command does not unmount these file systems: root (/), `/dev/fd`, `/proc`, `/usr`, `/var`, `var/adm`, and `/var/run`.

8. ☑ **A** and **C**. A file system can be unmounted with the `umount` command by specifying either the device name or the mount point.
☒ **B** is incorrect because the command is `umount`, not `unmount`. **D** is incorrect because you cannot unmount a file system by specifying just the file type.

9. ☑ **B** and **D**. The command `mount` uses the block device, and the command `fsck` uses the raw device.
☒ **A** is incorrect because the command `mount` uses the block device. **C** is incorrect because the command `fsck` uses the raw device and the raw device name in the answer is not specified.

10. ☑ **A** and **B**. The `dmesg` command displays the mapping between the instance device names and the physical device names, and the `/etc/path_to_inst` file also contains this mapping.
☒ **C** and **D** are incorrect because the `prtconf` and `sysdef` commands display the instance device names but not their mapping to the physical device names.

11. ☑ **B**. The `-f` and `-o` options are required. The logical device name for the slave device on the primary IDE channel is `c0t1d0`, which makes the block device file including slice 1 as `/dev/dsk/c0t1d0s1`. The mount point used for the CD-ROM is the directory `/cdrom`.
☒ **A** is incorrect because the device name is not given. **C** and **D** are incorrect because both the `-F` and `-o` options are required. In addition, **C** does not specify the mount point.

6

Performing User Administration

CERTIFICATION OBJECTIVES

6.01	Basics of User Accounts	✓	Two-Minute Drill
6.02	Managing User Accounts	Q&A	Self Test

Managing users on a Solaris system, a significant responsibility of a system administrator, includes creating, modifying, and deleting the user accounts on the system by using both the command and the GUI tools. In addition to learning how to accomplish this task, you will also explore the files in which the user accounts live after you create them. Furthermore, each user works on a system in a certain environment with a global component and a customized local component. We will explore the shell initialization files that are used to set up this environment when the user logs in.

The central issue to think about in this chapter is the Solaris 10 user administration. To understand user administration, we will explore three thought streams: the structure of a user account and how it is managed, the files in which the user accounts live, and the initialization files that are used to create the work environment for a user. In other words, you create and maintain a user account, the account information is stored into some files, and the initialization files create the work environment for a user when the user logs into the account that you created.

CERTIFICATION OBJECTIVE 6.01

Basics of User Accounts

Exam Objective 4.1: *Explain and perform Solaris 10 OS user administration, and manage user accounts and initialization files.*

Before a user can access and use a system, you need to create an account for that user on the system. A user account contains the identification and the permissions attached to it, which allows the user to access and use the system. After logging on to a system, a user can do things such as accessing files and directories according to the permissions granted to that user by the system administrator. Multiple users who need identical permission can be organized into a group, and the permissions can be granted to the group. A permission granted to a group applies to all the users who are members of the group. This makes security management more efficient. In this section, we will explore the structure of a user account and the files in which the user accounts live. Let's begin with exploring the structure of a user account.

Structure of a User Account

A user is required to have a user account on a system in order to log in and use system resources. A user account contains a set of components, such as the user login name and password. The components of a user account, described in the following sections, are summarized in Table 6-1.

Multiple users can be organized into a logical group that has a group name, a group ID (GID), and of course a list of users. A user must belong to a primary group and can belong to a maximum of 15 secondary groups. Any permission for a resource granted to the group apply to each user in the group. A user must belong to at least one group called the user's primary group.

Let's further explore the components of a user account, beginning with the component called user name or login name.

User Name

A user name, also called a login name, is a mandatory component of a user account, which you, the system administrator, create. The user employs the user name and the password associated with it for logging into a local or a remote system. You should establish an organization-wide standard for specifying user names, such as the

TABLE 6-1 Components of a user account explained

Component	Description
User login name	A unique name for a user on a system; two to eight characters in length. The characters can be letters and numerals; the first character must be a letter and at least one character must be a lowercase letter.
Password	A component of a user account that must be kept secret and known only to the user. The user uses it to log into the system along with the user login name.
User ID (UID)	A required unique integer associated with the user name. The numbers from 0 to 99 are reserved for system accounts. Regular users should be assigned UIDs from 100 to 60,000, but they can go as high as the largest 32-bit signed positive number: 2147483647.
Group name	A collection of users who share the same set of permissions to the resources. The maximum length of a group name is eight characters. A group has a name, a group ID, and a list of users that belong to it.
Home directory	The root of the subtree of the file system that belongs to the user.

first letter from the user's first name followed by the last name truncated after seven letters (e.g., opuri for Om Puri, and sspielbe for Steven Spielberg).

You should not use a user name identical to a mail alias known to the system or an NIS domain because it may deliver the user's mail to the alias.

You must exercise the following rules in specifying a user name:

- Each user name on a system must be unique.
- A user name should be two to eight characters long; a character being a letter or a numeral.
- A user name should begin with a letter, and it should contain at least one lowercase letter.

Although allowed, it is not recommended to include a period (.), an underscore (_), or a hyphen (-) in the user name because these characters can cause problems with some software products.

In order to log in to a system, a user needs a password in addition to a login name. Let's take a closer look at the password component.

Password

A password is a secret component of a user account that is known only to the user of the account. As a system administrator, you have two choices: specify a password when you create a user, or force the user to specify a password when the user logs into the system for the first time. The following are the rules for specifying a password:

- The password length, by default, may be six to eight characters long, including letters, numerals, and special characters.
- The minimum and maximum allowed length mentioned previously may be changed by editing the files `/etc/default/passwd` and `/etc/policy.conf`, respectively.
- The first six characters of a password must contain at least one numeric or special character, and at least two alphabets.

A good password is a tradeoff between two opposing requirements: the password should be easy enough for the user to remember but hard enough to keep a hacker from guessing. With this in mind, here are some general guidelines for choosing a good password:

- Do not use the word "password" as your password, as it is too trivial to crack even if you replace the character "s" with the symbol $.
- Avoid the use of proper nouns, login names, the names of a spouse or pet, or anything related to the user that can be easily guessed.
- Avoid using car license numbers, telephone numbers, employee numbers, and Social Security numbers.
- Avoid using words related to a hobby or interest.
- Avoid using any word in the dictionary.
- Avoid using any of the preceding choices spelled backwards.
- Words with numbers or special characters embedded in them make good passwords—for example, goofyboys is a bad password but g00fyboy$ is a good one.

Each user account has a user ID, and each group of users has a group ID, both of which we explore next.

User ID and Group ID

The user ID (UID) is a unique integer associated with a user and is used by the system to keep track of the user account. Theoretically speaking, a UID is any positive integer that you can make out of a signed 32-bit (i.e., $2^{31} - 1$ = 2147483647). However, some of these numbers are reserved, as shown in Table 6-2.

The numbers from 0 to 99 are reserved for system accounts such as root, daemon, sys, and bin: 0 for root, 1 for daemon, 2 for bin. The accounts with UID number greater than 60,000 do not have full functionality—for example, 60,001 for the anonymous user nobody, 65,534 for the anonymous user nobody4, and 60,002 for the

TABLE 6-2 Integers used to specify user ID

UID	Accounts
0–99	System accounts such as root, sys, daemon, and bin.
100–60,000	General-purpose accounts for regular users.
60,000–2,147,483,647	Accounts that do not have full functionality such as anonymous users.

exam watch

The maximum value of a UID can be $2^{31} - 1$. A regular user account has a UID number within the range of 100 to 60,000, and the UID numbers in the range from 0 to 99 belong to the system accounts—for example, the root account has a UID of 0.

non-trusted user noaccess. A general-purpose user account should be assigned a UID number within the range from 100 to 60,000.

Just like a user, a group has an ID too, called the group ID (GID). The rules for the GID numbers are the same as for the UID numbers; a GID on a system should be unique and should not be greater than 60,000.

A user account is created to let the user use the system resources including the file system. The user enters the file system through the home directory, which we explore next.

Home Directory

Users have their own subtrees, which are parts of the whole directory tree on the system. The home directory for a user makes the root of this subtree. The user can access the home directory locally or remotely. The naming convention for the home directory is: `/export/home/<username>`; thus, a user jkerry on a system will have the home directory `/export/home/jkerry`.

A user should access the home directory through a mount point `/home/<username>`. Furthermore, because `/export/home/<username>` is machine specific, the home directories should always be referred to by the environment variable $HOME in order to use them anywhere on the network. The symbolic links created in the user home directory should use relative paths and not absolute paths to make them independent of the home directory's mount point. In this case, changing the mount point will not invalidate the links.

on the job

If you have a large number of user accounts on a server, distribute them over different file systems and use a different name `/export/<homen>` for each file system for the home directories—for example, `/export/home1` on one file system, `/export/home2` on another file system, and so on. This facilitates tasks such as backing up and restoring the home directories.

You will learn further on in this chapter how to create user accounts. First, let's explore where the existing user accounts are stored on the system.

Where User Accounts Live

Once a user account has been created, the account information is saved in three files in the `/etc` directory: `passwd`, `shadow`, and `group`. Let's examine these files one by one.

The `passwd` File

Most of the information about a user account is stored in the `/etc/passwd` file. Each line in this file represents a user account and contains multiple fields with the following syntax:

```
<username>:<password>:<uid>:<gid>:<comment>:<home directory>:<login shell>
```

Any two fields are separated by a colon (:). For example, an entry in the `passwd` file is explained in Figure 6-1. The fields of an entry in the `passwd` file are described in Table 6-3.

The default `passwd` file created by Solaris 10 is shown here.

```
root:x:0:1:Super-User:/:/sbin/sh
daemon:x:1:1::/:
bin:x:2:2::/usr/bin:
sys:x:3:3::/:
adm:x:4:4:Admin:/var/adm:
lp:x:71:8:Line Printer Admin:/usr/spool/lp:
uucp:x:5:5:uucp Admin:/usr/lib/uucp:
nuucp:x:9:9:uucp Admin:/var/spool/uucppublic:/usr/lib/uucp/uucico
smmsp:x:25:25:SendMail Message Submission Program:/:
listen:x:37:4:Network Admin:/usr/net/nls:
gdm:x:50:50:GDM Reserved UID:/:
webservd:x:80:80:WebServer Reserved UID:/:
nobody:x:60001:60001:NFS Anonymous Access User:/:
noaccess:x:60002:60002:No Access User:/:
nobody4:x:65534:65534:SunOS 4.x NFS Anonymous Access User:/:
```

FIGURE 6-1

Entry in the `/etc/passwd` file corresponding to a user account

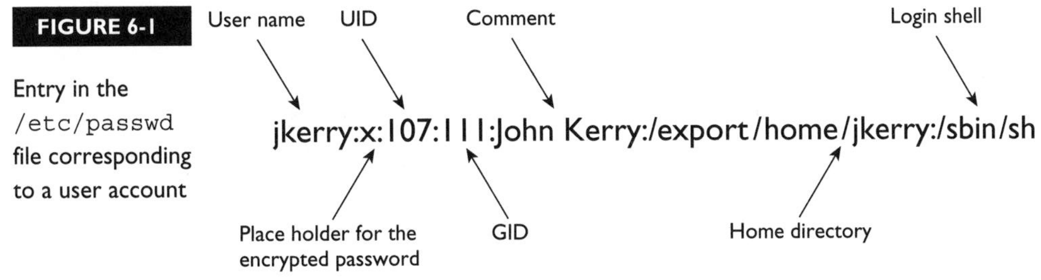

TABLE 6-3 Fields of an entry in the passwd file

Field Name	Description
<username>	The unique user name, also called the login name, for the account.
<password>	The user password for this account.
<UID>	A unique user ID number for the user account. Each account has a UID.
<GID>	A unique group ID number for the group to which the user of this account belongs.
<comment>	An optional informational field. You can basically type any information here; usually it contains the user's full name.
<home directory>	Home directory for the user of this account.
<login shell>	The default login shell for the user such as /bin/sh or /bin/csh.

The comment field in the passwd file is also called the GECOS field for historical reasons; it was originally used to hold the login information needed to submit batch jobs to a mainframe computer running the operating system called GECOS (for General Electric Computer Operating System) from UNIX systems at Bell Labs.

The default passwd file contains entries for standard processes, also called daemons, that are usually started at boot time to perform system-level tasks such as printing, network administration, and port monitoring. Two adjacent colons (::) in the passwd file represents a blank field. This is also true for other files such as the shadow file and the group file.

If the password for a user is encrypted, the entry in the passwd file contains only an x. The encrypted password along with other user information goes into the shadow file, which we examine next.

The shadow File

The shadow file contains detailed information about the password. The syntax for an entry in the shadow file is similar to that of the passwd file and is shown here:

```
<username>:<password>:<lastchg>:<min>:<max>:<warn>:<inactive>:<expire>
```

FIGURE 6-2

Entry in the `/etc/shadow` file corresponding to a user account

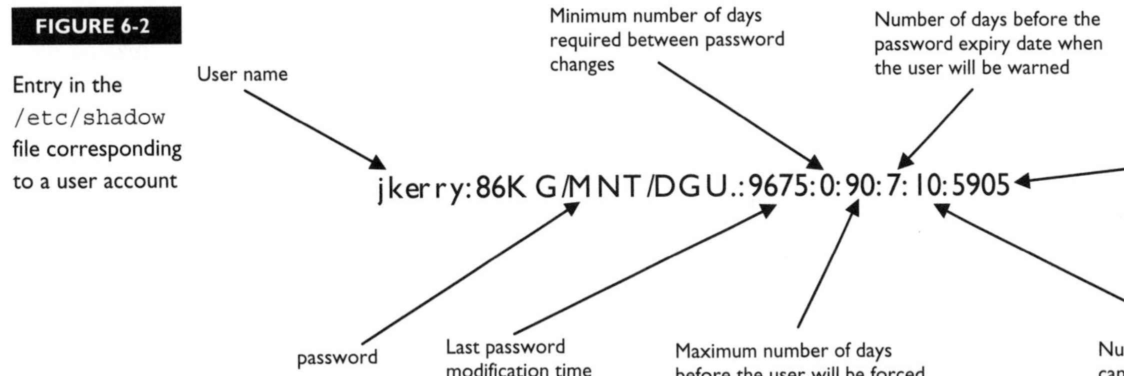

As an example, an entry in the `shadow` file is explained in Figure 6-2. The fields in the `shadow` file entries are described in Table 6-4.

Remember that the `shadow` file can be viewed only by a superuser (e.g., the root account).

The `/etc/passwd` file contains most of the user account information, including a place holder for the password, whereas the detailed password information is

TABLE 6-4

Fields in the `/etc/shadow` file entries

Field Name	Description
`<username>`	The unique user name, also called the login name, for the account.
`<password>`	The user password. May contain one of the following: an encrypted user password 13 characters long, the string *LK* indicating that the account is locked and hence not accessible, or the string NP indicating that this account has no password.
`<lastchg>`	The number of days between January 1, 1970, and the date when the password was modified last.
`<min>`	The minimum number of days required between two consecutive password changes.
`<warn>`	The number of days before the password expiration date when the user is warned.
`<inactive>`	The number of days for which a user account can be inactive before being locked.
`<expire>`	The user account expiration date, after which the user will be unable to log into the system using this account.

contained in the /etc/shadow file. The passwd file and the shadow file contain the user account information, and the group file contains the information about user groups. We discuss the group file next.

The group File

Multiple users can be organized into a group for ease of administration. Entries in the group file contain information about groups. The syntax of an entry in the /etc/group file is similar to an entry in the passwd file and is shown here:

```
<group name>:<group password>:<gid>:<user-list>
```

As an example, an entry in the group file is shown in Figure 6-3. The fields in a group file entry are described in Table 6-5.

The group password field is generally not used—that is, it is left empty. It is a legacy from the earlier days of UNIX. If a group does have a group password, the newgrp command will prompt the user to enter the password. However, note that there is no utility to set the group password. The default group file created by the Solaris 10 system is shown here.

FIGURE 6-3 Entry in the group file corresponding to a group of users

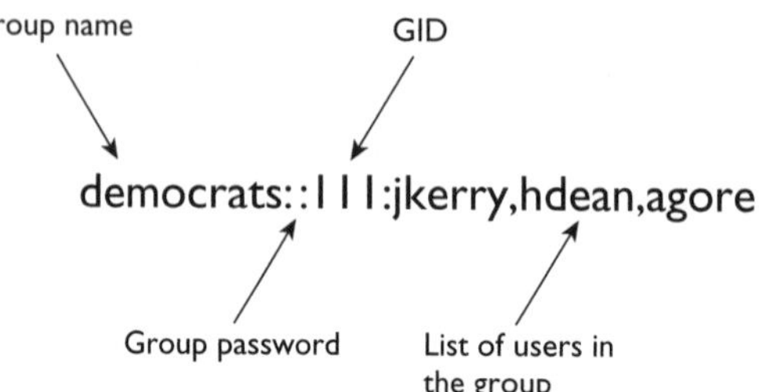

TABLE 6-5 Fields in the /etc/group file

Field Name	Description
<group name>	The name assigned to the group: maximum length eight characters.
<group password>	Optional field, usually contains an asterisk or is left empty.
<GID>	The group ID number.
<user list>	The list of users who are members of this group; any two members are separated by a comma.

```
root::0:
other::1:
bin::2:root,daemon
sys::3:root,bin,adm
adm::4:root,daemon
uucp::5:root
mail::6:root
tty::7:root,adm
lp::8:root,adm
nuucp::9:root
staff::10:
daemon::12:root
smmsp::25:
sysadmin::14:
gdm::50:
webservd::80:
nobody::60001:
noaccess::60002:
nogroup::65534:
```

The default `group` file contains the system groups that support some system level tasks—printing, network administration, and email. Note that many of these groups have corresponding entries in the `passwd` file.

Now that you have explored the structure of a user account and you know where the user account information is stored, it is time to get more practical, that is, to learn how to create, modify, and delete user accounts.

CERTIFICATION OBJECTIVE 6.02

Managing User Accounts

Exam Objective 4.1: *Explain and perform Solaris 10 OS user administration, and manage user accounts and initialization files.*

Managing user accounts includes creating, modifying, and deleting user accounts. In Solaris 10, you can use the command line and the Solaris Management Console (SMC) GUI for managing user and group accounts. The command line as usual provides more options and hence more flexibility, but it can be complex for a

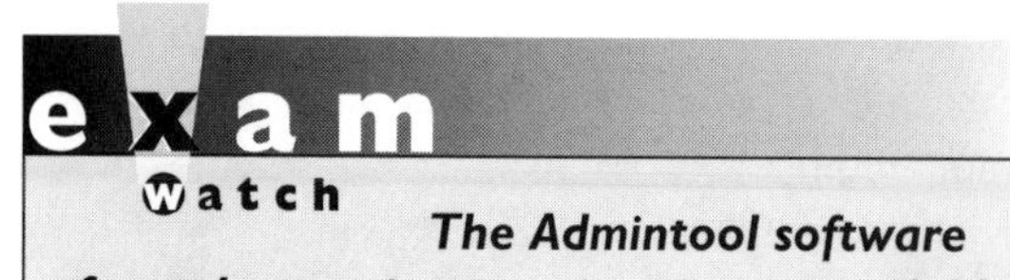

The Admintool software from the previous versions is not available in Solaris 10.

beginner. The SMC GUI on the other hand may be easier to use for a beginner but offers fewer options and less flexibility. However, people with Windows backgrounds may appreciate it.

Let's begin with exploring how to manage user accounts by using the command line.

Managing User and Group Accounts with the Shell Command Line

Solaris offers several shell commands to manage user and group accounts. In this section we explore these commands to create, modify, and delete user and group accounts.

The useradd Command

You use the useradd command to create a new user account—that is, to add a new user to the system. The account information will automatically go to the passwd, shadow, and group files as you create the account. The syntax for the useradd command is shown here:

```
useradd [-c <comment>] [-b <base_dir>] [-d <dir>] [-e <expire>] [-f <inactive>]
[-g <group>] [ -G <group, group...>] [ -m [-k <skel_dir>]] [-p <profile>]
[-A <authorization, authorization,...> [-R <role> ] [-s <shell>] [ -u <uid>]
<login-name>
```

The options for this command are explained in the following list:

- **-c <comment>.** It will take any text string, generally a short description of the user (e.g., full name of the user). The information entered here goes into the comment field of the corresponding entry in the /etc/passwd file.
- **-b <base_dir>.** Specifies the default home directory for the system which will contain the home directories of all the users on the system; for example, if the option -d <dir> is not used for a user with username jkerry, the home directory for jkerry will default to <base_dir>/jkerry.
- **-d <dir>.** Specifies the home directory of the user for whom the account is being created. If this option is not used, the home directory defaults to <base_dir>/<user_name>. This information goes to the passwd file.

- **-e <expire>.** Specifies the expiration date for the user account, after which the user will not be able to log on. The date can be entered using any of the formats specified in the template file `/etc/datemsk`, e.g., 5/9/2007 (the standard American way of referring to dates: month/day/year), or "May 9, 2007." Note that the date that includes spaces must be quoted. The default value for the expiration date on an account is null—that is, no expiration date. This information goes into the `shadow` file.
- **-f <inactive>.** Specifies the maximum number of days, expressed in integers, allowed between two consecutive logins; if the user does not log into the account for days more than the value of <inactive>, the account will be locked. The default for this option is 0. This information goes into the `shadow` file.
- **-g <group>.** Specifies the primary group for the user. The group may be identified by using the character string name of the group or by using the group ID. This information goes into the `passwd` file.
- **-G <group>.** Specifies a secondary group for the user. Multiple groups can be specified by using either the character string names or the group IDs separated by commas. A user cannot become a member of more than a maximum number of groups defined by the variable NGROUPS_MAX specified in the file `/usr/include/limits.h`. By default, a user may become a member of 15 secondary groups at maximum.
- **-k <skel_dir>.** Specifies the directory that contains the skeleton files for initializing the user account. The files are copied from this directory to the user home directory during the creation of the account. If you give the `-m` option along with the `-k` option, the home directory will be created if it does not already exist. The default skeleton directory is `/etc/skel`, and if you do use the `-k` option to specify a new skeleton directory, it must be created before you use the `useradd` command.
- **-p <profile>.** Specifies execution profiles, separated by commas, for the user. You will learn more about profiles further on in this book.
- **-A <authorization>.** A comma-delimited list of authorizations to be assigned to this account. You will learn more about it in Chapter 14.
- **-R <role>.** Specifies roles, separated by commas, for the user. You will learn more about roles in Chapter 14.

- **-s <shell>.** Specifies the user's login shell defined by providing the full path name to a program such as /bin/sh. This information goes into the passwd file.
- **-u <uid>.** Specifies the user ID for the account being created. The default is the next available number above the highest number already assigned to a user. This information goes into the passwd and shadow files.

As you have seen, there are quite a few options available for the useradd command. A reasonable question to ask is: what value would an option argument have if you did not specify it in the useradd command? In this case, the system would assign it a value called the default value listed in the /usr/sadm/defadduser file. The default values for various option arguments are shown in Table 6-6. You can see the default values by issuing the following command:

```
useradd -D
```

Now if you are picky (a wrong word for demanding), you can ask another question: if I don't like any of the system defaults shown in Table 6-6, can I change it? The answer is yes, you can overwrite the system default with your own default by using the -D option with the useradd command, as shown here:

```
useradd -D <option> <new_default>
```

For example, if you want to change the default for shell from /bin/sh to /bin/ksh, you would issue the following command:

```
useradd -D -s /bin/ksh
```

TABLE 6-6 Default values for some options in the useradd command (you can change these default values by using the -D option with the useradd command)

Option	Default Value
-b <base_dir>	/home
-e <expire>	Null
-f <inactive>	0
-k <skel_dir>	/etc/skel
-p <profile>	Null
-R <role>	Null
-s <shell>	/bin/sh

It can happen that after an account has been created, you want to specify an option that you weren't concerned about at the account creation time, or you want to change the value of an option. Solaris allows you to do that by offering the `usermod` command, which we explore next.

The `usermod` Command

You can use the `usermod` command to modify an account—that is, to modify the value for an option that either was specified by you when the account was originally created or a default value was assigned to it. Solaris lets you modify most of the options as follows:

```
usermod [-c <comment>] [-d <dir> [-m] ] [-e <expire>] [-f <inactive>]
[-g <group>][ -G <group, group...>] [-l <new_login_name>[ -m [-k <skel_dir>]]
[-p <profile>] [-A <authorization, authorization...>][-R <role> ] [-s <shell>]
[ -u <uid>] <login-name>
```

Note that the options used with the `usermod` command are the same as with the `useradd` command and they are used the same way except for the following two instances:

- **`-l <new_login_name>`.** Specifies the new login name for the user account.
- **`-m`.** Moves the user home directory to a new directory specified with the `-d` option as shown in the following example:

```
usermod -d /export/home/johnk -m jkerry
```

This command changes the home directory of the user jkerry to johnk. Two points to note here: if the new directory already exists, the user must have read, write, and execute permissions to it, and the files in the previous directory will not automatically be copied to the new home directory; they must be copied manually.

Now that you know how to add a user account to the system and modify it, see the next page for some practical scenarios and their solutions.

Anything in this universe that was created will eventually be destroyed, and a user account is no exception to this law of nature. Employees join and leave the organization, and when an employee leaves the organization, you must eventually delete the account for security reasons if nothing else. In order to accomplish this, the Solaris system offers the `userdel` command, which we explore next.

SCENARIO & SOLUTION	
Which command would you issue to create a user account for a new employee named Bill Clinton. Use bclinton as user name, `/export/home/bclinton` as home directory, which already exists, and execs as the primary group.	`useradd -g execs -d /export/home/ bclinton -s /bin/bsh bclinton`
In the next scenario, you need to add another user named Marlon Brando; you want to let the default group become his primary group and you want to make the `/export/home/mbrando` directory his home directory, which does not exist yet. Which command would you issue?	`useradd -d /export/home/mbrando -m mbrando`
Make the user Marlon Brando a member of another group named "actors."	`usermod -G actors mbrando`

The `userdel` Command

You use the `userdel` command to delete a user account from the system. The syntax for the `userdel` command is shown here:

```
userdel [-r] <login_name>
```

The option `-r` is used to delete the user home directory along with the account. For example, the following command deletes the account of user jkerry along with the home directory (and all directories underneath it recursively):

```
userdel -r jkerry
```

There may be important company files in the home directory of the employee who has just left. In that case, you can delete the user account without the `-r` option, and the user account will be deleted without deleting the home directory.

A user must have a primary group. In addition to this, a user can become a member of up to 15 (the default maximum number) secondary groups. Before a user can become a member of a group, the group account must exist. In the next section, we discuss how to manage group accounts.

Managing Group Accounts

You already know from the previous sections how to add users to a group by issuing the `useradd` and `usermod` commands with `-g` and `-G` options. Before you can add a user to a group, the group account must exist. In this section, you will explore how to add, modify, and delete group accounts.

Adding a Group A group account is created by using the `groupadd` command which has the following syntax:

```
groupadd [-g <gid> [-o]] <group_name>
```

The options supported by the `groupadd` are described as follows:

- **`-g <gid>.`** Specifies the group ID. If not used, the group ID will default to the next available number greater than the one already assigned to a group.
- **`-o.`** Specifies that the GID can be duplicated—that is, more than one group can share this GID, which is helpful in modifying the group.

The `<group_name>` obviously is the name of the group and is a character string that may contain lowercase letters and numerals. You can modify an existing group account, and this is discussed next.

Modifying a Group You modify a group by using the `groupmod` command, which has the following syntax:

```
groupmod [-g <gid> [-o]] [-n <new_name>] <group_name>
```

The options supported by the `groupadd` command are described here:

- **`-g <gid>.`** Specifies the new group ID.
- **`-o.`** Specifies that the GID can be duplicated—that is, more than one group can share this GID.
- **`-n <new_name>.`** Specifies a new name for the group.

The `<group_name>` is the name of the group for which the command is being issued. A group account is internally managed by its GID. If you just want to change the name of an existing group without changing its GID, you can issue the `groupmod` command in the following form:

```
groupmod -o -n <new_name> <existing_name>
```

There will be times when you want to get rid of a group. Next, we discuss the command to do exactly that.

Deleting a Group You can delete an existing group by using the `groupdel` command, which has the following trivial syntax:

```
groupdel <group_name>
```

For example, the following command will delete the group named gop:

```
groupdel gop
```

Note that the `groupdel` command deletes only the group account and not the users that belong to the group. That means that although the group membership of the users is deleted with the deletion of a group, the user accounts still exist.

Deleting a group does not delete the accounts of the users who were the members of the deleted group.

As opposed to Windows, in UNIX you always use the command line tools for system administration. Nevertheless, there are some GUI tools available for beginners. For example, on the Solaris 10 system, you can use the Solaris Management Console (SMC) GUI tool for user administration. We explore this tool next.

Managing User and Group Accounts with the SMC GUI

You can use the Solaris Management Console (SMC) to manage user and group accounts. In this section, you will do two hands-on exercises using SMC.

EXERCISE 6-1

Creating a User Account with the SMC GUI Tool

Perform the following steps to create a user account with the SMC GUI tool:

1. Become the superuser or assume an equivalent role (e.g., log in as root).
2. Start the SMC by issuing the following command:

```
/usr/sadm/bin/smc &
```

3. Click the This Computer icon under the Management Tools icon in the Navigation panel. A list of categories is displayed.

4. Click the System Configuration icon.
5. Click the User Accounts icon.
6. Type in your password.
7. Click the Users icon.
8. Select the Add User With Wizard from the Action menu. Click Next between each of the steps that follow.
9. Type in the user login name at the User Name prompt (following the rules for specifying the user names that you have learned in this chapter)—for example, agore.
10. Optional step. Type in the user full name at the Full Name prompt—for example, Al Gore.
11. Optional step. Type in a further description of this user at the Description prompt.
12. Specify the user ID at the User ID Number prompt—for example, 420.
13. Select the option: User Must Use This Password at First Login, and type in a password for the user at the password prompt. Confirm the password at the Confirm Password prompt.
14. Select the primary group for the user.
15. Create the home directory for the user by accepting the defaults at the Server and Path prompts.
16. Specify the mail server.
17. Review the information you provided and go back to correct the information, if necessary. Otherwise, click Finish.

Congratulations! You have a added a user to the system by using the SMC GUI tool. But before opening the champagne, attempt to log in as the user that you created to be sure that it works.

Groups contain users. You have two choices regarding adding users to a group: you can add the existing users to the group during the group creation, or you could add a user to the group when you create the user account.

Once a user has been created on the system, the user can log into the system and work. Each user works in a certain work environment on the system, which is set up when the user logs in. We explore this topic next.

Shell Initialization Files

As a part of setting up a user account, you need to set up some initialization files that will set up the work environment when the user logs in. These initialization files, also called the shell initialization files, are essentially the shell scripts that set up the characteristics of the user's work environment, such as search path, windowing environment, and environment variables. There are two kinds of initialization files: user initialization files, whose scope is a specific user; and site initialization files, whose scope is the system.

User Initialization Files

The user initialization files live in the home directory of a user. A user works in a specific shell. As shown in Table 6-7, each shell has its own set of initialization files, which exist in the home directory of the user.

A question arises: where do these files come from, and how do they end up in the user's home directory? Solaris 10 offers the skeletons for the user initialization files in the `/etc/skel` directory, as shown in Table 6-8.

When you create a user with the `useradd` command by using the `-k` and `-m` options, this set of skeleton files, depending upon the user's login shell, is copied into the user's home directory and renamed to the names shown in Table 6-7.

on the job

Including $path (C shell) and $PATH (Bourne and Korn shell) in the command that sets the path includes the existing path value before the command is issued. This is used to append the user's path settings to the ones that are already set in the site initialization file. If you do not use $PATH or $path, the existing path settings will be replaced with the new ones.

TABLE 6-7 User initialization files for the Bourne, C, and Korn shells (the files are copied into the user's home directory at the time the account is created)

Login Shell	User Initialization Files
Bourne	`.profile`
C	`.login` `.cshrc`

Korn	`.profile`
	`$ENV`
	It is the environment variable that specifies the file (usually `.kshrc`) that will define the user's environment

TABLE 6-8 Default user initialization files for the Bourne, C, and Korn shells (copied to the user's home directory when you create a user account)

Login Shell	Default Initialization Files
Bourne	`/etc/skel/local.profile`
C	`/etc/skel/local.login` `/etc/local.cshrc`
Korn	`/etc/skel/local.profile`

Of course, you can edit the initialization files in the `/etc/skel` directory and edit the initialization files in the home directory to customize them. Typically, the user will customize the local work environment by editing the user initialization files, whereas you will customize the user's work environment by providing the systemwide site initialization files, which we discuss next.

Site Initialization Files

Site initialization files allow you to add new functionalities to the work environments of all the existing users on the system. You would typically put these files on a server to make them accessible to all the users on the site. A user initialization file will access a site initialization file with a statement in the beginning of the file—that is, the site initialization file will be executed before the user initialization file. In case of a conflict, the value of a variable set in the user initialization file will override the one set in the site initialization file. Note that a user initialization file and the site initialization file that it refers to must use the same shell script.

The site initialization files on a system usually exist in the `/etc` directory. The standard site initialization files are `/etc/profile` for the Korn and Bourne shells and `/etc/.login` for the C shell. You can create any other site initialization file with any name on a server and then place its entry at the beginning of a user initialization file.

Order of Execution for the Initialization Files

When a user logs in, the work environment for the user is set up by automatically executing the initialization files in the order shown in Table 6-9.

Note that the C shell has two `.login` files, one in the `/etc/` directory that the system administrator—that is you—would manage, and the other one for individual users in their home directories. This way the users can customize their individual

TABLE 6-9 Order in which the initialization files are executed for C shell, Bourne shell, and Korn shell when a user logs in

Step	C Shell	Bourne Shell	Korn Shell
1	`/etc/.login`	`/etc/profile`	`/etc/profile`
2	`$HOME/.cshrc`	`$HOME/.profile`	`$HOME/.profile`
3	`$HOME/.login`	—	`$HOME/$ENV` It's usually the `.kshrc` file.

login environments. The same thing is true for Bourne shell and Korn shell; the file name in those shells is profile instead of login.

Now that you theoretically know how the initialization files work, here are some practical scenarios and solutions to consider.

SCENARIO & SOLUTION

You want the PATH variable of each user to include the paths /usr/bin and /usr/sbin. How will you do this?	Set this path in a site initialization file; for example, for the C shell enter the following line in the `/etc/.login` file:
	`set path=( /usr/bin /usr/sbin)`
	For the Bourne or Korn shell, enter the following line in the `/etc/profile` file:
	`PATH=/user/bin:/usr/sbin; export PATH`

The user Marlon Brando informs you that he wants to include his current directory and the `/usr/local/bin` directory into his path variable. What would you advise him to do?	If the user uses C shell, edit the `$HOME/.cshrc` file and enter the following line into it:
	`set path=($path /usr/local/bin .)`
	If the user uses the Bourne or Korn shell, enter the following line into the `$HOME/.profile` directory:
	`PATH=$PATH:/usr/local/bin:.; export PATH`

The three most important takeaways from this chapter are listed here:

- A user account can be created by using the `useradd` command, and it is composed of several components such as login name, UID, password, and home directory.

- Once a user account has been created, the information about the user account lives in the `/etc/passwd` and `/etc/shadow` files.
- When a user logs into the system by using the corresponding account, the work environment is created by automatically executing the site initialization files, followed by the execution of user initialization files.

Why would a user have an account on a system? The answer is obvious: to access and use system resources. Not every user needs to access everything on the system. So, once you have set up the user accounts on a system, the next obvious question would be: what can and cannot a specific user access on the system? This is a security issue whose importance cannot possibly be overstated This is true especially in the brave new world of the Internet whereby your system may be connected to the outside world, and it's a wild world out there. Yes, you can say "it's the security, stupid." The system's security is an integral part of user management. We explore the system security aspect of the user administration in the next chapter.

CERTIFICATION SUMMARY

A user account on the Solaris system consists of several components such as a user login name, a user ID, a user password, and a home directory for the user. User accounts can be added, modified, and deleted by using the `useradd`, `usermod`, and `userdel` commands, respectively, or by using the Solaris Management Console (SMC) GUI tool. The admin tool from the previous versions is not available in Solaris 10.

Most of the information about user accounts lives in the file `/etc/passwd`, which also holds a placeholder for the password, and the encrypted password and other password information lives in the file `/etc/shadow`. Multiple users can be organized into a group, and the information about the groups live in the `/etc/group` file. The work environment for a user is created by the shell initialization files, which are executed when the user logs into the system. There are two kinds of initialization files: site initialization files, which are available to all the users and set up the global part of the environment, and user initialization files, which a user can change to customize the environment locally. During the login procedure, first the site initialization files are executed, followed by the user initialization files.

System security is an integral part of user management. We explore the system security aspect of the user administration in the next chapter.

INSIDE THE EXAM

Comprehend

- How the initialization files are created; they are copied from the /etc/skel directory into the user's home directory.
- The order in which the initialization files are executed: the site initialization files followed by the user initialization files as shown here:
  - *C shell.* /etc/.login, $HOME/.cshrc, $HOME/.login
  - *Bourne shell.* /etc/profile, $HOME/.profile
  - *Korn shell.* /etc/profile, $HOME/.profile, $HOME/.kshrc

Look Out

- The passwd file does not contain the user password, but only a place holder: x. The encrypted password and other password information is stored in the /etc/shadow file.
- The usermod command contains the same options as the useradd command and is used mostly in the same way.
- A value of a variable set in the site initialization file will be overridden by the value set in the user initialization file.

Memorize

- The user name can be two to eight characters long.
- The numbers from 0 to 99 are used to specify UIDs for system accounts, and 100 to 60,000 for normal users. The largest UID can be $2^{31} - 1$.
- A user must be a member of one and only one primary group and may become a member of 15 secondary groups at maximum.
- The account information is stored in three files: /etc/passwd, /etc/shadow/, and /etc/group.
- The names of the initialization files for different shells, which are as follows:
  - *C shell.* /etc/.login, $HOME/.cshrc, $HOME/.login
  - *Bourne shell.* /etc/profile, $HOME/.profile
  - *Korn shell.* /etc/profile, $HOME/.profile, $HOME/.kshrc

TWO-MINUTE DRILL

Basics of User Accounts

A user account has the following components:

- *User login name*. It must be two to eight characters long, may contain letters and numerals, must begin with a letter, and must contain at least one lowercase letter.
- *Password*. It can be two to six characters long by default, and the first six characters must contain at least one numeric or special character and at least two letters. The default minimum (2) and maximum (6) length can be changed by editing the files `/etc/default/passwd` and `/etc/policy`, respectively.
- *UID*. This is a signed 32-bit positive integer associated with each user: 0–99 for system accounts, 100–60,000 for regular users, and higher numbers for accounts with incomplete functionality.
- *Home directory*. This makes the root of the directory subtree that belongs to the user. The path to the user home directory is included in the user's entry into the `/etc/passwd` file.
- *Group name and GID*. Multiple users can be logically organized into a group to share resources on the system. Each group has a group name, a group ID (GID), and a list of users that belong to the group.

The `/etc/default/passwd` file can also be used to change other default settings for the password such as the history parameter, which specifies how many previous passwords should be remembered so that a user cannot change the password to one of those. This is a security feature to prevent reusing recently used passwords. You will learn more about this file in the next chapter, in which we discuss security.

Managing User Accounts

- You can create new user accounts by issuing the `useradd` command. For example, the following command will create the user account with account name jkerry, primary group dems, and the default home directory `/home/jkerry`, which will be created if it does not exist:

```
useradd -g dems -m jkerry
```

- The `useradd` command can also be used to change the default value of an option; for example, the following command will change the default value for a base directory (`/home`) to `/home/export`:

  ```
  useradd -D -b /home/export
  ```

- You can modify an existing account by issuing the `usermod` command. The same set of options is available to both the `useradd` and the `usermod` commands; for example, the following command will assign a secondary group senate to the user jkerry, and will set the expiration date 2 November 2008 on the account:

  ```
  usermod -G senate -e 11/2/2008 jkerry
  ```

- You can delete an account by issuing the `userdel` command. For example, the following command will delete the user account jkerry along with its home directory:

  ```
  userdel -r jkerry
  ```

- You can create, modify, and delete the groups by using the `groupadd`, `groupmod`, and `groupdel` commands, respectively.
- Each entry in the `/etc/passwd` file contains information about a user account: login name, place holder for encrypted password, UID, GID, comment, home directory, and login shell.
- Each entry in the `/etc/shadow` file contains information about a user account: login name, UID, encrypted password, minimum number of days required between password changes, maximum number of days before the user will be forced to change the password, number of days before the password expiration date when the user starts getting warnings, number of days the account can be inactive before it will be locked, and the account expiration date.
- Each entry in the `/etc/group` file contains information about a group: group name, group password, GID, and the list of group members.

Shell Initialization Files

The following initialization files are used to set up the working environment for the user:

- *Bourne shell.* The `/etc/profile` site initialization file, which will be executed first, followed by the execution of the `$HOME/.profile`, which the user can customize.
- *Korn shell.* The `/etc/profile` site initialization file, which will be executed first, followed by the execution of the `$HOME/.profile` and `$HOME/.kshrc`, which the user can customize.
- *C shell.* The `/etc/.login` site initialization file, which will be executed first, followed by the execution of the `$HOME/.login` and `/$HOME/.cshrc`, which the user can customize.

SELF TEST

1. Consider the following entry in a passwd file of a user:

```
bgates:x:420:200:bill_gates:/export/home/bgates:/bin/sh
```

What is the user ID for this user?

A. 420

B. 200

C. x

D. Not possible to tell from a passwd file entry

2. Consider the following entry in a passwd file of a user:

```
bgates:x:420:200:bill_gates:/export/home/bgates:/bin/sh
```

What is the group ID for this user?

A. 420

B. 200

C. x

D. Not possible to tell from a passwd file entry

3. Consider the following entry in a shadow file of a user:

```
bgates:*LK*:abc12356thab1::::::
```

What does this entry indicate about the user account? (Choose all that apply.)

A. The account for this user is locked.

B. The user can type the following password to log into the account: abc12356thab1

C. The field *LK* represents an encrypted password.

D. No password is required to log into this account.

4. What is the maximum number of characters you can use in defining a user name?

A. Six

B. Seven

C. Eight

D. No limit

5. What is the maximum number of secondary groups a user can belong to?

A. Six

B. Eight

C. Fifteen

D. No limit

6. A user with username bobgone has left your organization. You want to delete the user account without deleting the files that belong to the user. Which of the following will you do?

A. Change the UID of the account.

B. Change the username for the account.

C. Issue the `userdel` command without the `-r` option (e.g., `userdel bobgone`).

D. Issue the `userdel` command without the `-d` option, but you can use `-r` option.

7. What is the maximum legal value a UID can have in Solaris 10?

A. 99

B. 60,000

C. 100,000

D. 2,147,483,647

E. No limit

8. A UID 0 can be assigned to which of the following accounts? (Choose all that apply.)

A. Any user account

B. root

C. No account

D. home

9. Which of the following is a site initialization file for the Bourne shell?

A. `/etc/.login`

B. `/etc/.profile`

C. `/etc/profile`

D. `$HOME/profile`

10. Which of the following files contains the encrypted password?

    A. `/etc/passwd`

    B. `/etc/shadow`

    C. `/etc/group`

    D. `/etc/password`

11. In order to create a user account, you issued the `useradd` command without specifying all the options. To find the default values for the unspecified options, the `useradd` command will look into which of the following files?

    A. `/etc/passwd`

    B. `/etc/default/useradd`

    C. `/etc/sadm/defadduser`

    D. `/usr/sadm/defadduser`

SELF TEST ANSWERS

1. ☑ **A**. The first field in the `passwd` file entry is the UID.
   ☒ **B** is incorrect because this is a GID, and **C** is incorrect because this indicates that the password is encrypted. **D** is incorrect because a `passwd` file entry does have information about the user ID.

2. ☑ **B**. The second field in the `passwd` file entry is the GID.
   ☒ **A** is incorrect because this is a UID, and **C** is incorrect because this indicates that the password is encrypted. **D** is incorrect because a `passwd` file entry does have information about the group ID.

3. ☑ **A**. The value *LK* of the `<password>` file in the `shadow` file entry means the account is locked.
   ☒ **B** is incorrect because this is the encrypted password; **C** is incorrect because this indicates that the password is locked; and **D** is incorrect because this account does have a password, which is represented in encrypted form in the second field.

4. ☑ **C**. A user login name can contain up to eight characters including uppercase or lowercase alphabets and numerals (0–9). It must begin with a letter, there should be no space, and it should include at least one lowercase letter.
   ☒ **A**, **B**, and **D** are incorrect because the maximum number of characters that can be used to compose a user name is eight.

5. ☑ **C**. A user can be associated with one primary group and 15 secondary groups at maximum.
   ☒ **A**, **B**, and **D** are incorrect because the maximum number of secondary groups that a user can belong to is 15.

6. ☑ **C**. If you want to delete the files along with the user account, you need to use the `-r` option with the `userdel` command.
   ☒ **A**, **B**, and **D** are incorrect because it will not delete the account. **D** is incorrect because it is the `-r` option, not the `-d` option, that deletes the user's home directory along with the user account.

7. ☑ **D**. The user ID is a positive integer that you can make out of a signed 32-bit (i.e., the maximum value is $2^{31} - 1$ = 2,147,483,647. However, the values for the UID should be in the range from 100 to 60, 000 for regular users.
   ☒ **A**, **B**, and **C** are incorrect because these are not the largest integers you can make with a signed 32-bit. **E** is wrong because there is a limit on the maximum value a UID can have.

8. ☑ **B**. The root account always has UID 0.
   ☒ **A** and **D** are incorrect because the UID 0 should be assigned only to the root account. **C** is incorrect because the root account always has the UID 0.

9. ☑ **C**. The site initialization file for the Korn and Bourne shells is `/etc/profile`, and the site initialization file for the C shell is `/etc/.login`.
   ☒ **A** and **B** are incorrect because these are not the site initialization files for the Bourne shell. **D** is incorrect because the site initialization files don't live in the home directories.

10. ☑ **B**. The `/etc/shadow` file contains the encrypted password information for each user account.
    ☒ **A** is incorrect because the `/etc/passwd` file only contains an x in the password field, indicating that the encrypted password exists in the `/etc/shadow` file. **C** is incorrect because the `/etc/group` file contains information about groups, not about individual users. **D** is incorrect because there is no such system file as `/etc/password`.

11. ☑ **D**. The `/usr/sadm/defadduser` file contains the default values for the options of the `useradd` command.
    ☒ **A** is incorrect because the `/etc/passwd` file contains the values assigned to the user account, which are not necessarily the default values. **B** and **C** are incorrect because there are no such files as `/etc/default/useradd` and `/etc/sadm/defadduser` that come with the Solaris OS.

7

Performing Security Administration

CERTIFICATION OBJECTIVES

7.01	Monitoring System Access	7.04	Restricting Access to Data
7.02	Performing System Security	✓	Two-Minute Drill
7.03	Controlling System Security	Q&A	Self Test

Solaris allows you to manage system security in order to ensure that the system resources are used properly. The security is applied at two access levels: access to the system and access to the resources on the system, such as files. Access to the system is secured both by managing access to it and by restricting it. Managing access involves password management, login management, and observing who is having access. Restricting largely involves restricting access from the remote machines.

The access to data on the system is managed by file permissions. The file permissions are set on a file for three kinds of users: the user who owns the file, the group that owns the file, and everyone else. Because executable files try to access other files, this access is controlled by special file permissions called setuid, setgid, and sticky bits.

The core issue to think about in this chapter is: how system security is performed on Solaris 10. To understand this, we will explore three thought streams: security issues in accessing the system, security issues in accessing the data on the system, and managing this security at both the data and system levels.

CERTIFICATION OBJECTIVE 7.01

Monitoring System Access

Exam Objective 4.2: *Monitor system access by using appropriate commands.*

A computer system is only as secure as its weakest point of entry. Both keeping unauthorized users away from the system and managing the authorized users who access the system are essential. In short, monitoring system access is an important task in the arena of system security. Monitoring system access involves both watching login activities and allowing or denying logins. In order to control the access, all the users must be required to have passwords, and the passwords must be managed. Therefore, password management and login management are key to monitoring system access, which we explore in this section.

Password Management

As you learned in Chapter 6, the password is an important component of a user account. In order to control system access, passwords must be managed, beginning with making sure that every user has a password. You can issue the following command to find the users who do not have passwords:

```
logins -p
```

A password has important parameters related to its age that you can manage. For example, you can force users to change their passwords in a periodic fashion, or you can prevent users from changing their passwords within a specific time period. Table 7-1 shows these parameters, which you can change by editing the file `/etc/default/passwd`, in order to set their default values.

The parameter values shown in Table 7-1 are the default values; they can be changed for an individual user by using the command `passwd`, which has the following syntax:

```
passwd <username> [<options>]
```

The following options are available for this command:

- **`-d`.** Delete the password; that means the logins will not prompt for a password.
- **`-f`.** Force the user to change password at the next login.
- **`-l`.** Lock the account; no more logins will be allowed.
- **`-n <min>`.** Specify the minimum number of days between two consecutive password changes.

TABLE 7-1 Parameters in the file `/etc/default/passwd`

Parameter	Description
HISTORY	Maximum number of previous passwords the system will remember for a user. Maximum allowed value for this parameter is 26.
MAXWEEKS	Maximum time for which the password is valid.
MINWEEKS	Minimum time before which the password can be changed.
PASSLENGTH	Minimum password length in characters: 6, 7, or 8.
WARNWEEKS	Time after which the system warns the user about the password's expiration date.

- **-s.** Display password attributes for this user.
- **-w <warn>.** Specify the number of days before the expiration date, when the user will get the warning.
- **-x <max>.** Specify the maximum number of days allowed between two consecutive password changes.

It's important to assign password to each user account, and users should be required to change passwords on a periodic basis. Use the `passwd -l` command to lock an account when it becomes necessary. Unmanaged passwords and accounts can create security holes in the system.

The accounts can be locked by using the `passwd` command with the `-l` option, and the accounts can be deleted with the `userdel` command. The `passwd` command with `-d` option will not lock or delete the account.

In addition to password management, you must perform login management, which we explore next.

Login Management

Login management involves watching login activities and restricting logins altogether. Watching login activities includes finding out who is logged in and monitoring failed login attempts.

Finding Out Who Is Logged In

You can find out who is currently logged into the system by using the `who` command, which has the following syntax:

```
who [<options>]
```

Following are the most common options for this command:

- **-b.** Show the time for the last reboot.
- **-d.** Show the processes that have expired.
- **-H.** Print column headings above the output.

- **-l.** List the processes that are waiting for someone to log in.
- **-q.** Quick display—show only the number of users logged in and their names. When this option is given, all other options are ignored.
- **-r.** Display the system run level.

Another useful command regarding logins and logouts is the `last` command, which looks into the `/var/adm/wtmpx` file that records all logins and logouts. It displays the sessions of the specified users and terminals. For example, to display all the sessions by the root user, issue the following command:

```
last root
```

When the system is shut down and rebooted, the pseudo-user reboot logs in automatically. So, to get the information about the reboots, issue the following command:

```
last reboot
```

The output of this command includes the time and date of each reboot.

Now you know how to take a snapshot of users logged onto your system. Even more interesting is the list of users who attempted to log in to the system but failed. You should scan that list on a regular basis; you never know what you will find. But how do you generate that list? We discuss it next.

Monitoring Failed Login Attempts

Failed login attempts are automatically recorded in the file `/var/adm/loginlog`. All you need to do is create this file, using the following command:

```
touch /var/adm/loginlog
```

Subsequently, each failed login attempt will create one entry into this file, which looks like the following:

```
gbush:/dev/pts/2:Tue Jan 25 10:21:21 2005
jashc:/dev/pts/2:Wed Jan 26 10:21:21 2005
```

It contains the account's login name, tty device, and time of the failed attempt. You can display the file with the `less`, `more`, or `cat` command:

```
less /var/adm/loginlog
```

Note that if a user makes fewer than five unsuccessful login attempts, no attempt is recorded into the `loginlog` file. A growing `loginlog` file means someone may be attempting to break into the system.

If you want to record each failed login attempt (that is, even if someone makes only one unsuccessful attempt to log in), edit the following file:

```
/etc/default/login
```

In this file, set the following parameter:

```
SYSLOG_FAILED_LOGINS=0
```

Now, every failed login attempt will be recorded into the `loginlog` file.

There will be situations in which you will need to temporarily disable all user logins except the root.

Temporarily Disabling User Logins

You may need to temporarily disable all user logins—for example, during system shutdown or system maintenance. In order to prevent all non-root users from logging in, you can create the file `/etc/nologin`:

```
touch /etc/nologin
```

If this file exists, the `sshd` will not allow any non-root user to log in. You can optionally type a message in the file that will be displayed to anyone who attempts to log in. The world should have only the read permission for the file.

Note that this will not disable the superuser login.

EXERCISE 7-1

Capturing Failed Login Attempts

1. Become superuser.
2. Create the `loginlog` file as follows:

```
# touch /var/adm/loginlog
```

3. Set the read and write permissions for the superuser on the `loginlog` file with the following command:

```
# chmod 600 /var/adm/loginlog
```

4. Change the group membership of the `loginlog` file to `sys` as follows:

```
# chgrp sys /var/adm/loginlog
```

5. Verify that the `loginlog` file works. For example, try to log in to the system five or more times with the wrong password. After each attempt display the `/var/adm/loginlog` file:

```
# less /var/adm/loginlog
```

You will see that after five attempts you will get the log for the failed attempts in the `loginlog` file, which would look like the following:

```
jkerry:/dev/pts/2:Fri Feb 4 11:25:10 2005
jkerry:/dev/pts/2:Fri Feb 4 11:25:20 2005
jkerry:/dev/pts/2:Fri Feb 4 11:25:30 2005
jkerry:/dev/pts/2:Fri Feb 4 11:25:41 2005
jkerry:/dev/pts/2:Fri Feb 4 11:25:55 2005
```

When you perform security tasks, you may need to switch from account to account. We discuss next how to do that efficiently.

CERTIFICATION OBJECTIVE 7.02

Performing System Security

Exam Objective 4.3: *Perform system security by switching users on a system, and by becoming root and monitoring su attempts.*

Let's now address what seems to be a prevalent confusion among beginners. That confusion relates to the relationship between the command `su` and the terms switching user and superuser. Read my lips—Becoming superuser and switching user (`su`) are not the same thing. Superuser denotes the administrative account, normally the root account. We use the terms *superuser* and *root* interchangeably in this book, just as those terms are used in the field. However, remember that the command `su` refers to switching user, and as you will see, you can use this command to switch to any user and not just the root.

Performing Security by Switching User

You must be logged in as root (that is, superuser) to perform several system administrative tasks, such as security administration. While logged on to a system and doing security administration, you may need to jump from account to account. One way of doing so is to log out from the current account that you are logged into and log in to the other account. An alternative and more efficient method is to use the `su` command, which allows you to switch from one account to another without logging out. If you are not logged in as root when you issue the `su` command, you need to give the password for the account you are switching to.

exam watch

If you are logged in as a root user, you can switch to other users using the `su` command, and you will not be asked for a password. If you are not logged in as root, you will be asked for a password when you want to switch to another account.

Furthermore, when you are logged in as root, the prompt turns to # (pound sign). Following is the syntax for the `su` command:

```
su [-] [<username> [<arg>...]]
```

For example, the following command will switch you to the sys account while retaining your current environment:

```
su sys
```

The following command will switch you to the bin account and will also switch the environment to what it would be if you were originally logged in as bin:

```
su – bin
```

The superuser access to the system is necessary for performing system administration tasks. But it is also the most dangerous access when an intruder succeeds in getting it. Therefore, it is essential to monitor superuser access attempts to the system, which we discuss next.

Monitoring Superuser Access Attempts

Given all the administrative capabilities a superuser has, monitoring superuser access to a Solaris system is very important from a security perspective. The monitoring can be performed in two ways: observing the accesses, and restricting them.

The root account is created by the system during installation as a superuser account. However, any account that has a UID of 0 will assume the capabilities of a superuser.

Observing Superuser Access

The system lists all the uses of the `su` command in the following file:

```
/var/adm/sulog
```

Remember, all attempts to switch users, not just the attempts to switch to superuser, are recorded in the `sulog` file. The entries in the `sulog` file look like the following:

```
SU 01/23 15:23 - pts/0 jkerry-root
MO 01/24 11:39 + pts/0 gbush-jkerry
TU 01/25 10:49 + pts/0 root-jkerry
```

The columns in the output mean the following:

- The first three columns indicate the time at which the attempt was made.
- The fourth column contains a minus sign (−) if the attempt was unsuccessful and a plus sign (+) if the attempt was successful.
- The fifth column lists the port from which the attempt was made.
- The sixth column lists the name of the original user and the switched identity.

Before the system starts logging the usage of the `su` commands into the `sulog` file, you need to set it up by editing the following file:

```
/etc/default/su
```

Uncomment the following entry in this file:

```
SULOG=/var/adm/sulog
```

Save the `sulog` file. You have just told the system in which file to log the `su` usage attempts. Of course, you have to be a superuser to perform this exercise.

In addition to logging the superuser access, you can also restrict it, which we discuss next.

Restricting Superuser Access

You can also prevent users from having a superuser access to the system remotely. If the system is set up for this, you can log in as a superuser only from the system console. In order to set up your system for this, edit the following file:

```
/etc/default/login
```

Uncomment the following line in this file:

```
CONSOLE=/dev/console
```

Remember that no value for the CONSOLE variable means no remote login for the root. Of course, you have to be a superuser to perform this exercise. All that means is that you cannot log in directly as a superuser from a remote machine. However, you can still log in as another user and then use the `su` command to switch to superuser. Note that when you install Solaris 10, remote superuser access is prevented by default.

EXERCISE 7-2

Becoming a Superuser

1. Log in as a non-root user.
2. Become the superuser by issuing the following command:

```
% su
Password: <root-password>
#
```

3. Now, switch to another user account by issuing the `su` command. Did it ask for a password?

If your system runs an ftp server, the remote users can access your system by logging on to the ftp server. This may also raise security issues which we discuss next.

CERTIFICATION OBJECTIVE 7.03

Controlling System Security

***Exam Objective 4.4:** Control system security through restricting ftp access and using /etc/hosts.equiv and $HOME/ .rhosts files, and SSH fundamentals.*

A user can also access the Solaris system through ftp. Even more dangerous access is through the `.rhosts` file. So, these accesses need to be controlled and restricted.

Restricting ftp Access

The ftp utility, based on the open Internet standard called File Transfer Protocol (FTP), is a standard tool used to transfer files across a network and across the Internet. If you leave your system with ftp enabled, the remote users may have access to your system by logging in through ftp. It is just another entryway into your system, and every entryway has to be guarded, from a security perspective.

You can restrict ftp access by using the following three files:

```
/etc/ftpd/ftpusers
/etc/ftpd/ftphosts
/etc/shells
```

The `ftpusers` file is used to restrict access at user level. This file contains a list of login names that you can see by issuing the following command:

```
# less /etc/ftpd/ftpusers
```

Any login name included in this list is prohibited from using ftp. So, if you want to deny a user access to your system through ftp, just edit the `ftpusers` file, type in that user's login name, and save the file. When a user attempts to start an ftp session, the system searches the user's login name in the `ftpusers` file. If a match is found, access is denied.

on the job ***The names in the `ftpusers` file must be the login names. In order to ensure that, make sure they exactly match with the login names in the `/etc/passwd` file.***

You can use the `ftphosts` file to restrict ftp access at host level in order to allow or deny access to a user coming from a specified host. For example, the following entry in the `ftphosts` file allows the user jkerry to connect to your system using ftp remotely from machines with IP addresses: 205.25.2.3, 195.26.3.4, and 210.23.4.5:

```
allow jkerry 205.25.2.3 195.26.3.4 210.23.4.5
```

However, the following entry denies user gbush an ftp access from the host machine with IP address 132.12.13.5:

```
deny gbush 132.12.13.5
```

A user interacts with the Solaris system through a shell, and there are several shells around. If the user is using a shell that the system does not support, obviously the user will be denied access. This indirect method can also be used to restrict ftp access. By default, the system supports a number of shells. You can restrict the number of shells supported by the system by creating the following file and typing in the shells that you want the system to support:

```
/etc/shells
```

Let's assume you made the following entries into this file:

```
/bin/sh
/bin/csh
/sbin/jsh
```

Now, if a user, for example, using the `/etc/ksh` shell attempts to gain ftp access, access will be denied.

Be careful about the combined effect of all these options. For example, if a user is using the allowed shell but the corresponding user name has included the `ftpusers` file, access will still be denied. The same is the case when the username is not in the `ftpusers` file, but the user is using the wrong shell.

exam watch

If you create the `/etc/shell` file, the shells listed in the file are the only permitted shells. The users listed in the `/etc/ftpd/ftpusers` files are the users who are not permitted to have ftp access.

The `.rhosts` File: A Major Security Risk

Each entry in the `$HOME/.rhosts` file contains the host-username pair. If a host-user exists in the file, that means the specified user from the specified host is allowed to log in remotely to this system without a password (yes, that's not a typo). However, for this to work, the `.rhosts` file must be in the home directory of the user at the top level; a file in a subdirectory of the home directory will not work.

Now, this is a severe security problem, because any user can create the `$HOME/.rhosts` file, not just the system administrator. You can disable `.rhosts` files altogether by commenting out lines in the following file that reference `am_rhosts_auth.so.1`:

```
/etc/pam.conf
```

If you do this, rlogin will still work, but it will ask for a password even from the users who are listed in the `.rhosts` files. The rlogin related entries in the `pam.conf` file look like the following:

```
rlogin auth sufficient pam_rhosts_auth.so.1
rlogin auth requisite pam_authtok_get.so.1
rlogin auth required pam_dhkeys.so.1
```

The hosts that are used in the `.rhosts` authentication are also listed in the `/etc/hosts.equiv` file, which is also used by the `rlogind` and `rshd` daemons. Why do we need these two files? The `/etc/hosts.equiv file` applies to the entire system, whereas each `$HOME/.rhosts` file is maintained by an individual user.

An entry in both the `.rhosts` file and the `hosts.equiv` file may have the following syntax:

```
<hostname> <username>
```

This means that a user specified by `<username>` can access this system from the host specified by `<hostname>` by using the same user name as on the `<hostname>`. An entry into these files may also have the following syntax:

```
<hostname>
```

This means that any user from the host specified by `<hostname>`, except the root user, can have access to this system on which this file (`.rhosts` or `hosts.equiv`) exists.

We have been talking about securing the system. The Internet has added another security dimension involving the communication lines between the computers. Communication with the system from another computer also needs to be secured, because it may contain sensitive information. Solaris offers communication-related security by implementing the secure shell (SSH), which we discuss next.

Secure Shell Fundamentals

The secure shell (SSH) implemented in Solaris enables users to securely access a remote system over an insecure network or Internet. SSH provides strong authentication and secure communication over the public (unsecure) Internet. Users can use the SSH to accomplish the following:

- Log in to a remote system by using the `ssh` utility. Without `ssh`, the user would use rlogin or rsh.
- Transfer files across the network by using sftp. Without `ssh`, the user would be using ftp.
- Run commands securely on the remote system.

The SSH protocol is based on the client/server communication model. The host that initiates the connection is called the client, and the host that accepts the connection and serves the requests made by the client is called the server. When the system is started, it starts the `sshd` daemon by running the following script:

```
/etc/init.d/sshd
```

It happens on both the client and the server machines. The `sshd` is configured on both machines by using the following file:

```
/etc/ssh/sshd_config
```

The `sshd` uses the variables in the `/etc/default/login` file and the `login` command. The variables values in the `/etc/default/login` file can be overridden by the values set in the `sshd_config file.`

The `ssh` command syntax is:

```
ssh [-l <login_Name>] <hostname>
```

or

```
user@hostname [<command>]
```

So far, we have explored the security issues related to system access. Once a user has accessed the system, the next things to secure are the resources on the system. Data is an important resource on the system, and we explore data security next.

CERTIFICATION OBJECTIVE 7.04

Restricting Access to Data

Exam Objective 4.5: *Restrict access to data in files through the use of group membership, ownership and special file permissions.*

So far, we have explored the security issues involved in accessing a system. Once a user has gained access to a system, the question arises: what resources on the system can the user use? After all, a user accesses a system to access its resources, and data is an important resource. Naturally, data access on a system needs to be managed. On computers, data lives in files; therefore, data security means file security. In other words, we can restrict data access by managing permissions on the files.

Solaris allows you to manage file access by managing file ownership and file permissions, which we explore in this section.

Permissions, Ownership, and Group Membership

In UNIX, everything is about files; there are regular files, and there are special files such as directories, devices, sockets, and named pipes. There is a uniform file permission system for all these file kinds. From a file's perspective, the world of users is divided into three continents: the user who owns the file (called *owner*), a group of users that has group ownership of the file, and everyone else (called *world* or others). Accordingly, the Solaris file permission system, akin to the traditional UNIX file permission system, has three levels of file access permissions:

- Access permission for the owner of the file
- Access permission for the group of users that has the group ownership of the file
- Access permission for all other users, called the world or others

These permissions are managed by a set of commands listed in Table 7-2.

Understanding File Permissions: The `ls` Command

The `ls` command can be used to find the current permissions on files. The command has the following syntax:

```
ls <options> <target>
```

where `<target>` is the name of the directory and its default value is the current directory. For example, the following command will display the list of all the files in the current directory with some information about the files:

```
ls -la
```

TABLE 7-2 Commands related to file security

Command	Used To
chgrp	Change the group ownership of a file.
chmod	Change permissions on a file.
chown	Change the ownership of a file.
ls	List the files along with information about them, including permission information.

An entry in the output of this command will look like the following:

```
-rwxrwxr-x 1 jkerry pres 11720 Nov 2 8:45 camp
```

Reading from the right, it means the name of the file is camp, the last time the file was modified was 8:45 A.M. on November 2, and the file size is 11,720 bytes. Next, the group ownership of the file is `pres`, and the login name for the owner is jkerry. The number 1 indicates that there is one link pointing to this file. The letters and hyphens indicate the permissions set on the file for the owner, the group, and the world (others).

There are ten characters in the first column (from the left) of the output of an `ls -l` command. The first character represents the file type. The symbols for the different file types are listed in Table 7-3.

The last nine characters in the first column of the `ls` output represent the file permissions for the owner, group, and others—three characters each and in this order. In each case (owner, group, and others), the first character tells whether the user has the read permission or not (`r` for yes, – for no), the second character tells whether the user has the write permission or not (`w` for yes, – for no), and the third character tells whether the user has the execute permission or not (again `x` for yes, – for no). For example, `rwxr-xr` means the owner of the file has read, write, and execute permission, the group of the owner has only read and execute permission, and all other users have only read permission to this file. These permission symbols are explained in Table 7-4.

TABLE 7-3 File types displayed by the `ls` command

Symbol	File Type
b	Block special file
c	Character special file
d	Directory
l	Symbolic link
s	Socket
D	Door
P	Named pipe
-(minus sign)	Regular file: text file, or a program

TABLE 7-4 The permission symbols displayed by the `ls` command

Symbol	Permission	For a file it means that the designated users	For a directory, it means that the designated users
r	Read	Can open the file and read its content.	Can list files in the directory.
w	Write	Can modify the content of the file or delete the file.	Can add files or links to and remove files or links from the directory.
x	Execute	Can execute the file.	Can open or execute files in the directory and can make this directory and the directories below it current.
–	Denied	Cannot read, write, or execute.	Cannot read, write, or execute.

Now that you have a good idea about how to find the file permissions with the `ls` command, here are some possible scenario questions and their answers.

SCENARIO & SOLUTION

The first column of a file entry in the output of the `ls` command is `drwxr-xr–`. What is the type of file that this entry represents?	A directory.
What kind of read permission any user in the group to which the owner belongs has, and what does that mean?	Any user in the owner's group has the read permission to the directory, and that means the user can list the files in the directory—for example, by using the `ls` command.
What kind of write permission a group user has to this file, and what does that mean?	A group user does not have a write permission to this directory, and that means a group user cannot add a file or link to or remove a file or link from this directory. The user also cannot change the names of the files or create new files in this directory.
What kind of permissions any other user (who is neither the owner nor a member of the owner's group) has to this file, and what does that mean?	Any other user only has a read permission to this directory, and does not have a write or execute permission; cannot execute files in this directory.

Now that you understand how to find the current file permissions, it is time to learn how to change them.

Changing File Permissions with chmod

Solaris offers a number of commands to change the file permissions. We explore three of these commands here: chmod, chown, and chgrp.

The chmod command is used to change the permissions shown in the first column of the output of an ls -l command. The syntax for this command is shown here:

```
chmod [-fR] <permission mode> <file>
```

The options are explained here:

- **-f.** Force; if the command cannot change the permission, it will not complain.
- **-R.** Recursively; descend through the directory and assign the specified permissions. When links are encountered, the permission mode of the target file is changed, but no recursion happens.

The permission mode can be defined in symbolic mode or in absolute mode. In symbolic mode, a permission mode in the command has the following three elements:

```
[<who>] <operator> [<permissions>]
```

The element <who> specifies whose permissions are to be changed, the <operator> specifies the assignment operation, and <permissions> specifies what kind of permission it is—read, write, or execute. Possible values of <who> are the symbols u, g, o, and a to refer to the user owner, the group owner, others, and all users, respectively. Possible values of <operator> are the symbols + to add permissions, = to assign permissions, and − to take away permissions. Finally, the possible values of <permissions> are r, w, and x, referring to read, write, and execute permissions, respectively.

For example, to grant the group write permissions to a file named politics, issue the following command:

```
chmod g+w politics
```

To prohibit users who are not in the group from changing and executing this file, issue the following command:

```
chmod o-wx
```

The = assignment overwrites the existing permissions. For example, the following command issued after the previous two commands will assign only the read permissions for the group and the other users and take away all other permissions:

```
chmod go=r politics
```

The symbolic mode options are listed in Table 7-5.

In the absolute mode, the permission symbols `r`, `w`, and `x` are represented by integers 4, 2, and 1, respectively. These integers are added to represent all the permissions granted for a user. For example, read-only permission is represented by 4; read and write by 6; and read, write, and execute together by 7. Because permissions for a user are represented by an octal (a number from 0 to 7), permissions in this mode are also called octal permissions. The overall permission on a file is represented by four octal digits, The digit at first place represents special permissions, which we discuss further on in this chapter. The digit at second place (from the left) represents the owner, third place represents the group, and fourth place represents the other users. Table 7-6 demonstrates this with some examples.

For example, the following command will grant all permissions for the owner, read and write permissions for the group, and only read permission for others, to the directory structure washington.

```
chmod -R 764 washington
```

TABLE 7-5 Symbolic mode options for the `chmod` command (the + means the permission is added, = means the permission is assigned, and − means the permission is taken away)

Permission	Owner (user)	Group	World (other)	All
Read	u+r	g+r	o+r	a+r
	u=r	g=r	o=r	a=r
	u−r	g−r	o−r	a−r
Write	u+w	g+w	o+w	a+w
	u=w	g=w	o=w	a=w
	u−w	g−w	o−w	a−w
Execute	u+x	g+x	o+x	a+x
	u=x	g=x	o=x	a=x
	u−x	g−x	o−x	a−x

TABLE 7-6 Examples for octal permissions using the absolute mode options for the `chmod` command

Permisssion	Owner (user)	Group	World (other)	Resulting Permission
Read	0400	0040	0004	0444
Write	0200	0020	0002	0222
Execute	0100	0010	0001	0111
Read, write	0600	0060	0006	0666
Read, write, execute	0700	0070	0007	0777

As you have realized by now, the permissions on a file are set not by the user name but by the user designation: owner, group, or other. In addition, the user acquires permissions to the files by acquiring one of these designations. One way of changing the file permissions is to change the permission bits on the file with the `chmod` command; and the other way of changing permissions for the user is to change the user designations—for example, to change the owner of the file, which we discuss next.

Changing the File Owner with `chown`

An indirect way of changing the file permissions without changing the permission bits on the file is to change the owner of the file. This is accomplished with the `chown` command, which has the following syntax:

```
chown [-fhR] <owner>[:<group>] <file>
```

The `<owner>` is the login name or the UID of the new owner, and the `<group>` is the group name or the GID of the new group. Note that you can change both the user ownership and the group ownership of a file with the `chown` command. The options for the command are listed here:

- **`-f.`** Force; do not report errors.
- **`-h.`** If the file is a symbolic link, this option changes the owner of the link. Without this option, the owner of the file to which the link points will be changed.

- **-R.** Change the ownership by recursively descending through the directory structure.

exam watch

If you are using the `chown` option on a symbolic link, use the `-h` option to change the owner of the link. If you want to change the owner of the file by using `chown` on the link that points to the file, leave out the `-h` option.

You have seen that you can change the group ownership of a file by using the `chown` command. You can also accomplish this by using the `chgrp` command, which we explore next.

Changing the Group Ownership with `chgrp`

The `chgrp` command is similar to the `chown` command and has the following syntax:

```
chown [-fhR] <group> <file>
```

The `<group>` is the group name or the GID of the new group, and the `<file>` is the file name (the full path) for which the ownership is being changed. The options for the command are listed here:

- **-f.** Force; do not report errors.
- **-h.** If the file is a symbolic link, this option changes the group ownership of the link. Without this option, the group ownership of the file to which the link points will be changed.
- **-R.** Changes the ownership by recursively descending through the directory structure.

So far, we have explored the permissions on a file thinking of the security of the data in that file. Now, let's look at the file permissions from a slightly different angle. Suppose a user has access to a file that is an executable, and when the user executes that file, the code in that file accesses other files. In this situation, how does the system determine whether an executable being executed by a specific user can access other files or not? We explore this issue in the next section by discussing special file permissions offered by Solaris.

Special File Permissions (setuid, setgid, and Sticky Bits)

In this section we explore three special permissions that can be set on a file: setuid, setgid, and sticky bits. Let's clear up a possible misunderstanding before it can arise: setuid and setgid are permissions that you set, not commands that you issue. These permissions are set on an executable file or a public directory.

When a user runs an executable on which any of these permissions are set, the executable file assumes the ID (UID or GID) of the owner of the file. The important point is that the user who started the execution of the file may not be the owner of the file.

The setuid Permission

When setuid permission is set on an executable file, the process that executes this file is granted permissions based on the owner of this file, not the user that started the execution of this file. This will give a user an access to the files and directories (through the process that execute the file) that will normally be available only to the owner.

The setuid permission can be set by using—well, your old friend, the `chmod` command with the following syntax:

```
chmod <4nnn> <filename>
```

As an example, consider the following command:

```
chmod 4755 speech
```

If you are not the owner of the file, you have to be a superuser to issue this command. This command sets these permissions on the file `speech`: read, write, and execute for the owner, read and execute for the group and other users; and it sets the setuid permission on the file. Now, if you issue the `ls -l` command on this file, the first column of the output file will look like the following:

```
-rwsr-xr-x
```

Note the use of the symbol `s` instead of `x` for the owner. Now suppose a user jbrown is neither the owner of this file nor a member of the group that owns this file. Further, assume there are other files to which the owner of this file does have a write permission but jbrown does not, and this file when executed tries to access those files and write into them. Once jbrown starts executing this file, the process that executes the file will have write permissions to those other files because the owner of this file has them. Do you see a security concern here?

Before setting setuid permission on a file, understand that it poses a security threat. For example, if the owner of an executable file is the root and you set the setuid permission on it, any user who executes this file can access the files (through the executable) that normally only the root could access.

With the permissions of the file owner, the process that executes the file may have too much access. It can be restricted by assigning the process the permission of the group that owns the file instead of the owner of the file. This is accomplished through the setgid permission, which we explore next.

The setgid Permission

The setgid permission is similar to the setuid permission. When the setgid permission is set on an executable file, the process that executes this file is granted permissions based on the group that owns the file, not the user that started the execution of the file. This will give a user access to the files and directories that would normally be available only to the group.

The setgid permission can be set by using the `chmod` command with the following syntax:

```
chmod <2nnn> <filename>
```

As an example, consider the following command:

```
chmod 2755 speech
```

If you are not the owner of the file, you have to be superuser to issue this command. This command sets these following permissions on the file speech: read, write, and execute for the owner and read and execute for the group and other users; it also sets the setgid permission on the file. Now if you issue the `ls -l` command on this file, the first column of the output file will look like the following:

```
-rwxr-sr-x
```

Note the symbol `s` instead of `x` for the group. When the setgid permission is applied to a directory, some users can use a process to create files in the directory that they otherwise cannot use. However, the created files always belong to the group to which the directory belongs, no matter who created them.

Now that you know the setgid permission, let's consider some scenarios and their solutions involving the setgid permission.

SCENARIO & SOLUTION	
You would like to set the setuid permission on a directory `/home/lib`. You would also like to assign read, write, and execute permissions for the owner and the group, and read and execute for others. What command would you issue?	`chmod 2775 /home/lib`
The user gbush is neither the owner of the directory nor a member of the group that owns the directory. How can gbush create files in this directory?	By executing a script that creates files in the directory `/home/lib` and to which gbush has the execute and write permissions, and the script is owned by the same group that owns the directory `/home/lib`.
Do the files created in the directory `/home/lib` belong to the group to which gbush belongs, or do they belong to the group that owns the directory `/home/lib`?	The newly created files belong to the group that owns the directory `/home/lib`.

The Sticky Bit Permission

While setuid and setgid pose a security threat, sticky bit improves the security. If this permission bit is set, a file in a directory can be deleted only by the file owner, the directory owner, or a privileged user. A sticky bit is useful to prevent users from deleting other users' files from public directories such as `/tmp`.

The sticky bit is set by assigning the octal value 1 to the first of the four octal digits in the `chmod` command while using the absolute permission mode. For example, the following command will set the sticky bit permission on the `/tmp` directory:

```
chmod 1777 /tmp
```

Now the first column of the output of the `ls -l` command on the `/tmp` directory will be:

```
drwxrwxrwt
```

Note the symbol `t` for the sticky bit permission. Remember, while setuid and setgid loosen the security on a file, stick bit tightens it.

EXERCISE 7-3

Setting Special Permissions on a File

1. Become superuser and create a file `countvote` using the following command:

```
# touch countvote
```

2. Issue the following command to set the setuid on the file:

```
# chmod 4755 countvote
```

3. Issue the following command:

```
# ls -l countvote
```

   Note that the first column of the output is: `-rwsr-xr-x`.

4. Now, set the setgid permission on the file by issuing the following command:

```
# chmod 2755 countvote
```

   Now issue the `ls -l` command and verify that the first column of the output is `-rwxr-sr-x`.

The three most important takeaways from this chapter are the following:

- You need to secure access to the system.
- Once a user accesses the system, you need to secure resources on the system such as files.
- You perform the security tasks by either using commands or creating files.

CERTIFICATION SUMMARY

System security is performed at two access levels: access to the system and access to the resources on the system such as files. System access is secured by monitoring and controlling it. You can monitor system access by making sure that each user has a password and by managing login by monitoring failed login attempts in the `/var/adm/loginlog` file or by disabling all non-root user logins by creating the `/etc/nologins` file in the event of system maintenance or system shutdown. You can also improve system security by restricting remote access to the system, such as ftp access, by using the `/etc/ftpd/ftpusers` and `/etc/ftpd/ftphosts` files.

System security is performed either by issuing the command `chmod` or by creating files such as `/etc/nologins`. In order to perform most security-related tasks, you must be logged in as superuser: the root account created by default will do it.

Everything on a Solaris system, as in any UNIX-based system, is file, as files represent regular files, directories, sockets, and devices. The Solaris file permission system divides the world of users into three continents: the user that owns the file called owner, the group of users that owns the file called group, and the rest of the world called others. The permissions on a file are assigned to these continents, and you can move the users in and out of these continents with the `chown` and `chgrp` commands. The executable files when executed can access other files, and this access is managed by special file permissions called setuid, setgid, and sticky bits.

Files are an important resource on the system. In addition to using files, users also employ the system to use printers and to run programs (processes). In the next chapter we discuss managing processes and printers.

INSIDE THE EXAM

Comprehend

- If you are logged in as a root user, you can switch to other users using the `su` command, and you will not be asked for a password. If you are not logged in as root, you will be asked for a password when you want to switch to another account.
- A user can take advantage of the setgid permission to create files in the directory on which the setgid permission is set, even if the user does not normally have the permission to do so. However, the created files will still belong to the group to which the directory belongs, not the group to which the user belongs.

Look Out

- The `passwd` command with `-d` option will delete the password, not the account. It means that the system will not prompt for a password.
- All attempts to switch users by using the `su` command, not just attempts to switch to *superuser*, are recorded into the `/var/adm/sulog` file.
- The users listed in the `/etc/ftpd/ftpusers` files are denied ftp access, whereas the users using the shell not listed in the `/etc/shell` file are also denied access to the system. If you do not create an `/etc/shell` file, the system supports all the default shells.
- The = operator in the `chmod` command overwrites the permission bits for the user.
- The `chown` command can also be used to change the group ownership of a file.
- If you want to change the ownership of a file by using `chown` on the link that points to the file, do not use the `-h` option.
- The *setuid* and *setgid* options pose security threats, but the *sticky bit* enhances the security on a file.

Memorize

- The command `su` refers to switching users and it does not necessarily mean switch to superuser.
- The term *superuser* is commonly used for the account named *root*, which is created by default. There is no account named *supersuser* created by default.
- When you are logged in as root, the prompt sign is # (a pound sign).
- When the remote superuser access is disabled, you can still log in as another user and then switch to the superuser account with the `su` command.
- The existence of the `/etc/nologin` file will not prevent a superuser from logging into the system.

✓ TWO-MINUTE DRILL

Monitoring System Access

- ❑ The command to find users who do not have passwords is: `logins -p`.
- ❑ A user can be denied login by using the `passwd` command with the `-l` option.
- ❑ Each failed login attempt is recorded in the `/var/adm/loginlog` file.
- ❑ If you want each failed login attempt to be recorded into the `loginlog` file, set the parameter SYSLOG_FAILED_LOGINS=0 in the `/etc/def/login` file.
- ❑ All non-root user logins can be disabled by creating the file `/etc/nologin`.

Performing System Security

- ❑ The system lists all the uses of the `su` command into the following file:

```
/var/adm/sulog
```

- ❑ In order to enable the logging of the superuser access attempts, you need to uncomment the following line in the `/etc/def/su file`:

```
SULOG=/var/adm/sulog
```

- ❑ In order to prevent superuser access remotely, uncomment the following line in the /`etc/default/login` file:

```
CONSOLE=/dev/console
```

Controlling System Security

- ❑ In order to prevent some users from having ftp access to your system, create the following file, enter their login names into the file, and save the file:

```
/etc/ftpd/ftpusers
```

- ❑ In order to prevent a specific user from a specific host from having ftp access to your system, use the `/etc/ftpd/ftphosts` file, instead.

- The Solaris system supports a number of shells by default. If you want to be selective in shell support, enter the names of the shells in the /etc/shell file; only those shells would be supported.
- The users listed in the $HOME/.rhosts file can log in to the system remotely without using the password.
- The configuration file for the sshd daemon is: /etc/ssh/sshd_config.

Restricting Access to Data

- The permissions on a file can be listed with the command: ls -l.
- The chmod command is used to change the permissions on files.
- The relationship between the symbolic and octal permissions is r = 4, w = 2, x = 1; and you calculate the octal number for overall permission by adding the correspond number. For example, the octal permission for read, write, and no execute is 4 + 2 = 6.
- You can use the command chown to change both the owner and the group of the file; and you can use the chgrp command to change the group of the file.
- The chmod command can also be used to set the setuid, setgid, and sticky bit permissions.
- The setuid and setgid options pose a security threat, but sticky bit improves security.

SELF TEST

The following questions will help you measure your understanding of the material presented in this chapter. Read all the choices carefully because there might be more than one correct answer. Choose all correct answers for each question.

1. Which of the following is the correct name for the administrative account on a Solaris 10 system created by default? (Choose all that apply.)

   A. superuser

   B. root

   C. administrator

   D. admin

   E. manager

2. You are a system administrator of your organization, and you suspect that some users have attempted to switch to the root user by using the `su` command. Which of the following files will you inspect?

   A. `/var/adm/log`

   B. `/var/adm/sulog`

   C. `/etc/adm/syslog`

   D. `/etc/adm/loginlog`

   E. `/etc/adm/superlog`

3. Which of the following commands can you use to change the group ownership of a file?

   A. `chown`

   B. `chmod`

   C. `chgrp`

   D. `passwd`

4. The first column of a file entry in the output of the `ls -l` command is:

   ```
   -rwxr-x---
   ```

Which permissions does the file have?

A. No execute permission for the owner.

B. In order to have an access to the file, you either have to be the owner or a member of the group that owns the file.

C. Write permission for both the owner and the group.

D. Execute permission for the owner.

5. The first column of a file entry in the output of the `ls -l` command has the form:

```
-rwsr-xr-x
```

What kind of permissions does the file have?

A. No execute permission for the owner.

B. The sticky bit is set on the file.

C. The setuid permission is set on the file.

D. The group has no write permission to the file.

6. Which of the following commands can be used to set the setgid permission on a file?

A. `setgid`

B. `setuid`

C. `chmod`

D. `chgrp`

7. The first column of the output of the `ls -l` command on a file has the form:

```
-rwsr-xr-t
```

What are the octal permissions set on the file?

A. 5755

B. 654

C. 4755

D. 755

8. A user listed in which of the following files will be able to log in remotely to your system without having to type the password?

   A. `/etc/hosts`

   B. `$HOME/.rhosts`

   C. `/home/.rlogin`

   D. `/var/syslog`

9. Shell scripts that have their setuid and setgid permission set enhance the security of the file system.

   A. True

   B. False

10. Directories that have their sticky bits set compromise the security of the directory.

    A. True

    B. False

11. Which of the following commands will display information about the last three reboots of your system?

    A. `last reboot -3`

    B. `last reboot | head -3`

    C. `last reboot | tail -3`

    D. `who -r | head -3`

    E. `who -r | tail -3`

12. You are looking for the name of the log file that contains the log of attempts made to use the `su` command. Which file contains the full path to this log file?

    A. `/etc/default/su`

    B. `/etc/default/sulog`

    C. `/var/adm/sulog`

    D. `/etc/default/login`

SELF TEST ANSWERS

1. ☑ **B**. Root is the administrative account created by default when you install the system.

   ☒ **A**, **C**, **D**, and **E** are incorrect because there are no such accounts created by default.

2. ☑ **B**. All the usages of the `su` command are listed in the `/var/adm/sulog` file.

   ☒ **A**, **C**, **D**, and **E** are all incorrect because they do not specify the file that records the usage of the `su` command.

3. ☑ **A** and **C**. You can change the group ownership with the `chgrp` command. You can also change the group ownership with the `chown` command by optionally giving the GID along with the UID when you issue the command.

   ☒ **B** is incorrect because the `chmod` command is used to change permissions on the file, not the ownership. **D** is incorrect because the `passwd` command is used to manage `passwd`-related things, not to change the group ownership of a file.

4. ☑ **B** and **D**. The last three hyphens represent that the world has no permissions to the file. The first hyphen represent the file type, and the following three characters—`rwx`—specify that the owner has read, write, and execute permission to the file.

   ☒ **A** is incorrect because the permission bits for the owner are `rwx`. **C** is incorrect because the write bit for the group contains a hyphen, not a `w`.

5. ☑ **C** and **D**. When you set the setuid permission on a file, the `x` is replaced with `s` for the user execute permission, so **C** is correct. D is correct because there is a hyphen (`-`) instead of a `w` in the write permission bit for the group.

   ☒ **A** is incorrect because `s` represents that the owner still has execute permission, but when any user executes this file, the running process will acquire the permissions of the owner. **B** is incorrect because `s` in the output does not stand for sticky bit; the sticky bit would be set in the last permission bit and is represented by the character *t*.

6. ☑ **C**. `chmod` is the command that is used to set the setuid and setgid permissions and also to set the sticky bit.

   ☒ **A** and **B** are incorrect because setuid and setgid refer to set user identification and set group identification; they are not the commands to accomplish this task. **D** is incorrect because the `chgrp` command is used to change the group, not to set the setgid permission.

7. ☑ **A**. Both setgid and sticky bit are on and they amount to 5000 (4000 for setgid + 1000 for sticky bit). Other permissions are 755.

   ☒ **B** and **D** are incorrect because the setgid and sticky bit are not accounted for. **C** is incorrect because it does not account for the sticky bit.

8. ☑ **B**. Each entry in the `$HOME/.rhosts` file contains the host-username pair. If a host-user exists in the file, that means the specified user from the specified host is allowed to log in remotely to this system without a password.

   ☒ **A**, **C**, and **D** are incorrect because these are the wrong names for the files to accomplish this task.

9. ☑ **B**. The setuid and setgid permissions allow the user to execute the files with these permissions to acquire the owner's permissions. Hence they compromise security instead of improving it.

   ☒ **A** is incorrect because setuid and setgid permissions compromise security.

10. ☑ **B**. When sticky bit is set on a directory (e.g., a public directory), nobody other than the file owner, the directory owner, or a privileged user can delete a file in the directory.

    ☒ **A** is incorrect because sticky bit improves the security by allowing only the directory owner, or the file owner, or a privileged user to delete a file in the directory on which the sticky bit is set.

11. ☑ **C**. The `last reboot` command generates the list of all the reboots, which is piped into the `tail -5` command that displays the last three entries from the list.

    ☒ **A** is incorrect because this form of the command is the wrong form for the results you want. **B** is incorrect because it will display the first three reboots, not the last three. **D** and **E** are incorrect because the `who -r` command displays the system run level, not the reboot information.

12. ☑ **A**. The log for the `su` command usage is stored in the file whose full path is shown by the value of the SULOG field in the `/etc/default/su` file.

    ☒ **B** is incorrect because the `/etc/default/sulog` file does not exist by default. **C** is incorrect because the `/var/adm/sulog` file is the default file in which the `su` log attempts will be stored, not the file that contains the full path to the log file. **D** is incorrect because the `/etc/default/login` file is used to store the security policy regarding the logins, not the `su` command attempts.

8

Managing Network Printers and System Processes

CERTIFICATION OBJECTIVES

8.01 Managing System Processes

8.02 Managing Printers

✓ Two-Minute Drill

Q&A Self Test

One of the services operating systems offer is to manage the execution of programs submitted by a user. A program can launch more than one process. A process is a piece of a program that has its own execution thread and address space. The processes use system resources such as CPU and disk space, and they can damage the system, depending on what they are set to do. Therefore the processes need to be managed. As a system administrator, you need to perform process management, which includes viewing, controlling, and scheduling processes.

There are two kinds of processes: the processes that a user starts (such as a script or a command), and the processes that run in the background and perform tasks for the system. The latter kind of processes is called daemons—for example, the `lpsched` daemon that manages print requests on a system. As a system administrator, you need to administer the print service on the Solaris system, as well.

The central question to think about in this chapter is: how are the processes administered on a Solaris 10 system, including the processes for managing the print service? In search of an answer, we will explore three thought streams: viewing and controlling processes, scheduling processes, and managing the LP print service.

CERTIFICATION OBJECTIVE 8.01

Managing System Processes

Exam Objective 5.2: *Control system processes by viewing the processes, clearing frozen processes, and scheduling automatic one-time and recurring execution of commands using the command line.*

Managing system processes is one of the tasks you will be performing often as a system administrator. It includes listing the processes, getting detailed information about a process, deleting a hung process, and scheduling a process. Some common commands for managing processes are listed in Table 8-1.

Before we can control a process, we need to find some information, such as the process ID. Now, let's find out how Solaris identifies a process and how to view it.

Viewing Processes

In order to manage (or control) processes on your system, you need to know what processes exist on the system, and you need to have some information about those processes such as process IDs. Therefore, process management starts with the

TABLE 8-1 Some commands to manage processes

Command	Description
ps	List the active processes on a system and obtain information about them.
pgrep	Display information about selective processes.
prstat	Display information about selective processes that must be refreshed periodically.
pstop	Stop processes.
prun	Start processes.
kill, pkill	Terminate processes.

commands that let you view the processes. The ps command lets you check the status of active processes on the system and obtain some technical information about them.

Viewing Processes with the ps Command

You can view the active processes on the system by using the ps command, which has the following syntax:

```
ps [<options>]
```

If no <options> are specified, the output of the ps command includes only those processes that have the same effective user ID and terminal as the user who issued the command. Some common options for this command are described here:

- **-a.** Display information about the most frequently requested processes. Processes not associated with a terminal will not be included.
- **-A.** Display information about every process currently running.
- **-e.** Identical with the -A option.
- **-f.** Full listing. Display additional information about each process.
- **-l.** Generate a long listing.
- **-P <procList>.** Display information only about those processes whose process IDs are specified by <procList>.
- **-u <uidList>.** Display information only about those processes whose effective user IDs or login names are specified by <uidList>, which could be a single argument or a space or comma-separated list.
- **-U <uidList>.** Display information only about those processes whose real user IDs or login names are specified by <uidList>, which could be a single argument or a space or comma separated list.

Remember that the ps command takes a snapshot of the processes running at the moment the command is issued, and therefore the values of some of the fields in the output may not be good even right after the command is executed.

exam watch

The state of a running process is represented by the value O of the state field, not by the value R of the state field. A process with the value of the state field equal to R is not running, but is ready to run and is in the queue for running. This state is called runnable.

The output samples of the ps command are shown in Exercise 8-1. The fields displayed in the output of the ps command depend on the command options. A large set of these fields is described in Table 8-2.

TABLE 8-2 Summary of fields in the output of the ps command

Field	Required Option	Description
ADDR	-l	The memory address of the process
C	-f or -l	The processor utilization for scheduling (not displayed if -c option is used)
CLS	-c	The scheduling class to which the process belongs (e.g., system, time sharing)
CMD	None	The command that generated the process
NI	-l	The *nice* number for the process that contributes to its scheduling priority (Nicer means lower priority.)
PID	None	The process ID, a unique identifier for each process
PPID	-f or -l	The parent process ID (i.e., the unique identifier of the process that spawned this process)
PRI	-l	Scheduling priority for this process (Higher number means higher priority.)
S	-l	State of the process (For example, R indicates that the process is running, and S indicates that the process is sleeping.)
STIME	-f	The starting time of the process in hours, minutes, and seconds.
SZ	-l	Size (total number of pages the process has in the virtual memory)
Time	None	The total CPU time the process has used since it began
TTY	None	The terminal from which the process of its parent process was started

If the output of the `ps` command is several pages in size, it will quickly scroll down to the end: hence it may not be convenient to view a particular process. In this case, you can pipe the output to the `more` (or `less`) command as shown here:

```
ps -f | more
```

Now, you can display the output page by page. If you know what process or processes you are looking for and you can figure out a string of characters, say xyz, in their entries in the output, then you can pipe the output into a `grep` command as shown here:

```
ps -f | grep xyz
```

The most important two fields in the output of the `ps` command are the PID, which represents the process ID (the unique identifier for the process), and S, which represents the current state of the process. The possible values for the field S are described in Table 8-3.

Note that it is the O state, not the R state, that indicates that the process is running. The R state indicates that the process is Runnable, and is in the queue for running. The S state means that the process is sleeping—for example, waiting for resources or some other event to happen before it is put into the Runnable state. The T state indicates that the process has been terminated—for example, by a stop command or a CTRL-Z pressed by the user when the process was running. The Z state identifies a zombie process, which is a dead process whose parent did not clean up after it and it is still occupying space in the process table.

on the job

A zombie process, recognized by the state Z, does not use CPU resources, but it still uses space in the process table. There is no parent process to clean up after it.

TABLE 8-3 Summary of process states

Value of Field S	Process State	Description
O	Running	The process is running.
R	Runnable	The process is ready and is in the queue for running.
S	Sleeping	The process is waiting for some event to complete.
T	Traced	The process has been stopped, either by a job control signal or because it's being traced.
Z	Zombie state	The process has been terminated, and the parent process is not waiting; it is an uncleaned dead process.

Even in the ps command, you can be somewhat selective in viewing the processes—for example, by specifying the list of PIDs or UIDs. However, the pgrep command lets you be even more selective in viewing the processes or in searching for the processes that you want to view.

Viewing Processes with the pgrep Command

Previously in this chapter we showed how by using the grep command along with ps you can restrict the displayed output to certain processes. Solaris 10 offers the pgrep command to handle such situations. The pgrep command lets you specify the criteria and then displays the information only about the processes that match the criteria. The syntax for the pgrep command is shown here:

```
pgrep [<options>] [<pattern>]
```

For example, the following command will select all the processes whose real group name is poli or tics:

```
pgrep -G poli,tics
```

You can also specify multiple criteria, and a logical AND will be assumed between the criteria. For example, consider the following command:

```
pgrep -G poli,tics -U gbush,jkerry
```

This command will select the processes that match the following criteria:

```
(group name is poli OR tics) AND (user name is gbush OR jkerry)
```

Now that you have a handle on how the pgrep command works, let's look at some of its options:

- **-d <delim>.** Specify delimiter string to be used to separate process IDs in the output. The newline character is the default.
- **-f.** The regular expression pattern should be matched against the full process argument string, which can be obtained from the pr_psargs field of the /proc/nnnnn/psinfo file.
- **-g <pgrpList>.** Select only those processes whose effective process group ID is in the list specified by <pgrpList>. If group 0 is included in

the list, this is interpreted as the process group ID of the `pgrep` or `pkill` process.

- **`-G <gidList>.`** Select only those processes whose real group ID is in the list specified by `<gidlist>`.
- **`-l.`** Use the long output format.
- **`-n.`** Select only the newest (i.e., the most recently created) process that meets all other specified matching criteria. Can't be used with the `-o` option.
- **`-o.`** Matches only the oldest (i.e., the earliest created) process that meets all other specified matching criteria. Cannot be used with the `-n` option.
- **`-P <ppidList>.`** Select only those processes whose parent process ID is in the list specified by `<ppidList>`.
- **`-s <sidList>.`** Select only those processes whose process session ID is in the list specified by `<sidList>`. If ID 0 is included in the list, this is interpreted as the session ID of the `pgrep` or `pkill` process.
- **`-t <termList>.`** Select only those processes that are associated with a terminal in the list specified by `<termList>`.
- **`-T <taskidList>.`** Select only those processes whose task ID is in the list specified by `<taskidList>`. If ID 0 is included in the list, this is interpreted as the task ID of the `pgrep` or `pkill` process.
- **`-u <euiList>.`** Select only those processes whose effective user ID is in the list specified by `<euiList>`.
- **`-U <uidlist>.`** Select only those processes whose real user ID is in the list specified by `<uidList>`.
- **`-v.`** Reverse the matching logic—that is, select all processes except those which meet the specified matching criteria.
- **`-x.`** Select only those processes whose argument string or executable file name exactly matches the specified pattern—that is, all characters in the process argument string or executable file name must match the pattern.

Remember that in these commands, as anywhere else, a user ID may be specified either by the user name or by the numeric ID. This is also true for group IDs.

Now that you know how to use the `ps` and `pgrep` commands, here are some practical scenarios and their solutions.

SCENARIO & SOLUTION	
How would you issue the `pgrep` command to list all the processes except the one with user name `jmccain` or `bboxer`?	`pgrep -v -U jmccain,bboxer` The `-v` option reverses the matching logic.
If you want to select only the oldest process on the system, what command would you issue?	`pgrep -o`
Which command would a user issue to get the list of all processes with the same UID and the terminal as that user?	`ps` The `ps` command without any option and argument will accomplish this task.

Both the `ps` and `pgrep` commands display a snapshot of the processes. The situation might have changed immediately after the output of these commands was displayed. In order to find the current information you will need to re-issue the command. If you want to monitor the processes continuously without having to reissue the command, use the `prstat` command, which we explore next.

Viewing Processes with the `prstat` Command

The `prstat` command displays information about the processes similar to that displayed by the `ps` and `pgrep` commands. However, a unique feature of the `prstat` command is that it refreshes (updates) the output in a periodic fashion. You can determine the frequency of updates.

The `prstat` command has the following syntax:

```
prstat [<options>] [<interval> [<count>]]
```

The `<interval>` argument specifies the time lapse between two consecutive display updates, and the default is five seconds. The `<count>` argument specifies how many times the display will be updated in total, and the default is infinity—that is, until the command process is terminated. Some values of `<options>` for this command are described here:

- **-a.** Display information about processes and users.
- **-c.** Display new reports below the previous displays instead of overwriting them.

- **-n. <number>.** Display information about only the first x number of selected processes where the value of x is specified by `<number>`.
- **-p <pidList>.** Display information about only those processes whose process ID is in the list specified by `<pidList>`.
- **-s <key>.** Sort output lines by the field specified by `<key>` in descending order. Only one key can be used as an argument. The key has five possible values:
  - **cpu.** Sort by CPU usage by the process. This is the default.
  - **pri.** Sort by the process priority.
  - **rss.** Sort by resident set size.
  - **size.** Sort by size of process image.
  - **time.** Sort by the process execution time.
- **-S <key>.** Sort output lines by the field specified by `<key>` in descending order.
- **-u <euiList>.** Select only those processes whose effective user ID is in the list specified by `<euiList>`.
- **-U <uidList>.** Select only those processes whose real user ID is in the list specified by `<uidList>`.

You may be wondering at this point how you are going to remember all these options for these commands. Well, note that some options are related to the properties of a process and are repeated for more than one command. Those options along with the process properties they are related to are described in Table 8-4.

TABLE 8-4 A list of process properties that appear as options in various process management command

Option	Process Property	Description
-p	Process ID	The unique identifier for a process
-u	Effective user ID	The user ID whose permissions are being used by the process
-U	Real user ID	The user ID for the user that started the process
-g	Effective group ID	The group ID for the group whose group permissions are being used by the process
-G	Real group ID	The group ID of the group that owns the process

To understand the difference between real and effective, suppose a user hillary starts a process passwd that is owned by the user root. The executable passwd has its setuid and setgid bits set—that is, its permission mode is 6555. Therefore, although hillary started the process passwd, it's running with privileges associated with the root. In this case, hillary is called the real user of this process, and root is called the effective user. Accordingly hillary's user ID is the real user ID for the process, and root's user ID is the effective user ID for the process.

EXERCISE 8-1

Using the `ps` Command to View Processes

1. Use the process command without any options:

```
$ ps
```

The output will look like the following:

```
PID TTY TIME COMD
1664 pts/4 0:06 csh
2081 pts/4 0:00 ps
```

2. Now, use the process command with the `-e` and `-f` options:

```
$ ps -ef
```

The output will look like the following:

```
UID PID PPID C STIME TTY TIME CMD
root 0 0 0 Dec 20 ? 0:17 sched
root 1 0 0 Dec 20 ? 0:00 /etc/init -
root 2 0 0 Dec 20 ? 0:00 pageout
root 3 0 0 Dec 20 ? 4:20 fsflush
root 374 367 0 Dec 20 ? 0:00 /usr/lib/saf/ttymon
```

3. Try other options and understand the output.

By using the `ps`, the `pgrep`, or the `pstat` command, you obtain some information about the processes. That information may tell you which process needs a control action, and that same information (such as PID) also gives you the handle that you can use to control the process.

Controlling Processes

Processes use the resources on your system such as CPU, memory, and disk space. If they remain unmonitored, they may fill your disk space or bring your system to a halt. Therefore, you need to control processes—for example, by clearing a hung process, terminating a process that has fallen into an infinite loop, stopping a process, or restarting a process.

Controlling a Process

You control a process by taking these three steps:

1. Obtain the process ID of the process that you want to control—for example, by issuing the following command:

   ```
   D#pgrep <processName>
   ```

2. Issue the appropriate command to control the process. For example, issue the following command to stop the process:

   ```
   #[[CD]]pstop <pid>
   ```

   `<pid>` is the process ID that you discovered in step 1.
3. Verify the process status to make sure you have accomplished what you wanted to; for example, issue the following command:

   ```
   # ps -ef | grep <pid>
   ```

   Repeat steps 2 and 3 if you need to. If you want to restart the stopped process, issue the following command:

   ```
   # prun <pid>
   ```

   Verify that it is actually running.

There will be some hung processes that you will need to clear.

Clearing a Hung Process

Solaris supports the concept of communicating with a process by sending it a signal. Sometimes, you might need to kill (stop or terminate) a process. The process, for example, might be in an endless loop, it might be hung, or you might have started a large job that you want to stop before it has completed. You can send a signal to a process by using the `kill` command which has the following syntax:

```
kill [<signal>] <pid>
```

The `<pid>` is the process ID, and `<signal>` is an integer whose default value is -15 (SIGTERM). If you use -9 (SIGKILL) for the `<signal>`, the process terminates promptly. However, do not use -9 signal to kill certain processes, such as a database process, or an LDAP server process, because you might lose or corrupt data contained in the database. A good policy is first always use the `kill` command without specifying any signal, and wait for a few minutes to see whether the process terminates before you issue the `kill` command with -9 signal.

As a superuser, you can kill any process. However, killing any of the processes with Process ID 0, 1, 2, 3, and 4 will most likely crash the system. Now, why would you do that?

You will mostly be using the SIGHUP, SIGSTP, and SIGKILL signals. Table 8-5 describes these and some other commonly used signals for controlling the processes.

You can issue the following command to get a list of all the supported signals:

```
kill -l
```

TABLE 8-5 Most common signals used for controlling processes

Signal	Number	Description
SIGHUP	1	Hangup. Usually means that the controlling terminal has been disconnected.
SIGINT	2	Interrupt. Pressing CTRL-D or DELETE will generate this signal.
SIGQUIT	3	Quit. This signal causes the process to quit and generates a core dump. You can generate it by pressing CTRL-.
SIGABRT	6	Abort.
SIGKILL	9	Kill the process promptly. Process is not allowed to clean up after itself, so you can lose or corrupt data with this command.
SIGTERM	15	Terminate. Terminate the process and give the process a chance to clean up after itself. This is the default signal sent by `kill` and `pkill`.
SIGSTOP	23	Stop. Pauses a process.
SIGCONT	25	Continue. Starts a stopped process.

If you are going to use the `pgrep` command to find some processes matching some criteria and then use the `kill` command on them, you would do better to use the `pkill` command, which has the functionality of both the `pgrep` and `kill` commands. For example, consider the following command:

```
pkill -9 -U gbush, jkerry
```

This command will find all the processes owned by gbush and jkerry and kill them. You can also use (`pkill` instead of `kill`) to send a signal to a known process:

```
pkill [<signal>] <processName>
```

Note that in the `kill` command, you use the process ID and in the `pkill` command you use the process name to refer to a process.

A hung up process can also freeze the system.

Dealing with a Hung System

You will find at times that the system has hung because of some software process that has become stuck. To recover from a hung system, try the following actions:

1. If the system is running a window environment, perform the following steps:
   - Make sure the pointer is in the window in which you are typing the commands.
   - Press CTRL-Q if the screen is frozen because the user accidentally pressed CTRL-S.
   - Log in remotely from another system on the network, and use the `pgrep` command to look for the hung process. Identify the process and kill it.
2. Press CTRL- to force a "quit" on the running process.
3. Press CTRL-C to interrupt the program that might be running.
4. Log in remotely, identify the process that is hanging the system, and kill it.
5. Log in remotely, become superuser, and reboot the system.
6. If the system still does not respond, force a crash dump and reboot.
7. If the system still does not respond, turn the power off, wait a minute or two, then turn the power back on.
8. If you can't get the system to respond at all, contact your local service provider for help.

You can always start a process instantly by issuing a command. However, Solaris allows you to schedule processes that will start executing at a later time.

Scheduling Processes

The motivation for scheduling processes is three pronged: to start executing a job at a time when you will not be physically present at the system to manually start a job, to distribute the job load over time, and to execute a job repeatedly in a periodic fashion without having to start it each time manually.

Like everything else in Solaris, you do process scheduling through files. The management in this area includes writing and maintaining these files and determining who can write them.

Scheduling Processes with the `cron` Utility

The automatic scheduling of processes (also called jobs) is handled by the *cron* utility, named after the Greek god of time Chronos. The job schedule is set up in the `/var/spool/cron/atjobs` directory files for jobs that will be executed only once, and in the `/var/spool/cron/crontab` directory files for jobs that will be executed repeatedly. The `cron` daemon manages the automatic scheduling of the processes (commands) listed in these files by performing the following tasks:

- Check for new `crontab` (and `atjob`) files.
- Read the commands and their scheduled times inside these files.
- Submit the commands for execution at the scheduled times.
- Listen for the notifications from the `crontab` commands regarding updated `crontab` and `atjobs` files.

Each entry in a `crontab` file contains the command name and the time at which it should be executed. The structure of an entry in a `crontab` file is shown in Figure 8-1.

FIGURE 8-1 An example of an entry in the `crontab` file that specifies that the script `diskchecker` will be executed at 9:15 A.M. on each Sunday and Wednesday every week, every month

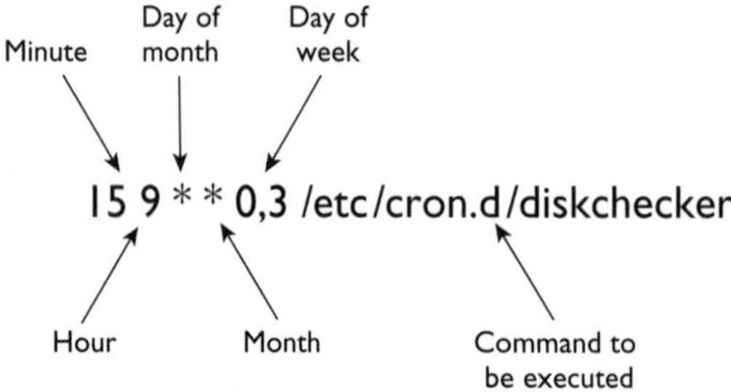

There is one entry in each line in `crontab` file. The beginning of each entry contains date and time information that tells the `cron` daemon when to execute the command, which is listed as the last field in the entry. The fields are described in Table 8-6.

While writing an entry in a `crontab` file, follow these rules:

- Use a space to separate any two consecutive fields.
- Use a comma to separate multiple values for a field.
- Use a hyphen (-) to specify a range of values for a field.
- Use an asterisk (*) as a wildcard to indicate all legal values of a field.
- Use a pound sign (#) at the beginning of a line to indicate comment or a blank line.

on the job

Each entry in a `crontab` file must consist of only one line, even if that line is very long, because the `crontab` file does not recognize extra carriage returns. This also means that there should be no blank lines (without a # sign) in between any two entry lines.

For example, you get a `crontab` file named `root` during SunOS software installation. Consider the following two entries in this file:

```
10 3 * * * /usr/sbin/logadm
15 3 * * 0 /usr/lib/fs/nfs/nfsfind
```

TABLE 8-6 Acceptable range of values for the `crontab` time fields

Field Position (from left)	Field	Range of Values
1	Minute	0–59 A * means every minute.
2	Hour	0–23 A * means every hour.
3	Day of month	1–31 A * means every day of the month.
4	Month	1–12 A * means every month.
5	Day of week	0–6 A * means every day of the week.
6	Command	Command to be executed.

The first entry schedules the logadm command to be run at 3:10 A.M. every day, and the second entry schedules the nfsfind script to be executed at 3:15 A.M. every Sunday.

The jobs that need to be run repeatedly are scheduled by using the crontab files. A user with the appropriate privileges can create a crontab file, whereas the system administrator can create a crontab file for any user.

Managing the crontab Files

As a system administrator, you will need to manage the crontab files. The crontab files are created and edited by using the crontab command with the following syntax:

```
crontab -e [<userName>]
```

The <username> is the login name of the user for whom you want to create the crontab file, and it defaults to the login name of the user who issued the command. You must be a superuser to create (or edit) the crontab file for other users, but you don't need to be a superuser to create the crontab file for your own account.

You can verify that the crontab file exists from the output of the following command:

```
ls -l /var/spool/cron/crontabs
```

You can display the content of a crontab file by using the crontab command with the following syntax:

```
crontab -l [<userName>]
```

The <username> specifies the login name of the user whose crontab file you want to display, and it defaults to the login name of the user who issues the command. You will need to be a superuser to display the crontab file of another user.

You can remove a crontab file by using the crontab command with the following syntax:

```
crontab -r [<userName>]
```

The <userName> specifies the login name of the user whose crontab file you want to remove and defaults to the login name of the user who issued the command. You need to be a superuser to remove a crontab file of another user.

Processes running on a system consume system resources, and they can also damage the system depending on what they are launched to do. A regular user has a right, by default, to create a crontab file and thereby to schedule processes. However, as a system administrator, you can determine which users can have the privilege to create crontab files.

Controlling Access to crontab Files

You can control access to the crontab command by using the following two files:

```
/etc/cron.d/cron.deny
/etc/cron.d/cron.allow
```

These files allow you to specify users who can (or cannot) use the crontab command for performing tasks such as creating, editing, displaying, or removing their own crontab files.

The cron.deny and cron.allow files consist of a list of user names, one user name per line. The permission to use the crontab command is determined by the interaction of both files as described here:

- If the cron.allow file exists, only the users listed in this file can create, edit, display, or remove crontab files.
- If the cron.allow file does not exist, all users except those listed in the cron.deny file can submit the crontab files.
- If neither cron.allow nor cron.deny exists, only a superuser can execute the crontab command.

To be more specific, there are only four possible combinations of the existence or absence of the cron.allow and cron.deny files. The crontab access corresponding to each of these combinations is listed in Table 8-7.

TABLE 8-7 Access to the crontab command managed by the cron.allow and cron.deny files

Does cron.allow exist?	Does cron.deny exist?	Who has access to crontab?
Yes	Yes	Users listed in the cron.allow file, and superuser
Yes	No	Users listed in the cron.allow file, and superuser
No	Yes	All users except those listed in the cron.deny file
No	No	Only the superuser

When the cron.allow file exists, the existence or absence of the cron.deny file does not matter—that is, the cron.deny file is not even checked.

Furthermore, only a superuser can create or edit the cron.deny and cron.allow files. When you install SunOS software, a default version of the cron.deny file is created, but no cron.allow file is created. You can display the content of the cron.deny file with the following command:

```
$ cat /etc/cron.d/cron.deny
```

The output of this command would look like the following:

```
Daemon
bin
smtp
nuucp
listen
nobody
noaccess
```

None of the user names listed in the cron.deny file can access the crontab command, but all other users can. Of course, you can edit this file to add other user names that will be denied access to the crontab command, and you can create the cron.allow file as well, in which case the cron.deny file will be ignored.

Scheduling a Process for One Time Execution

The processes for one time execution at a later time are scheduled by using the at command. You can schedule a job for time execution by performing the following steps:

1. Issue the at command with the following syntax:

   ```
   $ at [-m] <time> [<date>]
   ```

   The -m option will send you an email after the job is completed. The <time> specifies the hour at which you want to schedule the job. Add am or pm if you do not specify the hours according to the 24-hour clock. Acceptable keywords are midnight, noon, and now. Minutes are optional. For example, 1930 means 7:30 P.M. The <date> specifies the first three or more letters of a month, a day of the week, or the keywords: today or tomorrow.

2. At the at prompt, type the commands or scripts that you want to execute: one per line. You can type more than one command by pressing RETURN at the end of each line.
3. Press CTRL-D to Exit the at utility and save the at job.

Your at job is assigned a queue number, which is also the job's filename in the /var/spool/cron/atjobs directory. You can control access to the at command by using the following file:

```
/etc/cron.d/at.deny
```

This file is created when you install SunOS software and has the following list of users, one user name per line:

```
Daemon
bin
smtp
nuucp
listen
nobody
noaccess
```

The users who are listed in this file cannot access the at command, but all other users can. As a superuser, you can edit this file and add more user names to it.

EXERCISE 8-2

Scheduling a cron Job by Creating and Editing a crontab File

1. Issue the following command to edit your crontab file:

   ```
   crontab -e
   ```

   If you did not have a crontab file, this command will create an empty crontab file and let you write into it.
2. Write the following entry into your crontab file:

   ```
   * * * ls -l /etc >> cron_test.log
   ```

This command will execute the `ls -l` command on the directory `/etc` every minute and dump the output into the file `cron_test.log`. Save the file. Provide the full path for the file `cron_test.log`, so that you know for sure where to find it.

3. After each minute, verify that the output from the `ls -l` command is being appended to the `cron_test.log` file.
4. After a few minutes, edit the `crontab` file and remove the entry that you made. Verify that no more output is being appended to the `cron_test.log` file.

Remember that you can also use the process tool of the Solaris Management Console (SMC) GUI to view and manage processes.

Processes use system resources such as CPU, memory, and disk space. There is another important resource that users often use on a system—the printing service that the Solaris system offers. You will need to manage the printing service on the Solaris system to allow the users to share the printers on the network.

CERTIFICATION OBJECTIVE 8.02

Managing Printers

Exam Objective 5.1: *Configure and administer Solaris 10 OS print services, including client and server configuration, starting and stopping the LP print service, specifying a destination printer, and using the LP print service.*

The Solaris printing software provides an environment for setting up and managing client access to printers on a network by providing a graphical user interface (GUI) tool called Solaris Print Manager, and by providing the LP print service commands.

Understanding the Solaris Print Process

The Solaris print process uses the LP print service, which is a set of software utilities that automate the process of sharing printers to print files. The print process includes print clients and print servers. A print client is a machine that has the print client software installed on it, which enables it to accept print requests from a local user and send them to a remote print server. A print server is a machine with the print server software installed on it that enables it to accept print requests from remote print clients and process them. Any machine with the Solaris system on it and having enough resources, such as disk space, can be connected to a local printer to make it a print server.

Figure 8-2 illustrates the print process starting with a user issuing a print request on a print client and ending with the printed output from a printer.

The steps in this process are listed here:

1. A user submits a print request from a print client machine by issuing either the SVR4-based `lp` command or the BSD-based `lpr` command. The user may or may not specify a printer name in the command.
2. The print command processes the request, for example, it checks a hierarchy of print configuration resources to determine where to send the print request.
3. The print command sends the print request directly to the appropriate print server. A print server can be any server that accepts the Berkley Software Distribution (BSD) printing protocol, including SVR4 (lp) print servers and BSD lpr-based print servers.
4. The print server sends the print request to the appropriate printer.
5. The print request is printed.

FIGURE 8-2 Overview of the Solaris print process

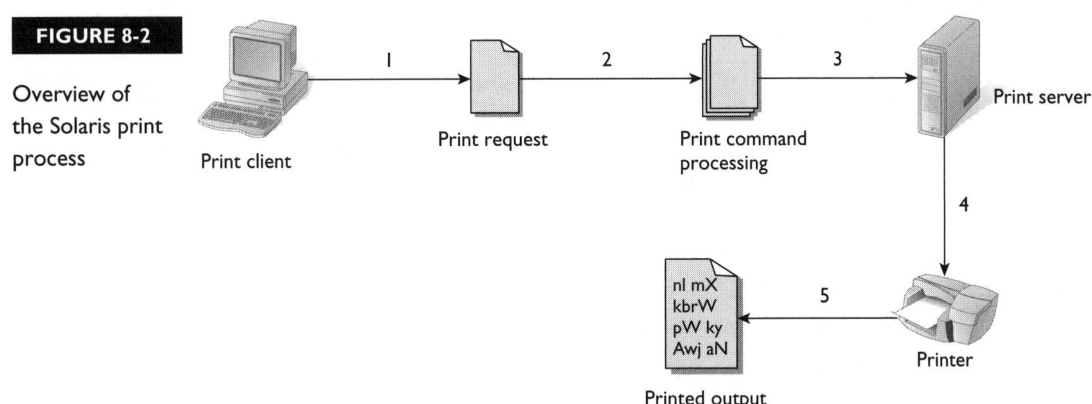

Step 2 in the print process needs further explanation. If the user does not specify a printer name (or class), the command does the following:

1. Checks the values for the user's environment variables PRINTER and LPDEST for the default printer.
2. If none of these environment variables is defined, it checks the `.printers` file in the user's home directory for a default printer.
3. If no default printer alias exists in the `.printers` file, it checks the print client's `/etc/printers.conf` file for configuration information.
4. If the printer is still not found, it checks the name service such as NIS.

Files that belong to the print requests in the queue are stored in the* `/var/spool/lp` *directory and stay there until they are printed. You must have enough disk space for this directory, depending on the print load.

A new feature for printing on a network is the Internet Printing Protocol listener, ipp-listener, which works in conjunction with the Apache web server shipped as part of the Solaris software. You can use this feature to print a web page over the Internet. The IPP listener listens on port 631 for print-related HTTP requests and communicates the requests to the printing system. The listener is managed by the Service Management Facility (SMF) under the following FMRI:

```
svc:/application/print/ipp-listener
```

Now, that you have a view of how the print process works, let's explore how to administer the printers.

Administering Printers

After you set up print servers and print clients in your network, you may need to perform the following administrative tasks frequently:

- Check the status of printers.
- Restart the print scheduler.
- Delete remote printer access.
- Delete a printer.

Checking Printer Status

Checking the printer status is at the heart of many routine printer administration tasks that require information about the status of the LP print service or a specific printer. For example, you may need to determine which printers are available for use, and you may need to know the characteristics of those printers.

The `lpstat` is your command to obtain status information about the LP print service or a specific printer offered by the service. The syntax for this command is shown here:

```
$ lpstat [-d] [-p <printerName>] [-D] [-l] [-o <list>] [-t]
```

The options are listed as follows:

- **-d.** Show the system's default printer.
- **-D.** Show the description of the printer specified by `<printerName>`; usually used with other options such as `-p`.
- **-l.** Show the characteristics of the printer specified by `<printerName>`.
- **-o [<list>].** Display the status of the output requests specified by `<list>`, which could be an intermix of printer names, class names, and request IDs. If you do not specify a list, the status of all requests is displayed.
- **-p [<printerName>].** Show whether the printer specified by `<printerName>` is active or idle, when the printer was enabled or disabled, and whether the printer is accepting print requests. You can specify multiple printer names in a comma-separated list, or a space-separated list enclosed in quotation marks. If you do not specify a printer, the status of all the printers is displayed.
- **-t.** Show the status information about the LP print service. It includes the status of all printers, including whether they are active and whether they are accepting print requests.

So, you can use the `lpstat` command to determine the status of a print request, a printer, and many other aspects of the print service such as print scheduler.

Starting and Stopping Print Scheduler

The print scheduler daemon, `lpsched`, handles print requests on print servers. When it is stopped, print requests are neither accepted nor printed. In Solaris 10, the `lpadmin` command automatically enables the `lpsched` service when a local printer is added to the system and disables it when the last local printer is removed. However, sometimes you will need to stop the scheduler and to restart a stopped scheduler manually.

on the job

If a print request was being printed when the print scheduler stopped, the print request will be printed in its entirety from the beginning when you restart the print scheduler.

To determine whether the print scheduler is running, you can use the following command:

```
lpstat -r
```

If the print scheduler is not running, the following message is displayed:

```
scheduler is not running
```

You can start (or restart) the scheduler by using the following command:

```
/usr/lib/lpsched
```

You can stop the scheduler by using the `lpshut` command.

watch

The LP print service (the `lpsched`) is automatically started when you add a printer to the system with the `lpadmin` command.

Because the print service in Solaris 10 is run under SMF, you can also use the SMF `svcs` and `svcadm` commands to manage the print scheduler, which is controlled by the SMF service with FMRI:

```
svc:/application/print/server
```

Therefore, to find out whether the scheduler is running or not, issue the following command:

```
svcs svc:/application/print/server
```

To start the print scheduler, issue the following command:

```
svcadm enable svc:/application/print/server
```

To stop the print scheduler, issue the following command:

```
svcadm disable svc:/application/print/server
```

To keep track of the print requests, the print scheduler keeps a log of the print requests in the /var/spool/lp/requests/<systemName> and /var/spool/lp/tmp/<systemName> directories, where <systemName> specifies the name of the system. Each print request has two log files: one in each of these two directories. The /var/spool/lp/requests/<systemName> directory is accessible only to the superuser and the lp service, whereas the information in the /var/spool/lp/tmp/<systemName> directory can be accessed by the superuser, the lp service, and the user who submitted the request. Although the print scheduler manages print requests, on occasion you may need to intervene—for example, to cancel a print request.

Knowing and Canceling Print Requests

If you want to cancel a print request, you will need to know the request ID for the request. You can find the request ID by becoming the superuser and issuing the following command:

```
#lpstat [-o <list>] [-u <userList>]
```

The <list> can specify a list of printer names, class names, or print request IDs. The list may have multiple values in it separated by commas or spaces. If you use spaces, enclose the list in double quotes. If you don't specify <list>, the status of print requests submitted to all printers is displayed.

The <userList> specifies user login names. Use this option to check the status of requests from specific users. The list may have multiple values in it separated by commas or spaces. If you use spaces, enclose the list in double quotes. If you don't specify <userList>, the status of print requests made by all users is displayed.

To cancel a request, you can issue the following command:

```
# cancel <requestID> | <printerName>
```

The <requestID> specifies the request ID of a print request that you want to cancel. You can specify multiple request IDs in a comma-separated or space-separated list. If you use spaces, enclose the list in the double quotes.

You can use the `cancel` command to cancel both kinds of requests—those that are in the queue and those that are currently being printed.

The `<printerName>` specifies the printer for which you want to cancel the print requests. You can specify multiple printer names in a comma-separated or space-separated list. If you use spaces, enclose the list in double quotes.

Printing is an important and very expensive resource on your system. In addition to using system resources such as disk space, it also consumes printer paper, which can cost your organization a great deal, depending on the print load. Solaris helps here by allowing you to control access to printing. You can perform the access control and many other tasks by configuring the LP print service accordingly.

Configuring the LP Print Service

You can configure the LP print service to accomplish the following:

- Add printers to the service.
- Change the configuration of existing printers.
- Remove printers from the service.
- Set or change the system's default destination printer.
- Define alerts for printer faults.
- Control access to the print service.
- Mount print wheels.

You can configure the LP print service by using the `lpadmin` command, which has many forms. The aspects of printer configuration that we will explore in this chapter include adding a new printer, deleting a printer, and controlling access to the print service.

Adding a New Printer

The command to add a new printer or to change the configuration of an existing printer has the following syntax:

```
lpadmin -p <printerName> <options>
```

This command also starts the print scheduler. When you add a new printer, the `<options>` must specify at least one of the following three options:

- **`-s <systemName> [<printerName>]`.** Make a remote printer accessible to users on your system.
- **`-U <dialInfo>`.** Allow (not enable) your print service to access a remote printer. The `<dialInfo>` specifies the phone number for a dial-up connection or a system name for other kinds of connections.
- **`-v <deviceName>`.** Associate a device with the printer. The `<deviceName>` specifies the full path for the device file.

Distinguish between a printer and the printing device. You can associate the same device with more than one printer.

Note that adding the printer adds the printer information to the print server's configuration files only, and the print clients do not automatically know about the printer. You are required to add the printer information to each print client that wants to use the printer.

As an example of using the `-s` option in the `lpadmin` command, if you want to access a remote printer named `printerR` on a system named `systemR` and you want it called locally `printerL` on your system, you would issue the following command:

```
lpadmin -p printerL -s systemR!printerR
```

When you are adding a new printer, only one of the following three options can be supplied:

- **`-e <printer>`.** Copy the interface program of an existing printer specified by `<printer>` to be the interface program for the printer being added.
- **`-i <interface>`.** Establish a new interface program for the printer. `<interface>` specifies the pathname of the new program.
- **`-m <model>`.** Select the model interface program specified by `<model>`, provided with the LP print service, for the printer.

Once you have added a printer to the service, you can control the client access to it.

Controlling Client Access to Printing

You can control access to printing by disabling access to printing at various levels. For example, you can delete the printer information on a client machine by issuing the following command:

```
# lpadmin -x <printerName>
```

It will delete the information about the printer specified by `<printerName>` from the print client's directory: `/etc/lp/printers`.

You can stop accepting print requests for a printer by issuing the following command on a print server:

```
# reject <printerName>
```

This will stop accepting requests for the printer specified by `<printerName>`. You should always issue this command before removing the printer, because it will prevent any new requests from entering the printer's queue. The following command will stop the print requests from printing:

```
# disable <printerName>
```

Later, when you want to start printing the print requests for that printer, you can issue the same command by replacing the command name `disable` with `enable`.

Finally, the following command will delete the printer from the print server:

```
# lpadmin -x <printerName>
```

It will delete the configuration information for the printer from the print server's directory: `/etc/lp/printers`.

Access to printing can also be controlled at the user level.

Controlling User Access to Printing

By default, all users have access to a printer. However, you can limit their access by using the following form of the `lpadmin` command:

```
# lpadmin -p <printerName> -u allow:<userList> [deny:<userList>]
```

These options are described here:

- **-p <printerName>.** Specify the name of the printer to which the allow or deny access list applies.
- **-u allow:<userList>.** Specify the user login names to be added to the allow access list. You can specify multiple user names in a comma-separated or space-separated list. If you use space, enclose the list in double quotes.
- **-u deny:<userList>.** Specify the user login names to be added to the deny access list. You can specify multiple user names in a comma-separated or space-separated list. If you use space, enclose the list in double quotes.

Table 8-8 provides the valid values for the `<userList>`.

The users specified in the command are added to the allow or deny list for the printer in one of the following files on the print server:

```
/etc/lp/printers/<printerName>/users.allow
/etc/lp/printers/<printerName>/users.deny
```

Obviously, the users in the allow file have access to the specified printer, and the users in the deny file do not have access. When determining user access, an empty allow or deny file is equivalent to or does not exist. Having said that, if both allow and deny files exist, the deny file is ignored. The combined effect of allow and deny files on the access is described in Table 8-9.

TABLE 8-8 Values for the `<userList>` in the allow or deny files

Value for `<userList>`	Description
all or all!all	All users on all systems
all!<user> <user>	A user specified by `<user>` on any system
!all	All users on the local system
None	No user on any system
<system>!all	All users on a system specified by `<system>`
<system>!<user>	A user specified by `<user>` on a system specified by `<system>` only

TABLE 8-9 The allow and deny access rules

State of Allow and Deny Lists	Access Consequence
Neither allow nor deny file exists.	All users can access the printer.
Either allow, or deny, or both files exist but they are empty.	All users can access the printer.
The value of `<userList>` for the allow file is all.	All users can access the printer.
The value of `<userList>` for the deny file is all.	No user except root and lp can access the printer.
Any entry in the allow list.	The deny list will be ignored and the only entries in the allow list will have the access.
Non-empty deny list exists, allow list either does not exist or is empty.	Only the users in the deny list are denied the access to the printer.

You can perform various administrative tasks by configuring the LP print service. The configuration information goes into the files underneath the `/etc/lp` directory. For example, the following file contains configuration information for an individual printer:

```
/etc/lp/printers/<printerName>/configuration
```

The configuration files should never be edited directly. Change the configuration only by using the `lpadmin` command. The `lpsched` daemon administers the updates for the configuration files.

Now that you know how to perform printer administration, here are some practical scenarios and their solutions.

SCENARIO & SOLUTION

Which command will you issue to view the description of a printer named cornell?	`lpstat -D -p cornell`
You want to see the status of all print requests received by the LP print service. Which command will you issue?	`lpstat -o`
You have a list of users in the `users.allow` file to whom you have given access to a printer. What will you need to do if you want to deny access to another user, bkerry.	Ensure that an entry for bkerry does not exist in the `allow` file. Because the `allow` file exists, the `deny` file will be ignored. Therefore, there is no point in creating the `deny` file.

In summary, there are five basic functions that the LP print service performs:

1. Initializing the printer so that the print jobs can be submitted and processed
2. Administering files and scheduling local print requests
3. Tracking the status of the print jobs
4. Filtering files, that is, converting print jobs to the correct format for the destination printer
5. Delivering alerts about printing problems

The three most important takeaways from this chapter are as follows:

- You can view the processes on a Solaris system with the `ps`, `pgrep`, and `prstat` commands, and you can control a process by sending it a signal through the `kill` or `pkill` command.
- You can schedule the processes by using the `crontab` and `at` commands.
- You can find the status of the LP print service with the `lpstat` command, and you can configure it with the `lpadmin` command.

CERTIFICATION SUMMARY

Before you can control a process by issuing a control command, you will need to obtain some information about the process, such as process ID, which you do by viewing the process. Therefore, process management begins with viewing the processes on the system, which can be accomplished with the `ps`, `pgrep`, and `prstat` commands. The `ps` command displays information about the active processes on the system, and the `pgrep` command can be used to display only those processes that match specific criteria. If you want the displayed process information updated at a specified interval, use the `prstat` command. You can use the `pgrep` command to find out the process ID and use the process ID in the `kill` command to send the process a signal; alternatively, you can accomplish both tasks with one command: `pkill`.

You can schedule processes that need to be run repeatedly by making their entries in the `/var/spool/cron/crontab` directory files, called `crontab` files. You can manage these files by using the `crontab` command. You can schedule processes that need to be run only once by making their entries in the `/var/spool/cron/atjobs` directory files, called `atjobs` files. You can manage these files by using the `at` command interactively. The access to the `crontab` command can be controlled by creating the `cron.deny` and `cron.allow` files.

You can view the status of the LP print service on Solaris by using the `lpstat` command, and you can configure the service by using the `lpadmin` command. A component of the LP print service, the `lpsched`, manages print requests on the local system. By default, each user on the system has access to the printers on the system. You can control that access by using the `users.allow` and `users.deny` files.

Printers are important resources on the system, and the LP print service provides access to them. However, the most important resource that needs to be protected in case of a disaster or a crash is the data on the disks. The solution to a data loss resulting from a disaster or a disk crash is backup and recovery. This is the subject we explore in the next chapter.

INSIDE THE EXAM

Comprehend

- When the `cron.allow` file exists, the `cron.deny` file is not even checked, so its content plays no role in determining access to the `crontab` command.
- When the `users.allow` file exists, the `users.deny` file is ignored to check access to printers.
- You can first find a process and then send it a signal by using the `/usr/bin/kill` command, or you can use the `pkill` command, which will find the process for you that matches a criteria and send it a signal.

Look Out

- The value R for the S (state) field in the output of the `ps` command does not mean the process is running. It means the process is runnable—it is in the queue and ready for running.
- Use the signal 9 (kill -9) with caution, because it kills the process without giving it a chance to clean up after itself. It may cause data loss or data corruption.
- When neither the `cron.deny` file nor the `cron.allow` file exists, nobody except the superuser has access to the `crontab` command. In contrast, when neither the `users.allow` nor the `users.deny` file exists, all users have access to the printer on the system.
- When the print scheduler is restarted, a partly finished print job is printed in its entirety.

Memorize

- The `ps` and `pgrep` commands take a snapshot, whereas the `prstat` command refreshes its output at a specified interval.
- The default signal sent by `kill` and `pkill` is -15 (i.e., terminate the process and give it a chance to clean up after itself).
- The print scheduler, `lpsched`, is automatically started when you add a printer to the system with the `lpadmin` command.
- You can use the cancel command to cancel a print request waiting to be printed or currently being printed.
- By default, all users have access to a printer on the system they are logged on to.

TWO-MINUTE DRILL

Viewing Processes

- The ps command without any option and argument only displays the information about those processes whose effective UID and the terminal is the same as the user who issued the command.
- The pgrep command can be used to display information only about selective processes.
- You should use the prstat command to display the process information if you want the output refreshed periodically.

Controlling Processes

- You can control a process by using the pgrep command to get its process ID, and then using a control command such as pstop, and prun.
- You can also control a process by sending it a signal with the kill command.
- Instead of using pgrep and kill, you can just use pkill, which finds the process and sends it the signal.

Scheduling Processes

- You schedule a process for repeated execution by entering a command in a crontab file, and you schedule a process for one-time execution in the future by issuing the at command.
- If the cron.allow file exists, only the users listed in this file can create, edit, display, or remove crontab files.
- If the cron.allow file does not exist, all users except those listed in the cron.deny file can submit the crontab files.
- If neither cron.allow nor cron.deny exists, only a superuser can execute the crontab command.

Managing Printers

- ❑ The `lpstat` command displays the status of the LP print service.
- ❑ The print scheduler, `lpsched`, is started with the `/usr/lib/lpsched` command and stopped with the `lpsut` command.
- ❑ You can use the `cancel` command to cancel a print request.
- ❑ You can use the `lpadmin` command to configure the LP print service. Do not edit the configuration files manually.

SELF TEST

The following questions will help you measure your understanding of the material presented in this chapter. Read all the choices carefully because there might be more than one correct answer. Choose all correct answers for each question.

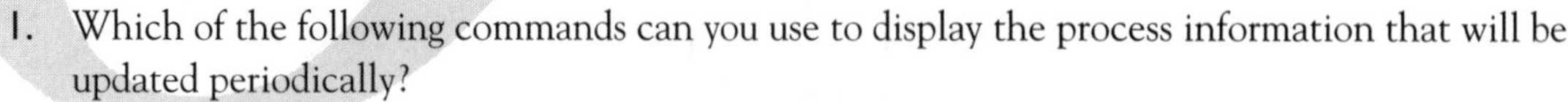

1. Which of the following commands can you use to display the process information that will be updated periodically?

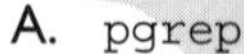

   A. `pgrep`

   B. `ps`

   C. `plist`

   D. `prstat`

2. In the output of the `ps` command the S field for a running process will display which of the following values?

   A. O

   B. R

   C. S

   D. A

   E. Running

3. Which of the following commands will display all the processes that go in the process argument string?

   A. `ps -ef grep go`

   B. `pgrep -l -f go`

   C. `ps -a go`

   D. `prstat go`

4. Which of the following commands will kill a process with process ID 24387 and process name pass2?

   A. `kill 24387`

   B. `kill pass2`

   C. `pkill 24387`

   D. `pkill pass2`

5. Which of the following commands or actions will kill the process with process ID 24387 and let it clean up after itself?

   A. `Kill -9 24387`

   B. `Kill -15 24387`

   C. `sigterm 24387`

   D. Press CTRL-D

6. Which of the following commands can you use to schedule a command to be executed repeatedly?

   A. `crontab`

   B. `at`

   C. `cron`

   D. `run`

7. Which of the following entries in a `crontab` file instructs the system to execute the diskchecker script at 9:10 A.M. each Sunday and Tuesday?

   A. `0 2 * * * 9:10 /etc/cron.d/diskchecker`

   B. `10 9 * * * 0,2 /etc/cron.d/diskchecker`

   C. `10 9 * * * 1,3 /etc/cron.d/diskchecker`

   D. `9 10 * * * 0,2 /etc/cron.d/diskchecker`

8. When you installed the SunOS software, you deleted the `cron.deny` file that the system created, and you did not create a `cron.allow` file. Which of the following is true?

   A. All users have access to the `crontab` command to manage all the `crontab` files.

   B. No user except the superuser has access to the `crontab` command.

   C. All users have the permission to use the `crontab` command only to manage their own `crontab` files.

   D. Users can edit their `crontab` files but cannot remove them.

9. Which of the following is a correct statement? (Choose all that apply.)

   A. If neither the `cron.allow`, nor the `cron.deny` file exists, no user without superuser privilege can have access to the `crontab` command.

   B. If neither the `users.allow`, nor `users.deny` file exists, no user except the superuser has access to a printer on the system.

C. When you install the Solaris OS software, a `cron.deny` file is created automatically.

D. When you install the Solaris OS software, a `cron.allow` file is created automatically.

10. How do you configure the print service on Solaris? (Choose all that apply.)

A. Edit the configuration files underneath the directory `/etc/lp/printers`.

B. Use the `lpadmin` command.

C. Use the `lpsched` command.

D. Use the `printerconfig` command.

11. The CEO of your company complains that she cannot print a web page. You suspect a problem with the print server and want to ensure that the listener service for the web print requests is running. What is the name of this service?

A. http-listener

B. ipp-listener

C. ippd

D. http-listen

12. You discover that the print scheduler, `lpsched`, has stopped on your system. Which SMF command would you issue to restart the scheduler?

A. `svcs enable svc:/application/print/server`

B. `svcadm start svc:/application/print/server`

C. `svcadm enable svc:/application/print/lpsched`

D. `svcadm enable svc:/application/print/server`

SELF TEST ANSWERS

1. ☑ **D**. The `prstat` command refreshes the output at a specified interval.
   ☒ **A** and **B** are incorrect because the `pgrep` and `ps` commands take a snapshot of the system and do not update the output. **C** is incorrect because `plist` is not a command.

2. ☑ **A**. The state O indicates that the process is running.
   ☒ **B** is incorrect because R means the process is runnable—that is, in the queue for running. **C** is incorrect because S means the process is sleeping. **D** and **E** are incorrect because there are no state values A and running.

3. ☑ **A** and **B**. The `ps` command with `-f` option generates the full listing of the processes, and the `grep` command selects the process from the output whose argument string contains the string go. The `pgrep` command accomplishes the same thing.
   ☒ **B** is incorrect because R means the process is runnable—that is, in the queue for running. **C** and **D** are incorrect because the `ps` and `prstat` commands are being used with the wrong syntax.

4. ☑ **A** and **D**. You use the process ID in the `kill` command and the process name in the `pkill` command.
   ☒ **B** and **C** are incorrect because you use the process ID in the `kill` command and the process name in the `pkill` command.

5. ☑ **B**. Signal 15 kills the process and gives it a chance to clean up after itself.
   ☒ **A** is incorrect because signal 9 kills the process without giving it a chance to clean up after itself. **C** is incorrect because it is the wrong command syntax. **D** is incorrect because pressing CTRL-C will interrupt the process but will not kill it.

6. ☑ **A**. The `crontab` command is used to edit a `crontab` file in which you can enter a command that you want to execute repeatedly.
   ☒ **B** is incorrect because the `at` command is used to schedule a command to be executed at a future time only once. **C** and **D** are incorrect because there are no such commands as `cron` or `run` to schedule a process.

7. ☑ **B**. This is the correct use of the command. This first field is minute, the second field is hour, and the last field represents days: 0 for Sunday and 2 for Tuesday.
   ☒ **A** is incorrect because the first two fields have the wrong values for the minute and the hour, and the last field has the value in the wrong format. **C** is incorrect because it will schedule the job for Monday and Wednesday. **D** is incorrect because it will schedule the job at 10:09 A.M., not 9:10 A.M.

8. ☑ **B**. When neither the `cron.allow` nor the `cron.deny` file exists, only the superuser has access to the `crontab` command.
   ☒ **A** is incorrect because no user except the superuser ever has access to all the `crontab` files. You need to be a superuser to access other users' `crontab` files. **C** and **D** are incorrect because when neither `cron.allow` nor `cron.deny` exists, no user except the superuser has access to any `crontab` file.

9. ☑ **A** and **C**. When neither the `cron.allow` nor the `cron.deny` file exists, only the superuser has access to the `crontab` command, and the `cron.deny` file is created during installation.
   ☒ **B** is incorrect because each user has access to printers on the system if neither the `users.allow` nor the `users.deny` file exists. **D** is incorrect because only the `cron.deny` file, not the `cron.allow` file, is created during the Solaris OS software installation.

10. ☑ **B**. You use the `lpadmin` command to configure the LP print service.
    ☒ **A** is incorrect because you should not edit the configuration files directly. **C** is incorrect because the `lpsched` is the scheduler that manages the print requests. **D** is incorrect because there is no such command as `printerconfig` to configure the LP print service.

11. ☑ **B**. The name of the service that listens to the print related HTTP requests is `svc:/application/print/ipp-listener`.
    ☒ **A**, **C**, and **D** are all incorrect because there are no such services as http-listener, ippd, and http-listen.

12. ☑ **D**. The SMF service manages the print scheduler under the FMRI `svc:/application/print/server`. Therefore the `svcadm enable svc:/application/print/server` command will start the print scheduler.
    ☒ **A** is incorrect because `svcs` is the SMF command to determine the status of a service. **B** is incorrect because the correct argument in the command is enable, not start. **C** is incorrect because the FMRI contains the word `server`, not `lpsched`.

9

Performing System Backups and Restores

CERTIFICATION OBJECTIVES

9.01	Performing Scheduled Backups of an Unmounted File System
9.02	Performing Backup of a Mounted File System
9.03	Restoring File System Backups
9.04	Restoring a UFS Snapshot
✓	Two-Minute Drill
Q&A	Self Test

The most important asset on a computer system is the data, which must be protected from a possible disaster. This involves copying the data from the system to storage media—a process called backup—and, when a need arises, copying the data back to the system—a process called restoration or recovery. Solaris offers tools for backup, such as the `ufsdump` command, and tools for restoration, such as the `ufsrestore` command.

When you plan to back up a whole file system or all the file systems on a Solaris system, you need to make sure that all the files are copied to the media correctly. To ensure this, you should make the file system or the Solaris system unavailable to users by unmounting the file system or bringing the Solaris system to single-user mode. Because this is inconvenient for the users, in some situations you will want to make a backup without making the file system unavailable to them and just take a snapshot of an active file system. Your backup strategy will affect how easy or difficult it will be to restore the data.

The core issue to think about in this chapter is: how do we make efficient use of the Solaris tools available for backup and restoration? To understand this, we will explore the following three thought streams: backing up unmounted file systems, backing up mounted file systems, and restoring the backups.

CERTIFICATION OBJECTIVE 9.01

Performing Scheduled Backups of an Unmounted File System

Exam Objective 6.1: *Given a scenario, develop a strategy for scheduled backups, and backup an unmounted file system using the appropriate commands.*

The most important asset on a computer system is the data on its hard disk. The disks can and do crash, and disasters such as fire do happen occasionally. These occurrences result in loss of data, and that can cost a company a great fortune. Therefore, backups are your protection against a disaster. Backing up a file system means copying the file system to a removable medium such as a tape; restoring a file system means copying the files from the removable medium back to the working directories. Because backup and restore is a serious business, you should develop a backup strategy based on the needs of your organization.

Developing a Backup Strategy

Because backing up files is one of the most crucial and important tasks that you will perform as a system administrator, the importance of developing a backup strategy cannot be overestimated. In order to develop a sound strategy according to your organization's needs, you first need to realize that regularly scheduled backups are performed as a protection against data loss that may occur as a result of the following types of problems:

- Accidental removal of files
- Hardware failures
- Natural disasters such as earthquakes, fire, or hurricanes
- Problems that occur during reinstalls or upgrades
- System crashes

Developing a backup strategy includes deciding which file systems to back up and how often, and which backup type and backup media to use.

Determining Which File Systems to Back Up

The question is which file systems should be backed up and how frequently? You should back up any file system that has critical data, and the frequency of backup depends on how frequently the data changes.

For example, consider the root file system that has the `/var` directory in it. Because it may contain important information such as the log files and the mail directory, it must be backed up. If you add and delete users quite frequently on the system or change the important files in this file system for some other reasons, a weekly backup would be a safe bet. If your system has a mail server running that stores user mail in `var/mail`, you should perform daily backups. Some examples of file systems that are candidates for backup are presented in Table 9-1.

Once you have decided which file systems to back up, you need to figure out which backup type you are going to use.

TABLE 9-1 Some standard file systems to back up

File System to Back Up	Content	Backup Frequency
`root (/)` slice 0	Kernel, and possibly the `/var` directory which may contain frequently changing system accounting and mail files	Regularly, such as daily or weekly
`/usr` slice 6	Executables and other software-related files	Occasionally
`/export/home` slice 7	Directory subtrees for users	Could be daily depending on the needs

Determining the Backup Type

Solaris offers you several backup types to choose from. You can use the full backup or an incremental backup by using the `ufsdump` command. The full backup copies the whole file system or directory, whereas the incremental backup copies only those files from a file system or directory that have changed since a previous backup. Which previous backup? That can be determined by using the dump level, which we will discuss when we explore the `ufsdump` command later in this chapter.

A full backup takes longer and uses more tapes, but it's simple to perform. Furthermore, it is a very efficient way to restore the data in case of a crash or disaster. Simply take the most recent full backup and copy it to the system. An incremental backup takes less time and requires fewer tapes to copy the data from the system; however, it may take longer and require a greater number of tapes (or sets) to restore the entire data back to the system.

Before using the `ufsdump` command for a backup, your system should be in single-user mode, or the file system should be unmounted, to preserve data integrity. If you are backing up file systems while users are creating, removing, or editing files, some data will not be included in the backup. However, if you do want to make a backup of a file system while it is active, you can take a snapshot of it by using the `fssnap` command without putting the system into single-user mode. Then, you can back up the snapshot. These various backup types are compared in Table 9-2.

A good backup strategy is to choose a mix of these backup types based on your needs—for example, a weekly full backup combined with incremental backups on weekdays, as opposed to a full backup every day.

TABLE 9-2

Comparison of various backup types

Backup Type	Function	Advantages	Disadvantages
Incremental	Copies only those files in the specified file system that have changed since a previous backup.	Fewer files to back up, hence smaller number of backup tapes required.	Lengthens the restore process; more data sets needed to restore the entire data.
Full	Copies the whole file system under backup.	Easy to restore because all data is in one set.	Larger amount of backup data, and longer time needed for backup.
Snapshot	Creates a temporary image of the file system under backup.	System can remain in multiuser mode.	System performance may suffer when the snapshot is being created.

The data will be backed up on a removable medium that you need to choose.

Determining Which Backup Device to Use

You will need to choose an appropriate tape device depending on the volume of data that needs to be backed up. You will typically use the tape media listed in Table 9-3 for backups from the Solaris system. As shown, these drives differ by their storage capacity.

The amount of data you will be backing up partially determines which storage device you should use. Your choice of backup media also depends on the availability of the equipment (that supports it) and the media (usually tape) on which you store

TABLE 9-3

Typical tape devices used for backup

Backup Media	Storage Capacity
1/2-inch reel tape	140MB
1/4-inch cartridge (QIC) tape	2.5GB
4-mm DAT cartridge tape (DDS3)	12–24GB
8-mm cartridge tape	14GB
1/2-inch cartridge tape (DLT)	35–70GB

the data. Another criterion for choosing backup media might be the data transfer speed supported by the equipment and the media. Supposedly, you could perform backups with diskettes, but why would you? It would be so cumbersome and time consuming. But again, it depends on the backup needs of your site.

Once you know which media you are going to use for backup, you can determine your backup schedule.

Determining Backup Schedule

A backup schedule is the schedule that you put in place to execute regular backups—for example, by running the `ufsdump` command. In a nutshell, your backup strategy will be based on the business requirements of your site along with applicable regulatory requirements. In that context, while creating a backup schedule you should consider various issues related to your site's needs, including the following:

- Do you need to minimize the number of tapes used for backups?
- How much time do you have at your disposal to make backups?
- How much time will be available to perform a full restore should you lose a file system?
- How much time will be available for retrieving individual files that have been accidentally deleted?

The frequency of backups depends on your need to minimize the number of tapes used and the time needed for the backup (and restore) process. For example, if you have an unlimited number of tapes and unlimited time available for backup and restore operations and you have critical data, you should make a full backup every day. However, this is not realistic for most sites. Typically, you want to make enough backups to enable you to restore files from the last four weeks. Let's work through an example to design a strategy to meet this requirement. Consider the following elements of the strategy:

- Each month, use at least four sets of tapes: one set for each week—say a full backup on Friday and incremental backups on other days of the week. By the fifth week of the year you will start reusing the tapes from the first week.
- The last full backup of the fourth Friday would be considered the monthly backup. You archive the monthly backups for a year.

- The full backup of the 52nd week will be the yearly backup. You can archive it for a number of years.

As Figure 9-1 illustrates, you will need 18 sets of tapes (4 weekly, 13 monthly, and 1 yearly) for the year for this scheme. In the figure, we refer to a period of four weeks as a *monthlet*, for convenience.

Once you have a backup strategy in place, you need to figure out how to use the commands for performing backups.

Performing Backups of an Unmounted File System

To perform full and incremental backups, Solaris offers the `ufsdump` command, which should be used only on the unmounted or read-only mounted file systems.

FIGURE 9-1

A yearly backup strategy to meet the requirement of being able to restore files from the past four weeks

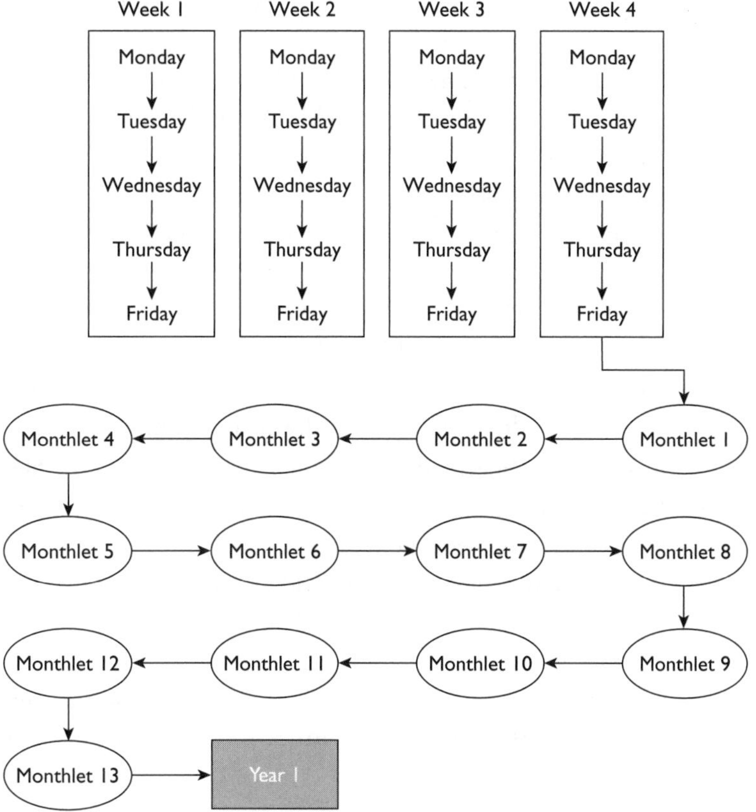

If you attempt to dump a mounted read-write file system, it may cause system disruption or inability to restore the backed up files.

Using the `ufsdump` Command

The `ufsdump` command has the following syntax:

```
ufsdump [<options>] [<arguments>] <files>
```

An option is a one-character single string. An argument may be a list of multiple strings whose association with the option is determined by order. The `<files>` argument is mandatory and must appear last in the command. It is used to specify a whole file system or files within a file system that will be copied to a magnetic tape, a diskette, or a disk file. Some common options and arguments for the `ufsdump` command are listed here:

- **`0-9.`** Specify the backup (dump) level. 0 for a full backup, 1–9 for incremental backups.
- **`a <archiveFile>.`** Store a table of contents for the backup in a file specified by `<archiveFile>`. This file will be used by the `ufsrestore` command to determine whether a file is there for a restore.
- **`D.`** Dump to a diskette.
- **`f <dumpFile>.`** Specify the device to which the files will be dumped. The default value is the first tape drive: `/dev/rmt/0`. Possible values for `<dumpFile>` are a local tape drive or disk drive, a remote tape drive or disk drive, or—for dumping to standard output.
- **`n.`** Notify all operators in the sys group in case the `ufsdump` needs attention.
- **`o.`** Take the drive offline when the backup completes.
- **`s <size>.`** Specify the size of the volume to which the files are being copied.
- **`S.`** Estimate the amount of space in bytes needed to perform a backup without actually performing the backup.
- **`u.`** Update the dump record by adding an entry to the `/etc/dumpdates` file. The entry contains information about when a file system was backed up and at which dump level.
- **`v.`** Verify the content on the backup media against the source file after a tape (or a disk) has been written. Can't be used when the dump is done to the standard output.

- **w.** Warn by listing the file systems that have not been backed up within a day. This information is retrieved from the /etc/dumpdates and /etc/vfstab files. When this option is specified, all other options are ignored and the command exits immediately after producing the list.

- **W.** Warn by highlighting all the file systems that have not been backed up within a day, but produce a list of all the file systems in the /etc/dumpdates file.

on the job ***The ufsdump command can detect the end of media. Therefore, the s <size> option is not required.***

Remember the following about the ufsdump command:

- It backs up data only from the raw disk slice.
- If the file system is still active during copying, any data in memory buffers will not be copied.
- The backup performed by the ufsdump command does not include the free blocks—that is, the blocks that are not being used as storage blocks, inodes, or indirect address nodes.
- The ufsdump command does not make an image of the disk slice.
- If symbolic links on the slice that's being backed up point to files on other slices, only the links are copied.

Make sure you understand the effects of various options that can be issued with the ufsdump command.

The ufsdump command has built-in support for incremental backups.

Using the Dump Levels in the ufsdump Command

You can use the ufsdump command to make full backups or incremental backups. The support for this characteristic is built into the command though dump levels. By specifying dump level 0, you tell the command to make a full backup. Dump levels 1 to 9 are used for backing up the files that have changed since the last backup was performed. Which backup? It's the last lower-level backup. For example, if you backed up on Monday by using dump level 1, on Tuesday using dump level 3, and on

Wednesday using dump level 2, then the command entered on Wednesday will copy the files that have been changed since Monday. As you can see, the dump levels give you lots of freedom to design a backup scheme according to your need. Two such schemes are presented, as examples, in Table 9-4.

The scheme presented in the first row of the table will make a full backup on each Sunday, and on any other day of the week it will back up only the files that have changed since the backup made on the previous day. The scheme presented in the second row will make a full backup on each Sunday, and on any other day of the week it will back up the files that have changed since the last full backup was made. This scheme is called differential backup. Let's assume it takes one tape to make a backup on each day, and further assume that the system crashes on Friday morning before the Friday backup. How many tapes will you need to restore the data? You will need five tapes if you were using the incremental scheme and only two tapes (Sunday and Thursday) if you were using the differential scheme. Accordingly, it takes more effort to back up using a differential scheme and less effort in restoring, as compared to an incremental scheme.

You may need to keep the backup information so that you could use it later to restore the data. The backup information can be automatically maintained by using the `/etc/dumpdates` file.

Purpose of the `dumpdates` File

The `ufsdump` command issued with the `-u` option maintains the `/etc/dumpdates` file. The command updates the `/etc/dumpdates` file by adding an entry into it that contains the following information:

- The file system backed up

TABLE 9-4 Examples of incremental and differential backups

Day	Sunday	Monday	Tuesday	Wednesday	Thursday	Friday	Saturday
Dump level: incremental backup	0	1	2	3	4	5	6
Dump level: differential backup	0	9	9	9	9	9	9

- Dump level of the backup
- The day, date, time, and year of the backup

So, the entries in an `/etc/dumpdates` file will look like the following:

```
/dev/rdsk/c0t0d0s3 0 TUE APR 12 15:25:13 2005
/dev/rdsk/c0t0d0s5 0 MON APR 18 14:12:30 2005
```

When you perform an incremental backup, the `ufsdump` utility does the following:

1. Checks the `/etc/dumpdates` file to find the date of the most recent backup of the next lower dump level.
2. Copies to the backup media all the files that were modified since the date of the lower-level backup.
3. After the backup is complete, a new information line, which describes the backup you just completed, replaces the information line for the previous backup at that level.

You can also take a look at the `/etc/dumpdates` file to verify that backups are being performed as scheduled. If a backup has not completed—for example, due to an equipment failure—the backup is not recorded in the `dumpdates` file. You may also need information from the `dumpdates` file for restoring the data. For example, assume you need to restore an entire disk. To determine which tapes you need to restore, you would check the `dumpdates` file for a list of the most recent backup dates and levels of backups.

on the job

Note that the `/etc/dumpdates` file can be edited, because it is a text file. However, you should not edit it under normal circumstances, because inaccurate information or accidental deletion or change of information can only cause confusion when you want to find the correct tapes to use for restoration.

When you need to back up complete file systems to a backup device and you want to use the combination of full backups and incremental backups, use the `ufsdump` command. There are many other kinds of backups that you may be interested in. For example, you might just want to copy or move individual files or groups of files to another directory, to an archive file, or to another disk or tape. In that case, you can use an appropriate command from a set of commands discussed in the following section.

Using Other Backup Utilities

You can use the cpio, pax, and tar commands to copy files and file systems to tapes, and you can use the dd command to copy files and file systems between disks. The choice of the command depends on the flexibility and precision required for the copy. You do not need to format or make a file system on tapes before you use any of these commands, because all three commands use the raw device.

The cpio Command

You can use the cpio (copy in and out) command to transfer individual files or groups of files from one file system to another. The syntax for this command is shown here:

```
cpio <mode> [<options>]
```

The <mode> specifies the mode in which the command will run, and <options> specify the options. There are three possible modes in which the cpio command can be used:

- **-i.** This specifies the copy-in mode used to read an archive. It reads an archive from the standard input, conditionally extracts the files contained in it, and places them into the current directory tree according to the options.
- **-o.** This specifies the copy-out mode, which is used to create an archive. It reads a list of file path names from the standard input and copies those files to the standard output in the form of a cpio archive according to the options.
- **-p.** This specifies the pass mode used to copy the content of one directory to another. It reads a list of file path names from the standard input and copies those files into the specified destination directory tree according to the options.

The options for the cpio command are described in Table 9-5.

For example, consider a combination of the find command and the cpio command:

```
find . -print -depth | cpio -pdm /tmp/data1
```

TABLE 9-5

Options for the cpio command

Option	Description
-a	Resets access times on files after they have been copied. Access times on links cannot be reset.
-A	Appends files to an existing archive; valid only with -o mode.
-c	Read or write header information in ASCII text format.
-d	Creates directories as needed.
-m	Retains previous file modification times.
-t	Prints a table of content in the input; no files are extracted.
-v	Verbose. Prints a list of file names.

In this example, the `find` command pipes the file names to the `cpio` command, which copies those files to the directory `/tmp/data1`. This was an example of a pass mode. Consider an example of `cpi` command used in the `-o` mode:

```
ls | cpio -oc > /tmp/testfile.backup
```

It takes all the files piped to it by the `ls` command, groups them together, and sends them to a single file `/tmp/testfile.backup`. The following example demonstrates the `cpio` command in the `-i` mode:

```
cat /tmp/testfile.backup | cpio -icd "notes/pol*" "notes/sen*"
```

This command takes the output file of the previous command and extracts only those files that match the pattern `notes/pol*` or `notes/sen*`. The directories will be created as needed because of the `-d` option.

The tar Command

You can use the `tar` command to archive files to a single file in the tape archive (tar) format, or extract files from a tar file. This is a very popular archiving and backup command, as most of the software for UNIX platforms is distributed in the `tar` format. The syntax for the `tar` command is shown here:

```
tar <options> <tarfileName> <filesToBackup>
```

The options are listed here:

- **c.** Create the tar file with the name specified by `<tarfileName>`.
- **f.** Use the file name or device name specified by `<tarfileName>` as a name of the archive.
- **t.** List the names of files in the archive.
- **u.** The files are added only if they do not already exist in the archive or if they have been modified since they were archived to that tar file last.
- **v.** Verbose.
- **x.** Extract the files from the archive file with the name specified by `<terfileName>`.

As an example, the following command will copy the `/home/jkerry` directory to the tape device `/dev/rmt/0`:

```
tar cvf /dev/rmt/0 /home/jkerry
```

You can extract the files from the tape by issuing the following command:

```
tar xvf /dev/rmt/0
```

As the following command shows, you can also create the archive file on the disk:

```
tar cvf jkerry.tar /home/jkerry
```

You can extract the files from the tar file as follows:

```
tar xvf jkerry.tar
```

While using the `tar` command, remember the following:

- Archiving files to a tape with the `-c` option destroys any files already on the tape at or beyond the current tape position.
- You can use the substitution wildcards (`?` and `*`) to specify the names of the files to be archived. For example, *.doc means copy all files with the .doc extension.
- You cannot use substitution wildcards in the file names to specify which files to extract from a tar file.

- The tar command does not transport user permissions and timestamps along with the files.

There is another command you can use to handle the archive files: the pax command.

The pax Command

You can use the pax (portable archive interchange) to perform the following tasks: read and write the members of an archive file, make a list of the members of an archive file, and copy directory hierarchies. It supports multiple archive formats such as cpio and extended tar. The syntax for the pax command is shown here:

```
pax [<mode>] [<options>]
```

The <mode> specifies the mode in which the pax command operates. The four available modes are described here:

- **-r.** Read mode when -r is specified and -w is not. Read an archive file from the standard input and extract the files with the path names that match specified patterns.
- **-w.** Write mode when -w is specified, and -r is not. Write the specified files into the standard output in a specified archive format. If no file operands are specified, a list of files (one per line) to archive are read from the standard input.
- **-rw.** Copy mode when both r and w are specified. Copy the specified files to the destination directory. If no file operands are specified, a list of files (one per line) to archive are read from the standard input.
- **<mode> not specified.** List mode when neither -r and nor -w is specified. Write to the standard output the names of members of an archive file that matches the patterns specified in the standard input.

Some common options for the pax command are described in Table 9-6.

For example, the following command copies the contents of the current directory into a tape device /dev/rmt/0:

```
pax -w -f /dev/rmt/0
```

TABLE 9-6 Options for the pax command

Option	Description
-a	Append the files to an existing archive.
-b <blockSize>	Specify block size.
-f <archive>	Specify the path name of the input or output archive.
-I	Rename the archive members in an archive.
-k	Do not overwrite the existing files.
-v	Verbose mode.
-x <format>	Specify the archive format. Possible values of <format> are pax, cpio, ustar, and xustar.

As another example, the following command copies the directory subtree with the top directory specified by <sourcedir> to the directory specified by <destdir>:

```
pax -rw <sourcedir> <destdir>
```

The pax archive can span across multiple volumes, and it has better portability than the tar and cpio commands across POSIX-compliant systems. The cpio, pax, and tar commands are compared in Table 9-7.

TABLE 9-7 Comparison of cpio, pax, and tar commands

Command	Task	Advantage	Disadvantage
cpio	Copy files or file systems that require multiple tape volumes.	Copies data to tape more efficiently than the tar command, and skips over any bad spots in the tape when restoring.	More complicated command syntax as compared with the tar and pax commands.
pax	Copy files or file systems that require multiple tape volumes.	Offers better portability for POSIX-compliant systems as compared with the tar and cpio commands.	Not aware of file system boundaries; maximum limit of 255 characters on the path name.
tar	Copy files and subtrees to a single tape.	Widely used on most flavors of UNIX OS and freely available in the public domain.	Not aware of file system boundaries; maximum limit of 255 characters on the path name; cannot be used to create multiple tape volumes.

If you simply want to clone a disk, the dd is the command to use.

The dd Command

The dd command is used to copy files or file systems between disks. In addition, by using this command you can make a copy of a complete file system from the hard disk to a tape. Note that the dd command makes a literal block-level copy of a complete UFS file system to another file system or to a tape.

Because the dd command copies at block level, you should not use it with variable-length tape drives without first specifying an appropriate block size.

The syntax for the dd command is shown here:

```
dd if=<inputFile> of=<outputFile> [<options>]
```

`<inputFile>` specifies the path for the input, and `<outputFile>` specifies the path for the output. The default values for the if and of arguments are standard input and standard output, respectively. Of course, you can specify appropriate input and output devices. For example, to make a literal copy of a file system on a diskette to a file in the /tmp directory, you can issue the following command:

```
dd if=/floppy/floppy0 of=/tmp/floppydump.file
```

As another example, the following command will copy the entire content of one hard disk to another hard disk:

```
dd if=/dev/rdsk/c0t0d0s2 of=/dev/rdsk/c0t1d0s2 bs=128k
```

The option bs=128k specifies the block size. The source disk and the destination disk must have the same geometry.

The cpio archive may span across multiple volumes. The cpio archive created using one UNIX system can be read by many other UNIX systems. Here is a summary of when to use these various commands:

- Use cpio, or pax, or tar to transport file systems from one disk to another.
- Use dd to clone a disk.
- Use tar to copy files to a diskette, or to make an archive of files for distribution on the Internet.
- Use ufsdump to perform full and incremental backups.

TABLE 9-8

Comparison of various backup commands

Command	Aware of File System Boundaries?	Supports Multiple Volume Backups?
`cpio`	No	Yes
`dd`	Yes	No
`pax`	Yes	Yes
`tar`	No	No
`ufsdump`	Yes	Yes

Another criterion to distinguish one backup command from another is whether the command is aware of the file system boundaries and whether it supports multiple volumes. You can check these properties from the information supplied in Table 9-8.

You have learned that you cannot use the `ufsdump` command for making backups of mounted file systems that are not in single-user mode. However, there will be situations in which you do want to make a backup of a file system while it is in use (an active file system). Next, we explore how to accomplish this.

CERTIFICATION OBJECTIVE 9.02

Performing Backup of a Mounted File System

Exam Objective 6.3: *Backup a mounted file system by creating a UFS snapshot and performing a backup of the snapshot file.*

As you already know, you cannot use the `ufsdump` command to make a backup of an active file system. However, if for some reason you do want to make a backup of an active file system, the first step is to take a snapshot of the system. A UFS snapshot is a temporary image of a UFS file system made for backup purpose. Solaris offers the `fssnap` command to create a read-only snapshot of a file system. The advantage of this command, of course, is that it can be used while the system is in multiuser mode and the file system is mounted: the disadvantage is that it may impede system performance when the snapshot is being taken.

The `fssnap` command creates a virtual device, and you can use the `tar` or `cpio` command to back up the snapshot to a storage device such as a tape. The syntax of the `fssnap` command for taking the snapshot of a file system is:

```
fssnap [-F <fileSystem>] [-V] -o backing-store=<destPath>,
[<specificOptions>] <mountPoint>
```

exam watch

The `fssnap` command can be used when the system is in multiuser mode and the file system is mounted. This command does not back up data to an external device, but creates a virtual device on the disk that can later be backed up to an external device by using commands such as `ufsdump`, `tar`, or `cpio`.

The `<mountPoint>` specifies the directory name to which the file system (that is to be snapshot) is mounted. You must also specify the path for the backing-store file, `<destPath>`. The backing-store file(s) are used by the snapshot subsystem to save the old file system data before it is overwritten. The name specified by `<destPath>` must not match an existing file name. If `<destPath>` specifies the name of an existing directory, the backing-store file will be created in that directory and a file name will be provided automatically. You can use the abbreviation `bs` for the backing-store option.

The `<specificOptions>`, which are not required, are described here:

- **`unlink`.** Unlink the backing-store file when the snapshot is created.
- **`chunksize=<n>`.** Specify the granularity of the data that will be sent to the backing file in units of kilobytes (k), megabytes (m), or gigabytes (g). For example, the value of `<n>` would be 32k to specify a granularity of 32 kilobytes.
- **`maxsize=<n>`.** Specify the allowed maximum value for the sum of sizes of all the backing-store files. The units for `<n>` are the same as in the `chunksize` option. When the sum of sizes of the backing-store files exceed the size specified by maxsize, the snapshot is automatically deleted.
- **`raw`.** Display to standard output the raw device name (instead of block device name) when a snapshot is created. The default is the block device name.

on the job

When you use the `unlink` option in creating a snapshot, the backing-store file will not be visible to you. That might make administration difficult. However, the file will be deleted automatically when the snapshot is deleted.

Remember that the backing-store files are the bitmap files that contain the copies of pre-snapshot data that has been modified since the snapshot was taken. Note the following about the backing-store files:

- The destination of the backing-store files must have enough free space to hold the file system data.
- The location for the backing-store files must be different from the file system that is being captured in the snapshot.
- The size of the backing-store files depends on the amount of activity on the file system.
- The backing-store files can reside on any type of file system, including another UFS file system or a file system mounted by NFS.
- In the `fssnap` command you may specify the name of a backing-store file. The `fssnap` utility automatically creates additional backing-store files on an as-needed basis after the first backing-store file. For example, multiple backing-store files are created when you create a snapshot of a UFS file system that is larger than 512GB.
- The additional backing-store files that will be automatically created will have the same name as the original file with suffixes of .2, .3, and so on.

Now that you know how the `fssnap` command works, here are some practical scenarios and their solutions related to using this command.

SCENARIO & SOLUTION	
How would you issue the `fssnap` command to take a snapshot of a UFS file system mounted to the directory `/export/home`? The backing-store files should be created in the `/var/tmp` directory.	`fssnap -F ufs -o backing-store=/var /tmp/export/home`
How will the command change if you want the backing-store files deleted automatically when the snapshot is deleted?	`fssnap -F ufs -o backing-store=/var /tmp,` `unlink /export/home`
How can you use the `ufsdump` command to back up the file system `/export/home` without unmounting it?	`ufsdump 0uf /dev/rmt/0 'fssnap -F ufs -o backing-stores=/var/tmp,` `raw /export/home'`

You make backups of file systems so that they can be restored to recover lost data in case of a disk failure or a disaster such as fire.

CERTIFICATION OBJECTIVE 9.03

Restoring File System Backups

Exam Objective 6.2: *Perform Solaris 10 OS file system restores using the appropriate commands, including restoring a regular file system, the /usr file system, the /(root) file system, and performing interactive and incremental restores for SPARC, x64, and x86 based systems.*

You can restore files by using various methods depending on the nature of the storage task at hand. For example, if you know which files or file systems you want to restore, you can restore them non-interactively (that is, by issuing the restoration command in non-interactive mode). On the other hand, if you do not know which files you want to restore and hence want to browse the content on the backup media, you will need to use the restoration command in interactive mode.

Before Restoring Backups

There are a few things you need to be aware of before you start restoring the backups. First, you should know that when you back up files, they are saved relative to the file system to which they belong. For example, consider the `/export` file system. The `/export/gov/senate` directory on the disk would be saved to the tape as `./gov/senate.` In other words, the path to the `jkerry` file in the `senate` directory on the tape would be: `./gov/senate/jkerry.`

Second, when you are restoring files, you should always be mindful of the possibility of overwriting the newer versions of files on disk thereby running into conflict with other users. To avoid such risks, it is a good idea to restore to a temporary location, say `/var/tmp`; after some verifications you can move files, a directory, or a subtree of directories from there to the actual location by using the `mv` command.

Third, it can happen because of a faulty disk drive or an accident, that you lose the most crucial file systems: `root (/)`, or `/usr`, or both. In that case, remember that restoring the `root (/)` or `/usr` file systems involves booting the system from a CD or the network.

When you want to restore files to a temporary location before moving them to their actual location, do not use the /`tmp` directory for this purpose. Recall that the /`tmp` directory is usually mounted as a TMPFS file system, which does not support attributes of a UFS file system such as ACLs.

You can use the `ufsrestore` command to restore your backups, which offers you both restoration methods: non-interactive, and interactive.

Using the `ufsrestore` Command

The `ufsrestore` command can be used to restore an individual file or a complete file system from a removable medium to a directory. This command has the following syntax:

```
ufsrestore <options> [<arguments>] [<filesToRestore>]
```

You can use `<options>` to specify one and only one of the following options:

- **`-i`.** Interactive. Specify to use the `ufsrestore` command in interactive mode.
- **`-r`.** Recursive. Restore a file system recursively.
- **`-R`.** Resume restoration (with `-r`) that was previously interrupted. This will prompt for the volume from which to resume.
- **`-t`.** Table of contents. List file names in the storage device, tape, or archive file.
- **`-x`.** Extract the files in non-interactive mode and restore them relative to the file system from which they were backed up.

The `ufsrestore` command used with the `-x` option will overwrite the existing files. If the file being overwritten is a currently running executable, think of the dire consequences it can have.

Note the following when you are using the -x option:

- The -x option is used to restore the partial file systems by using the <filesToRestore> argument.
- If <filesToRestore> specifies a directory name, the directory is extracted recursively.
- If you do not specify the value of <filesToRestore> or specify a dot (.) for it, the root directory is used by default—that is, the entire tape will be extracted.

The <arguments> in the ufsrestore command modify the effect of the option. For example, you can use the -f <dumpFile> argument to specify a source device for a restore.

Now that you know how the ufsrestore command works, here are some practical scenarios and their solutions related to using this command.

SCENARIO & SOLUTION	
How would you issue the ufsrestore command to display the content of an archive file myArchive.dump?	ufsrestore -tf myArchive.dump
How would you issue the ufsrestore command to display the content of a tape device /dev/rmt/0?	ufsrestore -tf /dev/rmt/0
How would you issue the ufsrestore command to extract all the files (the directory tree) on the tape drive /dev/rmt/0 and restore them to the current working directory?	ufsrestore -xf /dev/rmt/0

If you are restoring the whole file system and it was backed up by using incremental backups, you will need to understand the basic concept of incremental backups and how they are represented by dump levels. (We covered this issue in a previous section.) In this case, always begin restoring from the lowest dump level and work your way to the highest dump level tapes. If you are restoring only a partial file system, select the appropriate dump level tape and restore it.

Remember also that the ufsrestore command creates the restoresymtable file (in the directory in which the command was issued), which it uses to checkpoint the restore. The ufsretore utility uses it to store and retrieve information in order to coordinate the restoration of incremental backups on top of a full backup. This file is created automatically but is not deleted. You have to delete it manually after the restore is complete.

You can also use the ufsrestore command in interactive mode. For example, to restore files from the device /dev/rmt/0 to the current directory, issue the following command:

```
ufsrestore -if /dev/rmt/0
```

This will display the following prompt:

```
ufsrestore >>
```

This prompt accepts the commands listed in Table 9-9.

TABLE 9-9 Commands available for using the ufsrestore command in interactive mode

Command	Description
add <file>	Adds a file (or directory) specified by <file> to the list of files marked for extraction.
cd <directory>	Moves to the directory specified by <directory> in the backup directory hierarchy.
delete <file>	Unmarks a file (or directory) specified by <file> from the list of files to be extracted.
extract	Extracts all marked files. The ufsrestore command will prompt you for the volume number to be used.
help ?	Displays a list of available commands.
ls [<directory>]	Lists the contents of the current directory or the directory specified by <directory>. Entries marked for extraction are prefixed with a *.
marked <directoryName>	Same as ls except that only files marked for extraction are listed.
pwd	Displays the working directory in the backup directory hierarchy.
quit	Exit the ufsrestore utility.
verbose	Displays information about the files when they are extracted.

EXERCISE 9-1

Restoring the `root (/)` and `/usr` File Systems

In this exercise, you will learn how to restore `root (/)` and `/usr` file systems to the Solaris systems running on SPARC or x86.

1. Assume the role of a superuser.
2. Presumably you lost these file systems because the disk failed, and we assume you booted the system from a CD or from the network. In that case, perform the following steps:
   a. Add a new system disk to the system on which you want to restore the `root (/)` and `/usr` file systems.
   b. Create the file system by issuing the `newfs` command:

      ```
      newfs /dev/rdsk/<partitionName>
      ```

   c. Check the new file system with the fsck command:

      ```
      fsck /dev/rdsk/<partitionName>
      ```

3. Mount the file system on a temporary mount point:

   ```
   mount /dev/dsk/<deviceName> /mnt
   ```

4. Change to the mount directory:

   ```
   cd /mnt
   ```

5. Write-protect the tape so that you cannot accidentally overwrite it. This is an optional but important step.
6. Restore the `root (/)` file system by performing the following steps:
   a. Load the first volume of the appropriate dump level tape into the tape drive. The appropriate dump level is the lowest dump level of all the tapes that need to be restored. Issue the following command:

      ```
      ufsrestore -rf /dev/rmt/<n>
      ```

   b. Remove the tape and repeat step a, if there is more than one tape for the same level.

   c. Repeat steps a and b with the next dump level tapes. Always begin with the lowest dump level, and work your way to the highest dump level tapes.

7. Verify that the file system has been restored:

```
ls
```

8. Delete the `restoresymtable` file which is created and used by the `ufsrestore` utility:

```
rm restoresymtable
```

9. Change to the root directory and unmount the newly restored file system:

```
cd /
umount /mnt
```

10. Check the newly restored file system for consistency:

```
fsck /dev/rdsk/<deviceName>
```

11. If you are restoring the root file system, create the boot blocks as shown:
   a. On a SPARC system, issue the following command:

```
installboot /usr/platform/sun4u/lib/fs/ufs/bootblk /dev/rdsk/<deviceName>
```

   b. On an x86 system, issue the following command:

```
installboot /usr/platform/'uname -i'/lib/fs/ufs/pboot /usr/platform/'uname -i'
/lib/fs/ufs/bootblk /dev/rdsk/<deviceName>
```

12. Remove the last backup tape, and insert a new tape onto which you could write. Make a dump level 0 backup of the newly restored system by issuing the following command:

```
ufsdump 0ucf /dev/rmt/<n> /dev/rdsk/<deviceName>
```

   This step is necessary because `ufsrestore` repositions the files and changes the inode allocations; therefore, the old backup will not truly represent the newly restored file system.

13. Repeat steps 5 to 10 to restore the `/usr` file system.

14. Reboot the system:

```
init 6
```

The system is rebooted, and the restored file systems are ready to be used.

You may be wondering how you can restore a backup that was made from a UFS snapshot that you took by using the `fssnap` command. The next section provides the answer.

CERTIFICATION OBJECTIVE 9.04

Restoring a UFS Snapshot

Exam Objective 6.4: *Restore data from a UFS snapshot and delete the UFS snapshot.*

In a previous section you learned how to create a UFS snapshot and then back up the snapshot. The `fssnap` command creates a virtual device that you can backup by using a suitable backup command, such as `tar`, `cpio`, or even `ufsdump`. The backup created from the virtual device is essentially a backup of the original file system as it existed when the snapshot was taken. For all practical purposes, you can forget that a snapshot was ever taken and look at this backup as though it were any other backup. In other words, you can restore this backup just like any other backup by using the `ufsrestore` command. This relationship between direct backups, backups through snapshots, and restores is illustrated in Figure 9-2.

FIGURE 9-2 Relationship between direct backups, backups through snapshots, and restores

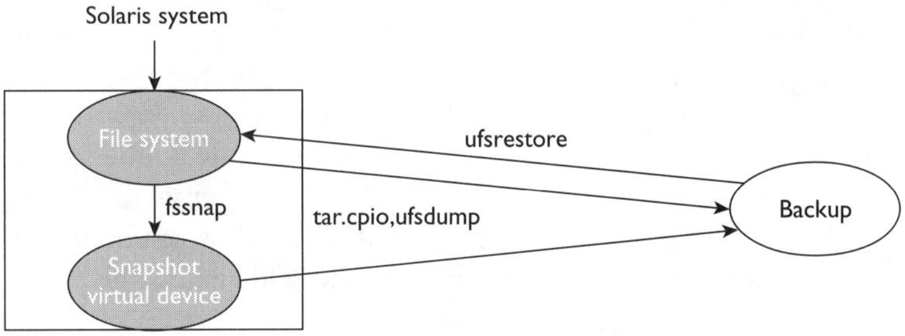

On occasion, you will need to delete a UFS snapshot, and before deleting you may need to get information about the snapshot. You can retrieve the information about the current snapshots on the system by using the fssnap command with the following syntax:

```
fssnap -i [<fileSystem>]
```

The <fileSystem> argument is to specify the file system whose snapshot you want to see. If you do not specify <fileSystem> in your command, information about all of the current UFS snapshots on the system is displayed. For example, the following command will display the information about the snapshot of the /export/home file system:

```
fssnap -i /export/home
```

The output of this command will look like the following:

```
Snapshot number : 1
Block Device : /dev/fssnap/1
Raw Device : /dev/rfssnap/1
Mount point : /export/home
Device state : idle
Backing store path : /var/tmp/home.snap0
Backing store size : 0 KB
Maximum backing store size : Unlimited
Snapshot create time : Fri Apr 15 17:15:25 2005
Copy-on-write granularity : 32 KB
```

You can delete a snapshot by using one of two methods: reboot the system or issue the fssnap command with the following syntax:

```
fssnap -d <fileSystem>
```

When you reboot the system, all snapshots are deleted.

You must specify the value of <fileSystem>, which is the path of the file system whose snapshot is to be removed.

If you used the -o unlink option in the command to create the snapshot, the backing-store file will automatically be deleted once you delete the snapshot. If you did not use the unlink option in the creation of the snapshot, you need to delete the backing-store file manually; you should, because it is occupying disk space.

The three most important takeaways from this chapter are the following:

- You can use the `ufsdump` command to make full and incremental backups of file systems. You use the `ufsdump` command when the file system is unmounted or the Solaris system is in single-user mode.
- If you need to make a backup of an active file system (mounted and in multiuser mode), you can take a snapshot of the system by using the `fssnap` command and then make a backup of the snapshot by using a backup command such as `cpio`, `tar`, or `ufsdump`.
- You can restore a backup by using the `ufsrestore` command.

CERTIFICATION SUMMARY

As a system administrator, you will be performing regularly scheduled backups as a protection against data loss. If you want to make sure that all the files in the system are backed up correctly, use the `ufsdump` command after unmounting the file system or after putting the Solaris system into single-user mode. The `ufsdump` command has a built-in capability for full and incremental backups. The `ufsdump` command creates the `/etc/dumpdates` file, which it uses to store and retrieve information to coordinate incremental backups on top of a full backup.

You cannot use the `ufsdump` command to back up an active file system—that is, a file system that is mounted and is in multiuser mode. However, if you do want to make a backup of an active file system, you can take a snapshot of the file system by using the `fssnap` command and then back up the snapshot by using an appropriate backup command, such as `ufsdump`, `tar`, or `cpio`. There are other backup commands available to meet varying needs. For example, you can use the `cpio` command to copy a file system from one disk to another, the `dd` command to clone an entire disk, and the `tar` command to package files (or directory subtrees) and transport them across UNIX systems.

You can use the `ufsrestore` command to restore an individual file or a complete file system from removable media to a directory. If you want to choose the files and directories from the backup file system that you want to restore, it's better to use the command interactively by specifying the `-i` option. If you are restoring the entire file system and it was backed up by using incremental backups, you will need to understand the basic concept of incremental backups and how they are represented by dump levels. You can restore the backup file system from a UFS snapshot the way you would restore any other backup.

INSIDE THE EXAM

Comprehend

- To make sure the entire data is backed up, you should put the system into a single-user mode or unmount the file system before backing up a file system by using the `ufsdump` command.
- The `fssnap` command does not back up the file system to an external device; it creates a snapshot on the disk.
- When you use the `fssnap` command with the unlink option, the backing-store file will not be visible to you, but it will be automatically deleted when the snapshot is deleted.

Look Out

- The destination for the backing-store files in the `fssnap` command must be on a file system different from the file system that is being captured in the snapshot.
- There are two ways of deleting a UFS snapshot: reboot the system or use the `fssnap -d` command.
- Do not use the `/tmp` directory as a temporary location for restoring a UFS file system, because `/tmp` is not usually mounted as a UFS file system.

Memorize

- The `ufsdump` command can be used only on unmounted or read-only mounted file systems. If you want to take the snapshot of an active file system, use the `fssnap` command, instead.
- The restoresymtable file is created and used by the `ufsrestore` utility to checkpoint the restoration. The `/etc/dumpdates` file is created by the `ufsdump` command, and backing-store file is created by the `fssnap` command.
- The `ufsrestore` command used with the `-x` option overwrites the existing files.
- Typical use of backup commands: `cpio` to copy a file system from one disk to another, `dd` to clone an entire disk, `tar` to package files (or directory subtrees) and transport them across UNIX systems, and `ufsdump` to perform full and incremental backups.

TWO-MINUTE DRILL

Performing Scheduled Backups of an Unmounted File System

- The `ufsdump` command supports full and incremental backups.
- You can store the backup information (the dump level and the dump date) for a successfully backed up file system in the `/etc/dumpdates` file by using the `-u` option with the `ufsdump` command.
- You can also issue the `ufsdump` command to get information rather than actually performing a backup. For example, the command with the `S` option estimates the amount of space in bytes needed to perform a backup.
- The `ufsdump` command is used to back up whole file systems. You can use the `cpio`, `pax`, and `tar` commands to copy individual files (and file systems) to tapes.
- You can use the `dd` command to copy files and file systems between disks.

Performing Backups of a Mounted File System

- You can take a snapshot of a mounted file system by using the `fssnap` command and then back up the snapshot onto an external device by using commands such as `tar`, `cpio`, or `ufsdump`.
- The backing-store file destination must be on a file system separate from the file system that is being captured in the snapshot.

Restoring File System Backups

- You can use the `ufsrestore` command to restore individual files or file systems.
- The backup from a UFS snapshot can be restored just like any other backup by using the `ufsrestore` command.
- The `ufsrestore` command can be used in the interactive mode by specifying the `-i` option.
- You can delete UFS snapshots either by using the `fssnap -d` command or by rebooting the system. If you did not unlink the backing-store file at the time of taking the snapshot, you need to delete the backing-store file manually.

SELF TEST

The following questions will help you measure your understanding of the material presented in this chapter. Read all the choices carefully because there might be more than one correct answer. Choose all correct answers for each question.

1. Which of the following commands would you issue to list the contents of a `tar` file specified by the argument `<tarFile>`?

   A. `tar cvf <tarFile>`

   B. `tar uvf <tarFile>`

   C. `tar xvf <tarFile>`

   D. `tar tvf <tarFile>`

2. Which of the following commands has a built-in capability to perform incremental backups?

   A. `ufsdump`

   B. `tar`

   C. `cpio`

   D. `pax`

   E. `dd`

3. Suppose your backup requires multiple tape volumes. Which of the following commands can you use?

   A. `cpio`

   B. `tar`

   C. `ufsdump`

   D. `pax`

4. Suppose while issuing the `ufsdump` command you do not use the `f` option to specify the tape drive to which the files will be dumped. Which tape device will the `ufsdump` utility look for, by default?

   A. `/dev/rmt/1`

   B. `/dev/rmt/0`

   C. `/dev/mt/0`

   D. `dev/tape/0`

5. Assume you have the following weekly backup schedule by using the `ufsdump` command:

   - Monday—dump level 1—tape1
   - Tuesday—dump level 2—tape2
   - Wednesday—dump level 3—tape3
   - Thursday—dump level 4—tape4
   - Friday—dump level 0—tape0

   Your system crashed on a Wednesday afternoon before starting the Wednesday backup. Which set of tapes would you use to restore the data as fully as possible?

   A. tape0, tape1, tape2, tape3, and tape4

   B. tape0, tape1, tape2, and tape3

   C. tape0, tape1, and tape2

   D. tape0

6. Assume you have the following weekly backup schedule by using the `ufsdump` command:

   - Monday—dump level 1—tape1
   - Tuesday—dump level 1—tape2
   - Wednesday—dump level 1—tape3
   - Thursday—dump level 1—tape4
   - Friday—dump level 0—tape0

   Your system crashed on a Thursday afternoon before starting the Thursday backup. Which set of tapes will you use in order to restore the data as fully as possible?

   A. tape0, tape1, tape2, and tape3

   B. tape0, tape1, and tape2

   C. tape0, and tape3

   D. tape0

7. You want to make a backup of a file system without putting the system into single-user mode and unmounting the file system. Which of the following options allows you to do that?

   A. Use the `ufsdump` command.

   B. First take a snapshot with `fssnap` and then backup the snapshot with `ufsdump` command.

C. First take a snapshot with the `fssnap` command and then backup the snapshot with the `cpio` command.

D. First take a snapshot with `fssnapshot` command and then backup the snapshot with `ufsdump` command.

E. Use the `fssnap` command to take the snapshot and perform the backup.

8. Which of the following files can the `ufsdump` command use to store or retrieve information?

   A. `/etc/dumpdates`

   B. `/etc/vfstab`

   C. `/etc/dumplog`

   D. `/etc/dumpinfo`

9. Which of the following are the necessary steps in restoring the root file system when your disk crashed and you added a new disk to the system?

   A. Boot the system from a CD or the network.

   B. Issue the `installboot` command.

   C. Use the `fsck` command.

   D. Use the `init 6` command.

10. Which of the following files are created by the `ufsrestore` command?

    A. `ufsrestore.log`

    B. `ufssymtable`

    C. `restoresymtable`

    D. `dumpdates`

11. You are a system administrator for a marketing firm that is very busy during the day and is closed on Sundays. Which of the following is an appropriate backup strategy?

    A. Full system backup each Sunday

    B. Full system backup on the last Sunday of each month and incremental backup on all other Sundays of the month.

    C. Full system backup daily at 9:00 A.M.

    D. Full system backup every Sunday and nightly incremental backups from Monday to Saturday.

SELF TEST ANSWERS

1. ☑ **D**. The `t` option will display the names of the files in the archive.
☒ **A** is incorrect because the `c` option creates the archive file, and **B** is incorrect because the `u` option is used to add the files to the archive. **C** is incorrect because the `x` option is used to extract the files from the archive.

2. ☑ **A**. The `ufsdump` command has dump levels that you can use to make incremental backups.
☒ **B**, **C**, **D**, and **E** are incorrect because the `tar`, `cpio`, `pax`, and `dd` commands all lack a built-in mechanism for incremental backups.

3. ☑ **A**, **C**, and **D**. The `cpio`, `pax`, and `ufsdump` commands support multiple tape volumes.
☒ **B** is incorrect because the `tar` command does not support multiple tape volumes and can be used to back up files and subtrees to a single tape.

4. ☑ **B**. The default tape drive for the `ufsdump` command is the first tape device: `/dev/rmt/0`.
☒ **A** is incorrect because the first tape device is `/dev/rmt/0`, not `/dev/rmt/1`. **C** is incorrect because `/dev/mt/0` is not the default backup device, and **D** is incorrect because there is no such device as `/dev/tape/0`.

5. ☑ **C**. You will need the last full backup, which is on tape0, along with all the files that have changed since then and were backed up, which are on tape1 and tape2.
☒ **A** and **B** are incorrect because tape3 and tape4 are from the previous week, before the last backup was taken. **D** is incorrect because some files may have changed after the last backup, and some of those files would be on tape1 and tape2.

6. ☑ **C**. You will need the last full backup which is on tape0 along with all the files that have changed since then and were backed up, which will be on tape3.
☒ **A** and **B** are incorrect because you do not need tape1 and tape 2; this is a differential backup. **D** is incorrect because some files may have changed and would have been backed up after the last backup; and all of those files would be on tape3.

7. ☑ **B** and **C**. First you make a snapshot of the file system, and then you can make a backup of the snapshot by using a suitable command, such as `tar`, `cpio`, or `ufsdump`.
☒ **A** is incorrect because to back up an active file system by using `ufsdump`, you need to unmount the file system. **D** is incorrect because there is no such command as `ufssnapshot`, and **E** is incorrect because the `fssnap` command takes the snapshot and stores it on the same disk.

8. ☑ **A** and **B**. The `ufsdump` command used with the `u` option updates the dump record by adding an entry to the `/etc/dumpdates` file, and the `ufsdump` command used with the `w` option warns by listing the file systems that have not been backed up within a day. This information is retrieved from the `/etc/dumpdates` and `/etc/vfstab` files.
   ☒ **C** and **D** are incorrect because there are no such files as `dumplog` or `dumpinfo`.

9. ☑ **A**, **B**, **C**, and **D**. Because your disk does not have the root file system, you cannot boot from the disk; you must boot from a CD or the network. You use the `installboot` command to install the boot blocks, and you issue the `fsck` command to check the consistency of the file system. You use the `init 6` command to reboot the system from the disk.

10. ☑ **C**. The `restoresymtable` file is created and used by the `ufsrestore` command to checkpoint the restore.
    ☒ **A** and **B** are incorrect because there are no files named `ufsrestore.log` and ufssymtable created by the `ufsrestore` command. **D** is incorrect because the `dumpdates` file is maintained by the `ufsdump` command and not by `ufsrestore`.

11. ☑ **D**. The full backup on Sunday would allow you to reuse the last week's media for the next week's incremental backups. The nightly incremental backups would not interrupt the busy days and would take less time than full backups.
    ☒ **A** and **B** are incorrect because they would not provide protection against loss of data during weekdays. **C** is incorrect because it would disrupt the busy days of the firm, as the system would be down every morning for backup.

Part II

Sun Certified System Administrator Examination for Solaris 10 Study Guide, Exam CX-310-202

CHAPTERS

10 Working with the Solaris Network Environment

CERTIFICATION OBJECTIVES

10.01	Understanding Network Fundamentals	✓	Two-Minute Drill
10.02	Working with Network Services	Q&A	Self Test

We are living in the dawn of the information age brought about by the Internet. Computing and communication technologies have been developing separately for decades. The unification of the two has started the information revolution, and at the center of this is the Internet: the global robust communication system being used by hundreds of millions of people around the world. Communication means exchanging data, and data lives on file systems (including databases) supported by operating systems such as Solaris. This is how important it is for a system administrator to learn how the Internet, or TCP/IP networking, works.

In order to make this chapter self contained we have covered the basic terms and concepts in networking that are required to enable you to start managing the Solaris networking environment. Your Solaris machine, like any other machine, is connected to the network through a network interface, which would need to be configured. Why does a machine become a part of the network (by using interfaces)? Well, to share resources, and the resources are offered in the form of services.

The core question in this chapter is: how do you get started with the Solaris networking environment? In search of an answer, we will explore three thought streams: understanding network fundamentals, managing network interfaces, and managing network services.

CERTIFICATION OBJECTIVE 10.01

Understanding Network Fundamentals

Exam Objective 1.1: *Control and monitor network interfaces including MAC addresses, IP addresses, network packets, and configure the IPv4 interfaces at boot time.*

To start managing the Solaris network environment, you need to understand the basic terms and concepts in networking. A computer network is a group of computers connected together to share resources such as printers and data. Remember, communication also involves the exchange of data. Under this basic definition, two computers connected together in your garage make a network, and the Internet, with millions of computers connected to it, is also a network. Not only by definition but also by practice, both the networks (the Internet and the garage net) work for the user in the same way—that is, the end user cannot tell whether the communication partner is sitting next door or on the other side of the globe.

This experience is made possible because networking technology is based on a set of global standards (protocols) called TCP/IP, and for that reason networking is also called TCP/IP networking.

TCP/IP Networking

From a user's perspective, the Internet is just a big network, even though we know that underneath it is a collection of various kinds of networks. So what makes a collection of heterogeneous networks one uniform network, called the Internet, to the end users connected to the net. The answer is the suite of protocols called TCP/IP, named after the two important protocols included in it—Transmission Control Protocol (TCP) and Internet Protocol (IP). In other words, the Internet is based on open standards called protocols. A protocol is not a piece of software itself; rather, it is a specification of what the software should do and how—the specifications for writing the relevant software.

In the case of TCP/IP protocols, these specifications lay out the syntactic and semantic rules for communication, such as the formats of requests and responses between computers. These specifications are written in a hardware-independent way so that the software based on these specifications will be independent of the underlying hardware. For example, a web browser and a web server are the software written based on the Hypertext Transfer Protocol (HTTP). However, for brevity, the terms like "this protocol is running" or "this protocol does this" are often used. Whenever you read or hear of a protocol running on something or a protocol doing something, always do the mental translation to "the software based on the protocol is running or doing something." A protocol by itself is just a specification; it is the software, written based on those specifications, that actually does something. Each computer connected to the net has TCP/IP (i.e., the software that implements the TCP/IP suite of protocols) installed on it.

The underlying ideas and principles of TCP/IP were developed during the late 1960s and 1970s as a result of research funded by the U.S. Department of Defense Advanced Research Projects Agency (ARPA), also known as the Defense Advanced Research Projects Agency (DARPA). The TCP/IP internet, also known as the Internet or just "the net," enables hundreds of millions of users around the globe to communicate with each other as though they were connected to one single network. In other words, the Internet appears the same to two communicating users regardless of whether they are connected to the same local area network (LAN) in the same building or to two different LANs on the opposite sides of the globe. A LAN is a network that is confined to a local area, such as a room, a building, or a group of local buildings. Because your Solaris system is more likely than not connected to the net (e.g., connected to a LAN, which in turn is connected to the Internet), you must learn the fundamentals of TCP/IP networking. We begin with looking at how the TCP/IP protocol suite is organized.

Network Protocol Layering Models

In the very beginning of the computer networking era, only computers from the same vendor could communicate with each other because of the different standards (or lack of standards) being used by different vendors. In the late 1970s, the International Organization for Standardization (ISO) created a reference model of Open Systems Interconnection (OSI). The protocols in the OSI model are organized into seven layers. Each layer is a group of related protocols that collectively (or alternatively) solve one part of the whole problem. Any two layers are placed next to each other based on which parts of the problem they solve and how those parts are related to each other. OSI is a very good theoretical model, and TCP/IP (the implementation of it) is the most practical system ever built closest to this model.

The OSI Model

The OSI reference model has seven interrelated layers of protocols shown in Figure 10-1. The data in these layers flows downward on the sender machine and upward on the recipient machine.

The seven layers of the OSI model are described here:

Layer 1: Physical The physical layer contains the specifications of the network hardware. In other words, it specifies standards for the physical signal and the media through which the signal travels from one computer to another. You can build all the layers you want, but at the end of the day the data travels on the wire, and the physical layer specifies the "wire." From the communication viewpoint, it has two tasks: to receive bits from other machines and to send bits to other machines on the wire. (By *wire* we simply mean the media used for transmission; of course there can be wireless media.) Cables, hubs, and connectors are some examples of network hardware specified in the physical layer. However, note that the physical layer supports a wide variety of standards that give rise to heterogeneous physical networks (LANs). For this reason a computer connected to one kind of network cannot communicate with a computer connected to another kind of network. One single task of TCP/IP is to solve this communication problem without demanding

FIGURE 10-1

The seven protocol layers of the OSI reference model

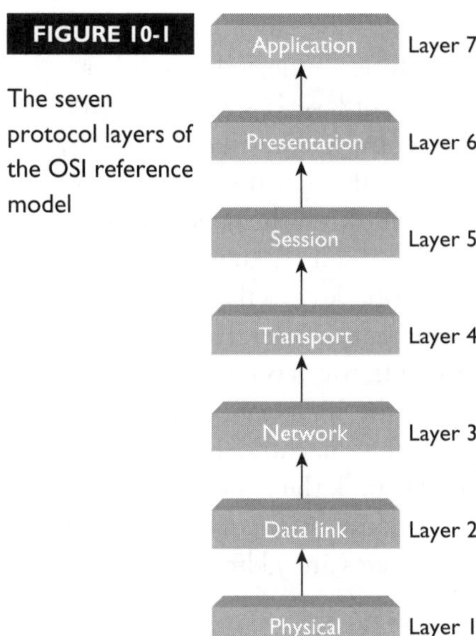

the elimination of differences between different LAN technologies. So the data is delivered on the physical media in a stream of bits that must be put together to make sense. This work begins at layer 2.

Layer 2: Data Link The layer 2 protocols specify how the bits of data are organized into a packet and addressed from one machine to another on a given physical network (LAN). In other words, these protocols define standards for data packets, called *frames*, and machine addresses, called *media access (MAC) addresses*. A MAC address is also called a hardware address, a physical address, or an Ethernet address (in an Ethernet LAN). The hardware can fail, and as a result transmission errors may occur. The data link layer also deals with transmission errors by providing mechanisms such as cyclic redundancy check (CRC). A network device aware of the MAC addresses (e.g., a switch or a bridge) is said to be operating at layer 2. Most of the LAN standards in the data link layer are defined by Institute of Electrical and Electronics Engineers (IEEE) and are known as IEEE 802.x standards; the varying value of x represents the varieties of physical networks supported at this level. Therefore, the format of the data packets and the frames, including the MAC address, will be different for different kinds of networks. This alone makes it impossible for two machines connected to two different kinds of networks to communicate with each other. This problem is solved by protocols in layer 3.

Layer 3: Network The network layer is responsible for delivery of data packets from a machine connected to one network to a machine connected to another network, even if the two networks are based on different layer-2 standards. This is accomplished by defining uniform standards for machine addresses, data packets, and routing. The machine addresses in this layer are called Internet addresses or IP addresses, and the data packets are called IP datagrams. Both the famous Internet Protocol (IP), one of the two protocols after which the TCP/IP suite is named, and the routing protocols are part of this layer. The network devices that deal with the IP addresses, such as routers, are said to be operating in this layer. However, there are two communication problems that are not addressed in this layer. First, an IP address is an address of a computer. Therefore, it will enable the IP datagram to reach the correct machine, but which application running on that machine should receive the data? The answer from layer 3 is I don't know. Second, the data delivery service offered by layer 3 is unreliable, which means that data can arrive out of order, can be delayed, and can get lost on the way. These two problems are addressed by layer 4.

Layer 4: Transport Layer 4 provides communication between two applications running on two machines connected to possibly two different networks. It accomplishes this task by introducing the concept of a port, which is a unique number assigned to a program running on the machine. A pair made up of an IP address and a port number uniquely identifies a source (or a destination), a program on a machine, and is called an *end point* or a *socket*. For this reason it is also said that layer 4 facilitates end-to-end communication. Some protocols in layer 4, such as the User Datagram Protocol (UDP) do not address the reliability issue. Others, however, such as the Transport Communication Protocol (TCP) do implement reliability by using acknowledgments to determine whether the data has been lost and re-transmitting the lost data. The data packets are called segments in TCP, and user datagrams in UDP. Communication using TCP is also called *connection-oriented communication*, because a virtual connection is established between the two machines that want to exchange data. This simply means that the two machines agree on a few things such as their readiness for communication in the beginning, and they mutually mark the end of communication, which is called closing the connection. In some applications, such as video broadcasts on the web, retransmission of lost data (frames) does not make sense and is not even desired. For such applications, UDP is an ideal choice. Therefore, the protocols in the transport layer enable an application on one computer connected to the net to communicate with another application running on another computer connected to the net from anywhere by using ports. The whole issue arises because there may be multiple applications running on a computer simultaneously. That raises another issue: who will keep the communication data (coming in or going out) of one application separate from the other application on the same computer? This is the responsibility of the next higher layer: the session layer.

Layer 5: Session Layer 5 protocols specify how to establish and maintain a session between two entities (programs) on two computers—for example, how to manage multiple logins to a remote computer. Security-related specifications such as authentication and passwords are dealt with in this layer. Some examples of session-layer protocols and standards include Network File System (NFS) supported by Solaris, Structured Query Language (SQL), and Remote Procedure Calls (RPC). Regardless of what kind of computer (Windows, Linux, or Mac) you are working on, an email message (or a web page) looks pretty much the same on all machines. However, the data does not travel in the same format in which an application (such as email or web browser) sends (or receives) it. Furthermore, different kinds of computers have different internal representations of high-level data such as a character or an integer. Who handles these differences to make the communication among different kinds of computers smooth? The answer is: the next higher layer, called the presentation layer.

Layer 6: Presentation The presentation layer acts as a format translator between the local standards on a specific kind of computer and the global standard that is used for transmission. It also deals with the issue of how the standard data should be formatted. For example, the following standards are part of layer 6: Tagged Image File Format (TIFF), Joint Photographic Experts Group (JPEG), Moving Pictures Experts Group (MPEG), and Rich Text Format (RTF). Remember that all these layers are means to an end: to enable two applications on different machines to communicate with each other. Who determines what kind of an application can use the network and how for communicating with another application? The answer is the protocols in layer 7.

Layer 7: Application A protocol in the application layer specifies how an application program on one machine connected to the net makes a request, and how another program running on another machine connected to the net responds to that request. The Hyptertext Transfer Protocol (HTTP), on which the World Wide Web is based, and the Simple Mail Transfer Protocol (SMTP), which is used to send email messages from one email server to another, are two examples of the many

exam watch

The network layer is responsible for delivering IP datagrams across multiple networks (LANs), whereas the data link layer is responsible for delivering frames over the same network.

protocols available in the application layer. The World Wide Web (based on HTTP) is so popular that it has become virtually synonymous with the Internet.

Each application uses either TCP or UDP in the transport layer and accordingly is identified either by a TCP port or a UDP port. Ports are just 16-bit integer numbers assigned to applications and maintained by the operating system. That means, in principle, you can assign any port number to your application in the range from 0 to 65535, but lower port numbers are reserved for well-known applications. Some of these reserved ports are listed in Table 10-1. The first column lists the protocols on which these applications are based.

TABLE 10-1 Reserved ports for well-known applications

Service Protocol	Port Number	Transport Protocol	Function
NETSTAT	15	UDP	Used to view a computer's inbound/outbound connections and the packet statistics.
FTP	21	TCP	File Transfer Protocol. Used to transfer files between two machines.
Telnet	23	TCP	Telecommunications Network Protocol. Used to work on a remote machine.
SMTP	25	TCP	Simple Mail Transfer Protocol. Used to carry email messages from client to server and from server to server.
DNS	53	UDP	Domain Name System. Resolves domain names to IP addresses.
TFTP	69	UDP	Trivial File Transfer Protocol. Thinned-out version of FTP, having no authentication and no file system navigation at the remote machine.
HTTP	80	TCP	Hypertext Transfer Protocol. Provides basis for the World Wide Web.
POP3	110	TCP	Post Office Protocol 3. Used by email clients to download email messages from email servers.
NNTP	119	TCP	Network News Transfer Protocol. Used to transfer (post, distribute, and retrieve) the Usenet messages on the Internet.
IMAP	143	TCP	Internet Mail Access Protocol. A popular alternative to POP3 with more features.
SNMP	161	UDP	Simple Network Management Protocol. Used to manage networks remotely.
NFS	2049	UDP	Network File System. Used to share files on a network.

The protocol-to-port mapping for services is listed on your system in the `/etc/services` file, which is actually a symbolic link to the `/etc/inet/services` file. The link is provided for BSD compatibility.

The OSI model, as elegant as it is, has never been exactly implemented. Nevertheless, the closest working system we have is the Internet which is based on the TCP/IP model.

The TCP/IP Model

Partly because of the way the Internet evolved, the TCP/IP protocols were never developed with the OSI layering model (or any other model for that matter) in mind; instead, a model evolved along with the Internet. Now that we have these protocols functioning together, we can look back and organize them into conceptual layers, and call them based on, say, the TCP/IP or Internet layering model. But there was no such model in front of the designers of the Internet protocols to follow. Most of the experts agree on the comparison between the TCP/IP layering model and the OSI model depicted in Figure 10-2.

The five layers of the TCP/IP layering model are listed here:

- **Layer 1: Physical.** Layer 1 deals with the network hardware and corresponds to the physical layer in the OSI model.
- **Layer 2: Network Interface.** This layer specifies how to organize data into packets called frames and how to address the machines in a LAN; it corresponds to the data link layer in the OSI model.

FIGURE 10-2

The five protocol layers of the TCP/IP layering model corresponding to the seven layers of the OSI model

OSI	TCP/IP
Application	Application
Presentation	
Session	
Transport	Transport
Network	Internet
Data link	Network interface
Physical	Physical

- **Layer 3: Internet.** This layer specifies the format of data packets called IP datagrams and is responsible for delivering these datagrams across the Internet. This layer corresponds to the network layer in the OSI model.
- **Layer 4: Transport.** This layer has protocols that specify end-to-end (application-to-application) communication and corresponds to the transport layer in the OSI model.
- **Layer 5: Application.** This layer corresponds to layers 6 and 7 in the OSI model.

Conceptually, as shown in Figure 10-3, a message from a sender machine begins at the application layer and travels down through the successive layers of protocol software, goes across networks through routers, eventually arriving at the destination machine at the physical layer and traveling upward to the application layer.

The protocol layers discussed in the OSI reference model and the TCP/IP layering model are summarized in Table 10-2.

Solaris 10 offers a completely rewritten TCP/IP stack. In previous versions of Solaris, TCP/IP across multiple CPUs was not very efficient and lagged behind the TCP/IP stack on Linux in performance. The Solaris 10 version of TCP/IP stack helps improve performance for all network applications, especially the web services.

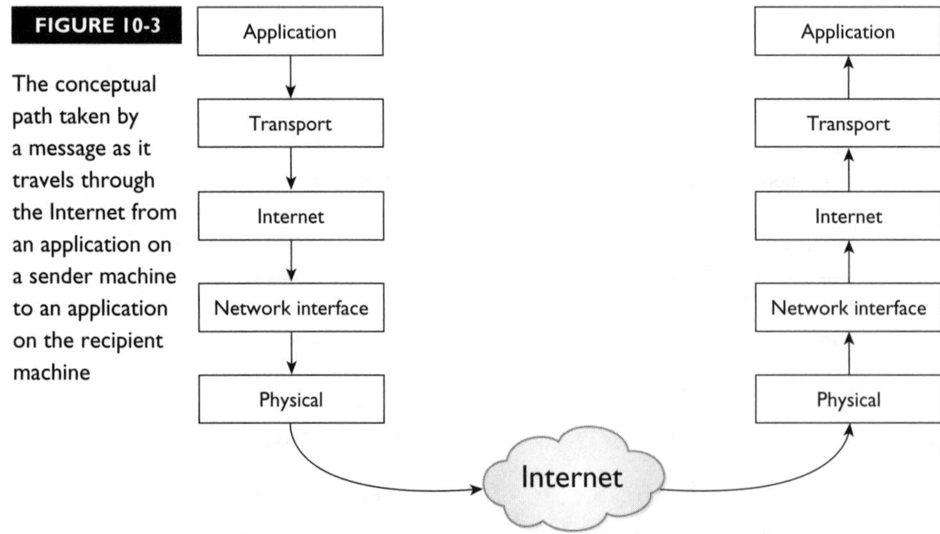

FIGURE 10-3 The conceptual path taken by a message as it travels through the Internet from an application on a sender machine to an application on the recipient machine

TABLE 10-2 Summary of layers of protocols in the OSI and Internet layering models

Layer	Protocols/Devices	Main Functionality
Physical	Hub, NIC, Repeater	Moves the bits of data from one device to another in form of specific signals.
Data link Network interface	Switch, Bridge	Organizes data into data packets called frames. Defines hardware (MAC) addresses.
Network Internet	Router IP, ARP, ICMP	Delivery of IP datagrams across networks. Organizes data into IP datagrams. Defines protocol (IP) addresses.
Transport	TCP, UDP	End-to-tend virtual connection. Defines ports, and optionally implements reliability.
Session	NFS, SQL	Creating sessions.
Presentation	MPEG, JPEG, UNICODE, ANSI	Presenting data in different formats. Encryption/decryption, compression/ decompression.
Application	HTTP, FTP, NIS, DNS, LDAP, telnet, SNMP	Specifies applications used by the end user.

Berkeley Software Distribution (BSD) UNIX released in 1983 from the University of California, Berkeley, was the first operating system ever to have the TCP/IP suite implemented on it. Of course, the TCP/IP protocol suite (containing these layers) is implemented on and is part of your Solaris system, which in turn is a part of a LAN. What kind of LAN?

LAN Topologies

As you already know by now, TCP/IP runs on top of a variety of LANs. These LAN technologies can be grouped into a few categories based on the design of their cable layouts, called LAN topologies. A LAN topology basically determines the pattern used to connect the computers and other devices in the network to each other through cables or other media. Three main topologies are discussed here:

Bus Topology

As shown in Figure 10-4, computers in a network based on bus topology share a single main cable (hence the name *bus*), and each computer is attached to this cable by using its own individual cable called a *drop cable*. The ends of the main cable

FIGURE 10-4 Layout of the bus topology (all computers are attached to a single shared cable)

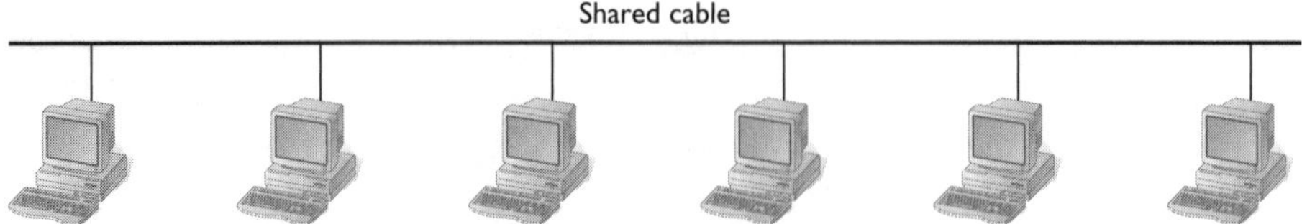

have terminators so that the signal is not reflected back. The disadvantages of this topology are that a single fault in the main cable can bring the whole network down, and it is difficult to troubleshoot.

Another way of connecting computers in a network is to connect a computer directly to another computer rather than through a single shared cable. This is done in ring topology.

Ring Topology

As shown in Figure 10-5, each computer in a network based on ring topology is connected directly to its two neighbor computers—a predecessor and a successor. As a typical example of how a computer in a star topology network communicates with another computer, assume computer A in Figure 10-5 is sending a data packet to computer D. The data packet travels in the ring from A to B, B to C, and C to D. Computer D copies the data and resets a few specific bits in the packet to indicate whether it copied the data successfully or not and puts the entire data back onto the cable. The packet keeps going until it completes the circle and reaches A. Computer A then looks at the bits reset by computer D to determine whether D received the packet correctly. Based on its findings, it may decide to re-send the packet. The point is that each computer and each cable in the ring is a single point of failure. Although a network based on this topology is easy to troubleshoot, it is not fault tolerant and it is difficult to reconfigure.

If the computers in a ring are not physically connected to each other as shown in Figure 10-5, but nevertheless the data travels in a ring as shown in the figure, the ring is called a logical ring.

Ring networks are not currently in common use. A topology that is commonly used today is the star topology.

Star Topology

As shown in Figure 10-6, all computers in a network based on the star topology are connected to a central device such as a hub. Data from the sender goes to

FIGURE 10-5

Layout of the ring topology (each computer is connected to its two immediate neighbors; the connection may be physical or logical)

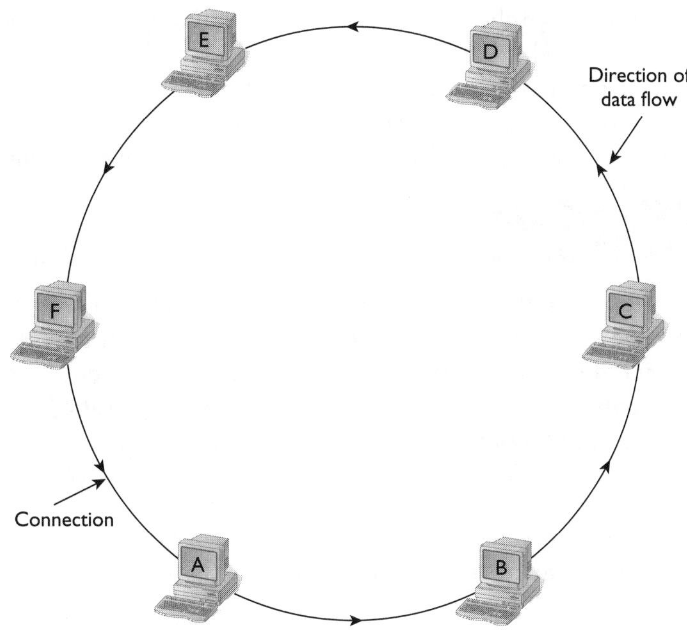

FIGURE 10-6

Layout of the star topology (each computer is connected to a central device)

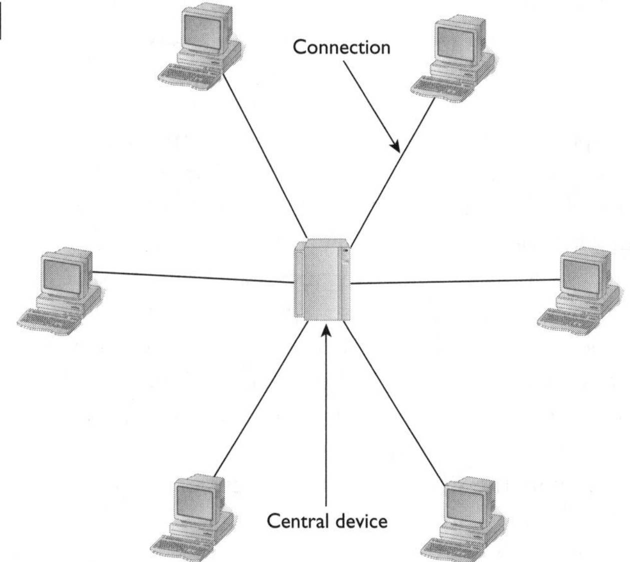

the recipient through the central point. The advantage of this topology is that new computers can be added to the network easily, and troubleshooting is relatively easy. It is fault tolerant in the sense that if a computer goes down or a cable connecting a computer to the central device goes down, the rest of the network still keeps functioning. However, the central device is the single point of failure.

exam watch

Note that a topology refers to the pattern of how the computers in the network are connected to each other through media such as cable. It does not necessarily refer to the actual physical shape of the network. For example, in a star network, all the computers connected to the hub may reside on the same side of the hub, and a snapshot of the network may not depict it as star shaped.

Bus topology and star topology are used by a class of LANs called Ethernet networks, which are the most commonly used LANs.

Ethernet Networks

As you already know by now, the protocols (standards) at the data link layer describe the specific LAN (physical network) technologies and prepare the outgoing data for transmission on a medium, for example, by organizing the data into frames. These protocols also receive the incoming data and, if necessary, pass on what is inside the frame to the appropriate network/Internet layer protocol.

The most popular LAN technology is called Ethernet, which was originally invented in Silicon Valley, California, at Xerox Corporation's Palo Alto Research Center in the early 1970s and was later adopted by (and now controlled by) the IEEE. Several variations of the Ethernet standards, summarized in Table 10-3, exist; they vary primarily because of the varying physical layer specifications included in the Ethernet standards, such as cable type. As a result the bandwidth and the maximum segment length vary as well. The bandwidth is the maximum data transmission rate that can be achieved and often is limited by the physical properties of the medium. The segment length, also called maximum cable length, is the distance the signal can travel in the cable before it disperses. Devices called repeaters can be used to amplify the signals and hence increase the maximum segment length of a network.

An Ethernet network has three main components: data packets, media, and media access (MAC) mechanism.

Data Packets

Data packets in data link layer are called frames. Each LAN technology has its own frame format. A frame, just like any other data packet, contains a data portion and a header portion. The header of a frame includes the MAC address of the source (sender) machine and the MAC address of the destination (recipient) machine. Data packets and addresses are described further on in this chapter. The frames travel from one computer to another on a LAN in the form of signals on a cable.

Cable Types

The cable types that you can use to build a network are described in the physical layer specifications included in the Ethernet standards. There are three main types of cable.

Coaxial Cables A coaxial cable (coax) contains two coaxial (one inside another) copper conductors separated by a layer of insulation and surrounded by an outer sheath. The signal travels through the inner conductor, and the outer conductor serves as the cable's ground. There are two types of coaxial cables: RG-58 standard, also called thick Ethernet (Thicknet), which is about 0.5 inch in diameter, and RG-8 standard, also called thin Ethernet (Thinnet), which is about 0.25 inch in diameter. A drop cable from a computer connects to the Thicknet cable by using the so-called vampire tap, which has a meta-tooth that sinks into the cable—hence the name *vampire tap*. Thinnet uses the Bayonet-Neil-Concelman (BNC) connector. Both types of coaxial cable are used in the bus topology, in which the coaxial cable is the cable shared by all the computers connected to the network. The two ends of the shared cable use terminators to terminate the signal and hence to eliminate the problem of signal bounce, called *echo effect*. Although coaxial cable is still used for the television network, it is no longer popular as a LAN medium, for which twisted-pair cables are commonly used.

Twisted-Pair Cables A twisted-pair cable has a multiple number of individually insulated copper wires (conductors) twisted together in pairs and surrounded by a sheath. There are two main kinds of twisted-pair cables: shielded twisted-pair (STP), which has a metallic shield around the protective sheath and is used in token-ring networks, and unshielded twisted pair (UTP), which has no outer shield and is used in star topology networks. The UTP cables are graded according to the following categories (also called *cats*):

- *Category 1.* A cable in this category has two twisted pairs (four wires) and can only carry voice. This is actually the telephone cable used in the Plain Old Telephone Service (POTS). It uses the RJ-11 connector.

- *Category 2*. A cable in this category has four twisted pairs (eight wires) and is suitable for a bandwidth of up to 4 Mbps. The UTP cables with four pairs use RJ-45 connectors.
- *Category 3*. A cable in this category has four twisted pairs (eight wires) and is suitable for a bandwidth of up to 10 Mbps. The Fast Ethernet protocol called 100Base-T4 was designed to use this category to achieve a bandwidth of 100 Mbps. This is made possible by using all the four twisted pairs in the cable, whereas most of other protocols use only two twisted pairs.
- *Category 4*. A cable in this category has four twisted pairs (eight wires) and is suitable for a bandwidth of up to 16 Mbps. It is used in token-ring networks.
- *Category 5*. A cable in this category has four twisted pairs (eight wires) and is suitable for a bandwidth of up to 100 Mbps. It is in common use today.
- *Category 6 (or 5e)*. A cable in this category has four twisted pairs (eight wires) and is suitable for a bandwidth of up to 1 Gbps. It is used in Giganet Ethernet.

Fiber-Optic Cables Coaxial and twisted-pair cables provide a segment length from 100 to 500 meters, because after traveling this distance the signal weakens (disperses) so much that it cannot be read accurately. Fiber-optic cable provides the solution to this problem, because it carries a light signal through a glass fiber that can travel up to 120 kilometers before weakening to a point at which it cannot be read.

These cable types are described in Table 10-3. Note that most Ethernet networks use only two pairs in the twisted-pair cable: one for receiving the data and the other for sending it.

Once we have a frame and the cable, we need a mechanism to access the cable in order to send the frame.

Media Access Mechanism: CSMA/CD

The issue of accessing the media for sending data arises because there is more than one computer on the network that would like to send data. In an Ethernet network with a shared medium, there is no central controller to coordinate the transmission from different computers and hence to avoid the traffic collision. The mechanism used for coordinating data transmission is called Carrier Sense Multiple Access (CSMA) and Collision Detection (CD); therefore, Ethernet networks are also called CSMA/CD networks.

To understand the CSMA/CD mechanism, consider an Ethernet network with a shared coaxial cable (Thicknet) as shown in Figure 10-7. Each computer is connected to the shared cable with a transceiver. Computer B wants to send data to

TABLE 10-3 Variations of Ethernet networks

Ethernet Name	Cable Type	Bandwidth	Maximum Segment Length	Comments
10Base5	Coax	10 Mbps	500 meters	0.5 inch in diameter. Also called Thicknet. Uses vampire taps to connect devices to cable.
10Base2	Coax	10 Mbps	185 meters	0.25 inch in diameter. Also called Thinnet. Uses BNC connector. Popular choice for Ethernet over coax.
10BaseT	UTP	10 Mbps	100 meters	Popular. Uses two pairs of Cat 3.
100BaseTX	UTP	100 Mbps	100 meters	Popular. Uses two pairs of Cat 5.
100BaseT4	UTP	100 Mbps	100 meters	Uses four pairs of Cat 3.
1000BaseT	UTP	1 Gbps	100 meters	Gigabit Ethernet. Cat 5.
10BaseF	Fiber optic	10 Mbps	500 meters to 2000 meters	Ethernet implemented over fiber optic.
100BaseFX	Fiber optic	100 Mbps	412 meters	—
1000BaseLX	Fiber optic	1 Gbps	550 meters to 5000 meters	—
1000BaseSX	Fiber optic	1 Gbps	220 meters to 5505 meters	—
FDDI	Fiber optic	100 Mbps	10 kilometers	—

computer D, so the transceiver of computer B will determine whether it can receive signal from the shared cable. This is called *carrier sensing* or listening to the cable. The computer will wait until the transceiver confirms that there is no signal in the cable; then it will start transmitting the data. As shown in Figure 10-7, the signal from computer B will propagate to both ends of the shared cable. The transceiver of

FIGURE 10-7 Flow of data across a shared Ethernet cable in the bus topology

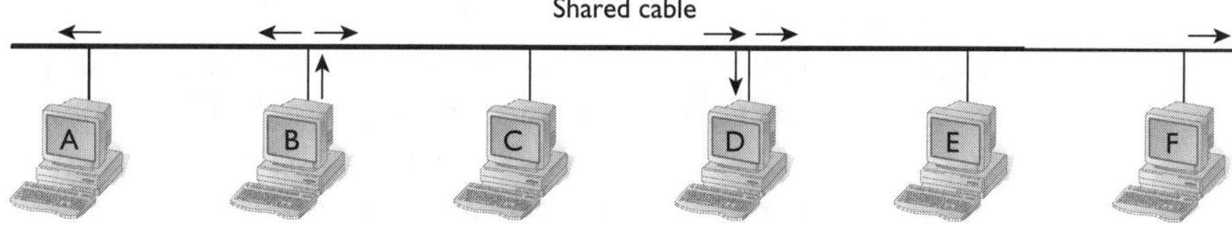

each computer on the network will sense the signal; the destination address in the frame header will be compared with the MAC address of the computer; and, if there is a match, the data will be accepted and processed by the computer. All computers that want to send data perform carrier sensing before accessing the cable on their own (without a central controller); hence the name *carrier sense multiple access*.

It can happen that at least two computers are sensing the cable, decide simultaneously that the cable is available, and start transmitting as a result. In this case the signals from the two computers will collide with each other in the cable. In other words, the possibility of a collision is built into the CSMA/CD mechanism. The philosophy behind this mechanism is to let the collision happen but if it does, detect it and recover from it. The transmitting computer detects the collision by comparing the incoming and outgoing signals at the transceiver. If the two (incoming and outgoing) are different, the collision has occurred. That means that the transmitting computer should still be transmitting when the distorted signal (as a result of collision) arrives at the transceiver of the transmitting computer. This is the origin of the requirement of a minimum Ethernet frame size.

After the two computers have detected a collision, the mechanism requires that each of the two computers select a random delay before attempting to re-transmit. If the delay chosen by the two computers happens to be the same, the collision will happen again. Every time this happens, each participating computer doubles the range from which to select the random delay, thereby reducing the possibility of collision. This recovery mechanism is called *exponential backoff algorithm*.

On a fiber-optic or UTP network, on which a computer has no transceiver, the computer senses the signal on a receive wire, and it assumes that a collision has occurred if it detects signals on both the receive and transmit wires simultaneously.

In a bus topology, the computers are directly connected to a single shared cable. But how do you connect a computer to a cable? In other words what else (other than cables) do we need to connect computers on a network? The answer is that we need network connectivity devices.

Network Connectivity Devices

A computer network is there to connect the computers. A computer connected to a network is called a computer, a machine, or a host. There are several devices other than computers, called *network connectivity devices*, that help connect different entities on the network (computers, printers, and the like) to one another. As a system administrator, you should be familiar with the various types of network connectivity devices. Some of them are described here.

Network Interface Card (NIC) As the name suggests, the network interface card provides an interface between the computer and the network media in order to connect a computer to the network. In its most common implementation, a NIC is an expansion card that fits into an expansion slot of the computer. However, a NIC can also be built into the computer's motherboard . It provides physical, electrical, and electronic connection for the computer to the network media. In other words, the data travels from the computer to the network and from the network to the computer through this device. On an Ethernet network, a hardware address is burned into a NIC, but the IP address is not. That means if you change the NIC of your computer, the hardware address of your machine changes. A machine may have more than one Ethernet card to connect to more than one network. A router is an example of such a machine. Although the MAC address assigned to different Ethernet cards by the manufacturers may differ, the Solaris system derives the MAC address from the NVRAM chip. Therefore, all the NICs on a Solaris machine will be using the same MAC address. This is not a problem as long as the cards are connected to different networks.

Hub A hub serves as the central device in a network that is based on the star topology. Each computer is connected to a different port on the hub. A hub receives signal on one port and repeats it on all other ports. If it simply provides the electrical connection between ports, it is called a passive hub, and it is typically unpowered. If it amplifies the signal it receives while repeating it on multiple ports, it is called an active port, and it is powered. Why do the hubs repeat received signal on all the ports even if it is supposed to go to only one computer connected to a specific port? That is because hubs have no awareness of hardware (MAC) addresses.

Repeater Repeaters are devices that can be used to amplify or to repeat an existing signal. Each cable type limits the maximum segment length (the maximum cable length between any two computers) of a network. This is because a physical signal can travel only so far before it disperses. Repeaters can be used to extend the segment length of a network by amplifying the weakening signals. As you have seen, a hub simply acts as a multiport repeater by repeating the received signal on multiple ports. A repeater, just like a hub and a NIC, operates at layer 1 (the physical layer).

Transceiver In a thick Ethernet network, each computer is connected to a single shared coaxial cable through a device called a transceiver, which can transmit data (signal) into the cable and receive data from the cable at the same time, hence the name transceiver. This capability of this device allows it to detect signal collision in the cable when it is transmitting data from the computer into the cable.

Switch As opposed to a hub, a switch repeats a received signal only on a port to which the intended recipient of the data is connected. When a switch is powered up, it starts off acting like a hub. However, with each frame it receives it learns the hardware address of the sender from the frame header and starts making a table in which each entry matches a port with the hardware address of the computer attached to that port. The switch then uses this table to repeat a received message only on the port to which the intended recipient is connected. Consequently, a switch knows hardware addresses whereas a hub does not. Because it has to know hardware addresses, a switch operates at layer 2 (data link layer), which defines hardware addresses.

Bridge Consider two networks based on the star topology implemented by a hub with one hub on each network. If you connect these two hubs with a cable, the two networks act like one big network—that is, a signal received from a sender will be repeated on all the ports on both hubs. Now assume that we connect the two hubs together through a device called a bridge. The bridge will stop all the traffic from a sender on one network (segment) from going to the second network (segment) if the intended recipient is not on the second segment. Therefore, a bridge can be used to combine two network segments together, or to split a network into two segments. Note the difference between a bridge and a switch: a bridge divides a network into two segments and stops the traffic from going into the wrong segment, whereas a switch stops the traffic from going to the wrong machine. Because it has to know hardware addresses, a bridge operates at layer 2 (the data link layer).

Router Whereas hubs, switches, and bridges manage the traffic inside a network, a router manages the traffic between two networks. A router receives a frame from a computer (or another router), retrieves the datagram from the frame, figures out (possibly with the help of the routing table) the recipient (which may be a local host or the next hop router), puts it into a new frame, and sends it. Because routers deal with IP datagrams, they are aware of IP addresses whereas bridges, switches, and hubs are not. Note that some of the switches (called layer-3 switches) also have the functionality of a router, which sometimes creates confusion about the term switch. Because it has to know IP addresses, a router operates at layer 3 (the network/Internet layer).

Gateway A gateway is a device (hardware, software, or a combination) that connects two different network environments by acting as a mediator. For example, a gateway may convert the traffic from one LAN protocol into another. An email gateway translates between two different email protocols so that the email servers based on those protocols can communicate with each other through the email gateway. A gateway can be regarded as a protocol translator and it may be operating at any layer depending on which protocols it's dealing with.

on the job

Do not confuse the TCP/UDP ports with the physical ports. The TCP/UDP ports are the software ports (the numbers), whereas the physical ports are the hardware ports used for physically connecting devices such as ports on a hub or ports on the back of your computer.

To sum up, a computer is connected to the network through a network interface, and each network interface must have an address in order to participate in network communication. This is analogous to your having your phone number, email address, and home address so people can communicate with you by using any of these addresses.

Network Addressing

A basic condition for network communication is that each machine on a network must have a unique address. On a LAN a machine is uniquely identified by its MAC address, and on the Internet a machine is uniquely identified by its IP address.

MAC Addresses

Media access (MAC) address is the address (a number) used to uniquely identify a computer on a LAN. It is also called a physical address, a hardware address, or an Ethernet address (on an Ethernet network). The MAC address on an Ethernet LAN, the Ethernet address, is a 48-bit number. Blocks of Ethernet addresses are purchased by the vendors from the IEEE and burned into the interface cards. That means that if the interface card of a computer changes, its MAC address will change. In general, network interface hardware recognizes three kinds of addresses:

- *Unicast address*. This is the unique address of a computer on a LAN.
- *Broadcast address*. This is the address used for broadcasting messages on a network. By convention, all 1's in an address make it a broadcast address. For example, if the destination hardware address in an Ethernet frame carries 48 bits, each set to 1, the frame will be delivered to and processed by all the computers on the LAN.
- *Multicast address*. This is the address that is used to broadcast a message to a subset of the computers on a network, and the subset is called a multicast

group. When the destination hardware address in the frame header is a multicast address, all the computers that have been assigned that address will accept and process the frame.

A MAC address is a layer-2 address and cannot uniquely identify a machine on the Internet.

IP Addresses

An Internet Protocol (IP) address is used to uniquely identify a machine on the Internet. IP (version 4) addresses are 32-bit numbers. In other words, think of the Internet as a big network (like a LAN) on which each machine is uniquely identified by a 32-bit integer. To understand IP address, note the following points:

- Each IP address has a structure—that is, it's composed of two parts, netid and hostid. All the computers on the same network (e.g., LAN) have the same netid but different hostids.
- The four bytes of an IP address are split between netid and hostid. The different ways we can split this address space between netid and hostid groups IP addresses into five categories called classes: class A, class B, class C, class D, and class E.
- The class of an IP address is identified by at most the first 4 bits of the address.

In order to route a datagram on its way from source to destination, the routers use only the netid of the destination IP address. Using the network address and not the host address of a destination helps to reduce the size of the routing tables.

In a class A address, the first byte (8 bits) belongs to the netid and the last three bytes belong to the hostid. In a class B network, the first two bytes belong to the netid, and the last two bytes belong to the hostid. In a class C network, the first three bytes belong to the netid and the last one byte belongs to the host ID. The class information is coded in the first few bits of an IP address. Look for the first appearance of a 0 bit in the address. It appears at the first (most significant) place in a class A address, at the second place in a class B address, and at the third place in a class C address. This information is summarized in Table 10-4.

Class D addresses are multicast addresses, and class E address space is reserved for future use. Note that the first few bits (one for class A, two for class B, and three for class C) of the first byte of an IP address are reserved to identify the class.

TABLE 10-4 Class structure of IP addresses

Class	netid	hostid	Fixed bits
A	First one byte	Last three bytes	First bit: 0
B	First two bytes	Last two bytes	First 2 bits: 10
C	First three bytes	Last one byte	First 3 bits: 110
D	—	—	First 4 bits: 1110
E	—	—	First 4 bits: 1111

The netid part of an IP address of a machine identifies the network of the machine to which it is connected. The common way of presenting IP addresses is called *dotted decimal notation*. In this notation, an IP address is written in four decimal integers separated by a dot, where each integer is the decimal value of the corresponding byte in the address. For example, consider the following IP address in binary format composed of four bytes:

```
10000100 00011100 00000011 00010100
```

Convert each byte into a decimal number individually and separate the decimal number by a dot and you obtain the following IP address in dotted decimal notation:

```
132.28.3.20
```

The network address is the IP address with the hostid replaced by all 0s. How would you know which bytes belong to the hostid? The bytes that do not belong to the netid belong to the hostid. But which bytes belong to the netid? That you determine from the class of the IP address. The first 3 bits of the IP address in our example are 100. The first 0 appears at the second place, hence it is a class B network address; as a result; the first two bytes belong to the netid. Therefore, the network address of the network to which the machine with this IP address (132.28.3.20) is connected is:

```
132.28.0.0
```

In class A addresses, the first byte belongs to the netid, and the first bit of the first byte is always 0. Therefore, the lowest non-zero netid is 00000001 (or 1) and the highest netid is 01111111 (or 127). However, the netid 127 is reserved for what is called a loopback address (used to test the TCP/IP stack on a machine), so the valid highest netid is 126. Therefore, the range of class A network addresses is: 1.0.0.0 to 126.0.0.0. Similarly, you can calculate the ranges for network addresses for the other classes, as listed in Table 10-5.

It is only the network addresses that are assigned by the Internet Corporation for Assigned Names and Numbers (ICANN). The network administrator is free to choose the hostid for a machine in the network. As you have already seen, all bits in a hostid set to 0 represent a network address, Furthermore, all bits in the hostid set to one represent a broadcast address. Therefore, an IP address with the hostid of all 0's or all 1's is not a valid IP address. Now let's do another exercise to understand the IP addresses. Consider again the IP address 132.28.3.20 in our example, and ask What is the maximum number of computers that can be connected to a network to which this computer with IP address 132.28.3.20 is connected? We have already determined that it is a class B network; therefore, the last two bytes belong to the hostid. That means you have 16 bits to make a hostid. Each hostid must be unique. How many unique numbers can you make with 16 bits? That would be 2^16 = 65536. Because all 0's and all 1's are not allowed in a hostid, the maximum number of machines that can be connected to a class B network is 65534.

What we have discussed is called the original IP addressing scheme, or a classfull addressing scheme, in which one network address is assigned to one LAN and each LAN has a class. In practice, these days, several LANs may be hidden behind one network address assigned by CANN. This is called subnetting and is accomplished by locally allotting a few bits from the hostid to represent several LANs for a given network address. However, discussion of this issue is beyond of the scope of this book.

Now that you know how the original IP addressing scheme works, see the next page for some practical scenarios and their solutions.

Having two addresses (IP and MAC) for a machine connected to a network may confuse a beginner. The right question to ask is How do we use both of these addresses? The point to remember is that an IP datagram is always addressed by an

TABLE 10-5 Network address ranges for different classes

Class	Lowest Network Address	Highest Network Address
A	1.0.0.0	126.0.0.0
B	128.1.0.0	191.255.0.0
C	192.0.1.0	223.255.255.0
D	224.0.0.0	239.255.255.255
E	240.0.0.0	255.255.255.254

SCENARIO & SOLUTION	
One of the machines connected to a TCP/IP network has an IP address of 195.23.3.16. What is the network address of this network?	The first byte 195 is 11000011 in binary. The first zero appears at the third significant place. So, it's a class C network, which means the first three bytes belong to the netid. Therefore, the network address is 195.23.3.0.
What is the maximum number of computers you can connect to this network?	There are 8 bits available for the hostid, which cannot contain all 0's and all 1's. Therefore, the maximum number of computers = 2^8−2 = 254.
What is the IP address on this network for broadcasting an IP datagram?	All 1's in the hostid makes the broadcast address 195.23.3.255.

IP address, and a frame is always addressed by a MAC address. These addresses are resolved into each other when necessary.

Address Resolution

You can build as many layers of protocols as you want, but ultimately the data will travel in some medium; it will always be delivered on a LAN in the form of a frame, and the frame is addressed by a hardware address. Consequently, it is always a frame that is delivered on a LAN. However, a frame cannot travel across networks. What travels across networks is the IP datagram, which is addressed by the IP address of the ultimate destinations and the original source. The IP datagram from original source to ultimate destination travels from router to router (i.e., from network to network) inside frames. The key point is that a router has more than one network interface—that is, it is connected to more than one network. It accepts the frame on one network, takes the IP datagram out of the received frame, puts it into another frame, and delivers it to the next router on the other network to which it is also connected. The new frame is compatible with the hardware of the network on which it will be delivered to the next router. This procedure is repeated until the datagram reaches its ultimate destination.

Each router on the way determines the IP address of the next router from the routing table, but to send the frame it needs the MAC address of the next router. So it broadcasts an address resolution protocol (ARP) message, which basically says

Any machine on this network whose IP address is this, please give me your MAC address. The next router responds to the sending router with its MAC address. This is how an IP address is resolved to a MAC address by using ARP.

Not just a router but any computer on a network can run ARP; as it learns the hardware addresses of other computers, it enters them into a table so that the next time it wants to send something to a computer it does not have to run ARP again. Because an ARP request is a broadcast, it consumes significant bandwidth. You can view the ARP table (the mapping of IP addresses to MAC addresses) maintained by a computer by executing the `arp` command on that computer.

Finally, note that the addresses are assigned to network interfaces, and a computer may have more than one network interface, which means more than one (hardware and IP) address. Consider an address as the address of a network connection for a computer. Computers need addresses so that they can send and receive data packets, also called network packets.

Network Packets

Computer networks are called packet-switched networks, because instead of transferring data as a string of bits, they deliver it organized into blocks called packets. In other words, a packet is a unit of delivery. A packet has two main parts—data and header, which is information about data—that is, how to interpret the data, who is the sender, where the data is going, and so forth.

Understanding Packets

Each layer in the protocol layering has its own view of the data packet. As shown in Figure 10-8, each layer on the sender machine gets a packet from the upper layer, prepends its own header to it, and passes it down to the next layer. As shown in Figure 10-9, each layer on the receiver machine does exactly the opposite; it receives a packet from the lower layer, removes the header (that the same layer prepended on the sender machine), and passes the packet on to the upper layer. Each layer has its own name for the packet—for example, *IP datagram* for the network layer and *frame* for the data link layer.

As listed here, each layer has a different name for its packet:

- *TCP segment and UDP datagram.* A data packet in the transport layer is called a TCP segment if it is composed by TCP, and it is called a user datagram or UDP datagram if it is composed by UDP. The most important header fields are the source port number and the destination port number, which uniquely identify the communicating applications at the sender machine and the

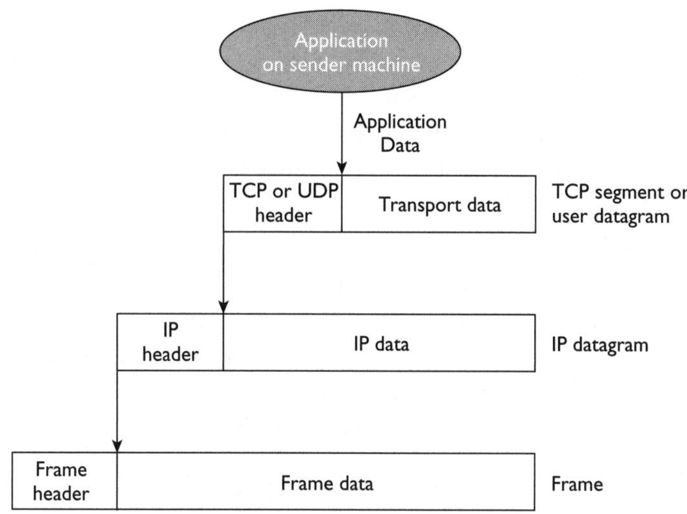

FIGURE 10-8 Data encapsulation on the sender machine (a packet in a layer becomes the data part for the packet in the lower layer)

destination machine, respectively. The TCP header has additional fields to implement reliability, such as acknowledgment number.

- *IP datagram.* A data packet in the network/Internet layer composed by IP is called an IP datagram. The most important fields in the IP datagram header are the source IP address, the destination IP address, and time to live (TTL). The source IP address and destination IP address are the addresses

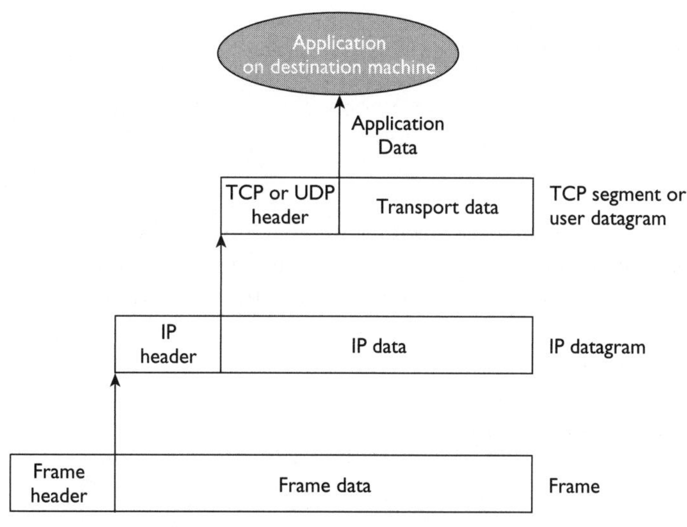

FIGURE 10-9 Data decapsulation at the recipient machine (a layer removes its header before passing the packet to the upper layer)

of the sender machine and the recipient machine, respectively. The TTL is a number that represents the maximum number of routers that a datagram can hop before it bites the dust. This is basically a protection against the datagrams becoming lost on the Internet (for example, put into loops), not going anywhere but wasting bandwidth.

- *Frame*. The data packet in the data link layer is called a frame. Its format depends on the hardware network technology being used by the LAN. The most important header fields in an Ethernet frame are source hardware address, destination hardware address, and cyclic redundancy check (CRC). The CRC field is calculated (from the content of the frame by using an algorithm) at the source machine and at the destination machine; if the two values are different, the data is probably corrupted.

Now that you have an understanding of network packets, you need to know how to monitor them on your Solaris system.

Monitoring Packets

You can view the packet statistics on your machine by using the `netstat` command. For example, issue the following command to display the packet statistics on your machine that has the IPv4 TCP/IP stack installed on it:

```
netstat -f inet
```

The output will look like the following:

```
Local Address Remote Address Swind Send-Q Rwind Recv-Q State
--------------------------------------------------------------
host49.850 host19.nfsd 49640 0 49640 0 ESTABLISHED
host49.38063 host19.32782 49640 0 49640 0 CLOSE_WAIT
host49.38146 host41.43601 49640 0 49640 0 ESTABLISHED
```

If you have trouble accessing another machine on the Internet or on your own network, you can use the `ping` (packet Internet groper) command, a utility based on Internet Control Message Protocol (ICMP), to determine whether the remote host is running or is dropping packets. You can issue the `ping` command by using the following syntax:

```
ping <host> [<timeout>}
```

The <host> argument specifies the remote host name and the <timeout> argument is the time in seconds for the ping command to continue trying reaching the host. The default value is 20 seconds. The ping command has several options. As shown here, you can use -s option to determine whether the remote host is dropping packets:

```
ping -s <host>
```

The output of this command will look like the following:

```
PING host1.domain6 : 56 data bytes
64 bytes from host1.domain6.COM (197.17.21.63): icmp_seq=0. time=70. ms
64 bytes from host1.domain6.COM (197.17.21.63): icmp_seq=1. time=72. ms
64 bytes from host1.domain6.COM (197.17.21.63): icmp_seq=2. time=75. ms
64 bytes from host1.domain6.COM (197.17.21.63): icmp_seq=3. time=73. ms
64 bytes from host1.domain6.COM (197.17.21.63): icmp_seq=4. time=73. ms
64 bytes from host1.domain6.COM (197.17.21.63): icmp_seq=5. time=72. ms
^
—host1.domain6 PING Statistics—
6 packets transmitted, 6 packets received, 0% packet loss
round-trip (ms) min/avg/max = 72/73/75
```

These statistics indicate whether the host has dropped packets. Note that depending on the <host>, the command may involve a network other than your network. In case the ping command fails, you can check the status of your network by using the netstat and ifconfig commands.

From the netstat command you know that the packets are being exchanged, and if you see a problem in communication, you can use the ping command for trouble-shooting. Now, suppose you get more ambitious and want to snoop into a packet. In technical terms, you want to monitor the data transfer by snooping into headers of the packets at various layer levels. You can do that by using the conveniently named snoop command. Without any specified option, only the application layer information is displayed; for example, for an NFS packet, only the NFS information will be displayed. However, you can turn on the appropriate verbose mode to receive the information about the UDP datagram, IP datagram, or frame. For example, if you want to inspect the telnet traffic coming to your system (assuming that the telnet application runs on TCP port 23), you would issue the following command:

```
snoop -v tcp port 23
```

This will start displaying the information from the TCP header, the IP header, and the frame header of packets from or to the first non-loopback interface of your machine. To halt the process, press CTRL-C.

You can also use the host names to capture the traffic between two hosts as in the following command:

```
snoop <hostName1> <hostName2>
```

You should use the `snoop` utility frequently to become familiar with normal system behavior. For analyzing packets carefully, you can capture the output of the `snoop` command in a file by specifying the file name as a command argument. For example, the following command will save the output of the `snoop` command in the `/tmp/snoopDump` file:

```
snoop /tmp/snoopDump
```

By now, you know that the hardware and the IP addresses of a machine define the network identity of the machine. The hardware addresses are burned into the interfaces, but the IP addresses have to be assigned. In other words, the network interfaces must be configured.

Configuring and Managing IP Network Interfaces

Configuring network interfaces basically means assigning IP addresses to them and defining some parameters such as whether the interface is up (online) or down. You get the first opportunity to configure the interfaces on your machine during the Solaris installation process. The installation program configures the first interface, and if it finds additional interfaces, it prompts you to configure. You can configure them then, or you can choose to configure them later. The configuration information is saved in a set of files that are used to configure the interfaces every time you boot the system.

Configuring an IP Network Interface at Boot Time

Every time you boot a Solaris system, the `ifconfig` utility is used to configure the interfaces; it uses the information from the configuration files described in the following list:

- The `/etc/nodename` file. This file contains one entry. For example, a system with the host name `tomdelay` will have one entry in the `/etc/nodename` file: `tomdelay`.

- The `/etc/hostname.<interface>` file. This file represents a physical interface to the system. Each functional (configured) physical interface on the machine must have its own `/etc/hostname.<interface>` file. The `<interface>` specifies the physical interface name which can be determined by using the `prtconfig` or `sysdef` commands. The names look like `<type><n>`, where `<type>` specifies the interface type and `<n>` specifies the interface number of a given type. For example, your machine may have two interfaces with names `hme0` and `hme1`. The host name files corresponding to these interfaces will be: `/etc/hostname.hme0` and `/etc/hostname.hme1`, respectively. What should be inside each of these files? Again, just one entry, the host name or the IP address of the host. For example, the `/etc/hostname.hme0` file may have an entry `tomdelay0`, and the `/etc/hostname.hme1` file may have the entry `tomdelay1`. These files contain the information that the interfaces hme0 and hme1 are installed on the machine and are associated with the host names `tomdelay0` and `tomdelay1`, respectively.
- The `/etc/inet/hosts` file. Now you have one file for each interface on your machine that contains the host name (or the IP address information) associated with that interface. Maybe you want to give a nickname to the host, or maybe you want to know the host names (and IP addresses) of the other machines on the system. The `/etc/inet/hosts` file let you organize that information. Each entry in this file contain the following fields:
  - **`<IPAddress>.`** Contains an IPv4 address corresponding to a host name, which in turn corresponds to a physical interface.
  - **`<hostname>.`** Contains the host name corresponding to this IP address.
  - **`<nickname>.`** Nickname for this host.
  - **`#.`** Comments
- The `/etc/inet/ipnodes` file. This file stores both IPv4 and IPv6 addresses. If you need to add (or change) the IPv4 address of your Solaris 10 system, you must make this change to both the `hosts` and the `ipnodes` files. If you are going to add an IPv6 address, you need to edit only the `ipnodes` file.

As an example, following are the contents of the `/etc/inet/hosts` file that exists on the machine with host names `tomdelay0` and `tomdelay1`, corresponding to two interfaces that this machine has.

```
# Little Network on the Hill
#
127.0.0.1 localhost
#
192.168.2.1 tomdelay0 tomy0 #This machine
192.168.2.2 tomdelay1 tomy1 #This machine
#
192.168.2.3 nancy # Nancy's machine. No nick name.
192.168.2.4 hillary smart # Hillary's machine
192.168.2.5 barbara boxer #This is Barbara's machine
```

The first entry corresponds to loopback address 127.0.0.1, which does not belong to any real physical interface and is used only to test TCP/IP installation on the machine. The entries with IP addresses 192.168.2.1 and 192.168.2.2 belong to the machine on which this file resides. The other entries with IP addresses 192.168.2.3, 192.168.2.4, and 192.168.2.5 belong to other machines on the network.

The `/etc/inet/hosts` file on your system needs entries about other machines only if the network is using the local files for the name service. Usually the network uses the NIS and DNS name services, which maintain host names and addresses on one or more servers. You will learn more about this in Chapter 11.

During the installation process, the Solaris installation program creates the `/etc/hostname.<interface>` file for the first interface that it finds during the installation. If the installation program finds additional interfaces, you will be prompted to configure them. You can choose to configure them then, or you may postpone it until later.

The `ifconfig` command configures each interface on the machine during boot time by using the corresponding configuration files. What if you want to change the configuration after booting, or you want to configure a new interface? You can do that as well with the `ifconfig` command.

Monitoring IP Network Interface Configuration

As you know by now, the `ifconfig` command configures each network interface at boot time. You can also use the `ifconfig` command manually to monitor the interface configuration after the system has been booted. Monitoring includes discovering the configuration information and changing the configuration. In other words, you can use the `ifconfig` command to manually assign an IP address to an interface and to manually configure the interface parameters.

By using the `ifconfig` command, you can get the following information about the interfaces:

- Device names of all interfaces on the system
- IP addresses assigned to an interface
- Whether an interface is currently configured or not

For example, to get information about all the interfaces, issue the `ifconfig` command with the `-a` option, as shown here:

```
ifconfig -a
```

It will display information about each interface, including the interface name, its hardware address, and its IP address. It will also tell you whether the interface is up (meaning configured and online), or down (meaning shut down). You can obtain information about a particular interface by specifying its name, say `hme1`, as shown here:

```
ifconfig hme1
```

If the interface is down, you can bring it up by issuing the following command:

```
ifconfig hme1 up
```

On the other hand, if it is up and you want to shut it down, you can issue the following command:

```
ifconfig hme1 down
```

To assign (or change) an IP address to an interface, you can issue the `ifconfig` command in the following format:

```
ifconfig <interfaceName> <ipAddress>
```

`<interfaceName>` specifies the interface name such as hme1. and `<ipAddress>` specifies the IP address to be assigned, such as 192.168.2.3.

EXERCISE 10-1

How to Monitor Packets by Using the snoop Command

To monitor network packets by using the `snoop` command, perform the following steps:

1. On your local host machine, become superuser.
2. You can use the `snoop` command without any argument to obtain the packet information from the first non-loopback interface, or you can specify an interface by its IP address. To find the IP addresses assigned to the interfaces, you can issue the following command:

   ```
   ifconfig -a
   ```

3. Issue the `snoop` command by specifying the file as an argument:

   ```
   snoop /tmp/snoopDump
   ```

   This will capture the packet information and store it into the file `/tmp/snoopDump`.
4. To display information about a specific interface of your choice, specify its IP address in the command argument. For example, the following command will display packet information from the interface with IP address 192.168.5.7:

   ```
   snoop 192.168.5.7
   ```

5. Once you issue the `snoop` command, it starts capturing the information about the packets to and from the specified interfaces. To terminate the process, press CTRL-C.

Now we have computers connected to the network through their interfaces, and the interfaces are all configured. Why would we go to all that trouble? Well, either to share or to use the shared resources, and resources are shared and used by offering and using network services.

CERTIFICATION OBJECTIVE 10.02

Working with Network Services

Exam Objective 1.2: *Explain the client-server model and enable/disable server processes.*

Networks are formed to share and use resources, and this is accomplished through services. The machine that offers a service is called a server, and the machine that uses the service is called a client.

Client/Server Model of Networking

Most of the network services are offered in a client/server environment. A client refers to a host that makes requests to another host on the network called a server. The client machine has a client program running on it to make these requests. Examples of clients are web browsers, such as Netscape Navigator and Internet Explorer, an email client, or an FTP client. A server is a machine that has resources to serve, such as files or web pages. A server program running on the machine accepts the incoming requests. It may ask other programs running on the machine to prepare the response and then will send the response back to the client.

Most networks (along with the Internet itself) are server centric. That means there are multiple clients per server. All the resources are on the server machines and the client machines make requests to the server machines. For example, think of a file server on a network, or a web server on the Internet. Because the resources are centered on the servers, security is also server centric.

There is another client/server environment in which the resources are not centered only on servers. Each machine has the resources to share. In other words, each machine is both a client and a server. Such a network is called peer to peer, because the resources are distributed over all the participating machines, and so is the security. Therefore the task of implementing security in peer-to-peer networks becomes very challenging.

As a system administrator, you will be managing network services on your Solaris system.

Working with Solaris Network Services

Solaris 10 offers a service-based startup facility named Service Management Facility (SMF), which provides an infrastructure that augments the traditional UNIX startup scripts, init run levels, and configuration files. SMF removes the `rc` startup script conventions in Solaris and creates a more Windows-like framework for services. Furthermore, SMF allows multiple services to start up concurrently, thereby dramatically reducing the boot time of a Solaris 10 server.

Still, during the system boot time, the `inetd` daemon is responsible for starting standard Internet services such as applications running on top of TCP, UDP, or SCTP, including RPC services. After the boot, you can manage services (modify the existing services or add new services) by using SMF commands.

In the SMF framework, multiple versions of the same service can run on a single Solaris system, each version with its own configuration. A specific configuration of a service is called an instance. For example, a web server offers web service, and a specific web server daemon configured to listen on port 80 is a web service instance. A service has a systemwide configuration, but each instance of the service may have its own configuration, which would override the service configuration when there is a conflict. This offers increased flexibility by allowing each instance to choose its own requirements.

Each service instance is named with a Fault Management Resource Identifier (FMRI)—a fancy term, indeed, for a combination of the service name and the instance name. For example, the FMRI for the `rlogin` service is `network/login:rlogin`, where `network/login` identifies the service and `rlogin` identifies the service instance.

You can use the `inetadm` command to manage inetd-controlled SMF services. The `inetadm` command has the following syntax:

```
inetadm [<option>] [<FMRI>]
```

The command without any option and without any argument will display the following information about each service that is currently controlled by inetd:

- FMRI of the service
- The run state of the service
- Whether the service is enabled or disabled

The following options specified by `<option>` are available:

- **`-e`.** Enable the service instance specified by `<FMRI>`.

- **`-d`.** Disable the service instance specified by the `<FMRI>`.
- **`-l`.** List the properties of the service instance specified by the `<FMRI>`.

SMF offers the `svcadm` command, which can be used to enable and disable the network services. The command has the following syntax:

```
svcadm<option> <FMRI>
```

You can specify the values for the `<option>`:

- **disable.** To disable the service.
- **enable.** To enable the service.
- **refresh.** To upgrade the running configuration with the values from the current configuration.
- **restart.** To restart the service.

Note that the service status change is recorded in the service configuration repository, which will persist across reboots. For example, if you have disabled a service and you reboot the machine, the only way to get the service running again is to enable it.

Now that you know how to enable and disable network services, here are some practical scenarios and their solutions.

SCENARIO & SOLUTION	
Which command would you issue to enable the rlogin service whose PMRI name is `network/login/rlogin`?	`svcadm enable network/login:rlogin`
Now, how will you disable this service?	`svcadm disable network/login:rlogin`

Table 10-6 presents some common services that have been converted to use SMF in Solaris 10. The table includes the following information for each service: the daemon name (service name), the FMRI, the run script used to start the service, and whether the service is started by inetd.

The three most important takeaways from this chapter are as follows:

- The TCP/IP protocol suite makes the Internet appear to be a single network, even though it is actually a collection of networks.

TABLE 10-6 Incomplete list of services converted to use SMF

Service Name	FMRI	Run Script	Inetd Service?
automount	svc:/system/filesystem/autofs:default	autofs	No
coreadm	svc:/system/coreadm:default	coreadm	No
cron	svc:/system/cron:default	cron	No
dumpadm	svc:/system/dumpadm:default	savecore	No
in.dhcpd	svc:/network/dhcp-server:default	dhcp	No
in.ftpd	svc:/network/ftp:default	None	Yes
in.named	svc:/network/dns/server:default	inetsvc	No
in.telnetd	svc:/network/telnet:default	None	Yes
inetd	svc:/network/inetd:default	inetsvc	No
ldap_cachemgr	svc:/network/ldap/client:default	ldap.client	No
nfsd	svc:/network/nfs/server:default	nfs.server	No
None	svc:/network/physical:default	network	No
nscd	svc:/system/name-service-cache:default	nscd	No
sendmail	svc:/network/smtp:sendmail	sendmail	No
sshd	svc:/network/ssh:default	sshd	No
syslogd	svc:/system/system-log:default	syslog	No
ypbind	svc:/network/nis/client:default	rpc	No
ypserv	svc:/network/nis/server:default	rpc	No

- A computer connects to a network through its network interface, which is assigned a hardware address and an IP address.
- The resources on the networks (or Internet) are shared through services. A client machine makes a request for a service, and a server machine serves the request.

CERTIFICATION SUMMARY

The TCP/IP protocol suite makes the Internet appear to be a big single network to millions of users, even though underneath it is a collection of heterogeneous networks. TCP/IP protocols are organized into five layers that closely correspond to the seven layers of the OSI reference model. Each machine has hardware (MAC) address (defined in the data link layer), which is its identity on a LAN, and an IP address (defined in the network layer) which is its identity on the Internet. Furthermore, a frame (data packet defined in the data link layer) can only be delivered locally, and an IP datagram (a data packet defined in the network layer) can be sent across multiple networks—that is, over the Internet. Each router on the way reframes the datagram as it hops from network to network on its route from source to destination.

You can view the packet traffic on the inbound/outbound connections of your machine by using the `netstat` command, and if you suspect a problem you can use the `ping` command to test the reachability of another host. You can also use the `snoop` command to look into the header of a packet. The packets that you can monitor by using these commands enter or exit through an interface that you can configure by using the `ifconfig` command.

Once your system is connected to the network through interfaces that you have configured, you need to manage the services running on your system. Standard Internet services are started by inetd at boot time. Solaris 10 offers Services Management Facility (SMF), which augments the traditional UNIX startup scripts and configuration files. The `inetadm` command is used to manage the inetd-controlled services, and `svcadm` is the SMF utility used to manage the network services.

It's easier to remember a machine on the network by a name rather than by IP address. An entry in the `/etc/inet/hosts` file on your system contains the following information about a host name associated with your machine: the host name, the corresponding IP address, and an alias for the host name, if any. This file needs entries about other machines on the network only if the network is using the local files for the name service. Usually the network uses the NIS and DNS name services, which maintain host names and addresses on one or more servers. We explore the name services in the next chapter.

INSIDE THE EXAM

Comprehend

- The node name of a machine can be found in a file /etc/<nodeName> on the machine, and the host name associated with an interface (specified by <interface>) of the machine can be found in the /etc/hostname.<interface> file.
- Each entry in the /etc/hosts contains the following information about a host: host name, IP address associated with it, and nickname (alias), if any.
- When you enable or disable a network service on your Solaris system by using, say, the svcadm command, the service status change is recorded in the service configuration repository and will persist across reboots.

Look Out

- Because a hardware address is burned into the Ethernet NIC, if you change the Ethernet card, the hardware address of your computer changes.
- Because every IP address has a network component in it, if you move your machine from one network to another, its IP address will change.
- The inetadm command is used to manage inetd-controlled services, whereas svcadm is the SMF command to manage the network services.

Memorize

- The netsat utility is used to view the network packets' activity (statistics) on inbound/outbound connections of your machine.
- The ping command is used to check the reachability of another host on the network (or the Internet).
- The snoop command is used to look into the incoming/outgoing packets on your machine (e.g., the values for the header fields).
- The ifconfig command is used to configure a network interface such as assign an IP address to it, bring it up, or shut it down. You can also use this command to obtain configuration information about an interface.

✓ TWO-MINUTE DRILL

Understanding Network Fundamentals

- ❑ Hardware addresses are defined by the data link (network interface) layer, and the IP addresses are defined by the network layer.
- ❑ The ports are defined by the transport layer.
- ❑ Hubs, repeaters, and NICs operate in the physical layer, switches and bridges in the data link layer, and routers in the network layer.
- ❑ An Ethernet network based on a bus topology uses a coaxial cable as a shared cable, and a network based on star topology uses unshielded twisted-pair (UTP) cables to connect computers to a central device.
- ❑ Computers on a Thicknet use a vampire tap to connect to the shared cable, and computers on a Thinnet use BNC connectors to connect to the shared cable.
- ❑ Ethernet networks based on the star topology and using UTP cables are the most commonly used LANs.
- ❑ Frames are delivered from one machine to another machine on the same network, whereas IP datagrams can be delivered across networks.
- ❑ The netsat utility is used to view the network packets' activity (statistics) on inbound/outbound connections of your machine, whereas the `ping` command is used to check the reachability of another host on the network (or the Internet).
- ❑ The `snoop` command is used to look into the incoming/outgoing packets on your machine (e.g., the values for the header fields).
- ❑ The `arp` command is used to resolve an IP address into the corresponding hardware address.
- ❑ The `ifconfig` command is used to configure a network interface (e.g., by assigning an IP address to it, bringing it up, or shutting it down). You can also use this command to obtain configuration information about an interface.

Working with Network Services

- Solaris 10 offers Services Management Facility (SMF), which augments the traditional UNIX startup scripts and configuration files.
- The `inetadm` command is used to manage the inetd-controlled services, and `svcadm` is the SMF utility used to manage the network services.
- Once you enable or disable an SMF service, the status change information goes into a configuration repository and persists across multiple boots.

SELF TEST

The following questions will help you measure your understanding of the material presented in this chapter. Read all the choices carefully because there might be more than one correct answer. Choose all correct answers for each question.

1. Which of the layers is responsible for establishing end-to-end communication between two machines?

   A. Network layer

   B. Transport layer

   C. Data link layer

   D. Application layer

2. What other terms are used for an Ethernet address of a machine?

   A. Hardware address

   B. Physical address

   C. MAC

   D. Internet address

3. Which of the following protocols provide reliable end-to-end communication?

   A. TCP

   B. UDP

   C. IP

   D. RELIABLE

4. At which TCP/IP layer does a router operate?

   A. Physical

   B. Network interface

   C. Internet

   D. Transport

5. Which of the following statements are true about a MAC address?

   A. A computer can have only one MAC address.

   B. When an Ethernet card of a computer is replaced, its MAC address changes.

C. A MAC address is a 32-bit number.

D. An IP datagram contains the source and destination MAC addresses in its header.

6. Which of the following files would you look into to find out the IP address associated with a host name on your machine?

   A. `/etc/hostname.<interface>`

   B. `/etc/hostname`

   C. `/etc/nodename`

   D. `/etc/inet/hosts`

7. Which of the following devices forwards data packets called IP datagrams from one network to another?

   A. Router

   B. Bridge

   C. Switch

   D. Hub

8. An Internet service—for example, rlogin—was started when you booted your Solaris 10 system. After the boot, you disabled the service with the `svcadm` command. Now when you reboot the machine, you will need to manually enable the service by using the `svcadm` command.

   A. True

   B. False

9. Which command would you use to check whether a remote host is reachable?

   A. `ping`

   B. `snoop`

   C. `ifconfig`

   D. `netstat`

10. Which command would you use to check what kind of information is being exchanged between two systems?

    A. `ping`

    B. `snoop`

    C. `ifconfig`

    D. `netstat`

SELF TEST ANSWERS

1. ☑ **B**. The transport layer provides protocols to establish end-to-end communication by defining port number to uniquely identify an application on a machine.
   ☒ **A** is incorrect because the network layer defines the IP address of a machine but not the port number; therefore, you cannot uniquely identify the communicating application on the machine. **C** is incorrect because the data link layer defines hardware addresses; it's not even aware of IP addresses. **D** is incorrect because the application layer is responsible for specifying the application functionality and does not concern itself with establishing connections.

2. ☑ **A**, **B**, and **C**. A machine on a LAN is uniquely identified by its Media Access (MAC) address, which is called a physical address or a hardware address. A MAC address on an Ethernet LAN is also called an Ethernet address.
   ☒ **D** is incorrect because an Internet address is an IP address, not the MAC address.

3. ☑ **A**. TCP offers reliable end-to-end communication by creating a virtual connection between the two communicating machines and by providing a mechanism for acknowledgment and retransmission.
   ☒ **B** is incorrect because UDP provides only ports but nothing for reliability or creating virtual connection. **C** is incorrect because IP offers unreliable data delivery service. Furthermore, it cannot even identify the correct communication application on the machine and it takes time to calculate parity information. **D** is incorrect because there is no protocol called RELIABLE.

4. ☑ **C**. A router deals with IP addresses, so it has to operate at the Internet layer, because that's where IP addresses are defined.
   ☒ **A** and **B** are incorrect because the physical layer and the network interface layer are not aware of IP addresses. **D** is incorrect because a router does not need to know what is in the data portion of an IP datagram.

5. ☑ **B**. A MAC address is burned into an Ethernet card, which is a NIC for an Ethernet network.
   ☒ **A** is incorrect because a computer can have more than one interface card and each interface card has its own MAC address. However, remember that multiple interfaces on a SPARC system have the same MAC address because it is derived from the NVRAM chip. **C** is incorrect because an Ethernet address is a 48-bit number, not a 32-bit number. An IP address (IPv4) is a 32-bit number. **D** is incorrect because a MAC source and a destination MAC address are in the frame header and IP addresses are in the IP datagram header.

6. ☑ D. An entry in the `/etc/inet/hosts` file on your system contains the following information about a host name associated with your machine: the host name, the corresponding IP address, and an alias for the host name, if any.
   ☒ A is incorrect because the `/etc/hostname.<interface>` file contains only the host name associated with the interface specified by `<interface>`. **B** is incorrect because there is no such file as `/etc/hostname`, and **C** is incorrect because the `/etc/nodename` contains only the node name of your machine.

7. ☑ A. A router receives a frame from one network, retrieves the IP datagram from the frame, encapsulate it in another frame, and delivers the frame on the other network.
   ☒ B is incorrect because a bridge is not aware of IP addresses; therefore, it cannot deliver data packets across networks. **C** is incorrect because in its original functionality, a switch is not aware of IP addresses; therefore, it can only deliver frames over the same network, not IP datagrams across networks. However, layer-3 switches are available from some vendors that have the functionality of a router. **D** is incorrect because a hub operates only in the physical layer and simply provides electrical connection between different physical ports. It's not aware of hardware addresses or IP addresses.

8. ☑ A. Once you enable or disable an SMF service, the status change information goes into a configuration repository and persists across multiple boots.
   ☒ B is incorrect because, according to the configuration repository, the rlogin service is disabled; therefore, it will not be automatically started at boot time until you change its status by enabling it again.

9. ☑ A. You use the `ping` command to test the reachability of another host on the same network or on another network.
   ☒ B is incorrect because the `snoop` command is used to view the packet headers at various layer levels coming in or going out of an interface. **C** is incorrect because the `ifconfig` command is used to configure the network interfaces. **D** is incorrect because the `netstat` command is used to view the packet statistics on inbound/outbound connections.

10. ☑ B. The `snoop` command is used to view the packet headers at various layer levels coming in or going out of an interface.
    ☒ A is incorrect because you use the `ping` command to test the reachability of another host on the same network or on another network. **C** is incorrect because the `ifconfig` command is used to configure the network interfaces. **D** is incorrect because the `netstat` command is used to view the packet statistics on inbound/outbound connections.

11

Managing Naming Services

CERTIFICATION OBJECTIVES

As you learned in the previous chapter, we build computer networks to share resources. To share or use the shared resources, the computers need some network information necessary to communicate over the network, such as machine addresses, user names, passwords, access permissions, printer names, and so forth. Each machine on the network can maintain this information on its own, but that would be a cumbersome task for a network administrator, a task prone to errors and inconsistencies. The solution to this problem is to maintain this information on a centralized machine called a *naming server* and let other machines retrieve this information from this server, which offers what is a called a naming service.

There are a number of naming services to support the varying needs of networks. Solaris supports the Network Information Service (NIS), Network Information Service Plus (NIS+), Domain Name Service (DNS), and Light Weight Access Protocol (LDAP) directory services. All these services are run in a client/server network environment where there are naming service clients and naming service servers. In network services, caching is often used to improve service performance. The naming service cache daemon, `nscd`, provides the caching service for the most frequent name service requests.

The core question in this chapter is: what are the naming services and how are they managed? In search of an answer, we will explore three thought streams: naming service servers, naming service clients, and naming service caching.

CERTIFICATION OBJECTIVE 11.01

Understanding Naming Services

Exam Objective 5.1: *Explain naming services (DNS, NIS, NIS+, and LDAP) and the naming service switch file (database sources, status codes, and actions).*

As you learned in the previous chapters, we build computer networks to share resources. To do that the computers need some network information necessary to communicate over the network and to share the resources. In principle, each machine can maintain its own information and the information about other machines and resources on the network locally. Still, this can be a cumbersome task and can lead to errors. Suppose you just installed a printer on the network; you then need to enter information about it individually on all the machines on the network. If information about one machine changes, you must update this information on all the machines individually. So it's not only a cumbersome task—the consistency is also at risk. This is where naming services come into the picture by offering centralized management of network information such as machine addresses, user names, passwords, access permissions, printer names, and so forth. Furthermore, naming services simplify machine addressing, by allowing you to refer to the machines with names that are easy to remember rather than numerical addresses such as IP address. The Solaris system supports a number of naming services.

Naming Services Supported by Solaris

In the beginning, there were files in the `/etc` directory that were used as a naming system for a standalone UNIX machine. This file-based naming service was also adapted for the network environment, where a machine needs to keep information not only about itself but about other machines and services on the network. Therefore, this local file-based service is not well suited for large, sophisticated networks, and only some old UNIX OSs and machines still use this as a primary choice. More suitable naming services supported by Solaris to use in today's network environment are DNS, NIS, NIS+, and LDAP.

Domain Name Service

The Domain Name Systems (DNS) naming service manages the machine names on the Internet. In Chapter 10, we talked about the data being transferred over the Internet by IP addresses. But when was the last time you had to use an IP address (such as 132.25.3.4) to send an email to your friend or to browse the web? Under normal circumstances end users always use names that are easy to remember (e.g., macgrawhill.com or cs.cornell.edu). These names are called domain names and are translated to corresponding IP addresses before the outgoing data leaves your computer. The process of translation is called domain name resolution, and the mechanism to maintain the domain names and to resolve them is called Domain Name System (DNS). The machines that participate in the resolution are called DNS servers. The collection of domain names, or the corresponding machines that use DNS, is called a DNS namespace.

As Figure 11-1 shows, DNS is a hierarchical namespace conceptually represented by an inverted tree with an unnamed root. Each node in the tree is called a domain, and you write the domain name for a domain by starting with its subname and making your way up to the tree root, separating one subname from the other with a dot. For example, the domain name for `cs` in Figure 11-1 is:

```
cs.sjsu.edu
```

In practice, `cs.sjsu.edu` is the domain name for the computer science department at San Jose State University. For conceptual understanding you can assume that each domain name is maintained (hosted) by a separate DNS server, but in practice the situation may be more complex. For example, a server can host more than one domain name, and a domain name may be supported by more than one server—a primary and a secondary server.

The lines in the figure represent communication that is done over the Internet. For example, suppose a student at a machine (one that uses the DNS server hosting unex.berkeley.edu to resolve names) sends an email message to his friend at myFriend@cs.sjsu.edu. The name resolution query will travel along the DNS servers corresponding to the following domains:

```
-> unex.berkeley.edu -> berkeley.edu -> .edu -> sjsu.edu -> cs.sjsu.edu
```

Finally when it reaches the cs.sjsu.edu (DNS) server, that server will resolve the name, and the response will travel back to the unex.berkeley.edu address and

FIGURE 11-1

Conceptual view of DNS naming hierarchy representing a very small part of the Internet

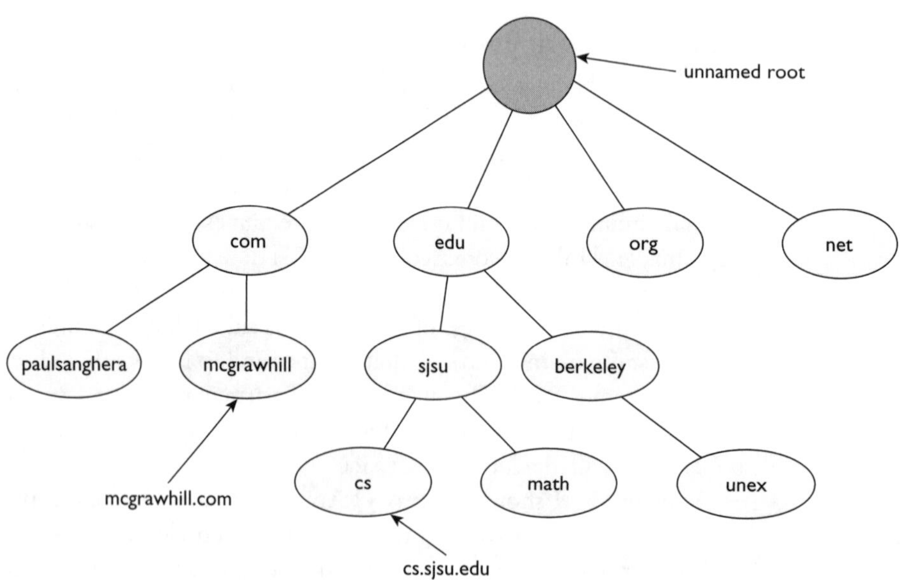

to the machine that sent the original query. However, the name may also be resolved by any server on its path from its cache. Further note that we have assumed one-to-one correspondence between a domain name and the DNS server just to clarify the concept, but it may not represent reality, which may be more complex, as stated previously.

DNS is a client/server system. A DNS server runs the daemon `in.named`. On the client side, DNS is implemented through what is called a *resolver*, whose function is to resolve naming queries by sending requests to the DNS server. The server can return either the requested information or the name of another DNS server that can be queried by the resolver.

DNS makes Internet communication simpler by letting you use domain names instead of IP addresses, and it manages the DNS namespace at Internet level. However, as you have seen, there are some names, such as local machine names and user names, that must be managed at a network level. In other words, the configuration information spread out in several files in the `/etc` directory on several machines in a network needs to be managed in a more efficient, consistent, and robust fashion. This is where Network Information Service (NIS) comes into the picture.

Network Information Service

The Network Information Service (NIS) manages, as the name suggests, the information specific to a network, such as information about machine names, user names, network services, and so forth. The focus of NIS is to make network administration easier by providing central management for distributed information. This is accomplished by providing a client/server environment. The principal terms in NIS are explained here:

- *NIS namespace*. The collection of network information managed by NIS.
- *NIS domain*. A set of NIS maps with some rules—for example, that a domain can contain one and only one master server. You can look at it as a well-defined subset of NIS namespace.
- *NIS maps*. The databases used to store the NIS namespace information. These maps were designed to replace the `/etc` files and other configuration files.
- *Master server*. The machines where you, the system administrator, originally create the NIS maps and then make any needed updates to them. The master server is also referred to as the primary server.

- *Slave servers*. These are the replications (or backups) of the master servers to provide fault tolerance and load balancing. Any NIS updates to a master server propagate to the corresponding slave servers. The slave servers are also referred to as secondary servers.
- *NIS clients*. Any host on the network that makes a request to an NIS server for NIS information is called an NIS client. The processes running on NIS clients make requests to the NIS servers for data from the maps. Note that a client does not make a distinction between a master server and a slave server. This applies to load balancing. Unlike DNS, the NIS namespace is flat, not hierarchical. Another naming service offered by Solaris is NIS+, which does offer a hierarchical namespace like DNS.

Network Information Service Plus

Network Information Service Plus (NIS+) is used to manage network information about machine addresses, mail, network interfaces, network service, and security. It is similar to NIS as to what and how it manages, such as central management for distributed information. However, it is not an extension to NIS. Unlike NIS, it is hierarchical and more dynamic (it can conform to the requirements of an organization), and it offers additional features such as security.

The fact that NIS namespace is hierarchical makes NIS more dynamic, because you can configure it to conform to the logical hierarchy of your organization. You can divide the namespace into multiple domains (corresponding to the organizational structure), which can be administered autonomously. Furthermore, you can control access to these domains in the hierarchy tree. NIS+ has primary servers and secondary servers just like NIS.

NIS and NIS+ store information in proprietary formats. To make the storage and retrieval of information system independent, the de facto Internet standard is called LDAP.

LDAP Service

The Light Weight Directory Access Protocol (LDAP) is an Internet protocol on which the LDAP service is based. The naming service NIS was originally called *yellow pages*. The idea behind the directory is the same as in the telephone directory, meaning that you can easily and quickly retrieve simple information such as a name, email address, phone number, and so forth. LDAP is a lighter version of the original directory protocol called X.500, which is a very complex protocol; its closest implementation is the original Novell Directory Service (NDS) which offers more features than LDAP and was made LDAP compatible because of the popularity of LDAP. A directory service is designed to be read intensive rather than write intensive, because fewer updates are expected to be made. You can store in LDAP all the information that you store in NIS or NIS+. Its namespace is hierarchical, and it does offer security.

You can use LDAP along with NIS or NIS+, because it allows data to be shared by different naming services. However, because of its wide acceptance, it will eventually replace NIS and NIS+.

on the job

Unlike an NIS server, an LDAP server cannot be its own client. In other words, a machine that is running as an LDAP server cannot be configured as an LDAP client.

The naming services are summarized in Table 11-1, and you will learn more about them in the remainder of this chapter.

TABLE 11-1 Comparison of various naming services

Characteristic	DNS	NIS	NIS+	LDAP
Namespace structure	Hierarchical	Flat	Hierarchical	Hierarchical
Data storage	Files resource records	Two-column maps	Multicolumn tables	Directories
Server kinds	Master/slave	Master/slave	Root master/ non-root master Primary/ secondary cache/stub	Master/ replica
Transport	TCP or UDP	RPC	RPC	TCP/IP
Scale	Global	LAN	LAN	Global
Security	Solaris 10 uses BIND 9.2, which offers some security features such as authenticated zone updates.	None (root or nothing)	Secure RPC	SSL

In selecting a naming service for your network, you have a number of options to choose from. You can even use more than one naming service for different types of information. The question is How does the naming service client (or an application that needs naming information) on your machine know which naming service is available to retrieve a specific piece of information? It looks into the naming service switch file, also known as *name service switch*, or simply *switch*.

Coordinating the Use of Naming Services

Because Solaris supports more than one naming service, you can use one or more than one naming service. You may find one naming service to be appropriate for one kind of information and another to be more appropriate for another kind of information. To enable the client to get specific network information from the correct naming service, you, the system administrator, maintain the name service switch file, which has the following name:

```
/etc/nsswitch.conf
```

Each entry (line) of this file lists a specific type of available information, such as host, password, or group, and identifies the source from which this information can be obtained. By looking into this file, a client can retrieve different pieces of the needed information from one or more sources (identified by one or more entries in the file)—for example, host name from the NIS table and password from a local file in the `/etc` directory, and so forth.

Creation of the `nsswitch.conf` File

Where does this `nsswitch.conf` file come from? It appears on your system during installation, as explained here:

1. During Solaris installation, the following four versions of the switch file (also called templates) corresponding to different naming services are loaded into the `/etc` directory:
   - `nsswitch.ldap`
   - `nsswitch.nis`
   - `nsswitch.nisplus`
   - `nsswitch.files`
2. The installer—that is, you—selects the machine's default naming service.

3. The template corresponding to your selection is copied to `nsswitch.conf`. For example, if you selected LDAP, the `nsswitch.ldap` file will be copied to `nsswitch.conf`.
4. You can edit and update the `nsswitch.conf` file, if needed.

The templates contain the default switch configuration for the LDAP, NIS, NIS+, and local files. The default template file copied to the `nsswitch.conf` file should be sufficient for normal operation in a typical environment. No template is provided for the DNS, but you can always edit the `nsswitch.conf` file and add the DNS information if you want to.

So, what is in the `nsswitch.conf` file?

Content of the Switch File

An entry in the `nsswitch.conf` file can have the following fields:

- The network information type.
- One or more sources from which the information can be obtained

Sixteen types of information are supported: aliases, bootparam, ethers, groups, hosts, ipnodes, netgroups, netmasks, networks, passwords, protocols, publickey, rpc, services, automount, and sendmailvars. The supported sources, also called information sources or database sources, are listed in Table 11-2.

TABLE 11-2 Database sources supported by the switch file

Database Source	Description
`compat`	Used for password and group information to support old-style + or − syntax in `/etc/group`, `/etc/passwd`, `/etc/shadow` files.
`dns`	Used to specify that the host information can be obtained from DNS.
`files`	Used to specify that the information can be obtained from files in the client's `/etc` directory, such as `/etc/passwd`.
`ldap`	Used to specify that the information can be obtained from the LDAP directory.
`nis`	Used to specify that the information can be obtained from an NIS map, such as a hosts map.
`nisplus`	Used to specify that the information can be obtained from an NIS+ table such as a hosts table.

An entry in the switch file may have more than one source; if it does, the information will be searched from sources in the order they are listed. Once the information is obtained, the search will be terminated—that is, the remaining sources will not be searched. This is the default that you can change by specifying the action options in the switch file.

When the information is searched in a source, the search may return any of the following status codes:

- SUCCESS. The requested information was found in the specified source.
- NOTFOUND. The requested information was not found in the specified source.
- UNAVAIL. The source either did not respond or was unavailable.
- TRYAGAIN. The information was not returned because the source was busy.

You can instruct the switch how to respond to any of these status codes (messages) by using what are called *switch action options*, which are listed here:

- *continue*. Try the next listed source. This is the default for NOTFOUND, UNAVAIL, and TRYAGAIN.
- *return*. Stop looking for the information. This is the default for SUCCESS.

You can change a default action value by specifying the action in an entry of the switch file. For example, consider the following entry in the switch file:

```
netmasks nis [NOTFOUND=return] files
```

If a client looking for netmasks information does not find it in NIS, it will not look in the files in the `/etc` directory. If the [NOTFOUND=return] was not in this entry, the client would look into files after failing to find netmask information in NIS.

As an example, the default switch file for NIS—that is, the template `/etc/nsswitch.nis`, looks like this:

```
passwd: files nis
group: files nis
# consult /etc "files" only if nis is down.
hosts: nis [NOTFOUND=return] files
networks: nis [NOTFOUND=return] files
protocols: nis [NOTFOUND=return] files
rpc: nis [NOTFOUND=return] files
ethers: nis [NOTFOUND=return] files
```

```
netmasks: nis [NOTFOUND=return] files
bootparams: nis [NOTFOUND=return] files
publickey: nis [NOTFOUND=return] files
netgroup: nis
automount: files nis
aliases: files nis
# for efficient getservbyname() avoid nis
services: files nis
sendmailvars: files
```

In summary, some of the functionalities of the naming services offer are listed here:

- Manage network information at a central place.
- Assign (bind) names to addresses of network entities, such as a computer.
- Resolve names to addresses.
- Delete bindings.
- Change the bindings.

Because from the user's perspective the Internet is also just a big network, in today's networks you need naming information related to your local network and the Internet. The information about your local network, such as machine names and users, can be managed by using NIS.

CERTIFICATION OBJECTIVE 11.02

Working with NIS

Exam Objective 5.5: *Configure the NIS domain: build and update NIS maps, manage the NIS master and slave server, configure the NIS client, and troubleshoot NIS for server and client failure messages.*

NIS is a distributed naming service that provides a mechanism for identifying and locating network entities and resources. It enables you to store and retrieve network information in a standard way and to distribute this information in the form of maps over master servers and slave servers. Then, you can update that information from a central location—that is, you don't need to log on to each server individually to update the information. This will ensure that all clients share the same naming service information, which is consistent throughout the network.

The main components of the NIS service are NIS maps and NIS master and slave servers.

Managing NIS Maps

As you know, NIS is used to manage network information. The set of files in which NIS keeps the information is referred to as NIS maps. These files are written in a binary format called `ndbm`. Historically speaking, network information was originally maintained in `/etc` and some other configuration files, and the maps were designed to replace those files. As you will see, the maps contain much more than just the names and addresses.

The information in NIS maps is stored in two-column tables, one column containing the key and the other column containing the information associated with the key. For example, a key may be the name of a host, and the information column may contain the IP address of the host with that name. Solaris offers a set of default maps for an NIS domain in the following directory of the NIS domain server:

```
/var/yp/<domainName>
```

For example, the maps for the domain capital.com will be in the `/var/yp/capital.com` directory. Some of these maps are listed in Table 11-3.

If you wanted to use the `/etc` files to manage network information, you would have to change the files on all the machines to reflect a change in the network environment. In the case of NIS maps, you only have to update the information on the master server, and the update will be propagated automatically to the slave servers. The client machines will get this information as needed from the servers (primary or secondary). As an example, suppose you add a new machine to your network, which is running NIS. You will do the following:

- Update the input file in the master server only (you will learn how further along).
- Run the `make` utility. This will automatically update the `hosts.byname` and `hosts.byaddr` files on the master server.
- These updates will be propagated automatically to the slave servers and will be available to the client machines.

Now you can see how NIS (as opposed to `/etc` files) simplifies the process of information management. But what is the input file and what is the `make` utility? The `make` is the utility that transforms the information in the input file into `ndbm`

TABLE 11-3 The default NIS files (the <key> in the file extension by<key> specifies the key in the file)

Map Name	Corresponding NIS Admin File	Description
auth_attr, exec_attr, prof_attr, user_attr	auth_attr, exec_attr, prof_attr, user_attr	Contains attribute information about profiles, users, and authorization; part of RBAC as discussed in Chapter 14.
bootparams	bootparams	Contains the path names for files that the client needs during boot: root, swap, and so forth.
ethers.byaddr, ethers.byname	ethers	Contain name-to-address mapping. The key in the ethers.byaddr file is the Ethernet address, whereas the key in the ethers.byname file is the machine name.
group.bygid, group.byname	group	Contain group security information with group ID as the key in the group.bygid file and group name as the key in the group.byname file.
hosts.byaddr, hosts.byname	hosts	Contain machine name and IP address with address as the key in the hosts.byaddr file and name as the key in the hosts.byname file.
ipnodes.byaddr, ipnodes.byname	ipnodes	Contain machine name and IP address with address as the key in the ipnodes.byaddr file and name as the key in the ipnodes.byname file.
mail.aliases, mail.byaddr	aliases	Contain alias and mail address with alias as the key in the mail.aliases file and address as the key in the mail.byaddr file.
netgroup, netgroup.byhost, netgroup.byuser	netgroup	Contain group name, user name, and machine name with group as the key for the netgroup file, host as the key for the netgroup.byhost file, and user as the key for the netgroup.byuser file.
netmasks.byaddr	netmasks	Contains the network mask information for IP addresses with IP address as the key.

TABLE 11-3 The default NIS files (the <key> in the file extension by<key> specifies the key in the file) *(continued)*

Map Name	Corresponding NIS Admin File	Description
networks.byaddr, networks.byname	networks	Contain network names known to your system and their IP addresses with IP address as the key for the networks.byaddr file and name as the key for the networks.byname file.
passwd.byname, passwd.byuid	passwd, shadow	Contain password information with user name as the key in the passwd.byname file and user ID as the key in the passwd.byuid file.
protocols.byname, protocols.bynbumber	protocols	Contain the network protocols known to your network with protocol name as the key in the protocols.byname file and protocol number as the key in the protocol.bynumber file.
rpc.bynumber	rpc	Contains the program number and the name of the RPCs known to your system with the RPC number as the key.
services.byname, services.byservice	services	Contain the list of network services known to the network with port (or protocol) on which the service is running as the key in the services.byname file and service name as the key in the services.byservice file.

format (i.e., the map format). The input file is a text file that simply contains the information that the /etc file will contain. For example, suppose you add a new user with user name agore; a line like the following will be added to the /etc/passwd file:

```
agore:x:123:10:User agore:/home/agore:/bin/csh:
```

You would copy this line to the password input file that the make utility will then transfer to the password map, such as passwd.byuid.

When you designate a machine as server during installation, a Makefile is stored in the /var/yp directory. When you run the make command, it is the instructions in the `Makefile` that are actually executed; they locate the input files and execute `makedb`, which creates or updates NIS maps from the input files.

You should always create maps on the master server, because they will be automatically pushed to the slave servers. If you create maps on a slave server, they will not automatically be pushed to the master server, or to other slave servers.

So it is the NIS master server on which you create or update maps. Let's explore how to manage the master server.

Managing the NIS Master Server

Recall that without NIS, we would have `/etc` files to manage network information on each machine. It is basically these files that make the source files for the NIS server. The goal is to convert these files on the server machine into NIS maps and then manage the NIS maps and serve the information from them.

Preparing the Source Files

The source files are the text files that will be converted to NIS maps, and they originally reside in the `/etc` directory. But you want to separate the view of the source files and the local files for various reasons. For example, local files also include `passwd` and `shadow` files, and if you use the `/etc` as the source file directory, the `passwd` file will also be converted to a NIS map and made available to the clients. Therefore, a good strategy is to use some other directory as a source directory and copy the necessary files from the `/etc` directory into this source directory. Edit the `passwd` file in the source directory, and remove the root entry from it. To find out in detail how to prepare the source files, check out the following exercise.

EXERCISE 11-1

How to Prepare Source Files for Conversion to NIS Maps

To prepare the source files for conversion into NIS maps, perform the following steps:

1. Log on to the machine that will be the primary NIS server. Become a superuser.

2. You need to make sure that the files in the `/etc` directory that will be the source files reflect an up-to-date picture of your system. To do this, check the following files:
   - `auto.home or auto_home`
   - `auto.master or auto_master`
   - `bootparams`
   - `ethers`
   - `group`
   - `hosts`
   - `ipnodes`
   - `netgroup`
   - `netmasks`
   - `networks`
   - `passwd`
   - `protocols`
   - `rpc`
   - `service`
   - `shadow`
   - `user_attr`
3. Copy all of these source files, except `passwd`, to the `<DIR>` directory that you have specified in the `/var/yp/Makefile` to be the source directory.
4. Copy the `passwd` file to the password directory `<PWDIR>` that you have specified in the `Makefile` as a source directory for the password file.
5. Copy the `audit_user`, `auth_attr`, `exec_attr`, and `prof_attr` to the selected `<RBACDIR>` directory that you have specified in the `Makefile`.
6. Check the `/etc/mail/aliases` file. Unlike other source files, you cannot move this file to another . However, make sure that it has all the mail aliases that you want to make available throughout the domain.
7. Weed out all the comments and other extraneous information from the source files. The `Makefile` does perform some file cleaning automatically, but it's good practice to examine and clean these files manually.
8. Check each source file and make sure the data is in the correct format.

The source files, once prepared, must be converted to NIS maps. The `Makefile` will do that. But you first need to make sure the `Makefile` will do the right thing.

Preparing the `Makefile`

When you designate a machine as server during installation, a `Makefile` is stored in the `/var/yp` directory. Because you are recommended to put the source files in a directory other than the `/etc` directory, you will need to make a few changes in the `Makefile`. Before making these changes, copy the original `Makefile` to some other name, to be on the safe side. Make any of the following changes in the `Makefile` if necessary:

- *DIR value.* The value of DIR in the `Makefile` is the `/etc` directory by default. If you have copied the source files to some other directory, change the value of the DIR field accordingly.
- *PWDIR value.* If you have copied the `passwd` and `shadow` files to a directory other than the `/etc` directory, change the value of the PWDIR field accordingly.
- *Domain name resolver.* If you want your server to use the domain name resolver for machines not in this domain, comment out the following line:

```
B=
```

and uncomment the following line:

```
B=-b
```

on the job

Make sure that the source password file on the master server that will be used to make the password map file does not have an entry for the root, and that the source file is in a directory such as `/var/yp` (not in the `/etc` directory); then change the value of PWDIR accordingly. When you change the values of DIR or PWDIR in the `Makefile`, make sure you do not indent the line.

Now that you have prepared the source files and modified the `Makefile` accordingly, you are ready to convert the source files into NIS maps. Solaris offers the `ypinit` command to accomplish that.

Setting Up the Master Server with the `ypinit` Command

The `ypinit` command is used to set up the master server, the slave servers, and the clients for NIS. It also builds a fresh set of NIS maps from the source files cited in the `Makefile`. After you issue the `ypinit` command to build NIS maps, the following steps are executed:

1. The `ypinit` script constructs the list of servers.
2. The `ypinit` command invokes the `make` command.
3. The `make` command cleans up the remaining comments in the `Makefile`.
4. The `make` command uses the `Makefile` to find out where the source files are and runs `makedbm` to convert the source files to the NIS maps.

Keep in mind that the `domainname` command is used on the master server to determine to which domain the maps will be pushed. If you are not sure it will do the right thing, you can hard code the domain into the `make` command in the `ypinit` script. For example, the following command in the `ypinit` script will push the `passwd` file to the domain senate.com:

```
make DOM=senate.com passwd
```

This way you can push a map file to the intended domain, even if the domain is different from that of the master server.

Check out the following exercise to see how you can use the `ypinit` command to set up an NIS master server.

EXERCISE 11-2

Setting Up a Master Server by Using the `ypinit` Command

You can set up the master server for NIS, by performing the following steps:

1. Log on to the master server machine as superuser.
2. Copy the `/etc/nsswitch.files` file to the `/etc/nsswitch.conf` file by issuing the following command:

   ```
   cp /etc/nsswitch.files /etc/nsswitch.conf
   ```

3. Edit the `/etc/hosts` and `/etc/inet/ipnodes` file and add the name and IP address of each of the NIS servers.
4. To build new NIS maps on this master server, issue the following command:

   ```
   /usr/sbin/ypinit -m
   ```

When you are prompted by `ypinit` for a list of other machines to become NIS slave servers, type the name of the server you are working on along with the names of other machines that you want to become NIS slave servers.

5. When you are asked by `ypinit` whether you want the procedure to terminate at the first nonfatal error or continue despite nonfatal errors, type `y`. If you choose `y`, and `ypinit` encounters a problem, it will exit. In this case, fix the problem and restart `ypinit`.
6. You are asked whether the existing files in the `/var/yp/<domainName>` directory can be destroyed. Obviously, this message would appear only if NIS was previously installed. At this point, the `ypinit` command executes the `make` command that triggers converting the source files to the NIS maps.
7. Issue the following command to enable NIS as the naming service:

```
cp /etc/nsswitch.nis /etc/nsswitch.conf
```

Note that by issuing this command you are replacing the existing switch file with the default NIS-oriented switch file. You can edit this file later if it becomes necessary.

Note that the `passwd` maps are built from the `/PWDIR/passwd`, `/PWDIR/shadow`, and `/PWDIR/security/passwd.adjunct` files, and the value for the `PWDIR` field is defined in `Makefile`. Make sure this field carries the correct value; otherwise, change it.

The NIS maps that will be created are listed under `all` in the `Makefile`. After the `makedbm` command has been executed, the information is collected in the following two files:

```
mapname.dir
mapname.pag
```

Both of these files reside in the `/var/yp/<domainName>` directory on the master server where the `<domainName>` specifies the domain. Once you set up the server with the `ypinit` command, it will automatically be started each time the machine is booted. However, situations may arise in which you will need to stop and restart the server when system is up and running.

Domains and Daemons

You can look at an NIS domain as a collection of Solaris machines that share a common set of NIS maps. A domain has a domain name, and each machine sharing the common set of maps belongs to that domain. Any machine on a network can be configured to belong to a given domain, as long as there is a server on the network to maintain the domain's NIS maps. An NIS client machine acquires its domain name and binds to an NIS server at boot time.

exam watch ***Make sure you understand that the NIS utilities are different from the NIS daemons and you know the function of each daemon and utility. In other words, you should be able to identify a daemon or a utility needed to accomplish a given task.***

The NIS service is managed by Service Management Facility (SMF), as discussed in Chapter 10, and the service itself is provided by five daemons (background processes running all the time) listed in Table 11-4.

In addition to the five daemons that keep the service running, a number of utilities, listed in Table 11-5, support the service.

You can administer (enable, disable, restart, and the like) these processes by using the `svcadm` command.

Starting and Stopping the NIS Service

Once you have configured the NIS master server by using the `ypinit` command, the server is started automatically during boot time by invoking the `ypstart` command. You can also stop and start (or restart) the server when the system is up and running.

You can stop the server by using either of the following two commands:

```
svcadm disable network/nis/server
ypstop
```

TABLE 11-4 The NIS daemons

Daemon	Description
`ypserv`	The NIS server process
`ypbind`	Binding process
`ypxfrd`	High-speed map transfer
`rpc.yppasswdd`	The NIS daemon to update the passwords
`rpc.ypupdated`	Modifies other maps such as public key

TABLE 11-5 NIS utilities

Utility	Description
`ypcat`	Lists data in a map.
`ypinit`	Initializes NIS client's server's list `ypservers`, and builds and installs an NIS database. Used to set up a client.
`ypmatch`	Looks up a specific entry in a map.
`yppoll`	Gets a map order number from a server by using the `ypserv` daemon.
`yppush`	Pushes an NIS map from the master server to the slave servers.
`ypset`	Sets binding of a machine to particular server.
`ypwhich`	Returns the name of the NIS server for this client as well as the nickname translation table.
`ypxfr`	Transfers NOS maps from a master server to the slave servers.

You can start the server by using either of the following two commands:

```
svcadm enable network/nis/server
ypstart
```

To restart (stop and immediately start) the server, you can issue the following command:

```
svcadm restart network/nis/server
```

Recall from Chapter 10 that the `svcadm` is an SMF (Service Management Facility) utility.

At this point, the master server is up and running and you know how to stop and restart it. Now you can set up a slave server. However, note that before you can configure a machine as a slave server for the first time, it must be configured as a client. With that said, let's first finish the server story before we move on to the clients.

Managing the NIS Slave Servers

You can have one or more slave servers for one master server. A slave server is the server that contains a copy of the network information from the master server. Remember, the updates are made only on the master server and then pushed to the slave servers. The slave servers are useful in two ways: they can balance the load by serving requests from the clients, and they offer fault tolerance by continuing to serve if the master server goes down.

To set up a slave server follow the instructions in the following exercise.

EXERCISE 11-3

Setting Up an NIS Slave Server

To set up an NIS slave server, perform the following steps:

1. Log in as superuser to the machine you want to set up as a slave server. Perform the following steps on this machine.
2. Add the names and IP addresses of all the other NIS servers to one of the following files:

   ```
   /etc/hosts
   /etc/inet/ipnodes
   ```

3. Change the directory to `/var/yp`.
4. Initialize the machine as a client by issuing the following command:

   ```
   /usr/sbin/ypinit -c
   ```

   The `ypinit` script will prompt you for a list of NIS servers. Enter the names in the following order: the server that you are setting up, the master server, and other NIS slave servers.
5. Determine whether the NIS client is running by issuing the following command:

   ```
   svcs network/nis/client
   ```

6. If you determined in step 5 that the client was running, restart the client service with the following command:

   ```
   svcadm restart network/nis/client
   ```

   If you determined that the client was not running, start the client by issuing the following command:

   ```
   svcadm enable network/nis/client
   ```

7. Initialize this machine as a slave by issuing the following command:

   ```
   /usr/sbin/ypinit -s <masterServer>
   ```

   The `<masterServer>` argument specifies the name of the master server that has already been configured (set up).
8. Repeat steps 1 to 7 for each machine you want to configure as an NIS slave server.

NIS is a network service offered in the client/server environment. Now that you know the server side of NIS, let's explore the client side.

CERTIFICATION OBJECTIVE 11.03

Configuring the Clients

Exam Objective 5.3: *Configure naming service clients during install, configure the DNS client, and set up the LDAP client (client authentication, client profiles, proxy accounts, and LDAP configurations) after installation.*

The naming services on Solaris works in terms of servers and clients. The client makes a request for the information, and the server provides the information. You need to know how to configure the clients for the naming services.

Configuring NIS Clients

You can configure your machine as an NIS client by using either of the two methods described here. The recommended method for configuring a client machine to use NIS is to log in to the machine as superuser and execute the following command:

```
ypinit -c
```

You will be asked for a list of NIS servers in the domain. You would name the master server and the other slave servers. It is a good practice to name the servers in ascending order of their distance (in terms of the network) from this machine—that is, the closest server first.

After logging on to the machine as superuser, you can use the following method (if you have to) from the good old days:

- Set the domain name with the `domainname` command:

```
domainname <domainName>
```

- Save the existing `ypservers` file:

```
mv /var/yp/binding/<domainName>/ypservers
/var/yp/binding/<domainname>/ypservers.bak
```

- Issue the `ypstart` command:

```
ypstart
```

- If the `/var/yp/binding/<domainName>/ypservers` file does not exist, the `ypstart` command will automatically invoke the NIS client in broadcast mode:

```
ypbind -broadcast
```

This is why you moved the `ypservers` file before issuing the `ypstart` command. The `ypbind` searches the local subnet for an NIS server. If the server is found, it binds to the server.

exam watch

You cannot set up an NIS client on a machine that has also been configured for a native LDAP client. In other words, Solaris does not support the coexistence of a native LDAP client and an NIS client on the same machine.

Once you have configured the clients, you can convert one or more of them to be slave servers, as shown in the previous section. Just like NIS, DNS is a client/server system, and you need to know how to set up a DNS client.

Configuring the DNS Client

Berkeley Internet Name Domain (BIND) is a freely available reference implementation of the Domain Name System (DNS) protocol for providing naming service on the TCP/IP networks and the Internet. The main function of DNS is to resolve domain names (such as www.cornell.edu) into IP addresses and vice versa. Solaris 10 ships with BIND 9 DNS server.

For example, when you type www.cornell.edu in the location bar of your browser, your machine makes a request to a DNS server to resolve the domain name cornell.edu to an IP address. However, before your machine can make this request, it needs to be configured as a DNS client.

The DNS configuration information on your machine is in the `/etc/resolv.conf` file, which contains the name of the local domain and the address of the DNS server. The configuration file contains the following lines (called directives) described in Table 11-6.

The `sortlist` directive is rarely used. It is useful only when a domain name may be resolved to multiple addresses. Normally, the resolver will send the addresses in the order they are received. However, if the sortlist option is in place and the

TABLE 11-6 The configuration directives in the `resolv.conf` file

Directive Name	Example	Description
`domain <domainName>`	domain cornell.edu	cornell.edu is the domain name registered with the Internet (DNS server).
`nameserver <DNSServer>`	nameserver 135.23.3.4	Here 135.23.3.4 is the IP address of the DNS server available to this client.
`sortlist <addressList>`	sortlist 132.121.17.3/255.255.240.0 143.25.3.4	Allows the addresses returned by the resolver to be sorted. A `sortlist` is specified by IP address/netmask pairs. The netmask is optional and defaults to the class netmask of the net. Up to ten pairs may be specified.
`options <options>`	timeout:30 attempts:5	Allows certain internal resolver variables to be modified; for example, `timeout` sets the time in seconds. The resolver will wait before retrying, and `attempts` specifies the number of times the resolver will send the query to the DNS server before giving up.

list of addresses that the resolver received contains the addresses specified in the sortlist, the resolver reorders the list of received addresses so that the addresses specified in the sortlist are placed in front of the other addresses. There is a space between the keyword (such as domain) and the value, and between two values when applicable. The keyword and the value (or values) must appear in the same line.

Watch ***The resolver is not a command or a process; it is a library of routines that can be called by network processes or applications.***

The `/etc/resolv.conf` file is used by the resolver, which is a collection of routines used for compiling and sending requests (queries) to a DNS server and interpreting the replies from the server.

If your network is running the LDAP service, you will need to set up LDAP clients to use the service.

Setting Up the LDAP Clients

The two main steps involved in setting up an LDAP client are initializing the client and setting up authentication for the client.

Initializing the LDAP Client

You can set up an LDAP client by using a utility called, well, `ldapclient` (can you figure out a simpler name?). Before a Solaris client machine can use the LDAP naming service, the following conditions must be met:

- You need to configure the client machine as LDAP client.
- The domain name that the client machine belongs to must be served by an LDAP server.
- The `nsswitch.conf` file must point to LDAP for the required services.
- The `ldap_cachemgr` must be running on the client machine.
- At least one server for which the client is configured must be up and running.

You can perform all these tasks, except starting the server, by using the `ldapclient` utility. You can initialize a client using either profile or proxy credentials. To initialize a client by using a profile, issue the following command:

```
ldapclient init -a profileName=<profile> -a domainName= <domain> <LDAP_SERVER>
```

<profile> specifies the name of the profile stored on the LDAP server specified by <LDAP_SERVER>, which could be an IP address of the server machine. The command uses the attributes in the specified profile to configure the client.

Alternatively, you can initialize a client to use the proxy credential by issuing the ldapclient command in the following form:

```
ldapclient init -a proxyDN=<DN> -a domainName=<domain> -a profileName=<profile>
-a proxyPassword=<password> <LDAP_SERVER>
```

DN stands for the distinguished name. If you do not specify proxy password in the command, you will be prompted for it. LDAP does provide authentication.

Authentication

Solaris uses the pam (http://www.kernel.org/pub/linux/libs/pam) module, pm_ldap, which enables Solaris servers and workstations to authenticate against the LDAP directories and to change the passwords in the directory. The pam API uses transport layer security such as Secure Socket Layer (SSL) or Transport Layer Security (TLS) to encrypt transactions between the workstation and the LDAP server and provide authenticated login.

An LDAP client authenticates to the LDAP server according to the client's credential level. The LDAP clients can be assigned three possible credential levels with which to authenticate to a directory server:

- *Anonymous*. A client with this access level can only access information that is available to everyone. Never allow write to anonymous—think of the implications if you do.
- *Proxy*. A client can be set up to authenticate or bind to the directory using a proxy account. A proxy account can be any entry that is allowed to bind to the directory. Obviously, this proxy account must have sufficient access to perform the naming service tasks on the LDAP server.
- *Proxy anonymous*. A client with this access level has the privileges of both the proxy and the anonymous levels. If a client with proxy anonymous access level attempts to log in as a proxy and the login fails, the client will be provided the anonymous access.

Null passwords are not allowed in LDAP.

Like LDAP, NIS+ also provides security, which we discuss next.

CERTIFICATION OBJECTIVE 11.04

The NIS+ Security

Exam Objective 5.4: *Explain NIS and NIS security including NIS namespace information, domains, processes, securenets, and password.adjunct.*

The NIS+ naming service provides security. Actually, the NIS+ security is such an integral part of the NIS+ namespace that you cannot set up security and the namespace independently. The security features of NIS+ are designed to protect both the information in the namespace and the structure of the namespace from unauthorized access. NIS+ security basically does two things: it authenticates the client, and, after successful authentication, it lets the client have appropriate access to NIS+ service entities such as tables of information.

Before exploring the NIS+ security process, let's take a look at the NIS+ security concepts.

NIS+ Security Concepts

The main NIS+ security concepts are described in the following:

- *NIS+ object.* NIS+ objects are the NIS+ entities (things) that are secured—for example, the server itself, the NIS+ table, the table entries, and so forth. The access rights (permissions) are set on an object, meaning who can do what to this object.
- *NIS+ principal.* An NIS+ principal is an entity that seeks access to an NIS+ object. In other words, all requests for NIS+ services will come from NIS+ principals. Note that a principal does not always have to be a user. For example, a request made by an ordinary user on a client machine would come from the client user, whereas a request made by the root user on a client machine would come from the client machine itself. NIS objects do not grant permissions to principals directly. To have access to an object, a principal must be a member of an authorization class.
- *Permission matrix.* A permission matrix is a set of permissions set on the objects and granted to principals. Once a principal has been properly authenticated to NIS+, its ability to read, modify, create, or destroy the NIS+ objects is determined by the applicable permission matrix.

- *Authorization class*. An authorization class is a type of principal to whom the permissions on an object are granted. There are four classes of principals:
  - *Owner*. A principal who is also the owner of the object gets the permissions set on the object for the owner class.
  - *Group*. A group is a collection of principals. Each NIS+ object has one group associated with it. You, the administrator, specify the principals for a given group, and each principal in the group enjoys the access permissions set on the object for the group class. Note that NIS+ groups are not the same as UNIX groups.
  - *World*. The world class is a collection of all principals that the server can authenticate. Any principal that belongs neither to the owner class nor to the group class but can be authenticated, belongs to the world class.
  - *Nobody*. Any principal that cannot be authenticated belongs to the nobody class.

When an NIS+ request from a principal is received, the system determines which class the requesting principal belongs to; the principal is then given the access rights belonging to that class. You, the administrator, can set on an object any combination of access rights for each of these classes—the permission matrix. Typically, however, a higher class (the owner class being the highest and the nobody class being the lowest) is assigned the same rights as all the lower classes, plus possible additional rights. For example, you could set on an object read access for the nobody class and the world class, read and modify access for the group class, and read, modify, create, and destroy access for the owner class.

How does a client go through the NIS+ security process?

NIS+ Security Process

NIS+ security is mainly a two-stage process:

1. *Authentication*. Authentication is the process to verify that a client is actually what the client claims to be. After a request (to access an NIS+ object) from a client is received, the client's identity and secure RPC password is verified. After the client's identity is validated, the authorization kicks in.
2. *Authorization*. Once a client's identity has been validated by the authentication process, NIS+ determines the class for the client. What a client (user or a machine) can do with a given NIS+ object depends on which class the client belongs to.

The entire security process can be broken down into the following steps:

1. A client (principal) requests access to an NIS+ object.
2. The server authenticates the client's identity by examining the client's credentials.
3. If the client is authenticated (credentials are validated), the client falls into the world class; otherwise, it falls into the nobody class.
4. The server looks into the target object's definition to make a final determination of the class that will be associated with the client (principal).
5. The client will get the permissions associated with the class of principal assigned to the client.

In any network service, caching is used to improve service performance.

CERTIFICATION OBJECTIVE 11.05

A Cache for the Naming Service

Exam Objective 5.2: *Configure, stop and start the Name Service Cache Daemon (nscd) and retrieve naming service information using the getent command.*

Generally speaking, a caching service is a process of saving (caching) information closer to the client and serving it from the cache (not from the original source) when a request arrives. This improves performance, but it also raises an issue of when the information gets stale and needs to be refreshed—that is, how to stay in synch with the original source of information (the server). The naming service caching is provided by the naming service cache daemon.

Managing the Naming Service Cache Daemon

The naming service cache daemon (`nscd`) provides cache for common naming service requests. The daemon automatically starts when the Solaris system is booted and provides caching for the following service databases:

- **`exec_attr.`** Contains execution profiles (RBAC).

- **group.** Contains group security information.
- **hosts.** Contains the machine name and IP address information.
- **ipnodes.** Contains IP address and machine name information.
- **passwd.** Contains password information.
- **prof_attr.** Contains profile attributes (related to RBAC).
- **user_attr.** Contains attributes for users and roles (related to RBAC).

The exec_attr, prof_attr, and user_attr are parts of Role Based Access Control (RBAC), which is discussed in Chapter 14.

If NIS+ is being used, the nscd checks the permissions on the passwd table to preserve NIS+ security. If this table cannot be read by an unauthenticated user, nscd makes sure that any encrypted password information from the NIS+ server is served only to the owner of that password.

You can also use the nscd command as an administration tool. Any nscd command you issue is passed transparently to an already running instance of nscd. The nscd command has the following syntax:

```
/usr/sbin/nscd [-e <cacheName>, yes | no] [-f <configurationFile>] [-g] [-i
<cacheName>]
```

The <configurationFile> specifies the configuration file that determines the behavior of nscd, and the default is /etc/nscd.conf. The <cacheName> specifies the name of the database from the list of databases supported by nscd such as group, hosts, and ipnodes. The options are described here:

- **-e <cacheName>, yes|no**. Enables (yes) or disables (no) the cache specified by <cacheName>.
- **-f <configurationFile>.** Instructs nscd to configure itself from the file specified by <configurationFile>, whose default value is /etc /nscd.conf.
- **-g.** Prints the current configuration information and statistics to the standard output. A non-root user can execute the nscd command only with this option.
- **-i <cacheName>.** Invalidates the cache specified by the <cacheName>.

Although nscd is started automatically when the system is booted, there will be situations in which you would like to stop and restart the daemon—for example, when the `nsswitch.conf` file is changed. You can use the following SMF commands to accomplish that:

```
svcadm disable $FMRI
svcadm enable $FMRI
```

where `$FMRI` specifies the `nscd` instance with a value like `system/name-service-cache:default`. You can also use the old commands:

```
/etc/init.d/nscd stop
/etc/init.d/nscd start
```

These scripts have been modified to eventually execute the `svcadm` command under the hood. Remember that the `nscd` daemon also caches the switch information.

There will be situations when you would like to examine the naming service databases. You can do it with the `getent` command.

Using the getent Command

You can retrieve the naming service information by using the `getent` command, which has the following syntax:

```
getent <database> [<key>]
```

The argument `<database>` specifies the name of the name service database to be examined. It could be any of the following:

- **/etc/ethers.** Database for Ethernet address to host name
- **/etc/group.** The group file
- **/etc/inet/hosts.** The database for IP version 4 host names
- **/etc/inet/ipnodes.** The database for IP version 4 and 6 host names
- **/etc/netmasks.** The database for network masks
- **/etc/networks.** The network name database
- **/etc/passwd.** The password file
- **/etc/project.** The project file
- **/etc/protocols.** The protocol name database
- **/etc/services.** Database for Internet services and aliases

The <key> argument specifies the key related to the database to be searched—for example, user name or numeric-uid for `passwd`. The `getent` command displays the database entries that match each of the supplied keys, one per line.

For example, consider the following command:

```
getent passwd danq
```

It will generate output like the following:

```
danq::30641:10:Dan Quale User:/home/danq:/bin/csh
```

The `getent` command retrieves information from the database sources specified for the <database> in the name service switch file, `/etc/nsswitch.conf`.

The three most important takeaways from this chapter are as follows:

- NIS is used to centralize the administration of network information such as machine names, user names, and network services, whereas DNS runs on the Internet to resolve domain names to IP addresses. LDAP manages the same kind of information as NIS, but it is based on an open Internet standard.
- You can use the `ypinit` command to set up master servers, slave servers, and clients for NIS, and the `ldapclient` command to set up clients for the LDAP service.
- The `nscd` daemon offers the cache service for most common naming service requests.

CERTIFICATION SUMMARY

Solaris supports a number of naming services to maintain network information on servers, which serve this information to the clients. DNS is the naming service running on the Internet to support TCP/IP networks. DNS makes communication simpler by using machine names (called domain names) instead of numerical IP addresses, whereas the focus of NIS is on making network administration more manageable and less error prone by providing centralized control over a variety of network information such as machine names, machine addresses, user names, and network services. Whereas NIS was developed in a proprietary environment, LDAP is based on an open standard and is poised to eventually replace NIS. Both LDAP and NIS+ offer security features. The `nsswitch.conf` file is used to coordinate the use of different naming services on your system.

You can use the `ypinit` command to set up the master server, the slave servers, and the clients for NIS. NIS is an SMF service under the identifier `/network/nis/server` and therefore can be started (enabled), stopped (disabled), or restarted by using the `svcadm` command. The NIS information is stored in files called maps in `ndbm` format. The maps are created and updated only on the master server from which they are propagated automatically to the slave servers. You can set up the LDAP client with the `ldapclient` command. The DNS client configuration information resides in the file `resolv.conf`. The naming service cache daemon, `nscd`, provides caching service for most common naming service requests. This daemon is managed by the SMF under the identifier system/name-service-cache and therefore can be started or stopped with the `svcadm` command, although initially it is automatically started at the boot time.

In addition to naming services, Solaris offers another important network service called network file system, which allows machines on a network to share files. This topic, along with some other issues related to file systems, is discussed in the next chapter.

INSIDE THE EXAM

Comprehend

- The `nsswitch.nis`, `nsswitch.nisplus`, `nsswitch.ldap`, and `nsswitch.files` are the templates for the corresponding naming services, and if during install you select a naming service, the corresponding file will be copied to `nsswitch.conf` file. Therefore, it is the `nsswitch.conf` file, but not any of these templates, that is used by the client.
- If you create an NIS map on a slave server, it will never be automatically pushed to the master server or other slave servers.
- NIS is an SMF service under the identifier `network/nis/server`, so it can be administered by using the `svcadm` command.

Look Out

- Make sure that the source password file on the NIS master server that will be used to make the password map file does not have an entry for the root.
- LDAP client and NIS client cannot coexist on the same machine.
- An LDAP server cannot be its own client—that is, you cannot configure a machine that is already running LDAP server to be an LDAP client.
- Null passwords are not allowed in LDAP.

Memorize

- The clients use the `nsswitch.conf` file to find out which naming service to use for a specific information type. You may list more than one naming service for an information type in this file.
- When you designate a machine as an NIS server during installation, a `Makefile` is stored in the `/var/yp` directory.
- The `make` command uses the `Makefile` to find out where the source files are, and runs `makedbm` to convert the source files to the NIS maps.

TWO-MINUTE DRILL

Understanding Naming Services

- The DNS is used to resolve IP domain names to IP addresses for any machine on the Internet.
- The NIS and NIS+ naming services are used to centralize the management of the network (LAN) information. NIS+ has a hierarchical namespace and offers additional features such as authentication, whereas NIS has a flat namespace.
- LDAP unifies the naming service and the directory service and is more appropriate in a read-intensive naming environment.
- The `nsswitch.conf` file is used to coordinate the use of different naming services on your system.

Working with NIS

- In NIS, network information is stored in files called maps, which are in the `ndbm` format.
- The maps are created and updated only on a master server, from which the information propagates to the slave servers.
- The `ypinit` command is used to set up the master server, the slave servers, and the clients for NIS. It also builds a fresh set of NIS maps from the source files cited in the `Makefile`.

Configuring the Clients

- You can set up an NIS client by using the `ypinit -c` command.
- The DNS configuration information used by the DNS client exists in the `resolv.conf` file.
- You can set up an LDAP client by using the `ldapclient` command.
- The naming service cache daemon is `nscd`, which is automatically started when the system is booted.
- You can use the `getent` command to get a list of entries from the administrative databases, such as `/etc/nsswitch.conf`, `/etc/passwd`, and `/etc/inet/hosts`.

SELF TEST

The following questions will help you measure your understanding of the material presented in this chapter. Read all the choices carefully because there might be more than one correct answer. Choose all correct answers for each question.

1. Which of the following files would a client use to determine which network service to use to get network information on a system that is running the NIS naming service?

   A. `nsswitch.conf`

   B. `nsswitch.nis`

   C. `nsswitch.nisplus`

   D. `nsswitch.ldap`

   E. `nsswitch.dns`

2. Solaris 10 ships with which DNS product?

   A. DNS 9.x

   B. BIND 9.x

   C. BIND 10.x

   D. DNS 10.x

3. Which of the following are the four authorization classes of principals in NIS+?

   A. owner, group, world, and nobody

   B. owner, group, all, and nobody

   C. read, write, execute, and no access

   D. principal, group, world, and nobody

4. Which of the following is the daemon for the DNS service?

   A. `dnsd`

   B. `nisd`

   C. `named`

   D. `nscd`

5. Which of the following commands is used to set up an NIS slave server?

   A. `ypinit -m`

   B. `ypserv`

C. `nisdm`

D. `ypinit -c` and `ypinit -s`

6. Which of the following naming services are offered by Solaris 10?

A. Active Directory

B. NDS

C. NIS+

D. DNS

E. LDAP

7. What is true about the NIS information databases?

A. These are the text files.

B. These are called objects.

C. These are the `ndbm` files called maps.

D. These are called tables.

8. Which of the following is the naming service cache daemon?

A. `nscd`

B. cached

C. named

D. cacheserver

9. You have just added a new machine to the network, and you want to update the information on the NIS server accordingly. You added this information into the source file and now you want to convert this source file to the `ndbm` map. Which command would you execute on the server?

A. `makedbm`

B. `Makefile`

C. `make`

D. `ypserv`

10. Which of the following statements about the naming services are not correct?

    A. The maps updated on an NIS slave server will not be pushed automatically to the NIS master server.

    B. The maps updated on the NIS master server will not be automatically pushed to the slave NIS servers.

    C. When you run a utility to convert the source files into NIS maps, it looks for the password source files in the directory specified by PWDIR in the `Makefile`.

    D. Resolver is the name of a command that is used by the client machine to resolve a domain name into an IP address.

SELF TEST ANSWERS

1. ☑ **A**. The nsswitch.conf file lists the naming services that can be used for a specific information type.
   ☒ **B**, **C**, and **D** are incorrect because these files are the templates, and if at install time you select to use a naming service corresponding to one of these files, that file will be copied to the nsswitch.conf file. **E** is incorrect because there is no such file as nsswitch.dns that the system presents.

2. ☑ **B**. Solaris 10 ships with BIND 9.x DNS server.
   ☒ **C** is incorrect because Solaris 10 ships with BIND 9.x and not with BIND 10.x. **A** and **D** are incorrect because there is no such product as DNS.

3. ☑ **A**. The four authorization classes in NIS+ are owner, group, world, and nobody.
   ☒ **B** and **D** are incorrect because there are no authorization classes named all and principal. **C** is incorrect because read, write, execute are permissions, not authorization classes.

4. ☑ **C**. The daemon that the DNS server runs is named.
   ☒ **A** and **B** are incorrect because there are no daemons named dnsd and nisd. **D** is incorrect because nscd is a naming service cache daemon.

5. ☑ **D**. You first set up a client with the ypinit -c command and then make it a slave server by using the ypinit -s command.
   ☒ **A** is incorrect because the ypinit -m command is used to set up a master server. **B** is incorrect because ypserv is an NIS server daemon, not a command to set up the NIS server. **C** is incorrect because there is no such command as nisadm.

6. ☑ **C**, **D**, and **E**. Solaris 10 supports NIS, NIS+, DNS, and LDAP.
   ☒ **A** and **B** are incorrect because Active Directory is the naming service supported on Windows and NDS is the directory service that is supported by various platforms even though it's not shipped with Solaris 10.

7. ☑ **C**. NIS contains information in ndbm files called maps.
   ☒ **A**, **B**, and **D** are incorrect because NIS databases are not text files and they are not called objects or tables.

8. ☑ **A**. The nscd daemon offers the cache service for the most common naming service requests.
   ☒ **C** is incorrect because named is the DNS daemon. **B** and **D** are incorrect because these are not correct names for the naming service cache daemon.

9. ☑ **C**. You would execute the `make` command, which automatically executes the `makedbm` and also uses the information from the `Makefile`.
   ☒ **D** is incorrect because `ypserv` is the NIS server daemon and is not the command to convert source files to maps.

10. ☑ **B** and **D**. These are false statements because a map created or updated on a primary server will be automatically pushed to the secondary servers, and resolver is not a command; rather, it's a collection of routines that help resolve the domain name.
    ☒ **A** and **C** are incorrect because these are true statements.

12

Managing Virtual File Systems and Core Dumps

CERTIFICATION OBJECTIVES

The processes running on the system use physical memory for their code instructions and data. Because a system may be running many processes (applications) concurrently, it may run low on memory because memory is a finite resource. In this case, a predetermined space on the disk, configured as swap space, is used as memory. Because the space being used is not real physical memory, it is called *virtual memory*. The file system that manages the swap space is called a *swap file system* (SWAPFS) and is a virtual file system. Another related virtual file system is TMPFS, which uses the memory for file read and write and is a default file system for the `/tmp` directory. This file system is used to improve the performance of the applications, and uses the space resources from the swap space.

Virtual file systems make the storage space transparent to the processes. The network file system (NFS) makes the location of the machine on which the file systems exist transparent to the users and the applications. Using NFS, a user can mount a file system that exists on a remote NFS server and use it as though it existed on the local machine.

Both the processes and the system can crash from time to time; when they do, they leave some information behind in the form of core files and crash dump files that you can use to diagnose the problem. The core issue to think about in this chapter is: how are the memory location and the file location made transparent for the processes and how do we manage the crash information of a process or the system? In search of an answer, we will explore three thought streams: virtual memory, network file system, and process and system crashes.

CERTIFICATION OBJECTIVE 12.01

Working with Virtual Memory

Exam Objective 2.1: *Explain virtual memory concepts and given a scenario, configure, and manage swap space.*

Solaris software uses some disk slices for temporary storage to support the physical memory rather than for regular file systems for the end users. These disk slices are called *swap slices*. Swap slices are used as virtual memory storage areas when the system does not have enough physical memory to support processes currently running on the system. The term *virtual* refers to the memory, because it is storage on disk as compared with physical memory. The virtual memory system maps physical copies of files on disk to virtual addresses in memory. The addresses are virtual because they give the impression to the process that it is a memory address, even though the data may be on the disk. In addition to virtual memory and swap space, you also need to learn how two file systems—TMPFS and SWAPFS—are related to the virtual memory.

Understanding Virtual Memory

Let us put the concept of virtual memory in the right context by exploring the basic concepts related to it:

- *Secondary storage.* This is the storage that is remote to the CPU and is usually used to store the programs and data that are currently not being used by the CPU. This space is provided by devices such as hard drives and CD-ROM. Access to the data on the secondary storage is slow, but the data survives even if the computer shuts down. For this reason it is also called *permanent storage.*
- *Physical memory.* The physical memory of a computer is the storage space provided by a physical device called random access memory (RAM) located on the motherboard (and in other circuit boards). This is also called *primary storage* because this is the storage that running programs often use and prefer, given that it is faster than secondary storage (disk). It holds the programs and the data currently being used by the CPU. When the computer is shut down or rebooted, the data in the physical memory is lost; this is why it is also called *volatile memory* or *temporary storage.*
- *Virtual memory.* The word *virtual* refers to something that is not really what it pretends to be. Virtual memory is the method of using the space on the hard drive as though it were the physical memory. It is used by the OS when it runs low on physical memory.
- *Swap space.* The disk slices being used for storing virtual memory are called the swap space or the swap slices. The address of the data in the virtual memory referred to by the running program is not the real address in the physical memory; this is why it is called a *virtual address.* The virtual memory system maps the data file on disk to the virtual addresses in the physical memory.

- *TMPFS file system*. The TMPFS is the memory-based file system that maps the /tmp directory on the hard disk to the memory. If there is sufficient RAM, the reads and writes will be faster. In other words, the TMPFS file system stores its files and the related information in the /tmp directory, which speeds up access to those files. As a result, the applications (such as compiler and database management systems products) that use the /tmp directory for storing and retrieving their data improve performance. However, TMPFS allocates space in the /tmp directory from the system's swap space resources. Consequently, if you are using the space in the /tmp directory, you are using the system's swap space. If the system starts getting low on memory, the files will be swapped to the disk, and then the read and writes will obviously be as slow as the disk. An entry in the /etc/vfstab file automatically activates the TMPFS file system. Because TMPFS is a memory-based file system, you will lose all the files in and underneath the /tmp directory when the system is shut down or rebooted.
- *Virtual swap space*. Virtual swap space is the opposite of virtual memory. Suppose your computer has enough memory (physical memory) that you do not need the swap space. Now, consider that you have a large number of processes running on your computer, and a swap space has to be allocated to each process to be on the safe side. That means that a large amount of physical swap space will have to be configured even if your computer has a large amount of physical memory. The solution to this problem is the space in the physical memory that acts as swap space—the virtual swap space. It is equivalent to saying, yes there is a swap space and here is the address for it, and the address actually lives in the memory; hence, the name *virtual swap space* address. This space is controlled by the SWAPFS file system, which provides virtual swap space addresses as opposed to physical swap space addresses in response to requests for reserving swap space, thereby reducing the need to configure a large amount of physical swap space.
- *Paging*. The memory space is allocated in units called pages—for example, a page is a chunk of 8KB memory in UltraSPARC architecture. When a program needs the data that has been stored into the swap space, the data cannot be found in the memory; this condition is called *page fault*. When the page fault occurs, the virtual memory system brings the page containing the requested data into the physical memory; this process is called *paging*.

Note that even if the virtual swap space is being used for virtual space addresses. When page faults start to occur, that indicates that the system is running low on physical memory. In this case, the SWAPFS converts the virtual swap space addresses to physical swap space addresses. Therefore, virtual swap space can be looked on as the sum of the actual physical swap space plus a portion of the remaining physical memory space.

on the job

If the applications on your system make heavy use of the /`tmp` directory, your system will run out of swap space if you fail to monitor swap space usage. You can set your compiler's `TMPDIR` environment variable to point to another directory with sufficient space. However, remember that this controls only which directory the compiler is using and has no effect on the use of the /`tmp` directory by other programs.

Because many applications count on swap space, you, the system administrator, should know how to manage swap space.

Managing Swap Space

Managing swap space includes the initial configuration, monitoring, and adding and removing of the swap space.

The Initial Configuration of the Swap Space

Swap space is initially set up (configured) during the Solaris installation process, and the default value is 512MB (which you can, of course, change). After the system has been installed, swap slices and swap files are activated by the `/sbin/swapadd` script each time the system is booted. The `/etc/vfstab` file contains the list of swap devices (slices and files). An entry for a swap device in the `/etc/vfstab` file contains the following:

- The full path name of the file or slice
- The file system type of the file or slice

Before a swap file is activated, the file system that contains the file must be mounted. Therefore, make sure that the entry that mounts the file system appears in the `/etc/vfstab` file before the entry that activates the swap file.

How much swap space should be set aside during installation? This largely depends on the requirements of the applications that will be running on your system. A complex application in areas such as computer-aided design and database management may require 200 to 1000MB of swap space. You can read the application documentation or consult the application vendor to find out the swap space requirement of a specific application. Overall general guidelines for swap space are presented in Table 12-1.

You initially configure the swap space based on your best estimate for the system requirements of the swap space. However, you can change it later on by adding or removing the swap space. How would you know you need to add or remove some swap space? You learn that by monitoring the swap space.

Monitoring the Swap Space

If your system does not have sufficient swap space, one or more of the applications running on the system may fail to start as a result of insufficient memory. If that were to happen, it would require manual intervention either to add additional swap space or to reconfigure the memory usage of these applications. Before this happens or to keep it from happening, you should be monitoring the swap space by using the `/usr/sbin/swap` command. To identify the swap area on your system and obtain some information about it, you can issue the command shown here:

```
swap -l
```

The output of this command will look like the following:

```
swapfile dev swaplo blocks free /dev/dsk/c0t0d0s1 136,1 16 1638608 1600528
```

TABLE 12-1 General guidelines for setting up the swap space on your system as a function of physical memory space

System Type	Physical Memory Size	Swap Space Size
Workstation	4GB	1GB
Mid-range server	8GB	2GB
High-end servers	16 to 128GB	4GB

The fields in this output are described here:

- **`swapfile.`** Full path name for the swap area
- **`dev.`** The device number for the swap device
- **`swaplo.`** Offset (in units of 512-byte blocks) where usable swap area begins
- **`blocks.`** Size of the swap area in units of 512-byte blocks
- **`free.`** The total amount of swap space, in units of 512-byte blocks, in this area that is not currently allocated

To get more information about the swap space, issue the command shown here:

```
swap -s
```

The output will look like the following:

```
total: 57416k bytes allocated + 10480k reserved = 67896k used,
833128k available
```

The fields in the displayed output are described here:

- **`bytes allocated.`** The total amount of swap space, in units of 1024-byte blocks, that is currently allocated as disk-backed swap space
- **`reserved.`** The total amount of swap space, in units of 1024-byte blocks, that is not currently allocated but is claimed by memory for possible future use
- **`used.`** The total amount of swap space, in units of 1024-byte blocks—that is, allocated plus reserved
- **`available.`** The total amount of swap space, in units of 1024-byte blocks, that is currently available for future use (i.e., for reservation and allocation)

These terms might be confusing if you are not clear about the process of allocating swap space, which is described here:

1. When a process requests additional memory, the system assigns it the memory pages from the physical memory.
2. Each page of physical memory is backed by swap space—that is, the swap space is reserved at this time. The reserved space has not really been allocated yet, just reserved for possible use in the future. This is because

the use of physical memory is a dynamic thing; there are many other processes running on the system, and when physical memory runs low, some memory pages are swapped out of the physical memory into the swap area.

3. When the process actually starts writing data to a reserved page, the system assigns a location on the physical swap space to the page. This is referred to as allocating the swap space.

Note that the used space plus the available space is equal to the total swap space on the system, which includes a portion of physical memory (think of virtual swap space) and swap files.

on the job

First, note that the `swap -l` command displays swap space in units of 512-byte blocks, whereas the `swap -s` command displays swap space in units of 1024-byte blocks—that is, in KB. Second, if you add up the blocks from the output of the `swap -l` and convert them to KB, the result is less than used + available (in the `swap -s` output). The reason is that `swap -l` does not include the physical memory part (virtual swap space) in its calculation of swap space.

Here is an example showing how you can use the amount of available and used swap space displayed by the `swap -s` command to monitor swap space usage. When system performance is good, use `the swap -s command` to determine how much swap space is available. Watch the system, and when performance slows down, check the amount of available swap space again and determine whether it has decreased. If it has, you have found a correlation between swap space and system performance, and you can identify the changes to the system that might have increased swap space usage.

Your analysis of swap space monitoring may suggest either that you need to add some swap space or there is too much unnecessary swap space that you should remove.

Adding and Removing Swap Space

The changing nature and load of the work on your system may require adding or removing swap space. For example, as new software packages are installed on the system, you may find that you need to add swap space. You can accomplish this without repartitioning a disk by using the `mkfile` and `swap` commands.

You basically designate a part of the exiting UFS or NFS file system as a secondary swap area. Here is the process:

- Create a swap file by issuing the `mkfile` command.
- Activate (add) the swap file by issuing the `swap` command.
- Add an entry for the swap file in the `/etc/vfstab` file so that the swap file is automatically activated when the system is booted.

Of course, an alternative is to repartition the disk or to use a new disk to add more swap space, using the `format` command. The following exercise demonstrates how to add swap space by using the `mkfile` and `swap` commands.

EXERCISE 12-1

How to Add More Swap Space without Repartitioning the Disk

To add more swap space, perform the following steps:

1. Become superuser.
2. Create a directory for the swap file, if needed—for example:

   ```
   mkdir /moreswap
   ```

3. Create the swap file by using the `mkfile` command, which has the following syntax:

   ```
   mkfile <number> [k|b|m] <filename>
   ```

   The `<number>` specifies the file size in KB, bytes, or MB specified by k, b, or m. For example, to create 500MB swap space, issue the following command:

   ```
   mkfile 500m /moreswap/swapFile
   ```

4. Activate the swap file by carrying on the same example:

   ```
   # /usr/sbin/swap -a /moreswap/swapFile
   ```

   You must use the absolute path name to specify the swap file. The swap file is now added, and activated. It is available until the file system is unmounted, the system is rebooted, or the swap file is removed. The swap file will be automatically activated each time the system is booted, if you perform the next step.

5. Add the following entry for the swap file to the /etc/vfstab file, again using the running example:

```
/moreswap/swapFile-- swap-no -
```

6. Issue the following command to verify that the swap file has actually been added:

```
/usr/sbin/swap -l
```

You can create a swap file without root permissions. However, if root is not the owner of the swap file, it could be easily overwritten by accident. You can remove a swap file by issuing the following command:

```
swap -d <swapFileName>
```

This will not remove the file, but it will make it unavailable for swapping. However, if you want the space occupied by the file, you can remove it by using the good old rm command:

```
rm <swapFileName>
```

You should also remove the entry for the removed swap file from the /etc/vfstab file.

We have used the swap command at several places so far. Now, let's take a look at its syntax:

```
swap <option> [<fileName>]
```

The options are described here:

- **-a <filename>.** Activate a swap file whose full path is specified by <filename>.
- **-d <filename>.** Make the file specified by <fileName> unavailable to swapping without removing the file.

- **-l.** Identify the swap space on the system: the device name and the total physical swap space—that is, it does not include any space from the physical memory.
- **-s.** Display the allocated, reserved, and available swap space. This swap space may include part of available physical memory (the virtual swap space).

The virtual memory and swap space make the location of the data storage transparent to the processes running on the system, whether it's stored in memory or on disk. What about making the location of the file systems transparent to the users and the processes: whether a file system is on the local machine or a remote machine? This is accomplished by using the network file system (NFS).

CERTIFICATION OBJECTIVE 12.02

Working with NFS

Exam Objective 2.3: *Explain NFS fundamentals, and configure and manage the NFS server and client including daemons, files, and commands.*

The network file system (NFS) is the system that can be used to access file systems over the network. NFS version 4 is the default NFS in Solaris 10. The NFS service is managed by the Service Management Facility covered in Chapter 10. That means NFS can be managed (enabled, disabled, or restarted) by the `svcadm` command, and the status of NFS service can be obtained by using the `svcs` command. The issue here is sharing files over the network among computers possibly running different operating systems.

Before learning how to manage NFS, you need to understand the fundamental concepts of NFS.

Understanding NFS

In order to work with the NFS service you need to understand the basic terminology and concepts described in this section.

The NFS Service

The NFS service is a network service that enables computers of different architectures running different operating systems to share file systems across the network. A wide spectrum of operating systems ranging from Windows to Linux/UNIX support NFS. It has become possible to implement the NFS environment on a variety of operating systems because it is defined as an abstract model of a file system, rather than an architectural specification. Each operating system applies the NFS model to its specific file system semantics. This means that file system operations such as reading and writing work for the users as if they were accessing a file on the local system.

The benefits of the NFS service are described here:

- It enables users on the network to share data, because all computers on the network can access the same set of files.
- It reduces storage costs by letting computers share applications and common files instead of needing local disk space on each computer for each common file and user application.
- It provides data consistency and reliability, because all users can read the same set of files, and whenever changes are made, they are made only at one place.
- It makes the mounting of file systems accessing the remote files transparent to users.
- It supports heterogeneous environments and reduces system administration overhead.

NFS is a network service offered in the client/server environment.

NFS Servers and Clients

The NFS is a client/server system. As you learned in Chapter 10, the terms *client* and *server* refer to the roles that computers assume in sharing resources (file systems in this case) on the network. In NFS, computers that make their file systems available over the network and thereby offer NFS service to serve the requested files are acting as NFS servers, and the computers that are accessing the file systems are acting as NFS clients. In the NFS framework, a computer on a network can assume the role of a client, a server, or both.

Here is how NFS works:

- A server makes a file system on its disk available for sharing, and the file system can then be accessed by an NFS client on the network.
- A client accesses files on the server's shared file system by mounting the file system.

- The client does not make a copy of the file system on the server; instead, the mounting process uses a series of remote procedure calls that enable the client to access the file system transparently on the server's disk. To the user, the mounting works just like a mount on the local machine.
- Once the remote file system (on the server) is mounted on the client machine, the user types commands as though the file systems were local.

You can mount an NFS file system automatically with autoFS, which we explore further on in this chapter.

The NFS File Systems

In most UNIX system environments, a file hierarchy that can be shared by using the NFS service corresponds to a file system or a portion of a file system. However, a file system resides on a single operating system, and NFS support works across operating systems. Moreover, the concept of a file system might be meaningless in some non-UNIX environments. Therefore, the term *file system* in NFS refers to a file or a file hierarchy that can be shared and mounted in the NFS environment.

An NFS server can make a single file or a directory subtree (file hierarchy) available to the NFS service for sharing. A server cannot share a file hierarchy that overlaps with a file hierarchy that is already being shared. Note that peripheral devices such as modems and printers cannot be shared under NFS.

Managing NFS

Since the release of Solaris 9, the NFS server starts automatically when you boot the system. Nevertheless, you do need to manage NFS, which includes administering the NFS service, working with NFS daemons, and making file systems available for sharing.

Administering the NFS Service

When the system is booted, the NFS server is automatically started by executing the `nfs.server` scripts. However, when the system is up, you may need to stop the service or start it again for whatever reason without rebooting the system. For that, you need to know that the NFS service is managed by the Service Management Facility (SMF) under the identifier `network/nfs/server`. By means of this identifier, you can find the status of the service by using the `svcs` command, and you can start (enable) or stop (disable) the service by using the `svcadm` command.

You can determine whether the NFS service is running on your machine by issuing the command shown here:

```
svcs network/nfs/server
```

This command displays whether the NFS service is online or disabled. If you want to stop (disable) the service, issue the following command:

```
svcadm disable network/nfs/server
```

You can start the service by issuing the following command:

```
svcadm enable network/nfs/server
```

When the system is up, some daemons are running to support the NFS service.

Working with NFS Daemons

Since the release of Solaris 9, NFS service starts automatically when the system is booted. When the system goes into level 3 (or multiuser mode), several NFS daemons are started to support the service. These daemons are listed in Table 12-2.

The `nfsd` daemon handles the file system requests from the client and is automatically started with option `-a`. You can change the parameters of the command by editing the `/etc/default/nfs` file. The syntax for the `nfsd` command is as follows:

```
nfsd [-a] [-c <#_conn>] [-l <listenBacklog>] [-p <protocol>] [-t <device>]
[<nservers>]
```

TABLE 12-2 Daemons automatically started in NFS version 4 when the system boots

Daemon	Description
`automountd`	Handles mount and unmount requests from the autofs service.
`nfsd`	Handles file system requests from clients.
`nfs4cbd`	Manages the communication endpoints for the NFS version 4 callback program.
`nfsmapid`	Provides integer-to-string and string-to-integer conversions for the user ID (UID) and the group ID (GID).

The options and parameters are described here:

- **`-a`.** Start the daemon over all available connectionless and connection-oriented transport protocols such as TCP and UDP. This is equivalent to setting the NFSD_PROTOCOL parameter in the `nfs` file to ALL.
- **`-c <#_conn>`.** Set the maximum number of connections allowed to the NFS server over connection-oriented transport protocols such as TCP. By default, the number is unlimited. The equivalent parameter in the `nfs` file is NFSD_MAX_CONNECTIONS.
- **`-l <listenBacklog>`.** Set the connection queue length (specified by `<listenBacklog>`) for the number of entries for the NFS TCP. The default value is 32. This number can also be determined by setting the `NFSD_LISTEN_BACKLOG` parameter in the `nfs` file.
- **`-p <protocol>`.** Start the daemon over the protocol specified by `<protocol>`. The default in NFS version 4 is TCP. The equivalent parameter in the `nfs` file is: NFSD_PROTOCOL.
- **`-t <device>`.** Start an `nfs` daemon for the transport specified by `<device>`. The equivalent parameter in the `nfs` file is: NFSD_DEVICES.
- **`<nservers>`.** Set the maximum number of concurrent requests from the clients that the NFS server can handle. The equivalent parameter in the `nfs` file is: NFSD_SERVERS.

exam watch

***The default NFS version is version 4 in Solaris 10. Unlike previous versions of NFS, NFS version 4 does not use these daemons:* `lockd`, `mountd`, `nfslogd`, *and* `statd`.**

If you want to issue the `nfsd` command for whatever reason, make sure you stop a previously running `nfsd` daemon invoked with or without options.

Before a user can use a file system on a remote computer (server), it needs to be made available for sharing.

Sharing File Systems

On the server machine, you can make a file system available for sharing by using the `share` command on the machine. You can use this command manually for testing purpose or to make a file system available only until the system is rebooted. If you want to make the sharing of a file system permanent and automatic, you should enter the `share` command into the `/etc/dfs/dfstab` file. Each entry of this file is a `share` command, and this file is automatically executed at boot time when the system enters run level 3. The syntax for the `share` command is shown here:

```
share [-F <FSType>] [-o <specificOptions>] [-d <description>] [<pathname>]
```

The options are described here:

- **-F <FSType>.** Specifies the file system type, such as `nfs`.
- **-o <specificOptions>.** The `<specificOptions>` specifies the options for controlling access to the shared file system. The possible values for `<specificOptions>` are as follows:
  - **rw.** Read/write permissions for all clients. This is the default behavior.
  - **rw = <client1>:<client2>**. . . . Read/write permission for the listed clients; no access for any other client.
  - **ro.** Read-only permission for all clients.
  - **ro = <client1>:<client2>**. . . . Read-only permission for the listed clients; no access for any other client.
- **-d <description>.** The `<description>` specifies the description for the shared resource.

If you want to know the resources being shared on the local server, issue the `dfshares` command without any arguments or options.

exam watch

Remember that two things need to happen on the server before the files can be shared: The `share` command has been issued or exists in the `/etc/dfs/dfstab` file, and the nfs server (the server and other daemons) are running.

If you decide to share more file systems permanently when the system is up, perform the following steps:

1. Add the `share` commands for the file systems in the `/etc/dfs/dsfstab` file.
2. Either reboot the system or issue the `shareall` command without any options or arguments.

The files related to the NFS service are described in Table 12-3.

TABLE 12-3 Files related to the NFS service

File Name	Function
`/etc/default/autofs`	Configuration information for autofs.
`/etc/default/fs`	Lists the default file system type for local file systems.
`/etc/default/nfs`	Configuration information for the `nfsd` daemon.
`/etc/dfs/dfstab`	Contains a list of local resources to be shared; the `share` commands.
`/etc/mnttab`	Lists file systems that are currently mounted.
`/etc/dfs/sharetab`	Lists the local and remote resources that are shared.
`/etc/vfstab`	Defines file systems to be mounted locally.

Now that you know how to manage NFS, here are some practical scenarios and their solutions.

SCENARIO & SOLUTION

Scenario	Solution
You are logged on to the server and want to share the `nfs` file system `/usr/libs` over the network. What entry would you make into the `/etc/dfs/dfstab` file so that all the clients have read-only permissions to this directory?	`share -F nfs -o ro /usr/libs`
How can you make this file system available without rebooting the system?	Issue the following command: `shareall`
How can you verify that the NFS service is running on your machine?	Issue the following command: `svcs network/nfs/server`

Now you know how the NFS servers share the file systems. But how do the clients access those file systems? They access those file systems the way any Solaris machine accesses any file system—by mounting it. To mount a shared file system on a client machine, you can use the same `mount` command that you learned in Chapter 5. However, when a network contains a fair number of file systems to share, the manual mounting may not be a very effective way to share the files. To help this situation, Solaris offers the AutoFS facility, which automates mounting.

CERTIFICATION OBJECTIVE 12.03

Working with AutoFS

Exam Objective 2.5: *Explain and manage AutoFS and use automount maps (master, direct, and indirect) to configure automounting.*

The clients can mount the file systems that the NFS servers share through the NFS service, either by using the mount utility or by using the automatic mounting offered by AutoFS, a client-side service. As a system administrator, you should understand how this service works and how to manage it.

Understanding AutoFS

AutoFS is a kernel file system that supports automatic mounting and unmounting of remote file systems. It is initialized by the `automount` service, which is started automatically when a system is booted. The automount daemon, `automountd`, runs continuously, mounting and unmounting remote file systems as necessary. An NFS resource (the remote file system) is automatically mounted when you access it, and it is automatically unmounted when it is left idle (i.e., not accessed) for a certain period. AutoFS offers the following benefits:

- NFS resources (the shared file systems) don't need to be mounted during the system boot, which saves booting time.
- Because mounting is done automatically, it avoids the problem of giving users the root password to mount and unmount NFS resources.
- Network performance might improve, because network traffic is being reduced by mounting the resources only when they are in use.

AutoFS allows you to specify multiple servers to provide the same file system. This way, if one of the specified servers is down, AutoFS can try to mount the file system from another server machine. This provides fault tolerance.

Note that the following three components work together to accomplish the task of automatic mounting:

- The `autofs` file system
- The `automountd` daemon
- The `automount` command

The automount service is managed by SMF under the identifier `svc:/system/filesystem/autofs`; it is automatically started when the system is booted. It reads the master map file named `auto_master` to create the initial set of autofs mounts, which are the points under which the file systems will be mounted in the future. These autofs mounts are also called trigger nodes, because when a file system request on one of these points is made, it triggers the file system mounting process. When autofs (the service that was started at the system boot time) receives a request to access a file system that is not currently mounted, it calls the `automountd` daemon, which mounts the requested file system. Although initial autofs mount points are set up during system boot time, the `automount` command is used to update the autofs mount points when necessary, after the system is up and running. The command makes the necessary changes after comparing the list of mounted file systems in the mount table file `/etc/mnttab` with the list of mount points in the `auto_master` map. It allows you to change mount information in the `auto_master` file and have those changes used by the autofs processes without stopping and restarting the `autofs` daemon.

In summary, the automount daemon `automountd` is started at boot time by the service `svc:/system/filesystem/autofs`. This service also uses the `automount` command to update the autofs mount points when the system is up and running. When a request is made to access a file system at an autofs mount point, it triggers the following process:

1. The autofs service intercepts the request and sends a message to the `automountd` daemon to mount the requested file system.
2. `The automountd daemon` locates the file system information in a map, creates the trigger nodes (autofs mount points) if necessary, and performs the mount.
3. The autofs service allows the intercepted request to proceed.
4. The autofs service unmounts the file system after a predetermined period of inactivity.

on the job

You should not manually mount or unmount the mounts that are managed through the autofs service. Even if your manual operation is successful, it may possibly generate inconsistencies, because the autofs service does not check whether the object has been unmounted. In addition, note that a reboot clears all of the autofs mount points.

Suppose you want to use AutoFS. How do you configure it?

Configuring AutoFS Using Maps

You configure the AutoFS environment by assigning values to keywords in the following file:

```
/etc/default/autofs
```

The behavior of autmounting is determined by the entries in the configuration files called maps used by `autofs`. These files (or the maps in them) fall into three categories: master maps, direct maps, and indirect maps. Sometimes the files themselves are referred to as maps. However, you will figure out from the context whether the term *map* refers to the file or to an entry in the file.

The Master AutoFS Maps

The master maps reside in the `/etc/auto_master` file, which contains the master list that specifies all the maps that autofs should check. The entries in the `auto_master` file looks like the following:

```
/net -hosts -nosuid,nobrowse
/home auto_home -nobrowse
/- auto_direct -ro
```

The syntax of an entry is:

```
<mountPoint> <mapName> [mountOptions]
```

These fields of an entry are described here:

- **`<mountPoint>`.** This specifies the path to a directory to which a file system will be mounted in the future. If the directory does not exist, autofs will create it. If it exists and has a content, autofs will hide this content when it mounts a file system to it. The value /- for the `<mountPoint>` may mean that this map is a direct map or that no particular mount point is specified for this map.
- **`<mapName>`.** This specifies the map name that the autofs service uses to find directions to locations or the mount information. The name is interpreted as a local file if it is preceded by a slash (/). Otherwise, autofs uses the `/etc/nsswitch.conf` file to search for the mount information.

- **<mountOptions>.** This specifies an optional, comma-delimited list of options that apply to the mounting of the entries that are specified in the <mapName>, unless the entries in the <mapName> list other options. Options obviously depend on the specific type of file system being mounted.

A line that begins with the pound sign (#) is considered to be a comment line and is ignored. The maximum number of characters allowed in an entry is 1024. You can use backward slash (\ ) as a continuation in order to split an entry into more than one line.

If the* `/etc/auto_master` *file contains more than one entry for the same mount point, the* `automount` *command uses the first entry and ignores the other entries.

AutoFS runs on all computers on the network and supports /net and /home (the automounted home directories) by default. The /home mount point is the directory under which the entries that are listed in the /etc/auto_home file are to be mounted. The following entry in the auto_master file makes this happen:

```
/home auto_home -nobrowse
```

The auto_home directory is an example of the indirect maps that we will discuss later in this chapter. Now, consider the following entry in the /etc/auto_master file:

```
/net -hosts -nosuid,nobrowse
```

It means that autofs mounts all the entries in the hosts map under the directory /net. Suppose a computer howard is listed in the hosts file, and it exports a file system. Further suppose that a client machine has the foregoing entry in its auto_master file. You can go to the root directory of the exported file system of computer howard by issuing the following command on the client computer:

```
cd /net/howard
```

When the system is booted, the automount command reads the master map file /etc/auto_master in which each entry defines either a direct map file name or an indirect map file name, along with the path of the mount point associated with the name and the mount options.

You can define the name of the direct map file in the `auto_master` file by using the /- value for the `<mountPoint>` as shown here:

```
/- auto_direct -ro
```

The mount point `/-` specifies that this is an entry for the direct maps file and that the full path to the mount point for each direct map will be defined in the direct maps file.

The Direct AutoFS Maps

A direct map is an automount point on the client associated with a directory on the server. The maps reside in the direct map file, whose name you can define in the auto_master file, typically `/etc/auto_direct`. These maps are called direct maps because they explicitly express the relationship of the mount point to the directory by specifying the full path. Entries in the `auto_direct` file look like the following:

```
/usr/local -ro
/bin senate:/export/local/sun4
/share senate:/export/local/share
/src senate:/export/local/src
/usr/man -ro blue:/usr/man
red:/usr/man \
white:/usr/man
/usr/games -ro congress:/usr/games
```

These entries are according to the following syntax:

```
<key> [<mountOptions>] <location>
```

The fields in the syntax are described here:

- **`<key>`.** This specifies the path name of the mount point to which file systems can be mounted.
- **`<mountOptions>`.** This specifies the options that will be applied to this particular mount.
- **`<location>`.** This specifies the full path of file systems that can be mounted to the mount point.

As in the master map file, a line that begins with the pound sign (#) is considered to be a comment line and is ignored, and you can use the backward slash (\) as a continuation to split an entry into more than one line.

A path name specified by* `<location>` *must be the legal absolute path to the file system on the server. For example, the location of a home directory for the user hdean on the senate computer should be listed as* `senate:/export/home/hdean`*, and not as* `senate:/home/hdean`*.

Note that the mount point `/user/man` in the example has three file systems associated to it. This feature can be used to implement fault tolerance. For example, you can associate multiple file systems configured as replicas to a mount point. In this case, if one file system fails, clients can be served from another one.

The mount points used in the direct maps file are specified in the named map, whereas the mount points defined in the master maps file are used by the indirect maps file.

The Indirect AutoFS Map

An indirect map uses the value of a key to identify the relationship of a mount point with a file system. Indirect maps are useful for accessing specific file systems, such as home directories. An example of an indirect map is the auto_home map that contains the entries to be mounted under `/home`. A typical `auto_home` file may look like the following:

```
hdean dnc:/export/home/hdean
jedward dnc:/export/home/jedward
hclinton dnc:/export/home/hclinton
crice -rw,nosuid gop:/export/home/crice
```

Entries in indirect maps file are in accordance with the following syntax:

```
<key> [<mountOptions>] <location>
```

The fields in the entry are described here:

- **`<key>`.** Specifies a simple name without any slashes. This name combined with the mount point defined in the master map file will make the full path name for the mount point.
- **`<mountOptions>`.** This specifies the options that will be applied to this particular mount.
- **`<location>`.** This specifies the full path of file systems that can be mounted to the mount point.

Let's go through an example in order to demonstrate the use of indirect maps. The story of the indirect maps starts from the master maps file. Consider the following entry in the master maps file, /etc/auto_master:

```
/home auto_home -nobrowse
```

It states that the indirect maps for the mount point /home will be defined in the file /etc/auto_home. Now, consider the following entry in the /etc/auto_home file:

```
crice -rw,nosuid gop:/export/home/crice
```

The key crice here is a mount point path relative to the mount point defined in the auto_home entry in the auto_master file—that is, /home. Therefore, the full path to the mount point is /home/crice. Now, let's assume that this map file exists on the machine washington where crice has her home directory listed in the passwd file as /home/crice. That means if crice logs into the washington machine, the autofs mounts the /export/home/crice directory on the gop machine as her home directory.

The master map file has entries for the direct map and indirect map files. The mount point for the direct maps specified in the master map file (auto_master) is /-, which means the full path of the mount points for direct maps will be defined in the direct maps file. In an entry for an indirect map file in the master maps file, the root of the mount point path is defined, such as /home. The rest of the path will be defined in the indirect maps file, and both paths together will make up the full path of a mount point.

Although initially the automount service is started automatically, there will be situations when you may need to stop it and start it again.

Starting and Stopping the Automount Service

The automount service is started automatically when the system is booted. When the system is up and running, for some reason (e.g., changing the configuration), you may need to restart the service. To do that, all you need to know is that the autofs service, like many other services in Solaris 10, is managed by SMF and hence can be administered by the svcadm command.

The SMF service identifier for the autofs command is shown here:

```
svc:/system/filesystem/autofs:default
```

That means, for example, that you can restart the automount service by issuing the following command:

```
svcadm restart system/filesystem/autofs
```

To stop or start the service you can replace the action restart with enable or disable, respectively, as shown here:

```
svcadm enable system/filesystem/autofs
svcadm disable system/filesystem/autofs
```

The NFS service running on your system, like any other service, may run into problems, in which case you will need to troubleshoot it.

CERTIFICATION OBJECTIVE 12.04

Troubleshooting NFS

Exam Objective 2.4: *Troubleshoot various NFS errors.*

The task of identifying and solving a problem is called troubleshooting, which is arguably the most difficult task in any area of computers. NFS is no exception. The good news is that the common steps used in troubleshooting work in all areas such as identifying the problem, isolating the causes of the problems by the process of elimination, and so on. The first step is always identifying the problem, and the error messages help in this step.

Common NFS error messages and their descriptions and possible solutions are presented in Table 12-4.

When trying to narrow down an NFS problem, remember the main suspects of a possible failure: the server, the client, and the network. Try to isolate each individual component to find the one that is not working. First of all, note that the `mountd` and `nfsd` daemons must be running on the server for remote mounts to succeed. To start the process of isolating the problem, perform the following initial steps:

- Check whether the client machine can access the server machine.
- Check whether the client can contact the NFS services on the server.
- Check whether the NFS services are running on the server.

TABLE 12-4 Common NFS errors and possible solutions

Error Message	Description	Possible Solution
Could not start <daemon>: <error>.	This message will be displayed if the `<daemon>` terminates abnormally or if a system call generates an error. The `<error>` string states the problem.	This error message is rare and has no straightforward solution. Contact the vendor, Sun in this case, for help.
Cannot establish NFS service over /dev/tcp: transport setup problem.	Probably the services information in the namespace has not been updated.	Update the services information in the namespace for NIS/NIS+, which was discussed in the previous chapter.
<daemon> running already with pid <pid>.	The daemon specified by `<daemon>` that you are trying to start is already running.	If you have to restart it, issue the `restart` command, or stop it first and then start it.
<filename>: File too large.	An NFS version 2 client is attempting to access a file that is larger than 2GB.	Do not use NFS version 2. Mount the file system with NFS version 3 or version 4.
NFS server recovering.	During the server reboot, some operations were not permitted, so the client is waiting for the server to permit this operation to proceed.	No action is required. Wait for the server to get to the point where it can permit the operation.
NFS server <hostname> not responding still trying.	NFS server specified by `<hostname>` is down, or there is some other problem with the server or the network.	Troubleshoot for connectivity.
NFS file temporarily unavailable on the server, retrying . . .	The server is recalling a delegation for another client that conflicts with the request from your client.	The server recall must occur before the server can process your client's request.
mount: . . . No such file or directory	Either the remote directory or the local directory does not exist.	Check the spelling for the directory names, and run the `ls` command for both directories.

In the process of checking these items you might discover problems with other parts of the network; in that case, continue isolating and narrowing down the problem.

As discussed in Chapter 10, you can use the `ping` command to check the reachability of a machine. Check the reachability of a client from a server and vice versa. Then, you can check whether the NFS services are running. For example, to check remotely whether the NFS service has started on the server, issue the following command:

```
rpcinfo -s <serverName>|egrep 'nfs|mountd'
```

To check whether the `nfsd` daemon on the server is responding, issue the following command on the client machine:

```
rpcinfo -t <serverName> nfs
```

This checks the NFS connection of the client with the server over TCP. If you want to check whether the daemon `mountd` is running on the server, issue the following command on the client machine:

```
rpcinfo -t <serverName> mountd
```

If the server is running, it prints a list of programs and version numbers.

You can also use the `rpcinfo` command by logging on to the server machine, such as the following:

```
rpcinfo -t localhost nfs
```

If the server is running, it displays a list of programs and version numbers associated with the TCP protocol.

Now that you know how to troubleshoot an NFS server machine, you may perform the following exercise, which demonstrates how to troubleshoot an NFS client machine.

EXERCISE 12-2

Troubleshooting an NFS Client Machine

Suppose you are troubleshooting the connectivity between the NFS client machine to which you are logged on with the server machine named senate. Perform the following steps.

1. Check the reachability of the server by issuing the following command on the client:

   ```
   ping senate
   ```

2. If the server is reachable, investigate the server—for example, with the `rpcinfo` command, as shown previously in this section. If the server was unreachable, continue investigating the client. Next, on the client, make sure that the local name service is running by issuing the following command:

```
/usr/lib/nis/nisping -u
```

3. If you find that the service is running, make sure that the client has received the correct host information by issuing the following command:

```
/usr/bin/getent hosts senate
```

The output of this command will look like the following:

```
132.17.3.5 senate.capital.government.com
```

4. Suppose the host information is correct, but you already found that the server was not reachable. In that case, try to reach the server from another client by using the `ping` command.
   a. If the server is not reachable from the second client, the server needs to be investigated—for example, by using the `rpcinfo` command, as shown previously in this section.
   b. If the server is reachable from the second client, continue investigating this client.
5. Issue the `ping` command on this client to check its connectivity with other machines on the network.
6. If the `ping` command fails, check the configuration files on the client, such as `/etc/netmasks`, and `/etc/nsswitch.conf`.
7. Issue the `rpcinfo` command on the client to see whether it displays something like the following:

```
program 100003 version 4 ready and waiting
```

If it does not display this, then NFS version 4 is not enabled. In this case enable the NFS service.

8. If you have not yet found the problem, you should check the hardware.

The main troubleshooting tools for NFS are the `ping` and `rpcinfo` commands. Of course, you can always use the `svcs` command to check whether the NFS service is running.

Systems do crash as a result of hardware or software problems, and as a system administrator, you must know how to manage crashes. The crash dump and core files are main components of system crash management.

CERTIFICATION OBJECTIVE 12.05

Working with Crash Dumps

Exam Objective 2.2: *Manage crash dumps and core file behaviors.*

The bad news is that the applications running on the systems do crash, and so do the systems. The good news is that the crash information is saved so that you can investigate the crash and take appropriate action to fix the problem. The information is stored in core files and crash dump files. Some folks confuse these two kinds of files with each other. So, let's make the distinction clear before we dive into the topic.

- The core files are those files that are created when an application crashes.
- The crash dump files are those files that are created when the system crashes.

Let's explore how to manage both of these file types.

Managing Core Files

Core files are generated when a process or an application running on the system terminates abnormally. An obvious question is Where are the core files saved and how are they named? They are saved, by default, in the directory in which the application was running. However, you may want to configure this location so that you can save all the core files to one central location. You will learn further on in this section how to do that.

The names of the core files can be more sophisticated than the names of the crash dump files that you will see in the next section. However, the default name of the core file is very simple: `core`. The following two file paths are available so that you can configure them independent of each other:

- *Process-based core file path.* This file path, also called the per-process file path, is enabled by default, and its default value is `core`. If enabled, it causes a core file to be produced when a process terminates abnormally. This path is inherited by a child process from the parent process. The owner of the process owns the process-based core file with read/write permission, and no other user can view this file.
- *Global core file path.* This file path is disabled by default, and its default value is also `core`. If enabled, this file will be created in addition to the process-based file (if that file path is enabled) and will contain the same content. However, the owner of this file is the superuser with read/write permissions, and no other user can view this file.

So, by default, a core file in the current directory of the process will be created if the process terminates abnormally. If the global core file path is enabled, a second core file will also be created in the global core file location. If more than one process is executing from the same directory and they terminate abnormally, there will be a name conflict for the file name `core`. The solution is to configure the expanded names for the core files by using the `coreadm` command, which, in general, is used to manage the core files. For example, consider the following command:

```
coreadm -i /var/core/core.%f.%p
```

This command sets the default process-based core file path and applies to all processes that have not overridden the default path. The pattern %f means the name of the process file, and the pattern %p means process ID. Assume that a process sendmail with process ID 101420 terminates abnormally. The core file name that the system will produce now is the following:

```
/var/core/core.sendmail.101420
```

A list of patterns that can be used in configuring the core file paths is presented in Table 12-5.

By default, a setuid process does not create any core file—neither a process-based core file nor a global-path core file.

TABLE 12-5 Patterns that can be used to configure the core file paths

Pattern	Description
%d	The directory name for the executable file (the process file)
%f	The name of the executable file
%g	Effective group ID for the process
%m	Machine name from the output of the `uname -m` command
%n	System node name from the output of the `uname -n` command
%p	Process ID
%t	Decimal value of time
%u	Effective user ID associated with the process
%z	Name of the zone in which the process is executed (Zones are discussed in Chapter 15.)
%%	The literal %

The main functionality of the `coreadm` command is to specify the name and location of core files produced by the abnormally terminating processes.

The `coreadm` command has the following syntax:

```
coreadm [-g <pattern>] [-i <pattern>] [-d <options>] [-e <options>]
```

The options are described here:

- **-d <options>.** Disable the options specified by `<options>`.
- **-e <options>.** Enable the options specified by `<options>`, which could be one or more of the following:
  - **global.** Allow core dumps that use the global core pattern.
  - **global-setid.** Allow setid core dumps that use global core pattern.
  - **log.** Generate a syslog message when there is an attempt to create a global core file.
  - **process.** Allow core dumps that use a per-process (process-based) core pattern.
  - **proc-setid.** Allow setid core dumps that use a per-process (process-based) core pattern.

- **-g <pattern>.** Set the global-core file path specified by <pattern>. Possible values for <pattern> are listed in Table 12-5.
- **-i <pattern>.** Set the per-process (process based) core file path specified by <pattern>. Possible values for <pattern> are listed in Table 12-5.

The configuration values set by the `coreadm` command are saved in the `/etc/coreadm.conf` file; hence, they survive across system reboots. Whereas the core files are created when a process crashes (terminates abnormally), the crash dump files are created when the system crashes.

Managing Crash Dumps

A system can crash for any of a number of reasons, including hardware malfunctions, I/O problems, and software errors. When the Solaris system crashes, it will do the following in order to help you:

1. Display an error message on the console.
2. Write a copy of its physical memory to the dump device.
3. Reboot automatically.
4. Execute the `savecore` command to retrieve the data from the dump device and write the saved crash dump to the following two files:
   - `unix.<n>`. Contains kernel's name list.
   - `vmcore.<n>`. Contains the crash dump data.

<n> specifies the dump sequence number. The files are saved in a predetermined directory; by default this is `/var/crash/<hostname>`, which you can change by reconfiguring, as you will see further on.

on the job

In the previous Solaris versions, the existing crash dump files were automatically overwritten when a system rebooted unless you manually enabled the system to do something about it. In Solaris 10, the saving of crash dump files is enabled by default.

The saved crash dump files provide useful information for diagnosing the problem. To manage the crash dump information, you can use the `dumpadm` command, which has the following syntax:

```
/usr/sbin/dumpadm [-nuy] [-c contentType>] [-d dumpDevice>]
[-m <n><unit>] [-s savecoreDir>] [-r rootDir>]
```

The options are described here:

- **-c <contentType>.** Modify the content options for the dump—that is, what the dump should contain. The `<contentType>` can specify one of the following values:
  - **all.** All memory pages.
  - **curproc.** Kernel memory pages and the memory pages of the currently executing process when the dump was initiated.
  - **kernel.** Only the kernel memory pages.
- **-d <dumpDevice>.** Specify the dump device. The `<dumpDevice>` can specify one of the following values:
  - **<devicePath>.** A specific device with an absolute path, such as `/dev/dsk/c0t2d0s2`.
  - **swap.** Select the most appropriate active swap entry to be used as dump device.
- **-m <n><unit>.** Specify the minimum free space that the `savecore` must maintain in the file system that contains the `savecore` directory. The parameter `<n>` specifies a number, and the parameter `<unit>` specifies the unit, which can be k for KB, m for MB, or % to indicate the percentage of the total file system size.
- **-n.** Do not run `savecore` automatically on reboot. This is not recommended, because you may lose the crash information.
- **-r <rootDir>.** Specify an alternative root directory relative to which the `dumpadm` command should create files. The default is /.
- **-s <savecoreDir>.** Specify the directory in which to store the files written by the `savecore` command. The default is `/var/crash/<hostname>`. The value of `<hostname>` is the name by which the system is known to the network; it can be retrieved by issuing the following command: `uname -n`.
- **-u.** Update the dump configuration based on the `/etc/dumpadm.conf` file. If the `/etc/dumpadm.conf` file is missing, it is created and synchronized with the current dump configuration.
- **-y.** Automatically execute the `savecore` command on reboot. This is the default.

Note that the system crash dump service is managed by SMF under the identifier:

```
svc:/system/dumpadm:default
```

Therefore, it is automatically started at system reboot. In addition, dumpadm is the name of the command that you can use to manage the configuration of the crash dump facility as described previously.

Now you know that a crash dump is just a snapshot of the memory when a fatal error occurred. At times, even when the system did not crash, you may want to investigate the memory content. Solaris 10 lets you take a memory snapshot of a live system by using the following command:

```
savecore -L
```

You can troubleshoot a running system by taking a snapshot of memory during some troubled state of the system, such as a transient performance problem or service outage. Before issuing the savecore command, make sure you have configured a dedicated dump device (by using the dumpadm command) to which the savecore command will save the information. Immediately after dumping to the dump device, the savecore utility writes out the crash dump files to your savecore directory.

Now that you know how to manage crash dump information, here are some practical scenarios and their solutions.

SCENARIO & SOLUTION	
You want to use the disk slice c0t1d0s2 as the dedicated dump device. What command would you issue to make that happen?	dumpadm -d /dev/dsk/c0t1d0s2
You want the crash dump files to be saved to the /var/dump directory instead of the /var/crash/<hostname> directory. What command would you issue?	dumpadm -s /var/dump
You discover that the crash dump service is not running. What command would you issue to start it without rebooting the system?	svcadm enable svc:/system/dumpadm:default (Remember that dump crash is an SMF service.)

The three most important takeaways from this chapter are the following:

- The file system SWAPFS is used by the kernel for swapping (using disk space for physical memory). TMPFS is used to improve the performance of applications by using physical memory for file read and write and is the default file system for the /tmp directory.

- Network file system (NFS) service is managed by the SMF under the identifier `network/nfs/server`.
- Core files are created when a process terminates abnormally, whereas crash dump files are created when the system crashes.

CERTIFICATION SUMMARY

The processes running on a system need random access memory (RAM), and when the system runs low on memory, some disk space is used in a way that the process views it as memory. This method of using disk space for memory is called virtual memory, and the disk space being used as memory is called physical swap space. In other words, virtual memory combines the swap space with memory. To avoid allocating unnecessary swap space, an address for the swap space that actually exists in the physical memory is assigned to the process when it asks for swap space. This is called virtual swap space. The SWAPFS file system is responsible for providing these virtual swap space addresses and translating them to real, physical swap space addresses when the system runs low on memory and the process needs to use the physical swap space. The TMPFS file system, a memory-based file system that stores its files in the `/tmp` directory in memory, is used to improve the performance of the applications. This system uses the space resources from the swap space. The `mkfile` and `swap` commands are used to manage the swap space.

The file systems are shared over the network by using the NFS service, which is automatically started when the system is booted. The `nfsd` daemon handles the file system requests from the client. A file system on the server that you need to share each time the system is booted should have a `share` command in the `/etc/dfs/dfstab` file. Because NFS service is managed by NFS, you can use the `svcs` command to determine the status of the service, and the `svcadm` command to enable and disable the service. The shared file systems can be used by the client machine by mounting them. For that purpose Solaris offers an automount SMF service called autofs, which is started automatically at boot time and has the daemon named `automountd`. The mount points on a client machine are mapped to the file systems on the server machines by three kinds of files on the client machine. These are the master maps file `/etc/auto_master` and the direct and indirect maps files defined in the `auto_master` file. The main steps in troubleshooting NFS services consist of: using the `ping` command to check the connectivity between the client and the server machines, using the `rpcinfo` command to check whether the client can access the NFS services running on the service machine, and using the `rpcinfo` command to check whether the NFS services are actually running.

Processes running on the system as well as the system itself do crash as a result of hardware failures or software errors. The problems that may have caused the crash can be diagnosed by examining the files that the crashes create: core dump files created when a process terminates abnormally and crash dump files created when the system crashes. These files can be managed by using the `coreadm` and `dumpadm` commands.

The network file system, and the virtual file systems help hide the boundaries from users. For example, a user does not have to worry about which machine has the data. From the end user's perspective, it is right there on the user's machine even if it is actually on another machine. There is another important boundary to consider—the limitation of having a file system on one disk. That is, a file system resides on a disk slice and hence cannot span across multiple disks. The volume management offered by Solaris eliminates this boundary for the end user as well. We explore this topic in the next chapter.

INSIDE THE EXAM

Comprehend

- Virtual memory is the storage space reserved on the hard disk for the system to use as memory when it runs low on physical memory. The disk space being used for the virtual memory is called swap space.
- The names of the direct maps file and the indirect maps files are defined in the master maps file: `/etc/auto_master`. An entry in the direct maps file provides the full path of the mount point The full path of the mount point in an entry in an indirect maps file is composed of the mount point defined in the indirect maps file and the mount point defined in the corresponding entry in the master maps file.
- Core dump files are created when processes running on the system terminate abnormally, whereas crash dump files are created when the system itself crashes.

Look Out

- When paging starts, the SWAPFS file system has to map the virtual swap space addresses to physical swap space addresses.

INSIDE THE EXAM (CONTINUED)

- The reserved swap space does not have any assigned location on the disk; the location is assigned when the process wants to write data and the reserved space is actually allocated.
- You don't need to repartition the disk to add secondary swap space by using the `mkfile` and `swap` commands.
- To share a file system, you must have issued the `share` command for the file system either manually or by making it an entry in the `/etc/dfs/dfstab` file, and the SMF server must be running.
- The default access to the shared file system is read/write for all clients.
- In the framework of automount service, only mount points are created at system startup times, and no file system is mounted on those points during the boot.
- Unlike `mount`, `automount` does not read the `/etc/vfstab` file for a list of file systems to mount. Remember that this file is specific to each computer.

Memorize

- TMPFS manages the swap space files, and SWAPFS manages the virtual swap space addresses.
- Virtual swap space is the sum of the actual physical swap space plus a portion of the available physical memory space.
- The swap devices (files and slices) are listed in the `/etc/vfstab` file.
- The swap slices and swap files are activated by the `/sbin/swapadd` script each time the system is booted.
- The parameters for the `nfsd` daemon are in the `/etc/default/nfs` file.
- The `coredump` files are managed by the `coreadm` command and the crash dump information is managed by the `dumpadm` command; the configuration files for these two utilities are `coreadm.conf` and `dumpadm.conf`.

TWO-MINUTE DRILL

Virtual Memory Concepts

- Virtual memory refers to using the disk space as if it were the physical memory of the computer, and this disk space is called swap space. Files in the swap space are managed by the TMPFS file system.
- Virtual swap space refers to the addresses that are in the physical memory and act as the addresses of the swap space and are called virtual swap space addresses, or just virtual addresses. They are used to avoid the problem of having to configure a large disk space as swap space.
- Virtual swap space is controlled by the SWAPFS file system, which provides virtual swap space addresses as opposed to physical swap space addresses in response to the requests for reserving swap space. SWAPFS also maps the virtual addresses to physical swap space addresses when the paging starts.

Managing Swap Space

- You use the `mkfile` command to create a swap file.
- You can use the `swap` command to manage the swap space: the `-l` and `-s` options display information about the swap space, the `-a` option activates the swap file, and the `-d` option makes the swap space unavailable.
- The `swapadd` script reads the list of swap space devices from the `/etc/vfstab` file and activates them by using the `swap -a` command each time the system is booted.

The NFS Service

- The NFS service is started automatically when the system is mounted.
- The `/etc/dfs/dfstab` file contains the `share` command for each file system on the server machine that needs to be shared.
- The daemon that handles the file system requests from the clients is `nfsd`, and its configuration file is `/etc/default/nfs`.
- The NFS service is managed by SMF; therefore, you can get its status by using the `svcs` command and you can start or stop the service by using the `svcadm` command on the SMF identifier `cvc:/network/nfs/server`.

Working with AutoFS

- ❑ AutoFS is a kernel file system that supports automatic mounting and unmounting of remote file systems.
- ❑ The autofs service is configured by the master maps file `/etc/auto_master`, and the direct and indirect maps files are defined in the master file.
- ❑ The maps files basically map the mount points on the client machines to the file systems on the server machine which will be mounted to these mount points when necessary. The mount point for a direct map is fully defined in the direct maps file; the full path of a mount point in an indirect map is defined partially in the master maps file and in the indirect maps file.
- ❑ The autofs is an SMF service under the identifier `svc:/system/filesystem/autofs`, and therefore can be administered with the `svcadm` command.

Troubleshooting NFS

- ❑ Use the `ping` command to check whether the client machine can reach the server machine and vice versa.
- ❑ Use the `rpcinfo` command on the client to check whether the client can access the NFS services running on the server.
- ❑ Use the `rpcinfo` command remotely and locally to check whether the NFS services are running on the server.
- ❑ Check the configuration files.

Managing Core Files and Crash Dumps

- ❑ Core files are generated when processes running on the system terminate abnormally, whereas crash dump files are generated when the system itself crashes.
- ❑ The `coreadm` command is used to manage the core files, and the `dumpadm` command is used to manage crash dump information. The configuration files for these two utilities are `coreadm.conf` and `dumpadm.conf`, respectively.
- ❑ By default, a core file in the current directory of the process is created if the process terminates abnormally. When the system crashes, two files, `unix.<n>` and `vmcore.<n>`, are generated and saved, by default, in the `/var/crash/<hostname>` directory. Here `<n>` specifies the dump sequence number, and `<hostname>` is the name of the machine node on which the system crashed.

SELF TEST

The following questions will help you measure your understanding of the material presented in this chapter. Read all the choices carefully because there might be more than one correct answer. Choose all correct answers for each question.

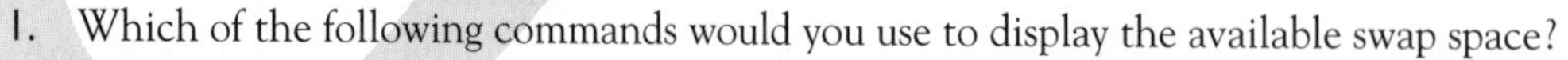

1. Which of the following commands would you use to display the available swap space?

   A. `swap -a`

   B. `swap -l`

   C. `swap -s`

   D. `prtconf`

2. Which of the following commands would you use to list the current swap area on your system?

   A. `swap -a`

   B. `swap -l`

   C. `swap -s`

   D. `prtconf`

3. Which of the following files must you modify so that the added swap space will be activated automatically each time the system is booted?

   A. `/etc/swapadd`

   B. `/etc/swap`

   C. `/etc/vfstab`

   D. `/etc/swapconf`

4. If you want to share a resource, you would add the `share` command for that resource into which of the following files?

   A. `/etc/dfs/sharetab`

   B. `/etc/dfs/dfstab`

   C. `/etc/default/nfs`

   D. `/etc/vfstab`

5. Which of the following daemons are used by NFS 4.0?

   A. `nfsd`

   B. `nfslogd`

C. `mountd`

D. `statd`

6. Which of the following commands displays the shared resources on the local server?

 A. `svcs network/nfs/server`

 B. `nfsshare`

 C. `share`

 D. `dfshares`

7. Which of the following map files contain all the direct and indirect map names?

 A. `/etc/auto_direct`

 B. `/etc/auto_indirect`

 C. `/etc/auto_master`

 D. `/etc/auto_all`

 E. `/etc/autofs`

8. What does the following line in the `/etc/auto_master` file on a client machine mean?

```
/share auto_share
```

 A. `auto_share` is the name of an indirect maps file, and all the path names of all the mount points in that file will be relative to the path `/share`.

 B. The directory `/share` on the client machine maps to the directory `auto_share` on the server machine.

 C. This is an invalid entry for the `auto_master` file.

 D. The `/share` directory on the server is mapped to the `auto_share` directory on the client.

9. What is the name of the daemon that handles the mounting and unmounting requests from the autofs service?

 A. `autofsd`

 B. `mountd`

 C. `automountd`

 D. `autofs`

10. Which of the following are true statements about core files and crash dumps.

    A. If you see a file such as `vmcore.123`, assume it was generated when a process terminated abnormally.

    B. A file that looks like `unix.123` must be created by a system crash.

    C. A file that looks like `core.politics.101` might have been created by a process named politics that terminated abnormally.

    D. `dumpadm.conf` is the configuration file for the utility that manages the core files.

11. Which of the following are the commands to manage core files and crash dump?

    A. `coreadm`

    B. `crashadm`

    C. `dumpadm`

    D. `dumpadmin`

SELF TEST ANSWERS

1. ☑ **C**. The `swap -s` command displays the reserved swap space, allocated swap space, and available swap space.
   ☒ **A** and **B** are incorrect because the `swap -a` command activates the swap file and the `swap -l` command displays the device name for the swap space and the swap space size but not the available swap space. **D** is incorrect because the `prtconf` command displays the total amount of memory and the configuration of system peripherals but not the available swap space.

2. ☑ **B**. The `swap -l` command lists the current swap area on your system.
   ☒ **A** is incorrect because `swap -a` is used to add (activate) the swap area. **C** is incorrect because the `swap -s` command displays the reserved swap space, allocated swap space, and available swap space, but not the full path of the swap area. **D** is incorrect because the `prtconf` command displays the total amount of memory and configuration of system peripherals but not the available swap space.

3. ☑ **C**. Each time the system is booted, the `swapadd` script reads the list of swap devices in the `/etc/vfastab` file to activate them.
   ☒ **A**, **B**, and **D** are incorrect because there are no files `/etc/swapadd`, `/etc/swap`, and `/etc/swapconf` that you need to change to make the swap area permanent.

4. ☑ **B**. The file systems listed in the `/etc/dfs/dfstab` file are automatically shared if the NFS server is running, because an entry in this file for a file system is actually a `share` command for that file system.
   ☒ **A** is incorrect because the `/etc/dfs/sharetab` file contains the list of the file systems currently being shared, but for a file system to be shared it must be entered in the `/etc/dfs/dfstab` file. **C** is incorrect because the `/etc/default/nfs` file contains the configuration information for the `nfsd` daemon, and **D** is incorrect because `/etc/vfstab` lists the file systems that are mounted automatically but are not necessarily shared.

5. ☑ **A**. The `nfsd` daemon handles the client requests for file systems.
   ☒ **B**, **C**, and **D** are incorrect because, unlike previous versions of NFS, NFS version 4 does not use the `lockd`, `mountd`, `nfslogd`, and `statd` daemons.

6. ☑ **D**. The `dfshares` command displays the list of shared resources.
   ☒ **A** is incorrect because the `svcs` command is used to display the status of the NFS service—that is, whether it's running or not. **B** is incorrect because there is no such command as `nfsshare`, and **C** is incorrect because the `share` command is used to share a resource and not to display the list of shared resources.

7. ☑ **C**. The `/etc/auto_master` file contains the names of all the indirect and direct map file names.
   ☒ **A** is incorrect because the `/etc/aut_direct` file contains the direct maps that are named in the `auto_master` file. **B** is incorrect because there is no such file as `auto_indirect`, but it could be named in the `auto_master` file. The same is true of the choices **D** and **E**.

8. ☑ **A**. Each indirect maps file must have its name declared in the `auto_master` file.
   ☒ **B** and **D** are incorrect because the `auto_master` file only defines the names of the direct and indirect maps files; it does not map directories between the clients and the servers. **C** is incorrect because the given entry is a valid entry for the `auto_master` file.

9. ☑ **C**. The `automountd` daemon on the client handles the mounting and unmounting requests from the autofs service
   ☒ **A** is incorrect because there is no daemon `autofsd` that handles requests from autofs. **B** is incorrect because the `mountd` daemon handles mount requests from remote systems. **D** is incorrect because autofs is not a daemon but a service managed by SMF.

10. ☑ **B** and **C**. When the system crashes it writes a copy of its physical memory to the dump device, reboots, and executes the `savecore` command, This command retrieves the data from the dump device and saves it in two files: `unix.<n>` and `vmcore.<n>`, where `<n>` specifies the dump sequence number. The files generated when a process terminates abnormally can have expanded names based on patterns involving process file names, node names, and so on.
    ☒ **A** is incorrect because a `vmcore.<n>` file is generated when the system crashes, not when a process terminates abnormally. **D** is incorrect because the utility that manages the core files is `coreadm` and its configuration file is `coreadm.conf`.

11. ☑ **A** and **C**. The `coreadm` command is used to manage the core files, whereas the `dumpadm` command is used to manage the crash dump information.
    ☒ **B** and **D** are incorrect because there are no commands named `crashadm` and `dumpadmin`.

13

Managing Storage Volumes

CERTIFICATION OBJECTIVES

13.01	Understanding RAID and SVM Concepts	✓	Two-Minute Drill
13.02	Creating State Databases and Mirrors	Q&A	Self Test

The system uses disks to store data, and you learned about disk management in Chapter 5. A file system resides on a slice of a disk and hence cannot span across multiple disks. In other words, the size of a file system is limited by the size of a single disk. Another drawback of treating disks individually and independent of each other is that if a disk crashes, we permanently lose the data that has not yet been backed up, and we cannot continue to serve the data until the disk has been replaced or repaired. In other words, our system is not fault tolerant, and this is not an acceptable environment for 24 × 7 services.

The solution to these problems begins with looking at the disks in terms of logical volume, which is a named chunk of disk space that can occupy a part of a disk or the whole disk; alternatively, it can span across multiple disks that are called a disk set. The concept of logical volume not only opens up practically unlimited disk space for a file system spanned across multiple disks: it also enables two more significant features. First, the availability of abundant disk space makes it possible to provide data replication, thereby implementing fault tolerance. Second, because a volume can span across multiple disks, we can write to multiple disks simultaneously to improve performance. These two features are implemented in a technology called Redundant Array of Inexpensive Disks (RAID). Different ways of implementing these features have given rise to what are called RAID levels. The volumes with these features are called RAID volumes, and Solaris offers a tool called Solaris Volume Manager (SVM) to manage these volumes.

The core issue to think about in this chapter is: how do we perform volume management in Solaris? In search of an answer, we will explore three thought streams: RAID levels, SVM concepts, and state databases, which hold the information about the disk sets and the volumes.

CERTIFICATION OBJECTIVE 13.01

Understanding RAID and SVM Concepts

Exam Objective 3.1: *Analyze and explain RAID (0,1,5) and SVM concepts (logical volumes, soft partitions, state databases, hot spares, and hot spare pools).*

The Redundant Array of Inexpensive Disks (RAID), also called Redundant Array of Independent Disks, takes the management of disk space from a single disk to multiple disks called a disk set. On a disk set, the data lives on a volume that can span across multiple disks. Solaris offers a tool called Solaris Volume Manager (SVM) to manage these volumes. In this section we explore the RAID and SVM concepts.

Implementing Disk System Fault Tolerance

Although you have a backup and restoration system as a protection against disasters such as a hard disk failure, it does not solve all the disk problems related to potential data loss. There are two cases that the protection provided by backup does not cover:

- The data stored between the last backup and the crash will be lost forever.
- There are situations where you want zero time between data loss and data recovery—that is, the end user should have no awareness that the disk has crashed. For example, think of a disk supporting a 24 × 7 web site.

These two cases are covered by implementing fault tolerance, which is the property of a system that enables the system to keep functioning even when a part of the system fails. Fault tolerance in a disk set is implemented through techniques called *mirroring*, *duplexing*, and *parity*.

Disk Mirroring

Disk mirroring is a process of designating a disk drive, say disk B, as a duplicate (mirror) of another disk drive, say disk B. As shown in Figure 13-1, in disk mirroring both disks are attached to the same disk controller. When the OS writes data to a disk drive, the same data also gets written to the mirror disk. If the first disk drive fails, the data will be served from the mirror disk and the user will not see the failure.

Note that the two disks don't have to be identical, but if you don't want to waste disk space, they should be identical. For example, consider two disks of size 5GB and 7GB. Using these two disks, you can make a mirrored system of only 5GB (each disk); hence, 2GB is wasted.

Note that mirroring has a single point of failure—that is, if the disk controller fails, both disks will become inaccessible. The solution to this problem is *disk duplexing*.

Disk Duplexing

You have seen that the fault tolerance in mirroring is vulnerable to the failure of disk controller. Disk duplexing solves this problem by providing each disk drive its own disk controller, as shown in Figure 13-1.

FIGURE 13-1

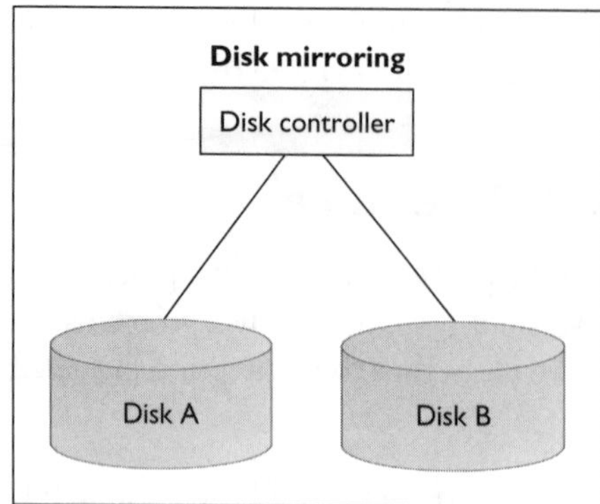

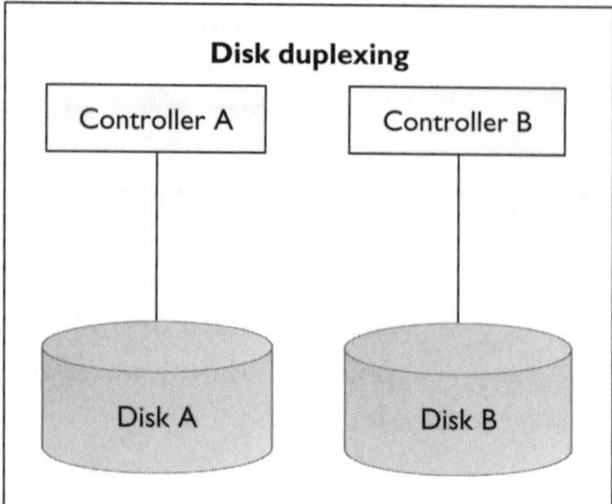

Comparison of mirroring and duplexing

As shown in Table 13-1, duplexing improves fault tolerance over mirroring. This is because in addition to disk redundancy there is also a controller redundancy. Therefore, duplexing is more fault tolerant than mirroring, and mirroring is more fault tolerant than a single disk.

There is another disk read/write technique that is related to disk volume, called *disk striping*.

Improving Performance through Disk Striping

When a disk volume spans across multiple disks, you fill up one disk before you start writing onto the next disk. Now that we have more than one disk in a volume, if we could write to all the disks in the volume simultaneously, we could improve

TABLE 13-1 Comparison of mirrored and duplexed disk systems

One Disk	Both Disks	One Controller	Is Mirrored System Fault Tolerant?	Is Duplexed System Fault Tolerant?
Fails	—	—	Yes	Yes
—	—	Fails	No	Yes
Fails	—	Fails	No	Yes if the failed controller belongs to the failed disk: otherwise, no.
—	Fail	—	No	No

performance. This is exactly what disk striping is all about. Disk striping breaks the data into small pieces called stripes, and those stripes are written to multiple disks simultaneously. Because the read/write heads are working simultaneously, striping improves read/write performance. This is depicted in Figure 13-2.

There is another technique to provide data redundancy called *parity*.

Data Redundancy by Parity

Parity is another technique that is used to implement fault tolerance. If you lose a part of data, you can reconstruct it from the parity information of this data. When a chunk (say a block) of data is stored on a disk, its parity information is calculated and stored on another disk. If this part of the data is lost, it can be reconstructed from the parity information. Note that parity provides fault tolerance at the cost of performance and disk space, because parity calculations take CPU time, and parity information takes disk space.

In this section, we have discussed concepts that can be used to implement disk fault tolerance and improve the read/write performance of a disk. In the next section, we explore a specific technology that implements these concepts.

Understanding RAID

Redundant Array of Inexpensive Disks (RAID), also known as Redundant Array of Independent Disks (RAID), refers to a technology that uses a set of redundant disks to provide fault tolerance. The disks usually reside together in a cabinet and are therefore referred to as an array.

FIGURE 13-2

Disk striping writes stripes of data on multiple disks simultaneously

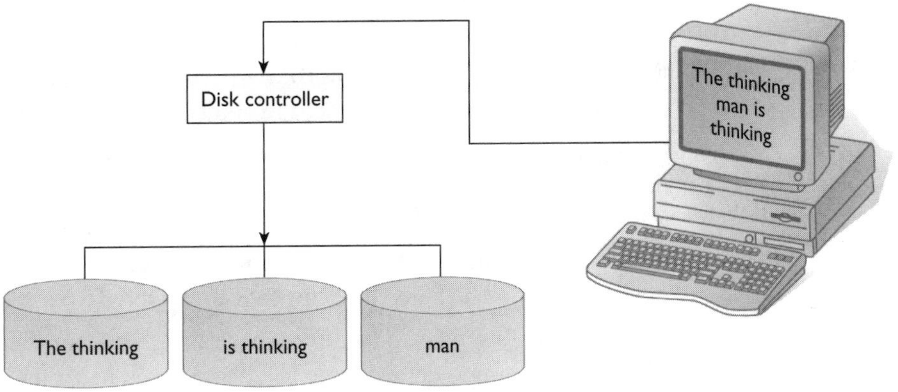

We have presented here a comprehensive coverage of RAID levels. However, note that Solaris supports only RAID 0, RAID 1, RAID 0 + 1, RAID 1 + 0, and RAID 5. So, for the exam, you need to remember only these RAID levels.

There are several methods that use an array of disks, and they are referred to as RAID levels, as described here:

- *RAID 0.* This level of RAID uses striping on multiple disks. This means that a volume contains stripes on multiple disks and the data can be written simultaneously to these stripes. In other words, the data is striped across multiple disks. Because you can write to various stripes simultaneously, RAID 0 improves performance, but it does not implement fault tolerance even though it uses multiple disks. Imagine a file written on various stripes residing on multiple disks. Now if one disk fails that contains a stripe of the file, you lose the file.
- *RAID 0 + 1.* This is the same as RAID 0, but the stripes are mirrored to provide fault tolerance in addition to performance improvement by striping. However, mirroring can slow down performance.
- *RAID 1.* This RAID level uses mirroring (or duplexing) on two disks to provide a very basic level of disk fault tolerance. Both disks contain the same data—that is, one disk is a mirror image of the other. If one disk fails, the other disk takes over automatically. This RAID level also provides performance improvement in data reads, because if one disk is busy, the data can be read from the other disk.
- *RAID 1 + 0.* This is the same as RAID 1, but the mirroring is striped to provide performance improvement in addition to fault tolerance.
- *RAID 2.* This RAID level implements striping with parity and therefore needs at least three disks, because parity information is written on a disk other than the data disks. The striping is done at bit level—that is, bits are striped across multiple disks. If a data disk fails and the parity disk does not, the data on the failed disk can be reconstructed from the parity disk.
- *RAID 3.* This is similar to RAID 2 (striping with parity). The main difference is that the striping is done at byte level as opposed to bit level—that is, bytes are striped across multiple disks. This offers improved performance over

RAID 2, because more data can be read or written in a single read/write operation.

- *RAID 4*. This is similar to RAID 2 and RAID 3 (striping with parity). The main difference is that the striping is done at block level as opposed to bit level or byte level—that is, blocks are striped across multiple disks. This offers improved performance over RAID 2 and RAID 3 because more data can be read or written in a single read/write operation.
- *RAID 5*. This RAID level implements striping with distributed parity—that is, parity is also striped across multiple disks. The parity function does not have a dedicated disk—that is, the data and parity can be interleaved on all disks. However, it is clear that the parity of a given piece of data on one disk must not be written to the same disk, which would defeat the whole purpose of parity. If a disk fails, the parity information about the data on the failed disk must exist on other disks so that the lost data can be reconstructed. If more than one disk fails, it's possible that you will lose parity information along with the data. If you use only two disks, you cannot distribute the parity information, because data and parity must be on separate disks. Therefore, RAID 5 requires three disks at minimum.

RAID 0, RAID 1, and RAID 5 are the most commonly used RAID levels in practice. However, in addition to these RAID levels, Solaris supports variations of RAID 0 and RAID 1, called RAID 0 + 1 and RAID 1 + 0, respectively.

The different RAID levels are distinguished from each other mainly by how much performance improvement and fault tolerance they provide and the way they provide it. This is summarized in Table 13-2.

exam watch

Remember that RAID levels are differentiated from each other according to the degree of read/write performance improvement and disk fault tolerance implemented by them. In choosing one RAID level against another for a given situation, always ask What is required here: read/write performance, disk fault tolerance, or both?

RAID technology takes disk space management from a single disk to a disk set. Instead of thinking of disk space in terms of a disk slice that resides on only one disk, now you can think of disk space in terms of a logical volume that can span

TABLE 13-2 Performance improvement and fault tolerance provided by various RAID levels

RAID Level of the Volume	Main Characteristics	Fault Tolerance?	Performance Improvement?
RAID 0	Striping, but no parity.	No	Yes
RAID 0 + 1	Striping with mirroring.	Yes	Yes
RAID 1	Mirroring or duplexing, but no parity.	Yes	Yes in reading
RAID 1+	Mirroring with striping.	Yes	Yes
RAID 2	Bit-level striping with parity.	Yes	Parity slows down performance, whereas striping improves it.
RAID 3	Byte-level striping with parity.	Yes	Parity slows down performance, whereas striping improves it.
RAID 4	Block-level striping with parity.	Yes	Parity slows down performance, whereas striping improves it.
RAID 5	Both data and parity are striped.	Yes	Parity slows down performance, whereas striping improves it.

across multiple disks. These volumes with RAID features are called RAID volumes. Solaris offers a tool called Solaris Volume Manager (SVM) to manage these volumes.

Understanding SVM Concepts

A volume is a named chunk of disk space that can occupy a part of a disk or the whole disk, or it can span across multiple disks. In other words, a volume is a set of physical slices that appears to the system as a single, logical device, also called a virtual (or pseudo) device or a metadevice in standard UNIX terminology. A volume is also called logical volume. In this book we use the terms volume and logical volume interchangeably.

Solaris offers Solaris Volume Manager (SVM) to manage disk volumes that may reside on multiple disks. In other words, SVM is a software product that helps you manage huge amounts of data spread over a large number of disks. Because SVM deals with a large number of disks, you can use it for the following tasks in addition to read/write performance improvement and disk fault tolerance:

- Increasing storage capacity
- Increasing data availability
- Easing administration of large storage devices

In the following, we describe important concepts related to SVM:

- *Soft partition.* With the increase in disk storage capacity and the invention of disk arrays, a user may need to divide disks (or logical volumes) into more than eight partitions. SVM offers this capability by letting you divide a disk slice or a logical volume into as many divisions as needed; these divisions are called *soft partitions*. Each soft partition must have a name. A named soft partition can be directly accessed by an application if it's not included in a volume, because in this case it appears to a file system (and the application) as a single contiguous logical volume. Once you include a soft partition in a volume, it cannot be directly accessed. The maximum size of a soft partition is limited to the size of the slice or the logical volume of which it is a part.
- *Hot spare.* A hot spare is a slice that is reserved for automatic substitution in case the corresponding data slice fails. Accordingly, a hot spare must stand ready for an immediate substitution when needed. The hot spares live on a disk separate from the data disk that's being used. By using SVM, you can dynamically add, delete, replace, and enable hot spares within the hot spare pool. An individual hot spare can be included in one or more hot spare pools.
- *Hot spare pool.* A hot spare pool is a collection (an ordered list) of hot spares that SVM uses to provide increased data availability and fault tolerance for a RAID 1 (mirrored) volume and a RAID 5 (striped data with striped parity) volume. You can assign a hot spare pool to one or more RAID 1 or RAID 5 volumes. If a slice failure occurs, SVM automatically substitutes a hot spare for the failed slice.
- *Disk set.* From the perspective of SVM, data lives in logical volumes. Where do the logical volumes (and hot spare pools that support improved data availability) live? They live on a set of disks called a disk set. In other words, a disk set is a set of disk drives that contain logical volumes and hot spare pools.

- *State database*. A state database contains the configuration and status information about the disk sets, and about volumes and hot spares in a disk set managed by SVM. SVM also maintains replicas (multiple copies) of a state database to provide fault tolerance. For example, if a replica gets corrupted during a system crash, other replicas would still be available. That means each replica should live on a separate disk. When a state database is updated, the update flows to all the replicas. If your system loses the state database, how does it determine which of the replicas contain valid data? This is determined by running the so-called majority consensus algorithm. According to this algorithm, a minimum majority (half + 1) replicas must be available and must be in agreement before any of them could be declared valid. This imposes the requirement that you must create at least three replicas of the state database. This way if one replica fails, we still have two of them to reach consensus. This means that the system cannot reboot into multiuser mode unless a minimum majority (half + 1) of the total number of state database replicas are available. However, the system continues to run if at least half of the state database replicas are available; otherwise the system panics.

Do not confuse redundant data (mirrored disk in RAID 1 or duplicate data in RAID 5) with hot spares. Both have their own roles to play. For example, consider a RAID 1 system that has two disks: Disk A and Disk B. Disk A is serving the data and Disk B is the mirrored disk—that is, a duplicate of Disk A; therefore your system is fault tolerant. Suppose Disk A fails; the system will automatically switch to Disk B for the data, and as a result the user does not see the failure. But here is the bad news: your system is not fault tolerant any more. If Disk B fails, there is no disk to take over. This is where a hot spare comes to the rescue; it keeps the system fault tolerant while the failed slice is being repaired or replaced. When a slice from the disk being used fails, the following happens:

- The mirrored disk takes over, but the system is no longer fault tolerant.
- The failed slice is automatically replaced with a hot spare, and the hot spare is synchronized with the data from the mirrored slice that is currently in use. Once again, the system is fault tolerant.
- You can take your time to repair (or replace) the failed slice and then free up the hot spare.

Ultimately, hot spares provide extra protection to the data redundancy that is already available without them.

exam watch

Because a hot spare must be synchronized with the current data, you cannot use hot spare technology in systems in which redundant data is not available, such as RAID 0. Furthermore, although you can assign a hot spare pool to multiple submirror (RAID 1) volumes or multiple RAID 5 volumes, a given volume can be associated with only one hot spare pool.

Earlier in this chapter, we discussed RAID levels in general. Next, we discuss how (and which of) these RAID levels are implemented in logical volumes supported by SVM.

Logical Volumes Supported by SVM

A logical volume is a group of physical disk slices that appears to be a single logical device. This means they are transparent to the file systems, applications, and end users—hence the name *logical volume*. Logical volumes are used to increase storage capacity, data availability (and hence fault tolerance), and performance (possibly including I/O performance).

In a previous section we provided a generic description of RAID technology, including RAID 0, RAID 1, and RAID 5 levels; in this section we discuss RAID 0, RAID 1, and RAID 5 volumes offered by Solaris and managed by SVM.

SVM has the capability of supporting a maximum of 8192 logical volumes per disk set. However, its default configuration is for 128 logical volumes per disk set.

RAID 0 Volumes

You can compose a RAID 0 volume of either slices or soft partitions. These volumes enable you to dynamically expand disk storage capacity. There are three kinds of RAID 0 volumes, which are discussed here:

- *Stripe volume*. This is a volume that spreads data across two or more components (slices or soft partitions). Equally sized segments of data (called *interlaces*) are interleaved alternately (in a round-robin fashion) across two or more components. This enables multiple controllers to read and write data in parallel, thereby improving performance. The size of the data segment is called the interlace size. The default interlace size is 16KB, but you can set the size value when you create the volume. After the volume has been created, you are not allowed to change the interlace value. The total capacity of a stripe volume is equal to the number of components multiplied by the size of the smallest component, because the stripe volume spreads data equally across its components.

- *Concatenation volumes*. Unlike the stripe volume, a concatenation volume writes data on multiple components sequentially. That is, it writes the data to the first available component until it is full; then it moves to write to the next component. There is no parallel access. The advantage of this sequential approach is that you can expand the volume dynamically by adding new components as long as the file system is active. Furthermore, no disk space is wasted, because the total capacity of the volume is the sum of the sizes of all the components, even if the components are not of equal size.
- *Concatenated stripe volume*. Recall that you cannot change the size of the data segments on the components in a stripe volume after the volume has been created. So how can you extend the capacity of a stripe volume? Well, by adding another component (stripe) and promoting the stripe volume to a concatenated stripe volume. In other words, a concatenated stripe volume is a stripe volume that has been expanded by adding components.

If you want to stripe an existing file system, back up the file system, create the stripe volume, and restore the file system to the stripe volume. You would need to follow the same procedure if you want to change the interlace value after creating the stripe volume.

Because there is no data redundancy, a RAID 0 volume does not directly provide fault tolerance. However, RAID 0 volumes can be used as building blocks for RAID 1 volumes, which do provide fault tolerance.

RAID 1 Volumes

A RAID 1 volume, also called a mirror, is a volume that offers data redundancy (and hence fault tolerance) by maintaining copies of RAID 0 volumes. Each copy of a RAID 0 volume in a RAID 1 volume (mirror) is called a submirror. Obviously, mirroring takes more disk space (at least twice as much as the amount of data that needs to be mirrored), and more time to write. You can mirror the existing file systems.

For a volume to be a mirror volume it must contain at least two submirrors, but SVM supports up to four submirrors in a RAID 1 volume. You can attach or detach a submirror to a mirror any time without interrupting service. In other words, you can create your RAID 1 volume with just one submirror, and you can subsequently attach more submirrors to it. To improve fault tolerance and performance, choose the slices for different submirrors from different disks and controllers. For example, consider a RAID 1 volume with two submirrors. If a disk contains slices belonging to both submirrors, we will lose both submirrors when the disk fails, hence there is no fault tolerance.

In a RAID 1 volume, the same data will be written to more than one submirror, and the same data can be read from any of the submirrors to which it was written. This gives rise to multiple read/write options for a RAID 1 volume. To optimize performance, you can configure read and write policies when you create a mirror, and you can reconfigure these policies later when the system is in use. The default write policy is the parallel write, meaning that the data is written to all the submirrors simultaneously. Obviously this policy improves write performance. The alternative write policy is the serial write—that is, the write to one submirror must be completed before starting a write to the second submirror. This policy is designed to handle certain situations—for example, if a submirror should become inaccessible as a result of a power failure. The read policies are described in Table 13-3.

Now that you know about the various read policies available in SVM, see the next page for some practical scenarios and their solutions related to configuring the read/write policies for a RAID 1 volume.

So, mirroring provides fault tolerance through data redundancy. There is another way to provide fault tolerance, and that is by calculating and saving the parity information about data. This technique is used in RAID 5 volumes.

TABLE 13-3

Read policies for RAID 1 volumes

Read Policy	Description
First	All reads are performed from the first submirror.
Geometric	Reads are divided among submirrors based on the logical disk block addresses.
Round robin (default)	Reads are spread across all submirrors in a round-robin order to balance the read load.

SCENARIO & SOLUTION	
While configuring a RAID 1 volume, you want to minimize the seek time for the reads. Which read policy would you choose?	Geometric
While creating a RAID 1 volume, you know that the disk drive supporting the first submirror is substantially faster than the disk drives supporting other submirrors. Which read policy will you choose if read performance is important?	First
You initially configured your RAID 1 volume for parallel write. One of the submirrors of this volume has become inaccessible as a result of a power failure. Which write policy should you switch to?	Serial

RAID 5 Volumes

A RAID 5 volume is a striped volume that also provides fault tolerance by using parity information distributed across all components (disks or logical volumes). In case of a component failure, the lost data is reconstructed from its parity information and data available on other components. The calculation of parity slows down system performance as compared with the striped volume. A striped volume offers better performance than a RAID 5 volume, but it does not provide data redundancy and hence is not fault tolerant. Note the following about RAID 5 volumes:

- Because parity is distributed across all components, and when we lose data we must not lose its parity information (data and its parity must not reside on the same component), a RAID 5 volume requires at least three components.
- A component that already contains a file system (that you don't want to lose) must not be included in the creation of a RAID 5 volume, because doing so will erase the data during initialization.
- If you don't want to waste disk space, use components of equal size.
- You can set the interlace value (size of data segments); otherwise, it will be set to a default of 16KB.

Because RAID 5 uses parity, which slows down performance, it may not be a good solution for write intensive applications. SVM also supports variations of RAID 0 and RAID 1 volumes.

RAID 0 + 1 and RAID 1 + 0 Volumes

You have seen that a stripe volume is beneficial for performance because it enables multiple controllers to perform read/write simultaneously, but it does not support data fault tolerance because there is no data redundancy. You can add data redundancy to the benefits of a stripe volume by choosing RAID 5. However, RAID 5 calculates the parity and impedes performance. There is a simpler solution—mirror your stripe. That is exactly what a RAID 0 + 1 volume is: a stripe volume that has been mirrored. The reverse is also supported by SVM—that is, a mirror volume that is striped. It is known as RAID 1 + 0.

EXERCISE 13-1

Accessing the SVM GUI

The SVM GUI is part of the Solaris SMC (Solaris Management Console). To access the GUI, perform the following steps:

1. Start the SMC by issuing the following command:

```
%/usr/sbin/smc
```

2. Double-click This Computer in the Navigation pane.
3. Double-click Storage in the Navigation pane.
4. Load the SVM tools by double-clicking Enhanced Storage in the Navigation pane. Log in as superuser (root or another account with equivalent access) if the login prompt appears.
5. Double-click the appropriate icon to manage disk sets, state database replicas, hot spare pools, or volumes.

The configuration and status information about volumes is contained in a database called a *state database*. In the following section, we describe how you can create mirrors and state databases.

CERTIFICATION OBJECTIVE 13.02

Creating State Databases and Mirrors

Exam Objective 3.2: *Create the state database, build a mirror, and unmirror the root file system.*

Solaris Volume Manager manages state databases and logical volumes. Such creation is one of many management tasks that can be performed by using SVM.

Creating State Databases

You can use either the SVM GUI or the `metadb` command to create, delete, or check the status of a state database. First, note that the default size for a state database replica in SVM is 8192 blocks (4MB), whereas the default size in Solstice DiskSuite (an older Solaris product for managing volumes) is 1034 blocks. Be sure to take extra precautions if you are upgrading from the DiskSuite to the SVM. For example, if you delete a default size DiskSuite replica and add a default size SVM replica, you are overwriting 8192 – 1034 (that is, 7158) blocks of file system data that is sharing the slice with the replica.

The `metadb` command has the following syntax:

```
metadb <action> [<options>] <component>
```

The argument `<component>` is used to specify the component that holds (or will hold) the replica. You can specify one of the following values for `<action>`:

- **`-a`.** Add a database replica. Used with the `-f` option when no database replica exists.
- **`-d`.** Delete all replicas located on the specified slice and update the `/kernel/drv/md.conf` and `/etc/lvm/mddb.cf` files accordingly.
- **`-f`.** Use with `-a` to create the database when no replica exists.
- **`-i`.** Inquire about the status of the replica.

The options specified by the value of `<options>` are described below:

- **`-c <number>`.** Specify the number of replicas to be added to a specified size. The default is 1.

- **`-l <replicaLength>`.** Specify the size in blocks of the replica that is to be created. The default is 8192.

Now that you know how to use the `metadb` command to create or delete state databases, here are some practical scenarios and their solutions.

SCENARIO & SOLUTION	
How would you issue the `metadb` command to create an initial (first) state database replica on a new system c0t1d0s7?	`metadb -a -f c0t1d0s7`
How would you add a replica to the c0t1d0s7 slice that already has the initial state database?	`metadb -a c0t1d0s7`
How would you delete the replica that you added to c0t1d0s7?	`metadb -d c0t1d0s7`

Next, we explore how to mirror and unmirror a file system.

Performing Mirroring and Unmirroring

A mirror is a RAID 1 volume that is composed of stripe (RAID 0) volumes called submirrors. In other words, a mirror is a volume that maintains identical copies of data in RAID 0 volumes—stripe or concatenation. You can create a mirror for an existing file system.

Building a Mirror

You can create a mirror (RAID 1 volume) from a mounted or an umounted file system. If you create a file system that cannot be unmounted, such as a `root (/)`, you will need to reboot the system after the mirror creation. However, a reboot is not necessary if the mirror creation was performed on an unmounted file system. You can create a mirror by performing the following steps:

1. First, identify the slice that contains the existing file system to be mirrored. In this example, we use the slice c0t0d0s0.
2. Create a new RAID 0 volume on the slice from step 1. You can do it by using SMC GUI:

```
metainit -f <volumeName> <numberOfStripes> <componentsPerStripe> <componentName>
```

You must use the `-f` option (which forces the command to continue), when the slice contains a mounted file system. The arguments are explained here:

- **<volumeName>.** Specify the name of the volume that you are creating.
- **<numberOfStripes>.** Specify the number of stripes to create in the volume.
- **<componentsPerStripe>.** Specify the number of components each stripe should have.
- **<componentNames>.** Specify the names of the components that will be used to create the volume, c0t0d0s0 in this example.

3. Create a second RAID 0 volume on an unused slice, say c1t1d0s0, to act as the second submirror.
4. Create a one-way mirror (a mirror that contains only one submirror) by using the SMC GUI, or the following command:

```
metainit <volumeName> -m <subMirrorName>
```

The argument `<volumeName>` specifies the name of the volume that you want to create, the `-m` option means create a mirror, and the `<subMirrorName>` argument specifies the name of the component that will be the first submirror in the mirror. In this example, it is the RAID 0 volume that contains the root slice.

5. If the file system you are mirroring is not the `root (/)` file system, you should edit the `/etc/vfstab` file to make sure that the file system mount instructions refer to the mirror, not to the block device. For example, an entry like the following in the `/etc/vfstab` file would be wrong:

```
/dev/dsk/<slice> /dev/rdsk/<slice> /var ufs 2 yes -
```

Change this entry to read:

```
/dev/md/dsk/<mirrorName> /dev/md/rdsk/<mirrorName> /var ufs 2 yes -
```

6. Remount your newly mirrored file system according to one of the following methods depending on the file system you are mirroring:

- If you are mirroring the `root (/)` file system, execute the `metaroot` command to tell the system to boot from the mirror, and then reboot:

```
metaroot <volumeName>
# reboot
```

- If you are mirroring a file system that is not the `root (/)` and that cannot be unmounted, just reboot your system:

```
reboot
```

If you are mirroring a file system that can be unmounted, you do not need to reboot. Just unmount and remount the file system:

```
umount <fileSystem>
mount <fileSystem>
```

7. Attach the second submirror by issuing the `metattach` command:

```
metattach <volumeName> <submirrorName>
```

`<volumeName>` specifies the name of the RAID 1 volume to which to add the submirror whose name is specified by `<submirrorName>`.

Once you create a one-way mirror with the `metainit` command, you should always attach another submirror with the `metattach` command. This is important because if you do not use the `metattach` command, resynchronization (the process of copying data from one submirror to another) will not happen.

There will be situations in which you would want to unmirror your mirrored file system.

Unmirroring a Mounted File System

Following is the procedure to unmirror file systems that cannot be unmounted during the normal operation, such as `root (/)`, `/usr`, `/opt`, and `swap` file systems:

1. Become superuser.
2. Issue the following command to verify that at least one submirror is in the Okay state:

```
metastat <mirror>
```

3. Issue the following command to detach the submirror that you want to continue using for the file system:

```
metadetach <mirror> <submirror>
```

4. Use one of the following commands depending on the file system you want to unmirror:
   - For the `root (/)` file system, execute the `metaroot` command to tell the system where to boot from:

     ```
     metaroot <rootSlice>
     ```

   - For the `/usr`, `/opt`, or `swap` file systems, change the file system entry in the `/etc/vfstab` file to use a non-SVM device (slice).
5. Reboot the system:

   ```
   reboot
   ```

6. Clear the remaining mirror and submirrors:

   ```
   metaclear -r <mirror>
   ```

This command will recursively delete the metadevices and hot spare pool specified by `<mirror>` but does not delete the one on which others depend.

The three most important takeaways from this chapter are listed here:

- Solaris supports RAID 0, RAID 1, RAID 5, RAID 0 + 1, and RAID 1 + 0 volumes. RAID 0 stripe volumes provide only improved I/O performance, whereas RAID 1 and RAID 5 provide fault tolerance through data redundancy.
- Hot spares provide additional fault tolerance, because a hot spare is a slice that stands ready to replace a failed slice automatically. A hot spare pool can be assigned to multiple volumes, but a given volume can be associated with only one hot spare pool.
- The configuration and status information of disk sets, hot spares, and logical volumes is contained in a database called a state database.

CERTIFICATION SUMMARY

The Redundant Arrays of Inexpensive Disks (RAID) technology takes disk space management from a single disk to multiple disks called a disk set and provides fault tolerance, and, in some cases, performance improvement. RAID 0 provides only performance improvement by enabling the disk controllers to write on stripes simultaneously. RAID 1 provides fault tolerance by duplicating data, and RAID 5 provides fault tolerance by saving the parity information about the data. Additional fault tolerance is provided by a hot spare, which is a slice that stands ready to automatically replace a failed slice.

A logical volume is a collection of physical disk slices that can span across multiple disks. RAID technology can be applied at volume level. The volumes are managed in Solaris by Solaris Volume Manager (SVM), which supports RAID 0, RAID 1, RAID 5, RAID 0 + 1, and RAID 1 + 0 volumes. A RAID 1 volume is also called a mirror, and it is composed of stripe (RAID 0) volumes called submirrors. These submirrors are replicas of each other. You can create a mirror of an existing file system, but you cannot include an existing file system in a RAID 5 volume because the initialization will erase the data. The configuration and status information about the disk sets and about volumes and hot spares in a disk set is contained in a database called a state database. State databases are also managed by SVM.

One of the main benefits provided by the RAID volumes is protection against faults such as a disk crash. However, no data protection method will work if the access to data is not controlled properly. We covered the basic access control in Chapter 7. In the next chapter, we explore advanced methods that provide a more granular approach to access control.

INSIDE THE EXAM

Comprehend

- Because a hot spare must be synchronized with the current data, you cannot use the hot spare technology in systems in which redundant data is not available, such as RAID 0.
- In order to provide fault tolerance, each state database replica should reside on a separate disk. For the majority consensus algorithm to work, you must create at least three replicas for the state database when you configure your disk set.

INSIDE THE EXAM (CONTINUED)

- Because data is written simultaneously on multiple components in a stripe volume, you cannot dynamically change the interlace (data segment size) value. You can dynamically add components to a concatenation volume because data is written on them sequentially.

Look Out

- Striping provides performance improvement but not fault tolerance.
- A soft partition included in a logical volume cannot be directly accessed by an application.
- A component that already contains a file system (that you don't want to lose) must not be included in a RAID 5 volume creation, because doing so will erase the data during initialization.
- You can include an existing file system in a RAID 1 volume.
- If you mirror a file system that cannot be unmounted, you must reboot your system after creating submirrors and before attaching the submirrors. If you can unmount the file system, then just unmount it and remount it after creating the submirrors.

Memorize

- You can assign a hot spare pool to multiple submirror volumes (RAID 1), or multiple RAID 5 volumes, but a given volume can be associated with only one hot spare pool.
- Stripe volume, concatenation volume, and concatenated volume are all RAID 0 volumes.
- SVM supports up to four submirrors in a RAID 1 volume called mirror.
- While building a mirror (RAID 1 volume), you create the submirrors with the `metainit` command, and you must attach the second submirror (and any subsequent submirror) to the mirror by using the `metattach` command, because without the `metattach` command the submirror will not be resynchronized.
- SVM has the capability of supporting a maximum of 8192 logical volumes per disk set. However, its default configuration is for 128 logical volumes per disk set.
- The default interlace value (size of data segments in stripe volumes and RAID 5 volumes) is 16KB.

TWO-MINUTE DRILL

Understanding RAID and SVM Concepts

- ❑ RAID 0 (striping) does not provide fault tolerance, but it can provide performance improvement by performing simultaneous read/write on multiple stripes.
- ❑ RAID 1 and RAID 5 provide fault tolerance by mirroring and parity, respectively.
- ❑ RAID 0 and RAID 1 both require a minimum of two disks, whereas RAID 5 requires a minimum of three disks.
- ❑ A hot spare is a slice of data that stands ready to be substituted for a failed data slice. A hot spare can be assigned to one or more hot spare pools.
- ❑ A hot spare pool is an ordered list of hot spares, and it can serve one or more RAID 1 and RAID 5 volumes.
- ❑ SVM can mange a maximum of 8192 logical volumes per disk set, but the default configuration is 128 logical volumes per disk set.
- ❑ SVM allows you to divide a disk slice (or a volume) into as many divisions as you want, and each division is called a soft partition.
- ❑ A stripe volume contains equally sized data segments across multiple components (slices or soft partitions), and the data is written in parallel on multiple components. Therefore, you cannot change the component size (interlace value) dynamically.
- ❑ A concatenation volume writes data to components sequentially—that is, it fills the first component first before moving to the next component.
- ❑ You can add new components to a stripe volume, and then it is called a concatenated volume.
- ❑ In SVM, the default read and write policies are round-robin read and parallel write.

Creating State Databases and Mirrors

- ❑ You can use either the SVM GUI or the `metadb` command to create, delete, or check the status of a state database.
- ❑ When a state database is lost, the majority consensus algorithm is run to determine which of the remaining replicas contain the valid data. This

imposes the requirement that you must create at least three replicas of the state database.

- The default size for a state database replica in SVM is 8192 blocks (4MB).
- To build a mirror (RAID 1 volume), you can create a submirror with the `metainit` command, and you must attach the second submirror to the mirror with the `metattach` command.

SELF TEST

The following questions will help you measure your understanding of the material presented in this chapter. Read all the choices carefully because there might be more than one correct answer. Choose all correct answers for each question.

1. What is the minimum number of disks required for a RAID 5 system?

   A. Two

   B. Five

   C. Three

   D. One

2. Consider an e-commerce application with mission-critical data. While configuring the volumes you do not need to be concerned about performance, but you cannot afford to lose data. How would you configure your disk set using the SVM?

   A. Stripe

   B. Mirror

   C. RAID

   D. RAID 3

3. Consider an application in which performance (including read/write performance) is most important. In configuring the volumes you do not need to be concerned about possible data loss. How would you configure your disk set using the SVM?

   A. Stripe

   B. Mirror

   C. RAID 5

   D. RAID 3

4. Which of the following provides data redundancy by using parity?

   A. RAID 1

   B. RAID 1 + 0

   C. RAID 5

   D. Hot spare

5. What is the maximum limit on the number of soft partitions you can create on a disk?
   A. Five
   B. One
   C. Eight
   D. No limit
6. When a slice in RAID 1 or RAID 5 volume fails, it is automatically replaced by a spare slice that stands ready to replace any failed slice. A collection of such spare slices is called:
   A. Hot spare pool
   B. Spare buffer
   C. Redundant slices
   D. Disk set
7. Which of the following is the default read policy for a RAID 1 volume?
   A. Parallel
   B. First
   C. Geometric
   D. Round robin
8. What is the maximum limit on the number of logical volumes that SVM can support on a disk set?
   A. Depends on the number of disks in the set
   B. 8192
   C. 8
   D. No limit
9. Which of the following volumes write data on components simultaneously?
   A. Stripe volume
   B. Concatenation volume
   C. Logical volume
   D. Serial volume

10. Which of the following commands would you use to add a second submirror (after creating it) to the mirror (RAID 1 volume)?

    A. `addmirror`

    B. `metainit`

    C. `metattach`

    D. `attachmirror`

11. What is the maximum number of submirrors that SVM can support in a RAID 1 volume?

    A. Four

    B. Two

    C. One

    D. No limit

SELF TEST ANSWERS

1. ☑ **C**. RAID 5 implements distributed (striped) parity with striping. You need a minimum of two disks for striping. Because the parity information cannot stay on the same disk where the corresponding data is; therefore, for the parity to be striped you need three disks at minimum.
   ☒ **A** is incorrect because the minimum number of disks you need for RAID 5 is three, not five. **B** is incorrect because two disks are enough just for striping the data or the parity, but not both. **D** is incorrect because with just one disk you cannot implement any RAID level.

2. ☑ **B** and **C**. Both Mirror and RAID 5 volumes support fault tolerance by providing data redundancy.
   ☒ **A** is incorrect because striping does not provide data redundancy, and **D** is incorrect because RAID 3 is not supported by SVM.

3. ☑ **A**. Striping helps improve performance because it enables multiple controllers to read/write data in parallel.
   ☒ **B** is incorrect because data must be written to more than one component, and **C** is incorrect because it takes time to calculate parity information. **D** is incorrect because RAID 3 is not supported by SVM.

4. ☑ **C**. RAID 5 provides data redundancy by calculating and storing the parity information about the data. When the data is lost, it is reconstructed from the parity information.
   ☒ **A** and **B** are incorrect because RAID 1 and RAID 1 + 0 provide data redundancy by mirroring and not by parity. **D** is incorrect because a hot spare is a slice that automatically replaces a failed slice, and it is useful only when data redundancy is already present.

5. ☑ **D**. You can create as many soft partitions as you like; disk space is the only limit.
   ☒ **A** and **B** are incorrect because there is no such limit as one or five. **C** is incorrect because the limit of eight partitions applies to a Solaris disk in a standard partition environment, not to soft partitions.

6. ☑ **A**. A slice that stands ready to replace a failed slice is called a hot spare, and a collection of such slices is called a hot spare pool.
   ☒ **B** and **C** are incorrect because there are no such terms as spare buffer or redundant slices in SVM. **D** is incorrect because a disk set is a group of disks that holds logical volumes and is not just a collection of hot spares.

7. ☑ **D**. Round robin is the default read policy for a RAID 1 volume. Reads are spread across all submirrors in a round-robin order to balance the read load.
☒ **A** is incorrect because parallel is a write policy and not a read policy. **B** and **C** are incorrect because First and Geometric are valid ready policies but neither of them is default.

8. ☑ **B**. SVM can support up to 8192 logical volumes per disk set.
☒ **A** is incorrect because the number of disks in the set may limit how many volumes you will practically be able to create, but it does not determine the maximum number allowed by SVM. **C** is incorrect because 8 is the maximum limit on the number of partitions you can create on a standard Solaris disk, not the limit on the number of logical volumes. **D** is incorrect because there is a limit on the number of logical volumes SVM can support, and that limit is 8192.

9. ☑ **A**. RAID 0 stripe volume writes data on components simultaneously and thereby provides performance improvement.
☒ **B** is incorrect because a RAID 0 concatenation volume writes data sequentially. **C** is incorrect because not all logical volumes write data across components simultaneously. **D** is incorrect because there is no such volume as serial volume.

10. ☑ **C**. Once a one-way mirror is in place, all the subsequent submirrors should be attached to the mirror by using the `metattach` command.
☒ **A** is incorrect because the `metainit` command is used to create a submirror, not to attach it. **B** and **D** are incorrect because there are no such commands as `addmirror` and `attachmirror`.

11. ☑ **A**. SVM supports up to four submirrors in a RAID 1 volume.
☒ **B** is incorrect because two is the minimum number (not the maximum number) of submirrors a RAID 1 volume must have. **C** is incorrect because just one submirror will not make a RAID 1 volume. **D** is incorrect because there is a limit on the maximum number of submirrors SVM can support, and that limit is four.

14

Managing Access Control and System Messaging

CERTIFICATION OBJECTIVES

14.01	Understanding Role-Based Access Control	✓	Two-Minute Drill
14.02	Managing RBAC	Q&A	Self Test
14.03	Managing System Messaging		

The conventional UNIX security model that we discussed in Chapter 7 is called the superuser security model, because there is only one almighty administrator with the root account, also referred to as superuser. The superuser has all the rights on the system, such as to modify the site's firewall, to read and modify confidential data, and to shut down the whole network. A program with the root privilege (or setuid program) can read and write to any file and send kill signals to any process running on the system. That means a hacker who hijacks the root account or a setuid program can do anything to the system—a frightening scenario indeed.

As a solution to this problem, Solaris offers a role-based access control (RBAC) security model for controlling user access to tasks normally restricted to the superuser. The RBAC model offers a more secure and flexible alternative to the superuser model by allowing the security rights to be assigned to what is called a *role*, and then assigning the role to a user. This way, you can distribute the administrative rights over a whole spectrum of roles, rather than centralizing all the power in one user (the superuser). One of the important (security-related) tasks for a system administrator is to "listen" to the system and take appropriate actions. The system communicates with the system administrator by using system message logging (syslog), which automatically saves (logs) various system errors and warnings in the message files.

The core issue in this chapter to think about is how to use the RBAC security model and the syslog. In search of an answer, we will explore three thought streams: understanding the fundamentals of RBAC and syslog, managing RBAC, and managing syslog.

CERTIFICATION OBJECTIVE 14.01

Understanding Role-Based Access Control

Exam Objective 4.1: *Configure role-based access control (RBAC) including assigning rights profiles, roles, and authorizations to users.*

Role-based access control (RBAC) is a security model that you, the superuser, can use for letting non-root users have access to tasks that would normally be restricted to superuser, the root account. You can use RBAC to apply security rights to processes and to users, and thereby distribute the security-related capabilities among several users, called administrators. This is accomplished through the following RBAC features: roles, rights profiles, and authorizations.

Understanding Roles

A role is a special type of account that can be associated with one or more users, and those users can subsequently assume that role; once they do, they assume all the rights assigned to the role. You create roles the same way you create normal user accounts, and just like a normal user account, a role has a home directory, a password, a group, and so on. The main characteristics of roles are described here:

- A user cannot initially log in as a role. Once logged into a normal user account, the user can assume a role by using the `su` (switch user) command (of course a role name and a password are required), or by using the SMC GUI.
- When a user assumes a role, all the user attributes are replaced with role attributes.
- Two or more users can assume the same role, and when they do, they have the same directory, access to the same files, the same operating environment, and so on.
- A user cannot assume more than one role at the same time. A user who has assumed a role must exit that role to be able to assume another role.
- The information about a role is stored in the `passwd`, `shadow`, and `user_attr` databases.
- Roles cannot inherit rights from other roles or users.

You can use roles to prevent a root login to your system from a remote machine. Just metamorphose the incoming root user into a role.

Note that assigning the role to a user and the user's assuming that role are two different things. Before a user can assume a role, the role must be assigned by the primary administrator (superuser) to that user.

The administrative capabilities are given to the roles by rights profiles and authorizations.

Understanding Rights Profiles

A *rights profile* is a collection of rights such as authorization, commands with assigned security attributes, and other rights profiles that can be assigned to a role. The rights profiles information is stored in the `prof_attr` and `exec_attr` databases.

Some typical rights profiles (and roles based on these rights profiles) are described here:

- *Primary administrator*. This rights profile consists of all the rights of a superuser.
- *System administrator*. This profile contains most of the rights except for security-related rights. It provides the ability to perform most non-security administrative tasks, such as printer management, cron management, device management, file system management, mail management, backup and restore, name service management, network management, software installation, and process and user management. However, it includes several other profiles, which makes it a powerful profile.
- *Operator*. This profile contains limited rights to manage files and offline media. It provides the ability to perform backups and printer maintenance. By default, it does not include the rights to restore files.
- *Printer management*. This profile consists of a limited number of authorizations and commands to handle printing.
- *Basic Solaris user*. This profile enables users to use the Solaris system within the security boundaries set up on the system. This profile is assigned, by default, to all the Solaris users.
- *All*. This profile consists of commands that do not have security attributes.

Note that these are typically used roles, and you can create profiles and roles based on those profiles according to the security needs of your organization. Although no roles are shipped with Solaris, there are three roles that can be easily configured: primary administrator, system administrator, and operator.

Roles are powered by profiles, and profiles are powered by authorizations.

Understanding Authorizations

An authorization is a discrete permission that enables a user (or a role) to perform a class of actions that could affect security. For example, the security policy gives ordinary users the `solaris.device.cdrw` authorization at installation, which enables users to read and write to a CD-ROM device. The authorizations are listed in the `/etc/security/auth_attr` file.

Although an authorization can be directly assigned to a role or a user, in the RBAC model, it is typically assigned to a profile from which it flows to a role and subsequently to the user who assumes that role. Profiles can also include commands with security attributes and other profiles.

Figure 14-1 puts all the pieces together to give you an overall picture of RBAC.

A role is assigned to a user, and a user can assume only one role at a time; when a user does so, that user automatically acquires the capabilities of the role. Roles, in turn, get their capabilities from the rights profiles, which consist of authorizations, privileged commands, and other rights profiles. A privileged command is a command that executes with special permissions. A privilege is a discrete right that a process requires to perform an operation. You can also assign privileges to a user, a role, or a system. A process executing with privileges executes within the bounds of the system's security policy and eliminates the need for a call to `setuid`, which runs outside the bounds of the system security. Recall that `setuid` and `setgid`, which we discussed in Chapter 7, are security attributes that you can assign to a process to perform an operation that is otherwise forbidden to ordinary users.

The superuser model and the RBAC model can coexist on the same system. For example, you can log in as an ordinary user or as root and then assume a role. A comparison of the two models is presented in Table 14-1.

FIGURE 14-1

Relationship between different elements of RBAC

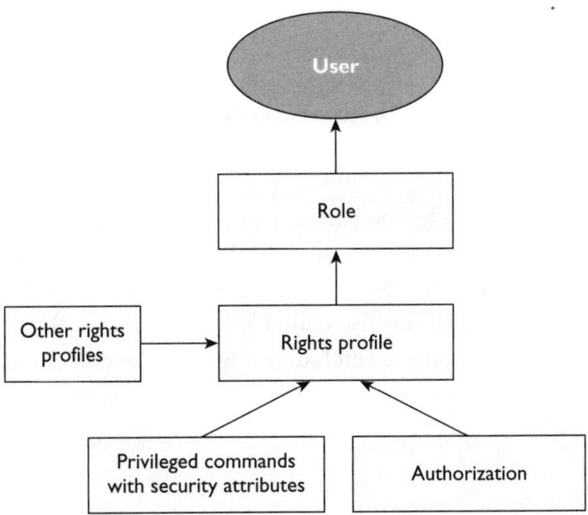

TABLE 14-1 Comparison of superuser and RBACK models (RBAC provides more options and flexibility)

User Capability on a System	Superuser Model	RBAC Model
Can become superuser with all superuser capabilities	Yes	Yes
Can log in as user with full user capabilities	Yes	Yes
Can log in as a user and acquire superuser capabilities	Yes, with setuid.	Yes, with setuid and using RBAC as well.
Once logged in as a user, can acquire limited superuser capabilities	No	Yes
Can log in as a user and acquire administrative capabilities but not full superuser capability	No	Yes
Can log in as a user and have fewer capabilities than an ordinary user	No	Yes

Now that you understand the different components of RBAC, it's time to explore how it is used.

CERTIFICATION OBJECTIVE 14.02

Managing RBAC

Exam Objective 4.2: *Analyze RBAC configuration file summaries and manage RBAC using the command line.*

In the previous section, you learned about how, conceptually, the authorizations are assigned to profiles, profiles to roles, and roles to users. All this information must reside somewhere and needs to be managed. This information resides in the configuration files, which are also called *RBAC databases*. We will be calling them databases and files interchangeably. You can edit these files, but it is recommended that you change the information in them through the commands whenever possible to avoid accidentally creating inconsistencies and inaccuracies.

Understanding the RBAC Configuration Files

The rights, rights profiles, roles, and users in RBAC are supported by the following four databases:

- **`auth_attr`.** Authorization attributes database. Defines authorizations and their attributes.
- **`exec_attr`.** Execution attributes database. Identifies the commands with security attributes that are assigned to specific rights profiles.
- **`prof_attr`.** Rights profile attributes database. Defines rights profiles and lists the assigned authorizations for the profiles.
- **`user_attr`.** Extended user attributes database. Associates users with roles and roles with authorizations and rights, typically through profiles.

These four databases also contain the relationships between rights, rights profiles, roles, and users. The `policy.conf` database contains authorizations, privileges, and rights profiles that are applied to all users.

The Authorization Attributes Database

An authorization is a discrete permission that enables a user (or a role) to perform a class of actions that could affect security. It can be directly assigned to a user or a role, but in RBAC it is typically assigned to a profile. The authorizations are stored in the `/etc/security/auth_attr` database. The fields in each entry of this database are delimited by a colon. An entry in this database has the following syntax:

```
<authname>:<res1>:<res2>:<short_desc>:<long_desc>:<attr>
```

The fields in this entry are described in Table 14-2.

When the `<authname>` field consists of a prefix and functional area (suffix) and ends with a period, it is not an actual authorization. For example, consider the following entry:

```
solaris.printmgr.:::Printer Manager::help=PrinterManager.html
```

It serves merely as a heading that, for example, can be used by an application in the GUI.

On the other hand, when `<authname>` ends with the word `grant`, it enables the user (that has this authorization) to delegate to other users authorizations with

TABLE 14-2 Fields in an entry of the `/etc/security/auth_attr` database

Field	Description
`authname`	A dot-delimited character string that uniquely identifies the authorization. The authorization for the Solaris OS starts with Solaris.[<suffix>], whereas any other authorization starts with the reverse domain name of the company that created the authorization, such as the com.novell.[<suffix>]. The <suffix> specifies what's being authorized, which is typically the functional area and operation such as printmgr. For example: solaris.printmgr.admin.
`res1` `res2`	Reserved for future use.
`short_desc`	A short name for the authorization that could be presented to the user, for example, in a GUI.
`long_desc`	Information about the authorization such as the purpose of the authorization, the types of users to whom the authorization may be assigned, and the applications in which the authorization can be used.
`attr`	A semicolon-delimited list of key-value pairs, which describe the optional attributes of the authorization. The keyword help, if it exists, identifies the help file in html format.

the same prefix and functional area. For example, consider the following value for the `<authname>` field:

```
solaris.printmgr.grant:::Grant Printer Manager Rights::help=PrintMgrGrant.html
```

This is a grant authorization. Any user who has this authorization is granted the right to delegate to other users such authorizations as:

```
solaris.printmgr.admin
solaris.printmgr.nobanner
```

Therefore, the user who has the "grant" authorization can replace the "grant" with any right for other users. To assign a grant authorization to a user is like signing a blank check. Here are some additional examples of the entries in the `auth_attr` database:

```
solaris.admin.printer.:::Printer Information::help=AuthPrinterHeader.html
solaris.admin.printer.delete:::Delete Printer::help=AuthPrinterDelete.html
solaris.admin.printer.read:::View Printer Information::help=AuthPrinterRead.html
```

The first entry is just a heading, not a real authorization, whereas the second and third entries are authorizations for deleting the printer and reading the printer information, respectively.

The authorizations can be assigned to a profile. You can also assign command with security attributes to a profile, and this is done in the execution attributes database.

The Execution Attributes Database

In addition to authorizations, a profile can contain commands that require security attributes in order to be executed successfully. You can assign these commands to a profile in the execution attributes database: /etc/security/exec_attr. The fields in each entry of this database are delimited by a colon. An entry in this database has the following syntax:

```
<profileName>:<policy>:<type>:<res1>:<res2>:<id>:<attr>
```

The fields in this entry are described in Table 14-3.

While defining the attr field in an entry of the exec_attr database, zero or more keys can be specified. The keys that can be used depend on the enforced policy: solaris or suser. For the solaris policy, the valid key is privs (for privileges), and the value is a comma-delimited list of privileges.

TABLE 14-3 Fields in an entry of the /etc/security/exec_attr database

Field	Description
profileName	The case-sensitive name of a rights profile that exists in the prof_attr database.
policy	Security policy associated with this entry. Currently, there are only two valid values: solaris means recognize privileges, and suser means do not.
type	The type of entity that is specified. Currently it has only one valid value: cmd means command.
res1 res2	Reserved for future use.
id	A string to uniquely identify the entity—for example, a full path for a command.
attr	A semicolon-delimited list of key-value pairs to describe optional security attributes applied to the entity, such as command. The keys that can be used depend on the security policy: solaris or suser.

For the `suser` policy, there are four valid keys, which are listed here:

- **`euid.`** The value may be a single user name or a numeric user ID (UID). The command runs with the supplied (real) UID, similar to setting the setuid bit on an executable.
- **`uid.`** The value may be a single user name or a user ID. The command runs with both the real UID and effective UID.
- **`egid.`** The value can be a single group name or a numeric group ID (GID). The command runs with the supplied GID, which is similar to setting setgid bit on an executable file.
- **`gid.`** The value can be a single group name or a numeric group ID (GID). The command runs with both the real GID and the effective GID.

We discussed effective UID and GID in Chapters 6 and 7.

As an example, following are a couple of entries from the `exec_attr` database:

```
File System Management:suser:cmd:::/usr/sbin/ff:euid=0
File System Management:solaris:cmd:::/usr/sbin/mount:privs=sys_mount
```

Note that the rights profile information is split between the `prof_exec` and `exec_attr` databases: the right profiles name and authorization are in the `prof_attr` database, while the rights profile name and the commands with the assigned security attributes are in the `exec_attr` database.

So, you can define the commands and the security attributes in the `exec_attr` database, and authorizations in the `auth_attr` database. The profile name in an entry of the `exec_attr` database must be defined in the profile attribute database. Furthermore, the authorizations defined in the `auth_attr` database can be assigned to a profile in the profile attribute database. Now, let's take a look at the profile attribution database.

The Profile Attributes Database

The profiles are defined in the `prof_attr` database. An entry in this database stores the profile name and assigns the authorizations to the profile; it has the following syntax:

```
<profileName>:<res1>:<res2>:<desc>:<attr>
```

The fields in the entry are described here:

- **profileName.** The case-sensitive name of the rights profile.
- **res1:res2.** Reserved for future use.
- **desc.** Information about the profile, such as the purpose of the profile and the types of users to whom the profile may be assigned.
- **attr.** A semicolon-delimited list of key-value pairs to describe optional security attributes that will be applied to the object to be executed. The two valid keys are described here:
  - **auth.** The value of this key is a comma-delimited list of authorization names, which must be defined in the `auth_attr` database. The authorization names can include a wild card (*) to indicate all authorizations. For example, solaris.admin.* means all solaris admin authorizations.
  - **help.** The value of this key specifies the help file in html format.

Remember that every rights profile defined on the system is listed by name in the `prof_attr` file, which also includes the authorizations and the supplementary rights profiles for each profile listed in it. Following is an example of an entry in the `prof_attr` file:

```
Operator::: Can perform some simple administrative tasks:profiles=Printer
Management, Media Backup,All; help=Operator.html
```

You can use the following command to display the profiles assigned to a user along with the security attributes:

```
profiles -l [<username>]
```

The Operator profile contains three other profiles: Printer Management, Media Backup, and All. The profiles defined in the `prof_attr` database can be assigned to roles in the user attribute database, which we explore next.

The User Attributes Database

The roles are assumed by the users, and the assignments of roles to the users are contained in the `user_attr` database, along with the assignment of profiles to the roles. The fields in each entry of this database are delimited by a colon. An entry in this database has the following syntax:

```
<user>:<qualifier>:<res1>:<res2>:<attr>
```

The fields in this entry are described here:

- **`user.`** The name of the user (or role) as specified in the `passwd` database. Remember that the roles are also accounts that are created just like users.
- **`qualifier:resel:res2.`** Reserved for future use.
- **`attr.`** A semicolon-delimited list of key-value pairs to describe optional security attributes that will be applied when the user runs commands. The four valid keys are described here:
  - **`type.`** Has two possible values: `normal` for an ordinary user, and `role` if this account represents a role.
  - **`roles.`** This key is used to assign roles to a normal user (you cannot assign a role to another role); that means the value for type must be normal for roles to have a valid value. The value for roles is a comma-delimited list of role names. The roles in this list must be defined in the same `user_attr` database, and those defining entries will of course have type = role.
  - **`profiles.`** The value of this key is a comma-delimited list of profile names defined in the `prof_attr` database.
  - **`auth.`** The value of this key is a comma-delimited list of authorization names defined in the `auth_attr` database. The authorization names can include a wild card (*) to indicate all authorizations. For example, solaris.admin.* means all solaris admin authorizations.

As an example, the following two entries in the `user_attr` database assign the Operator profile to the operator role, and assign the operator role to the normal user jedward.

```
jedward::::type=normal;roles=operator
operator::::profiles=Operator;type=role
```

Remember that in this case, the profile Operator must be defined in the `prof_attr database.bb.`

It is important to realize that all these files are connected to each other. The connection is shown through an example in Figure 14-2. In this example, a user jkerry defined in the `/etc/passwd` file is assigned a role filemgr in the `/etc/user_passwd` file. Also in the same file, `/etc/security/user_attr`, the role filemgr is assigned a profile File System Management, and this profile is defined in the `/etc/security/prof_attr` file, which lists the authorizations such as solaris.

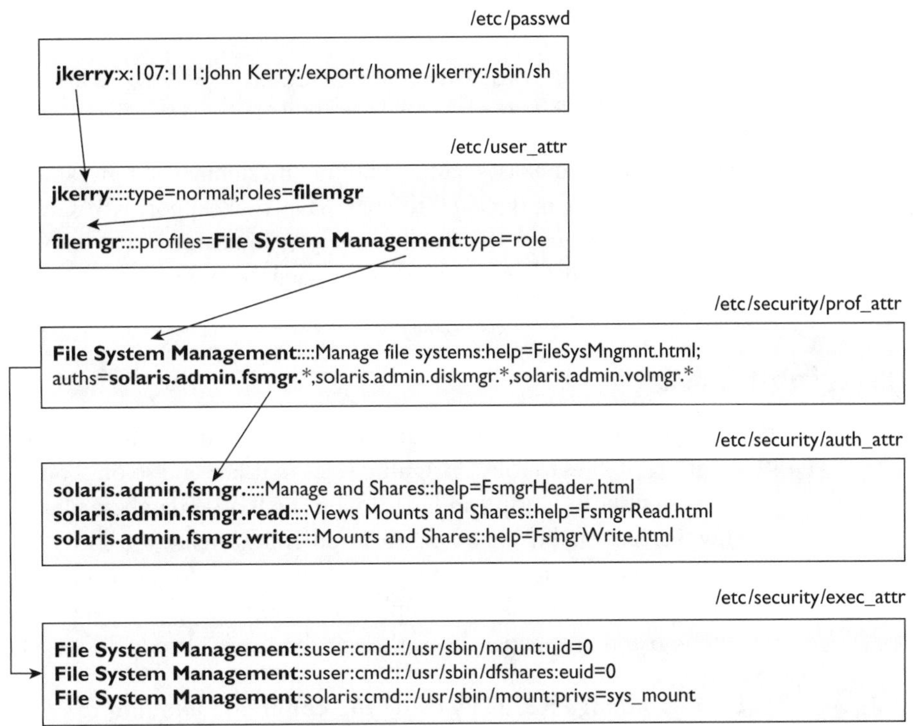
/etc/passwd
jkerry:x:107:111:John Kerry:/export/home/jkerry:/sbin/sh
/etc/user_attr
jkerry::::type=normal;roles=filemgr
filemgr::::profiles=File System Management:type=role
/etc/security/prof_attr
File System Management::::Manage file systems:help=FileSysMngmnt.html;
auths=solaris.admin.fsmgr.*,solaris.admin.diskmgr.*,solaris.admin.volmgr.*
/etc/security/auth_attr
solaris.admin.fsmgr.::::Manage and Shares::help=FsmgrHeader.html
solaris.admin.fsmgr.read::::Views Mounts and Shares::help=FsmgrRead.html
solaris.admin.fsmgr.write::::Mounts and Shares::help=FsmgrWrite.html
/etc/security/exec_attr
File System Management:suser:cmd:::/usr/sbin/mount:uid=0
File System Management:suser:cmd:::/usr/sbin/dfshares:euid=0
File System Management:solaris:cmd:::/usr/sbin/mount:privs=sys_mount

FIGURE 14-2 An example showing the relationships between different RBAC databases

edmin.fsmgr.*, which are subsequently defined in the `/etc/security/auth_attr` file. Furthermore, some commands are assigned to the profile File System Management in the `/etc/security/exec_attr` file.

In addition to these specific rights assigned to specific users through roles and profiles, there may be some rights that you want to assign to all users by default. This is accomplished through a policy configuration file.

The Policy Configuration File

You can use the `/etc/security/policy.conf` file to grant default rights profiles, authorizations, and privileges to all users. The relevant entries in the file are in the form of key-value pairs such as the following:

- **`AUTHS_GRANTED=<authorization>`.** The `<authorization>` specifies a comma-delimited list of authorizations.
- **`PROFS_GRANTED=<rightsProfiles>`.** The `<rightProfiles>` specify the comma-delimited list of rights profiles.

The corresponding entries in the policy.conf database looks like the following:

```
AUTHS_GRANTED=solaris.device.cdrw
PROFS_GRANTED=Basic Solaris User
```

All the RBAC databases discussed so far are summarized in Table 14-4.

Now, that you understand the databases that support RBAC you need to know how to manage RBAC. In principle, you can edit the database files and change them, but that is not recommended, because it can give rise to accidental inconsistencies and inaccuracies.

Managing RBAC

Managing RBAC includes adding, modifying, and deleting roles; creating profiles; assigning profiles to roles; assigning roles to users; and so on. You can accomplish all these tasks by editing and modifying the RBAC database files discussed in the previous section, but that is not recommend. Instead, you should use the SMC GUI or RBAC commands. Commonly used commands for managing RBAC are listed in Table 14-5. For the sake of completeness, we have also listed the useradd, userdel, and usermod commands, even though they were already discussed in Chapter 6.

on the job

Do not manage RBAC by using the command line and the SMC GUI simultaneously; if you do, you may end up making conflicting changes, and the results will be unpredictable.

TABLE 14-4 Files for RBAC databases

RBAC Database	File	Information
Authorization attributes	/etc/security/auth_attr	Defines authorizations.
Execution attributes	/etc/security/exec_attr	Defines the execution attributes for profiles. Assigns commands with security attributes to profiles.
Rights profiles attributes	/etc/security/prof_attr	Defines rights profiles.
User attributes	/etc/user_attr	Defines extended user attributes. Assigns roles to users and profiles to roles.
Policy configuration	/etc/security/policy.conf	Defines policy for the system, such as default rights profiles, authorization, and privileges for all users.

TABLE 14-5 Commands for RBAC management

RBAC Command	Description
`auths`	Displays authorizations for a specified user.
`profiles`	Displays rights profiles for a specified user.
`roleadd`	Adds a role to a local system. Uses (modifies) files: `/etc/passwd`, `/etc/shadow`, `/etc/user_attr`.
`roledel`	Deletes a role from a local system. Uses (modifies) files: `/etc/passwd`, `/etc/shadow`, `/etc/user_attr`.
`roles`	Displays roles that the specified user can assume.
`useradd`	Creates a user account on the system. You can assign an existing role to the user being created, with the `-R` option.
`userdel`	Deletes a specified user's login from the system.
`usermod`	Modifies a specified user account's properties.

You can create a role by using the `roleadd` command, which has the following syntax:

```
roleadd [-c <comment>] [-b <base_dir>] [-d <dir>] [-e <expire>]
[-f <inactive>] [-g <group>] [-G <group, group...>] [-m [-k <skel_dir>]]
[-p <profile>] [-A <authorization, authorization...>] [-s <shell>] [-u <uid>]
<roleName>
```

If you compare this command with the `useradd` command in Chapter 6, you will notice that the options are exactly the same except that there is a `-R` option in the `useradd` command that is missing in the `roleadd` command. Of course the `-R` option would not make sense in the `roleadd` command because we cannot assign a role to a role. All other options work the same way in both the commands `useradd` and `roleadd`.

The `rolemod` command has the same options as the `roleadd` command, and works the same way as `usermod`. The same is true with the `roledel` command, which works like the `userdel` command:

```
roledel [-r] <roleName>
```

If you use the `-r` option, the home directory for the role will be deleted, and the directory subtree under the home directory will not be accessible.

EXERCISE 14-1

How to Create a Profile and a Role and Assign a Role to an Existing User

In this exercise, we have used minimum options in the `useradd` and `roleadd` commands to emphasize the required options. You can add other options, such as the one for creating a home directory. To create a role and assign it to an existing user, perform the following steps:

1. Log on to the machine as root or assume the primary administrator role.
2. Edit the `/etc/security/prof_attr` file and add the following line to it:

```
PrintOpr:::Can perform printer related tasks:profiles=Printer Management, All
```

   Save the file and exit.

3. Create a role with name printRole and assign it the PrintOpr profile (remember, the profile name is case sensitive) by issuing the following command:

   ```
   roleadd -P PrintOpr printRole
   ```

4. Set the password for this role by using the `passwd` command:

   ```
   passwd printRole
   ```

5. Create a user with name testuser and assign it the role printRole:

   ```
   useradd -R printRole -d <dirName> testuser
   ```

   where `<dirName>` specifies the full path to the home directory that will be assigned to the user being created.

6. Set the password for testuser by issuing the `passwd` command:

   ```
   passwd testuser
   ```

7. Test that the role has been created and assigned to the user:
   - Log out, and log in as testuser.
   - Issue the `roles` command to see whether the testuser has the role assigned to it:

     ```
     roles
     ```

- Assume the role:

```
su printRole
```

- Display the profiles that are assigned to this role:

```
profiles
```

Even if you do a perfect job in controlling access to the system and the resources, things can still go wrong. The applications running on the system or the system processes will generate messages to report errors. The first step in correcting the errors is to learn about them. Solaris offers a UNIX native error-logging system, syslog, that you can use to learn about the errors.

CERTIFICATION OBJECTIVE 14.03

Managing System Messaging

Exam Objective 4.3: *Explain syslog function fundamentals, and configure and manage the /etc/syslog.conf file and syslog messaging.*

Applications (and processes) running on an operating system do malfunction from time to time, and generate errors. An application error may cause an operating system error, or the system may produce its own errors due to its own problems. The capability of capturing error-generating events and storing them (a process called logging) so that a system administrator can view and analyze them to take corrective action is an important requirement of any operating system.

Solaris uses the UNIX-native logging facility called syslog to handle system messaging. The system messaging function is run by the error-logging daemon, `syslogd`, which receives a message from a source (e.g., an application), adds some information to it such as a time stamp, and saves it in an appropriate message file. By default, the daemon displays these messages on the system console and stores them in the `/var/adm/messages.*` files. Of course, you can make changes to the default behavior by customizing the system message logging.

Fundamentals of System Message Logging

The `syslogd` daemon receives a message from the source and forwards it to a target such as the message log file. A system message consists of a single line of text, which in most cases includes the following information:

```
[ID <msgid> <facility>.<priority>]
```

For example:

```
[ID 746763 kern.notice]
```

This is the message that was originated in the kernel, and the kernel module name is displayed. The daemon may add a time stamp to the message. So the full displayed message may look like the following:

```
Sep 29 21:41:18 agore ufs: [ID 746763 kern.notice] alloc /: file system full
```

The two most important points about how system message logging works are:

- The `syslogd` daemon receives messages from the applications (processes) and sends them to the specified target: the system console or a file.
- The syslog allows you to capture messages by their source (e.g., type of process) and the level of priority (severity). Priorities are defined in the `/sys/syslog.h` file.

How are these two features implemented? In other words, how does the daemon know where to send the message, and how can you capture the messages based on source and priority level? This is accomplished through the configuration file:

```
/etc/syslog.conf
```

The `/etc/syslog.conf` file has two columns, which are described here:

- **`<facility>.<level>`.** The `<facility>` specifies the source of message (or error condition); it may be a list of comma-delimited names of sources. The `<level>` specifies the severity (or priority) of the condition being logged.
- **`<action>`.** This column specifies the comma-delimited list of targets (destinations) of the messages—that is, where the messages are being sent (e.g., the name of a file).

Examples of entries from the default /etc/syslog.conf file are shown here:

```
user.err /dev/sysmsg
user.err /var/adm/messages
user.alert 'root, operator'
user.emerg *
```

In all these entries, the facility source is the user that refers to the user processes. The first entry means that the message from the user processes with priority level should automatically be printed to the system console, while second entry means that these messages should also be logged to the /var/adm/messages file. The third entry means that the user messages with the alert priority level should be sent to the root and the operator, while the fourth entry means that the user messages with the emerg level (emergency messages) should be sent to the individual users.

The commonly used facility sources and priority levels are described in Tables 14-6 and 14-7, respectively.

You can activate a source facility in the /etc/syslog.conf file. There is no limit on how many facilities you can activate.

Now that you know how syslog works, you need to know how to manage it.

Managing Syslog

To manage syslog, you need to know how to handle the syslog.conf file and the syslog daemon. We have already covered the syslog.conf file in the previous sections. The syslog daemon, syslogd, is started during bootup, and the command has the following syntax:

```
/usr/sbin/syslogd [-d] [-f <configFile>] [-m <markInterval>] [-p <path>] [-t | -T]
```

TABLE 14-6 The most common error condition sources, called source facilities

Source Facility	Description
auth	Message comes from somewhere in the authorization system such as login and su.
daemon	Message source is a daemon such as httpd.
kern	Message generated by the OS Kernel.
lp	Message comes from the line printing spooling system.
mail	Message generated by the mail system.
user	Message generated by a user process.

TABLE 14-7 The most common priority levels for syslog messages

Priority Level	Description
emerg	System emergency. A panic condition.
alert	An error requiring immediate action to correct the situation.
crit	Critical error.
debug	The output used for debugging.
err	Other errors.
warning	Warning messages.
info	An informational message.
notice	Conditions that are not errors but may require special handling.
none	Specifies the do not log message for this system.

exam Watch ***Make sure you recognize the facility (source), the priority level, and the message target (where the message will go) in an entry of the `syslog.conf` file. You should be able to interpret the entries in this file.***

The options are described here:

- **`-d.`** Turn on debugging.
- **`-f <configFile>.`** Specify a configuration file. The default is `/etc/syslog.conf`.
- **`-m <markInterval>.`** Specify an interval in minutes between mark messages—that is, messages with a system time stamp. The default value is 20.
- **`-P <path>.`** Specify a log device name. The default is /dev/log.
- **`-T.`** Turn on logging of remote messages by enabling the UDP port of `syslogd`. This is the default behavior.
- **`-t.`** Turn off logging of remote messages by disabling the UDP port of `syslogd`.

The default settings reside in the `/etc/default/syslogd` file.

on the Job ***The `-d` option for the `syslogd` daemon to turn on debugging should only be used interactively in a root shell once the system is in multiuser mode. You should not use it in the system start-up scripts, because this will cause the system to hang when `syslogd` is started.***

Note that the `syslogd` service is managed by the Service Management Facility (SMF) under the service identifier:

```
svc:/system/system-log:default
```

That means you can perform administrative actions on this service, such as enabling, disabling, or restarting by issuing the following `svcadm` commands:

```
svcadm enable svc:/system/system-log:default
svcadm disable svc:/system/system-log:default
svcadm restart svc:/system/system-log:default
```

You can query the status of the service by issuing the `svcs` command:

```
svcs -l svc:/system/system-log:default
```

Now that you know how syslog works, here are some practical scenarios and their solutions.

SCENARIO & SOLUTION	

What command would you issue to generate messages recently generated by a reboot or a system crash?	`dmesg | more`
	or
	`more /var/adm/messages`

Consider the following line in the `syslog.conf` file: `*.alert root` What does it say about who will get the system alert messages?	The superuser (root) will get all the system alert messages.
You want all the user emergency messages and user alert messages to be sent to individual users as well as the root. What entry in the `syslog.conf` file will ensure that?	`user.emerg, user.alert 'root, *'`

The three most important takeaways from this chapter are the following:

- The role-based access control (RBAC) security model offers a more secure and flexible security system by allowing the superuser to create multiple administrators with different administrative capabilities.

- You can create, modify, and delete roles by using the `roleadd`, `rolemod`, and `roledel` commands, respectively, which work pretty much like the `useradd`, `usermod`, and `userdel` commands with the same options.
- The `syslogd` daemon is responsible for logging the messages into the message files. You can manage syslog either by using the `syslogd` command or by using the SMF command `svcadm` on the service identifier `svc:/system/system-log:default`.

CERTIFICATION SUMMARY

The role-based access control (RBAC) security model offers a more secure and flexible security system by allowing the superuser to create multiple administrators with different capabilities. This model is based on roles that can be assigned to non-root users. The roles get their power from profiles, which are collections of security rights such as authorizations and commands with security attributes. A user, once logged into the system, can assume the role that has already been assigned to that user. A user can assume only one role at a time; to assume another role, the user must exit from the current role.

The RBAC information resides in multiple files called databases. The `/etc/security/auth_attr` database defines the authorizations, whereas the `/etc/security/exec_attr` assigns the commands with security attributes to specific profiles. The `/etc/security/prof_attr` database defines the rights profiles and identifies the authorizations for the profiles, whereas the `/etc/user_attr` database assigns profiles to the roles and roles to the users. These users and roles are defined in the `/etc/passwd` and `/etc/shadow` files. The RBAC can be managed with a number of commands such as `roleadd`, `rolemod`, and `roledel`, which are used to create, modify, and delete roles; they work the same way as the `useradd`, `usermod`, and `userdel` commands.

Applications and processes create error messages when something goes wrong, and those messages are directed to message files or the system console by the `syslog` daemon, `syslogd`. The configuration file for this daemon is `syslog.conf`. You can manage syslog either through the `syslogd` command or through the SMF command `svcadm` by using the SMF service identifier for `syslog: svc:/system/system-log:default`.

In this chapter, we have explored how to control access to the system by using roles and how to monitor errors reported by the applications and the processes running on the system. One source of errors is the effect of one process on another running on the same machine. Solaris 10 offers a technology called zone partitioning, which allows you to create multiple zones on the same system. The processes running in one zone are isolated and secure from the processes running in other zones. We explore how to install and configure zones in the next chapter.

INSIDE THE EXAM

Comprehend

- Security rights (authorizations and commands with security attributes) are typically assigned to a profile, a profile to a role, and a role to a user. More than one profile can be assigned to a role.
- You can use the `/etc/security/policy.conf` file to grant default rights profiles, authorizations, and privileges to all users.
- The syslog is managed by the Service Management Facility (SMF); therefore, you can use the SMF command `svcadm` to manage it by the service identifier `svc:/system/system-log:default`. You can also use the `syslogd` command.

Look Out

- Assigning a role to a user and the user's assuming the role are two different things. A role must be assigned to a user before the user can assume that role.
- The rights profile name is case sensitive.
- You cannot assign a role to a role; that means you cannot use the `-R` option with the `roleadd` command, because unlike the `useradd` command, there is no `-R` option available for the `roleadd` command.

Memorize

- More than one user can assume the same role, but more than one role cannot be assumed by the same user simultaneously—that is, a user has to exit the current role before assuming another role.
- A user cannot log in as a role, but can assume a role after logging in as a non-RBAC user.
- The `user_attr` file lives in the `/etc` directory whereas the `auth_attr`, `exec_attr`, and `prof_attr` files live in the `/etc/security` directory.
- The `roleadd`, `roledel`, and `rolemod` commands work the same way as the `useradd`, `userdel`, and `usermod` commands—that is, they have the same options.
- The configuration information for the `syslogd` daemon resides in the `syslog.conf` file.

✓ TWO-MINUTE DRILL

Understanding Role-Based Access Control

- A role is a special type of account that can be associated with one or more users, and those users are said to have assumed the role.
- A rights profile is a collection of rights such as authorization, commands with assigned security attributes, and other rights profiles, that can be assigned to a role.
- An authorization is a discrete permission that enables a user (or a role) to perform a class of actions that could affect security. It is typically assigned to a profile; the roles acquire it through profiles, and users through roles.

Managing RBAC

- The `/etc/security/policy.conf` database contains default rights profiles, authorizations, and privileges that are applied to all the users.
- The `/etc/user_attr` database assigns the roles to the users and the profiles to the roles.
- The `/etc/security/prof_attr` database defines the profiles by specifying profile names and assigning them the authorization.
- The `/etc/security/auth_attr` database defines the authorizations.
- The `/etc/security/exec_attr` database assigns commands with security attributes to profiles.
- The `roleadd` command is used to create a role and works just like the `useradd` command.
- The `rolemod` command is used to modify a property of a role and works just like the `usermod` command.
- The `roledel` command is used to delete a role and works just like the `userdel` command.

Managing System Messaging

- The `syslogd` daemon automatically logs various system warnings and errors in message files whose location by default is the `/sys/adm` directory.
- The configuration file for the `syslogd` daemon is `/etc/syslog.conf`, which tells `syslogd` the name of the files to which the messages should be forwarded.
- You can manage syslog by using the SMF command `svcadm` on the service identifier `svc:/system/system-log:default`.

SELF TEST

The following questions will help you measure your understanding of the material presented in this chapter. Read all the choices carefully because there might be more than one correct answer. Choose all correct answers for each question.

1. Consider the following entry in the `auth_attr` database:

```
solaris.admin.:::Solaris Adminstration::help=SolarisAdmin.html
```

   Which of the following statements is true about this entry?

   A. It authorizes a user to administer a Solaris system.

   B. It grants a system administrator all the rights to the Solaris OS.

   C. It authorizes a user to grant any admin rights to any user.

   D. It is not really an authorization, but just a header that may be used in a GUI.

2. Which RBAC database assigns roles to the users?

   A. `auth_attr`

   B. `exec_attr`

   C. `prof_attr`

   D. `user_attr`

   E. `user_role`

3. Which RBAC database assigns privileged operations, such as commands with security attributes, to the rights profiles?

   A. `auth_attr`

   B. `exec_attr`

   C. `prof_attr`

   D. `user_attr`

   E. `prof_priv`

4. Which of the following files (databases) does RBAC use?

   A. `/etc/auth_attr`

   B. `/etc/exec_attr`

   C. `/etc/prof_attr`

   D. `/etc/user_attr`

5. Which of the following commands can be used to assign a role to a user?

   A. `roleadd`

   B. `rolemod`

   C. `useradd`

   D. `usermod`

6. Which of the following are the valid keys to specify security attributes in the `exec_attr` database of RBAC?

   A. `uid`

   B. `setuid`

   C. `euid`

   D. `gid`

   E. `egid`

7. Which of the following commands can be used to manage syslog?

   A. `syslogd`

   B. `svcadm`

   C. `syslogconfig`

   D. `syslog`

8. What does the following line mean in the `syslog.conf` file?

   ```
   *.alert *
   ```

   A. Send all the alert messages to the individual users.

   B. Ignore all the alert messages—that is, do not send them anywhere.

   C. Send all the alert messages to all the system administrators.

   D. Send all the alert messages to the log files, and the individual users.

9. Which of the following lines would you add to the `syslog.conf` file so that the user.alert and user.emerg messages are sent to both the root and the operator?

   A. `user.alert; user.emerg 'root; operator'`

   B. `user.alert, user.emerg 'root, operator'`

   C. `user.alert, user.emerg 'root operator'`

   D. `'user.alert, user.emerg' 'root; operator'`

10. Which of the following statements are true about the RBAC model?

    A. You cannot assign more than one role to a user.

    B. A user cannot assume more than one role at a time.

    C. You cannot assign more than one profile to a role.

    D. You can assign a role to another role just as you can assign a role to a user.

SELF TEST ANSWERS

1. ☑ **D**. When the `authname` field in an entry ends with a period, it means it is just a header, not an authorization.
   ☒ **A** and **B** are incorrect because an entry in the `auth_attr` database does not specify who is going to have this authorization. **C** is incorrect because a user (who has this authorization) will have the grant rights only if the `authname` field ends with the word grant.

2. ☑ **D**. The `user_attr` database assigns roles to users and profiles to roles.
   ☒ **A** is incorrect because the `auth_attr` database defines authorizations, and **B** is incorrect because `exec_attr` assigns privileged operations such as commands with security attributes to rights profiles. **C** is incorrect because `prof_attr` defines profiles by assigning authorizations to them, and **E** is incorrect because there is no RBAC database called `user_role`.

3. ☑ **B**. That is because `exec_attr` assigns privileged operations such as commands with security attributes to rights profiles.
   ☒ **A** is incorrect because the `auth_attr` database defines authorizations, and **C** is incorrect because `prof_attr` defines profiles by assigning authorizations to them. **D** is incorrect because the `user_attr` database assigns roles to users and profiles to roles, and **E** is incorrect because there is no RBAC database called `prof_priv`.

4. ☑ **D**. The databases that support RBAC are: `/etc/security/auth_attr`, `/etc/security/exec_attr`, `/etc/security/prof_attr`, and `/etc/user`.
   ☒ **A**, **B**, and **C** are incorrect because these database files should be in the `/etc/security` directory, not in the `/etc` directory.

5. ☑ **C** and **D**. A role can be assigned to a user by using the `-R` option, either at the time of user creation with the `useradd` command or later with the `usermod` command
   ☒ **A** and **B** are incorrect because you cannot use the `-R` option with `roleadd` or `rolemod` given that you are not allowed to assign a role to a role. In other words, the `-R` option is not available for the `roleadd` or `rolemod` command.

6. ☑ **A**, **C**, **D**, and **E**. The value for the keys `uid` and `euid` can be a single user name or a numeric user ID, and the value for the keys `gid` and `egid` can be a group name or a numeric group ID.
   ☒ **B** is incorrect because `setuid` is not part of RBAC.

7. ☑ **A** and **B**. You can use both the `syslogd` command and the SMF command `svcadm` to manage syslog.
   ☒ **C** and **D** are incorrect because there are no such commands as `syslogconfig` or `syslog`.

8. ☑ A. A * in the second column of an entry in the `syslog.conf` file means that destinations of the messages are the individual users, not any other destination.
   ☒ B, C, and D are incorrect because A * in the second column of an entry in the `syslog.conf` file means that the destinations of the messages are the individual users, not any other destination.

9. ☑ B. The list of facility sources, and the list of destinations has to be comma delimited.
   ☒ A, C, and D are incorrect because the lists should be comma delimited and not semi-colon delimited.

10. ☑ B. You can assign more than one role to a user, but the user cannot assume more than one role at a time.
    ☒ A is incorrect because you can assign more than one role to a user, but the user cannot assume more than one role at a time. C is incorrect because a role may contain more than one role. D is incorrect because you cannot assign a role to another role; you can only assign a role to a user.

15

Performing Advanced Installation

CERTIFICATION OBJECTIVES

- 15.01 Understanding JumpStart
- 15.02 Implementing JumpStart
- 15.03 Understanding and Using the Flash Archive
- 15.04 Booting and Installing with PXE
- 15.05 Managing Solaris Zones
- ✓ Two-Minute Drill
- Q&A Self Test

Installing an OS on a large number of machines can be a very time consuming and cumbersome activity. When you need to do the same thing over and over again, it is time for automation. Not only is doing the same thing manually over and over again time consuming but it can also lead to error. For example, if all 25 machines need to have the same value for a configuration parameter, some of these machines may end up having a different value due to human error. That's why the JumpStart installation method offers not only time saving but also a robust automated way to install Solaris on a group of machines that have identical configuration and software requirements. In a different situation, you may need to make a number of identical installations by using an image of an already installed system. This is accomplished through the flash archive installation method. Another installation situation is related to an x86 machine that does not have a local medium to boot from. This is addressed by the PXE installation method. If you want to install another application (or a set of applications) that require an isolated environment, you will need to install Solaris on another machine on which this set of applications will run. The question is: can I create multiple, isolated environments on one machine? The Solaris zone technology provides the answer to this question with a resounding yes.

So, the core issue in this chapter to think about is how to use the advanced installation methods offered by Solaris. To address this issue, we will explore three thought streams: JumpStart and files archive installation methods, the PXE method for booting an x86 machine, and Solaris zone technology.

CERTIFICATION OBJECTIVE 15.01

Understanding JumpStart

Exam Objective 6.4: *Explain custom JumpStart configuration including the boot, identification, configuration, and installation services.*

The custom JumpStart installation method allows automatic and identical installations or upgrades of several systems based on a profile that you create. The profile defines specific software installation requirements and choices. You realize the benefit of the JumpStart method when you have a large number of machines on which you want to make identical Solaris installations—that is, all installations use the same configuration. If you make these installations manually, one machine at a time, it will be very time consuming and also lead to errors. For example, the configurations of all the machines may not turn out to be identical as a result of some manual mistakes. For such a situation, JumpStart provides a robust and time-saving technique.

To understand clearly how JumpStart works, you need to comprehend the concepts and terminology involved in JumpStart installation.

The JumpStart Concepts

As you learned in Chapter 2, during manual installation, the installation program asks you some questions and gives you some options to choose from as it proceeds. You respond to the program by answering the questions and by making your choices. The JumpStart installation needs that information as well. However, because the JumpStart installation is automatic, you need to prepare and store that information for the JumpStart program before it starts. How is this information provided to the JumpStart program? (Or in other words, how do you help automate the installation process?) It is done by implementing some components described here:

- *Profile*. A profile defines specific software installation requirements. It specifies the elements of installation that you would otherwise determine interactively in a manual installation, such as the software group to install. You can create a profile by editing a text file and entering in the keyword-value pairs. For example, the value `initial_install` for the keyword `install_type` means it is the installation from scratch and not an upgrade, while the value SUNWCprog for the keyword `cluster` means the software group to be installed is SUNWCprog. You can give any meaningful name to the profile file. How does JumpStart know which machines belong to a given profile? In other words, how do you tell the JumpStart program: use this profile file to install Solaris on that group of machines? This is done by using the rules in the `rules` file.
- *Rule*. A rule is a statement that uses a set of system attributes to identify a group of machines and links it to a profile file. You define the rules in a text file whose name must be `rules`. You add a rule in the `rules` file for each machine or a group of machines on which you want to install the Solaris software. These machines are identified by the system attributes in the rule. So a rule does two things: it identifies a machine or a group of machines with a common set of system attributes, and it identifies the profile file that will be used to install Solaris on all the machines that belong to the group. The JumpStart

program looks at the `rules` file, and when it matches keyword-value pairs in the rule with a known machine, it installs the Solaris software on the machine according to the requirements specified in the profile file, which is listed in the profile field of the rule. For example, if there is a rule in the `rules` file that contains 192.168.2.0 as the value of the keyword network, and the word `network_prof` in the profile field of the rule, the JumpStart program will install the Solaris software according to the requirements specified in the `network_prof` file on all the machines connected to the subnet 192.168.2.0.

- *The* `check` *script*. Before JumpStart can use the `rules` file and the profiles, you need to perform a validation by running the `check` script. This script verifies that the rules in the `rules` files and the associated profiles are set up correctly; if they are, the script creates the `rules.ok` file, the file that is actually used by the JumpStart program.
- *JumpStart directory*. If you want to perform JumpStart installations for machines on a network, you need to create a directory on a network server, called a JumpStart directory. This directory contains all of the essential custom JumpStart files, such as the `rules` file, the `rules.ok` file, and profile files.
- *The servers*. If you are using JumpStart to install Solaris on one or more groups of machines, you will need a number of servers (which may live on the same machine) to provide common elements or information for these installations.
  - *Profile server*. A profile server is the server that contains the JumpStart directory, which must exist in the root (/) directory of the server.
  - *Boot server*. A boot server is the server that provides information that a JumpStart client (the machine on which JumpStart will install Solaris) needs to boot over the network.
  - *Install server*. An install server is the server that contains the Solaris installation files (an image of the Solaris operating environment from the installation CDs or DVD), which can be used for installation over a network.
- *JumpStart client*. This refers to the machine on which Solaris is to be installed by using the JumpStart program.
- *The* `sysidcfg` *file*. This is a text file used to pre-configure a machine on which you want to install Solaris by using JumpStart. When a JumpStart client boots for the first time (that is, during installation), the booting software attempts to get the configuration information, such as the host name, locale, and time zone from the `sysidcfg` file. You create and prepare

one `sysidcfg` file for a group of machines on which Solaris is to be installed with uniform configuration.

- *The* `begin` *and* `finish` *scripts*. These are the Bourne shell scripts, which are not required but can optionally be run at the beginning and end of a JumpStart installation. A detailed discussion of them is beyond the scope of this book.

You can give any name to a profile file, but it's a good idea to give a meaningful name. However, the name of the `rules` file must be `rules`.

Now that you know the basic elements of JumpStart, let's explore how they work together to jump start the installation.

Starting the JumpStart Installation

When you start a computer, two things happen before the OS takes over to help you work on your computer: a firmware (a software program on a chip) checks the hardware on the machine, and then a boot program boots the machine. These two things also happen when you attempt to install an OS such as Solaris. In this case, you direct the machine to boot from a device (CD, DVD, or net) where the installation software including the installation program is waiting. In the case of a JumpStart installation, you choose the JumpStart option for installation, but you must take some steps in advance to automate the installation.

Here is a high-level view of the steps that you must take before starting a JumpStart client for installation:

- Add rules in the `rules` file and create a profile corresponding to each group of systems on which you want to install Solaris.
- Save the `rules` file and the profiles in the JumpStart directory, which should live on one of the following two places:
    - Diskette, if you want to perform JumpStart installation on a standalone machine.
    - Server, if you want to perform JumpStart installations on machines connected to the network. Obviously, the machines must have access to the server.
- Validate the `rules` and profile files by executing the `check` script. It will generate the `rules.ok` file, which will be used by the JumpStart program to install Solaris.

- Set up the `sysidcfg` file to specify the values for some keywords in order to pre-configure the system.
- Start the JumpStart client to boot from a CD, a DVD, or a server on the network, and choose the JumpStart option.

After you choose the JumpStart option, the JumpStart program accesses the `rules.ok` file and browses through it to search for the first rule with defined system attributes that match the system on which the JumpStart program has been instructed to install the Solaris software. If it finds a match, the JumpStart program uses the profile specified in the rule to install the Solaris software on the system. This process is illustrated in Figure 15-1 in which there are two groups of systems (Engineering and Business) and an individual system with host name Barbara connected to the enterprise network.

FIGURE 15-1

An example of how the JumpStart installation starts on a network

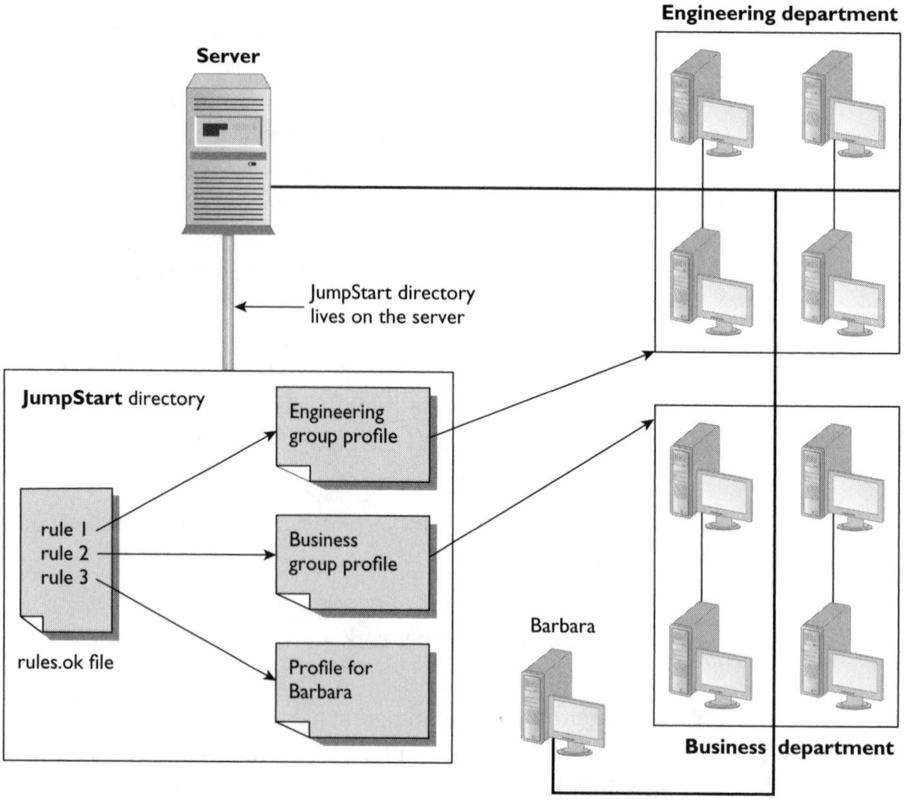

Engineering department
Server
JumpStart directory lives on the server
JumpStart directory
Engineering group profile
rule 1
rule 2
rule 3
Business group profile
rules.ok file
Profile for Barbara
Barbara
Business department

When the JumpStart program reads the `rules.ok` file, several scenarios may arise as shown in Figure 15-2, which also shows the order in which several steps are executed before the actual installation starts.

If the JumpStart program matches a rule with the system (on which the installation is to be performed), and finds the corresponding profile file specified in the rule, the JumpStart installation starts on the system; otherwise, an alternative installation method is used.

Now that you know how the JumpStart installation starts, see the next page for some practical scenarios and their solutions.

By now, you know how several elements such as the `rules` file, profile files, the `sysidcfg` file, and the install server work together to help JumpStart perform automatic installation. But how are these components built?

FIGURE 15-2

The process of starting JumpStart

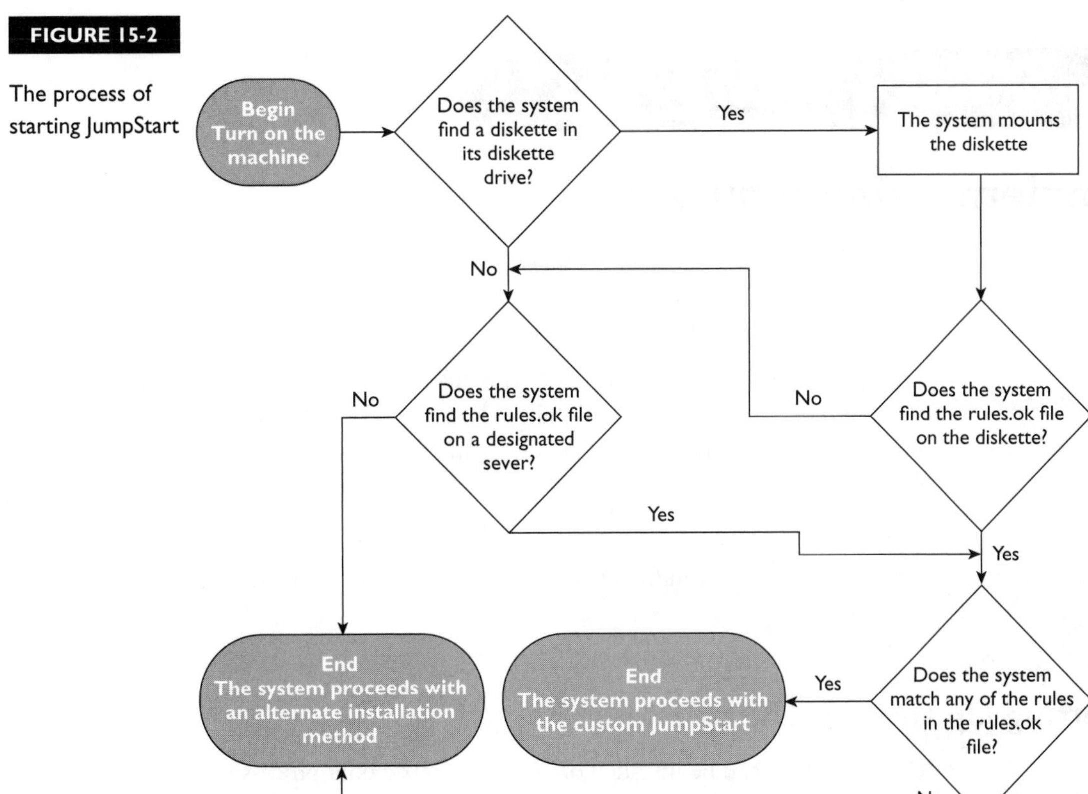

SCENARIO & SOLUTION	
The machines in the Engineering group shown in Figure 15-1 are connected to a subnet with IP address 192.168.3.0, and their group profile exists in the file `eng_prof`. Write an example for rule_1.	`network 192.168.3.0 - eng_prof -`
The machines in the Business group shown in Figure 15-1 are connected to a subnet with IP address 192.168.4.0, and their group profile exists in the file `bus_prof`. Write an example for rule_2.	`network 192.168.4.0 - bus_prof -`
Write an example for rule_3 in Figure 15-1, given that the profile for host Barbara is defined in the `barbara_prof` file.	`hostname Barbara - barbara_prof -`

CERTIFICATION OBJECTIVE 15.02

Implementing JumpStart

Exam Objective 6.5: *Configure a JumpStart including implementing a JumpStart server, editing the sysidcfg, rules and profile files, and establishing JumpStart software alternatives (setup, establishing alternatives, troubleshooting, and resolving problems).*

In the previous section, we read about the different JumpStart elements that facilitate the automation as promised by the custom JumpStart method. You make the automatic magic happen by implementing these elements, which involves the following:

- Writing the `sysidcfg`, `rules`, and profile files.
- Checking the validity of the `rules` and profile files by running the `check` script.
- Setting up servers such as install server, boot server, and configuration server.

Setting Up the `sysidcfg` File

Before anything can be installed on a machine, the boot process must be started. When a JumpStart client boots for the first time, it needs some information such as its host name and IP address before the installation can start. It's like: I would like to know who I am before you start installing things on me. That information is provided through the `sysidcfg` file.

The `sysidcfg` file pre-configures information, needed for installation, through a set of keyword-value pairs. You can pre-configure as much information as you want by specifying one or more keywords. Each group of machines that has unique configuration information must have its own `sysidcfg` file.

The syntax rules applied to writing keywords in the `sysidcfg` file are described here:

- You can define keywords in any order.
- The keywords are not case sensitive—for example, `hostname` and `Hostname` represent the same keyword.
- The keyword values can be optionally enclosed in single quotes (`'`) or double quotes (`"`).
- If a keyword appears multiple times in the file, only the first instance of the keyword is considered valid and used. The `network_interface` keyword is an exception to this rule, because a machine can have multiple network interfaces.

For example, the following keywords can be used for both SPARC and x86 machines:

- **`name_service`.** The possible values are DNS, LDAP, NIS, NIS+, and NONE.
- **`domain_name`.** The value is the name of the domain to which the machine belongs.
- **`name_server`.** The value is the host name or the IP address of the name server used by the machine under installation.
- **`root_password`.** To specify the root password. This is the encrypted password as it appears in the `/etc/shadow` file.
- **`system_locale`.** To specify the language for installation.
- **`time_server`.** To specify the time server.

The following keywords can be used only for x86-based machines:

- **`monitor`.** Specifies the monitor type.
- **`keyboard`.** Specifies the keyboard language.

- **display.** Specifies the graphic card.
- **pointer.** Specifies the pointing device.

The following is a sample sysidcfg file for a SPARC machine:

```
system_locale=en_US
timezone=US/Pacific
timeserver=localhost
terminal=sun-cmd
name_service=NIS {domain_name=committee.senate.congress.com
name_server=connor(172.17.111.4)}
root_password=WesMtQWing
system_locale=C
security_policy=Kerberos
{default_realm=Yoursite.COM
admin_server=krbadmin.Yoursite.COM
kdc=kdc1.Yoursite.COM, kdc2.Yoursite.COM}
```

This sysidcfg file is for a group of SPARC machines on which you want to install Solaris over the network. The host names, IP addresses, and netmasks of these systems have been pre-configured by editing the name service (discussed in Chapter 11). Because all the system configuration information has been pre-configured, an automated installation can be performed by using a custom JumpStart profile.

Where does the sysidcfg live and how do you send it to the JumpStart client? It can reside at one of the following places:

- For installation over a network, the sysidcfg file can reside on a shared Network File System (NFS) directory (the JumpStart directory). You can tell its location to the JumpStart client by using the -p option with the add_install_client command, which we will explore later in this section.
- For an installation on a machine locally, the sysidcfg file can reside on the root directory on a UFS or PCFS diskette in the machine's diskette drive. On an x86 machine, the sysidcfg file should reside on the Solaris Device Configuration Assistant (SDCA) diskette. Make sure the diskette is in the diskette drive when the machine boots.

So, you use the sysidcfg file to assign some system attributes to the machine or a group of machines. However, some installation questions and options have not yet been addressed. For example, what type of installation is to be performed—initial installation or upgrade? These questions are answered in a profile file.

Setting Up a Profile File

When the JumpStart program finds a rule that matches with the machine undergoing installation, the JumpStart program looks for the profile file specified in the rule. It is a text file that you create to tell the JumpStart program how to perform installations—for example, which installation group to install. In other words, it contains the responses that you would otherwise give by typing or clicking in an interactive installation. A profile file contains one or more profile keywords and their values. Each profile keyword is an answer to a question or a choice for an option related to how the Solaris software is to be installed on the machine. For example, the following profile keyword-value pair specifies that the JumpStart program is installing Solaris from scratch (initial installation) and not performing an upgrade:

```
install_type initial_install
```

The syntax rules for writing a profile file are described here:

- You can give any name to a profile file. However, it is a good idea to give a meaningful name (e.g., `eng_profile`) for a file that contains the profile of the machine that belongs to the engineering group.
- The first entry in the profile file must specify the `install_type` keyword.
- There must be one keyword-value pair in one entry (line).
- If a system that is being upgraded according to the profile contains more than one root (/) directory that can be upgraded, you must specify the `root_device` keyword in an entry.
- If a line begins with the pound symbol (#), the entire line is treated as a comment and is ignored by JumpStart.
- The file can have one or more blank lines.

on the job

Note that the profile keywords and their values are case sensitive, whereas the keywords in the `sysidcfg` file are not.

The following is an example of a profile file that specifies the installation type, the software group to install, the package to remove, and the remote file systems to mount:

```
install_type initial_install
system_type standalone
partitioning default
```

```
filesys any 512 swap # SWAP specification
cluster SUNWCprog
package SUNWman delete
```

The `filesys` entry specifies that the size of the SWAP area must be 512MB and it can be installed on any disk.

So, you have set up a profile for a machine (or a group of machines) that will tell the JumpStart program how to make an installation on that machine. But how does the JumpStart program running on the machine determine the name of the profile file that should be used to perform the installation? The answer is by reading the `rules` file (i.e., the `rules.ok` file, to be precise).

Setting Up the `rules` File

The JumpStart program performs installation on a machine according to the instructions in the profile file of the machine that is identified by the `rules.ok` file, which in turn is generated by the `check` script from the `rules` file.

The `rules` file is a text file that you write. The syntax for writing the `rules` file is described here:

- The name of the file must be `rules`.
- The file must contain one or more rules—that is, entries.
- If a line begins with a pound symbol (#), the entire line is treated as a comment and is ignored by the JumpStart program.
- If you want to continue a rule from one line to a new line, use the backward slash (\) at the end of the first line just before pressing RETURN.
- The file can have one or more blank lines.

The syntax for an entry in the `rules` file is as shown here:

```
<keyword-value pairs> <begin> <profile> <finish>
```

The fields in the entry are described in Table 15-1.

The <keyword-value pairs> and <profile> are the mandatory fields in an entry of the `rules` file. The following is an example of a `rules` file:

```
hostname eng-11—eng_prof -
network 192.168.3.0 && !model\
'SUNW,Sun-Blade-100'—net_prof -
model SUNW,SPARCstation-LX—lx_prof complete
```

TABLE 15-1 Fields in an entry of the `rules` file

Field in a `rules` File Entry	Description
`<keyword-value pairs>`	Specifies one or more keyword-value pair. If multiple pairs are specified, the pairs are separated by a double AND symbol (&&), and an exclamation point (!) is used to negate a pair.
`<begin>`	Specifies the name of an optional Bourne shell script to be executed before the installation begins. The hyphen (-) used instead of a name means no `begin` script exists. The `begin` scripts must reside in the JumpStart directory.
`<finish>`	Specifies the name of an optional Bourne shell script to be executed after the installation completes and before the machine is rebooted. The hyphen (-) used instead of a name means no `finish` script exists. The `finish` scripts must reside in the JumpStart directory.
`<profile>`	Specifies the name of the text file that defines how the Solaris software is to be installed on a machine whose system attributes match those in the rule. All profile files must be located in the JumpStart directory.

```
network 192.168.4.0 && karch i86pc setup x86_prof done
memsize 64-128 && arch i386—prog_prof -
any—- generic_prof -
```

There are six entries (mind the \ sign which means continue) in this file. The first entry instructs that if the host name of the machine is `eng-11`, the JumpStart installation should be performed on it according to the instructions in the `eng_prof` file. The second entry specifies that if the machine is connected to the subnet 192.168.3.0 and it's not a Sun-Blade0-100 machine, the JumpStart installation should be performed on it by using the profile in the `net_prof` file.

You create the `sysidcfg` file, `rules` file, and the profile files to automate the installation of Solaris software. But how will you make the Solaris software available for installation? The answer is by creating the install server.

Creating the Install Server

To make a machine the install server, you use the `setup_install_server` command to copy the images of the installation software to the local disk of the server machine. You can copy the images from either of the following media:

- Solaris 10 Software CDs and the Solaris 10 Languages CD
- Solaris 10 Operating System DVD

To convert the machine (SPARC or x86) into an install server, perform the following steps:

1. Insert the Solaris 10 Software for `<platformName>` Platforms-1 CD in the CD-ROM drive attached to the server machine, where `<platformName>` is SPARC for the SPARC machine and x86 for the x86 machine.
2. Make a directory on the server for the installation software by issuing the following command:

```
mkdir -p /export/install/solaris_soft
```

3. Go to the tools directory on the CD by issuing the following command:

```
cd /<cdMountPoint>/Solaris_10/Tools
```

   The `<cdMountPoint>` specifies the mount point for the CD. For example, the actual command may look like the following:

```
cd /cdrom/cdrom0/s2/Solaris_10/Tools
```

4. Set up the install server by issuing the following command:

```
/setup_install_server/export/install/solaris_soft
```

5. Insert the Solaris 10 Software for `<platformName>` Platforms-2 CD in the CD-ROM drive attached to the server machine, where `<platformName>` is SPARC for the SPARC machine and x86 for the x86 machine.
6. Go to the tools directory on the CD by issuing the following command:

```
cd /<cdMountPoint>/Solaris_10/Tools
```

   The `<cdMountPoint>` specifies the mount point for the CD.
7. Copy the image from the CD to the disk:

```
/add_to_install_server/export/install/solaris_soft
```

8. Repeat steps 5 through 7 for any CD that you want to copy to the disk for installation such as the Solaris 10 Languages CD.

Follow the same procedure to copy the Solaris 10 DVD to the disk. Because there is only one DVD, it will involve only the following three commands:

```
mkdir -p /export/install/solaris_soft
cd /<DVDMountPoint>/Solaris_10/Tools
./setup_install_server /export/install/solaris_soft
```

If the machines under installation need to be booted over the network, you must set up a boot server.

Creating the Boot Server

You can use a machine as a boot server for booting clients over the network. You can set up a machine to be a boot server by copying the boot image from the installation CD (or DVD) by using the following commands:

```
cd /<mountPoint>/Solaris_10/Tools
./setup_install_server -b /export/boot
```

The `<mountPoint>` specifies the mount point for the installation CD or DVD. Now that you have the install server and the boot server set up, you need to set up the JumpStart directory to store the files that will facilitate automatic installation as promised by JumpStart.

Setting Up the JumpStart Directory

As you already know, the JumpStart directory contains files, such as `rules` file and profile files, required for a custom JumpStart installation of Solaris. You, the system administrator, are responsible for setting up this directory before the installation. You can start working on this by copying the sample directory from the Solaris 10 software image that you have already copied to the `/export/install` directory on the disk from the Solaris 10 Software-1 CD or the Solaris 10 Operating System DVD.

To accomplish this task, issue the following two commands on your server machine:

```
mkdir /jumpstart
cp -r /export/install/solaris_soft/Solaris_10/Misc/jumpstart_sample /jumpstart
```

Now in the `/jumpstart` directory you can create or edit the `rules` file and the profile files for different JumpStart client machines or groups of machines. Obviously, you can move (or copy) these files to this directory if you have already created and prepared them elsewhere. After you set up the `rules` file and profile files, you must validate these files by running the `check` script on the server as shown here:

```
cd /jumpstart
./check
```

If the `check` script does not detect any errors, it creates the `rules.ok` file. This is the file that will be read by the JumpStart program running on a client to find out the rule for the client machine and hence to find out the name of the profile file that contains the information to be used for installation.

Use the `add_install_client` command on the server to inform the server about the clients that can use network installation. The `add_install_client` command must be run from the install server's Solaris installation image that you copied to the server machine's disk.

```
./add_install_client [-c <serverName>:<path>] [-p <serverName>:<path>]
<clientHostName> <clientPlatformGroup>
```

The options are described here:

- **`-c <serverName>:<path>`.** Specifies the path to the JumpStart directory: `<serverName>` specifies the host name or the IP address of the server on which the JumpStart directory resides, and `<path>` specifies the full path to the directory.
- **`-p <serverName>:<path>`.** Specifies the path to the `sysidcfg` file: `<serverName>` specifies the host name or the IP address of the server on which the `sysidcfg` file resides, and `<path>` specifies the full path to the file.
- **`<clientHostName>`.** The host name of a JumpStart client on which you want to install Solaris by using JumpStart. Ensure that the host name to IP address mapping is properly defined in DNS.
- **`<clientPlatformGroup>`.** Specifies the platform group of the machines (or group of machines) that use the `<serverName>`—for example, sun4u for ultra 5 systems.

JumpStart offers automation for installing Solaris on multiple machines with identical software and configuration requirements. Note that in JumpStart the source for each installation is the install server and a set of files such as `rules`, `sysidcfg`, and profile files. If the `sysidcfg` file does not have all the required configuration information, the program will prompt you for the information. Furthermore, you can change the information in the files between any two installations.

Now consider a slightly different kind of requirement. You have installed Solaris on a machine and then you say, I want exactly the same system running on a number of other machines. In other words, you want to clone it on other machines. This is accomplished by using the flash archive method.

CERTIFICATION OBJECTIVE 15.03

Understanding and Using the Flash Archive

Exam Objective 6.6: *Explain flash, create and manipulate the flash archive, and use it for installation.*

The Solaris flash archive, one of several available installation methods, is used to replicate a single reference installation on multiple machines. The replicas are called clones. From a given reference installation, you can create a replica (clone) in one of the following ways:

- *Solaris flash initial installation.* Overwrites all existing files on the system.
- *Solaris flash update.* Includes only the difference between two system images—the flash image and the image of the existing system.
- *Differential update.* Changes only the specified files.

Before we dive into the details, it's important to understand the basic concepts and the processes involved in the flash archive installation method.

Understanding the Flash Archive

Understand that flash archive is not a full-fledged new installation method independent of other methods. It is rather a different source of installation—an image of an already installed system, called flash archive. Once you have a flash archive, it can be installed by using methods you are already familiar with and fall into two broad categories: initial installation or upgrade. If you are using the initial installation, it could be any of the following: Solaris installation program, custom JumpStart, or WAN boot. The initial installation, called Solaris flash initial installation in this case, involves the following five steps:

1. Install the reference system, called the master system, by using any of the Solaris installation methods.
2. Prepare scripts to customize (or reconfigure) a clone system after or before installation.
3. Create a copy of the master system, called a flash archive. You can exclude some files that are not needed. This is the image that you will use for making clones.
4. Create a clone system by installing the flash archive on a machine. The machine with the clone system must have the same architecture as the machine with the master system.
5. Save a copy of the master image as protection against losing the master because of a system failure.

Obviously steps 2 and 5 are optional. You can create the master system by using any installation method that we have already discussed in this chapter and in Chapter 2. But how do you create the flash archive?

Creating a Flash Archive

As a system administrator, you will need to manage the flash archives, which include creating a flash archive from a master system, splitting an archive into different sections, combining different sections of an archive into one archive, and retrieving information about the archive. All these tasks can be accomplished by using the `flar` command with different subcommands such as `create` to create an archive, as shown in Table 15-2.

To create the flash archive for a master system, you should boot the master system and run it in the most inactive state possible. The first preference is to run the system in single-user mode. If this is not possible, you must at least shut down the applications that you want to include in the archive and the applications that are using extensive OS resources.

You can create a Solaris flash archive when the master system is in one of the following states:

1. Master system running in single-user mode.
2. Master system running in multiuser mode.

TABLE 15-2 Different subcommands that can be used with the `flar` command

Command	Description
`flar create` or `flarcreate`	Creates a flash archive from a master system.
`flar combine`	Combines the different archive sections in different files into one archive.
`flar info`	Provides information about an archive.
`flar split`	Splits an archive into sections with each section in a separate file.

3. Master system booted from one of the following:
   - Solaris 10 Software-1 CD
   - Solaris 10 Operating System DVD
   - An image of the Solaris 10 software

To create the archive from any of these sources, issue the `flar` command with the create subcommand, which has the following syntax:

```
flar create -n <archiveName> [<otherOptions>] <path>/<fileName>
```

The `-n` option is mandatory, where the argument `<archiveName>` specifies the name that you give to the archive. The `<fileName>` specifies the name of the archive file, and `<path>` specifies the full path of the directory in which the archive file resides. If you do not specify the path, the archive file will be saved in the current directory. Some other options that you can use with this command are described here:

- **`-a <authorName>.`** Specifies an author name for the archive identification section.
- **`-e <desc>.`** Specifies the description to be included in the archive as the value of the `content_description` identification key.
- **`-i <date>.`** Specifies the date to be included in the archive as the value of the `creation_date` field in the identification section. By default (that is, in the absence of this option), the current system date is included.
- **`-c.`** Compresses the archive by using the `compress` command.
- **`-m <masterName>.`** Specifies the name of the master system to be used as the value of the `creation_master` field in the identification section of the archive. By default, the name of the system on which the `flar create` command is issued is used as the value of this field.

- **-R <root>.** Specifies the root directory for the directory subtree to be archived. The default root is the system root (/).
- **-S.** Specifies to skip the disk space check and to keep the archive in memory. Without this option, the `create` command builds a compressed archive in memory, and checks the disk space before writing the archive to the disk.
- **-x <excludeDirFile>.** Exclude from the archive those files and directories whose names are specified by `<excludeDirFile>` on the command line.
- **-X <excludeList>.** Exclude from the archive those files and directories whose names are listed in the file the name of which is specified by `<excludeList>`. The list in the file should contain one name (file or directory) per line.
- **-y <includeDirFile>.** Includes in the archive those files and directories whose names are specified by `<includeDirFile>` on the command line.

Once you have a flash archive, you can check what is in the archive by issuing the following command:

```
flar info -l <fileName>
```

The argument `<fileName>` specifies the name of the archive file. The command displays the file structure of the archive.

Now that you know how to create and manipulate a flash archive, here are some practical scenarios and solutions:

SCENARIO & SOLUTION	
Create an exact copy of a master system, compress it, and store it in a file named `archive_exact.flar`. Name the archive: `archive_exact`.	`flar create -n archive_exact -c archive_exact.flar`
Display the file structure of the archive.	`flar info -l archive_exact.flar`
Create a flash archive from a master system and exclude all the content under the `/test` directory except the content in the `/test/scripts` directory. Name the archive as `archive_in` and the archive file `archive_in.flar`.	`flar create -n archive archive_in -x /test -y /test/scripts archive_in.fl`

Installing a Solaris Flash Archive

You can install a Solaris flash archive by using any of the methods that you already know: Solaris installation program, custom JumpStart, Solaris Live Upgrade, or WAN boot. To use the Solaris installation program to install a Solaris flash archive, perform the following procedure:

1. Begin the Solaris installation program and proceed through the steps described in Chapter 2.
2. When you reach the Specify Media panel, continue with the Solaris flash installation.
3. Specify the media you are using to install:
   a. Give the feedback that you are prompted for, depending on the selected media:
      i. DVD or CD. Insert the disk that contains the Solaris flash archive.
      ii. Network File System. Specify the path to the archive on the NFS.
      iii. HTTP. Specify the URL and the proxy information that is needed to access the archive.
      iv. FTP. Specify the FTP server and the path to the flash archive on it.
      v. Local tape. Specify the local tape device and the path to the flash archive on it.

   b. For flash archives stored on a disk or an NFS server, respond to the Select Flash Archives panel by selecting one or more archives to install.
   c. On the Flash Archives Summary panel, confirm the selected archives and click Next.

      The Additional Flash Archives panel is displayed. If you want to install an additional Solaris flash archive, specify the media on which the other archive is located. If you have no other archive to install at this time, select None.
4. Click Next and follow the steps for completing the installation.

What we have described is an initial installation that will overwrite everything on the system disk.

A Solaris flash archive provides you with choices in the source of installation—instead of installing the original Solaris installation software, you install the image of an already installed system. This offers a quick and robust way of installing a large number of identical systems. You can quickly clone an installed system.

Before you can install an operating system on a machine, the machine must start booting. A machine can boot either by using a local medium or over the network.

CERTIFICATION OBJECTIVE 15.04

Booting and Installing with PXE

Exam Objective 6.7: *Given a PXE installation scenario, identify requirements and install methods, configure both the install and DHCP server, and boot the x86 client.*

To install Solaris on your machine, it must start booting first. You can boot a machine either from local media (diskette, CD, or DVD), or over the network. If your computer implements Intel Preboot Execution Environment (PXE), you can boot your machine over the network by using what is called PXE booting.

Understanding Booting with PXE

If your x86 machine does not have a local medium to boot from, you can install Solaris on it by booting it over the network using PXE. Of course, like any other machine on any network, the client must access a DHCP (dynamic host configuration protocol) server to obtain an IP address before it can access any other machine. The following are the requirements for booting an installation client for installation over a network using PXE:

- *PXE support.* The client machine must support PXE to perform PXE boot. To find out whether your machine supports PXE network boot, check the hardware documentation. Also note that some early versions of PXE firmware do not support the Solaris system. In this case, you should upgrade the PXE firmware on the adapter, and you can obtain the upgrade information from the adapter manufacturer's web site.

- *DHCP server*. Your machine does not have a network connection until it has an IP address. For the sake of robustness, and a wise use of IP addresses, it is standard practice to use a DHCP server to assign IP addresses to machines on a network. Therefore, to make a PXE boot work, you will need to set up a DHCP server on your network. Note that PXE does not work well on subnets that use multiple DHCP servers; you should make sure that the subnet to which the installation client is connected has only one DHCP server.
- *Install server*. Because the installation is being done over the network, you must put the installation software on a machine and set it up as an install server.

You must perform the following steps to boot your machine using PXE and install Solaris on it over the network:

1. Verify that the installation client supports PXE—that is, that it can use PXE to boot without using any local media.
2. Set up an install server—that is, create an install server that contains the installation software (Solaris 10 for x86) to be installed over the network, and add install clients to the server.
3. Set up a DHCP server.
4. Boot the installation client.
5. Choose a Solaris installation method from the available methods, such as Solaris installation program, custom jumpstart, and flash archive.

Earlier in this chapter, you learned the procedure for setting up an install server and adding clients to it. Use the `-d` option with the `add_install` client to specify that the client will use the DHCP server to obtain the network install parameters. If you want to use this installation information only for a specific client, use the `-e <ethernetAddress>` option along with the `-d` option, where `<ethernetAddress>` specifies the hardware address of the client machine.

In addition to setting up an install server, you must set up and configure a DHCP server.

Configuring a DHCP Server

You can configure (and unconfigure) a DHCP server by using DHCP Manager on a machine if it is running an X Window system such as CDE or GNOME. You start the DHCP Manager by issuing the `/usr/sadm/admin/bin/dhcpmgr` command, which starts the DHCP Configuration Wizard. The wizard prompts you for the information needed to configure the server.

Perform the following steps to set up and configure the DHP server:

1. Select the system that you want to use as a DHCP server.
2. Gather the information needed to configure the DHCP server.
3. Become superuser on the machine you selected to be a DHCP server, and start the DHCP Manager by issuing the following command:

```
/usr/sadm/admin/bin/dhcpmgr &
```

4. Choose the option Configure as DHCP Server. At this point, the DHCP Configuration Wizard starts and queries to get the configuration information from you.
5. Interact with the wizard by making choices on the options, and typing information when requested.
6. At the end of the information-collection phase, click Finish to complete the server configuration.
7. At the Start Address Wizard prompt, click Yes to determine the IP addresses that the server will be managing, and respond to the prompts regarding IP address management.
8. Review your selections, and then click Finish to add the IP addresses to the network table maintained by the server.

As an alternative, you can also use the `dhcpconfig` command to configure the DHCP server by specifying the configuration information in the command line by using options.

Performing Boot and Installation on the Client

When you install an OS on a machine, you boot the machine from the device where the installation program is waiting to be started. So, to install over the network, you must instruct the install client to boot over the network. You must enable the PXE network boot on the client system by using the BIOS setup program in the machine's BIOS, the network adapter BIOS, or both. On some machines, you may need to change the boot device priority list to make network boot the highest priority: this way, the machine tries to boot from the network before attempting to boot from any other device. You can determine this by checking the manufacturer's documentation or by paying attention to the setup program instructions during boot.

Perform the following steps to boot an x86-based machine over the network by using PXE:

1. Turn on the machine. Press the appropriate key combination to enter the system's BIOS to enable the PXE boot. Some PXE-capable network adapters have a feature that allows you to press an appropriate key in response to a boot prompt, and this will enable the PXE boot. In that case, you can skip step 2.
2. In the system's BIOS, instruct the system to boot from the network. Check your hardware documentation to find out how to set the boot priority in the BIOS.
3. Exit the BIOS. The install client starts booting from the network.
4. When prompted, select an installation method:
   - To select the Solaris interactive installation GUI, type 1 and press ENTER.
   - To select a custom JumpStart installation, type 2 and press ENTER.
   - To select the Solaris interactive text installer in a desktop session, type 3 and press ENTER.
   - To select the Solaris interactive text installer in a console session, type 4 and press ENTER.
5. Answer the system configuration questions, if prompted.
6. After the system boot and installation over the network is complete, instruct the system to boot from the disk drive on subsequent boots, if that's what you want.

When you install Solaris and other software packages, you set up an operating environment isolated from other Solaris operating environments on other machines. If you want to install another application (or a set of applications) that require an isolated environment, you will need to install Solaris on another machine on which this set of applications will run. The question is Can I create multiple isolated environments on one machine? The answer is Yes, by using the Solaris zone technology introduced in Solaris 10.

CERTIFICATION OBJECTIVE 15.05

Managing Solaris Zones

In the good old days of computing, there was one operating system such as DOS (disk operating system) running on a machine and managing resources for one application and one user at a time. However, UNIX has been a multiuser and multi-process operating system from the very beginning. This means one operating system running on one machine and managing resources for multiple applications running concurrently and multiple users logged into the system at the same time.

The main advantages of running multiple applications on the same machine under one operating system are wise use of resources and ease of administration (it's easier to administer one machine as opposed to ten machines, for example). The main advantages of applications running on different machines under different copies (instances) of the same operating system such as Solaris are that the applications can communicate with each other only through network APIs. Hence, they are secured from each other, and a heavy use of resources by one application does not affect the performance of the other application on another machine.

Now that computer systems are increasingly becoming more powerful in resources such as disk space, memory, and CPU power, it makes sense to consolidate applications running on different systems to one system. The problem is that if you do that, the applications, though they may currently have no resource shortage, will lose the other benefits of running in an isolated environment. So the question is: how can I run multiple applications on the same machine and still provide each application (or a group of applications) the isolated environment as if it were running on a machine of its own? That means having more than one operating system environment on one machine. So the computing model we are talking about now is: multiple instances of an operating system running on the same machine, each instance providing an isolated environment to the processes running under it as if they were running on a machine of their own. These isolated environments are provided by Solaris 10 and are called zones.

Understanding Zones

Exam Objective 6.1: *Explain consolidation issues, features of Solaris zones, and decipher between the different zone concepts including zone types, daemons, networking, command scope, and given a scenario, create a Solaris zone.*

A Solaris zone is a virtual operating system environment created by one instance of the Solaris operating system. There may be more than one zone on the same machine, and processes running in one zone cannot monitor or affect the processes running in other zones. Processes running in different zones can interact with each other only through network APIs. In other words, the processes running in a zone are isolated from processes in other zones, as though each zone were a machine (box) on its own. Actually, zone technology provides an abstract layer that separates applications from the physical attributes of the machine, such as physical device paths, on which they are deployed.

on the Job

The maximum number of zones that you can create on a system is 8192. However, the number of zones that you can practically host on a system depends on the resources offered by the system and the resource requirements of the applications running in the zones.

Before diving into the details of zone technology, you should understand the basic concepts described here:

- *Zone types.* When we refer to zones, we mean the non-global zones unless specified otherwise. Each Solaris system has a default zone called the global zone that exists even before you create additional zones (i.e., non-global zones). Even after you create zones, the global zone continues to exist and can be used for systemwide administration. Table 15-3 compares the characteristics of a global zone with those of the non-global zones.
- *Networking.* The processes running in one zone can interact with processes running in other zones only through network APIs. Yes, each zone that needs network connectivity has one or more dedicated IP addresses. In other words, each zone (that provides network connectivity) has at least one logical network interface, and the application running in one zone cannot view (or monitor) the network traffic for another zone. So, you can run network services confined to a zone. You can use the `ifconfig` command from the global zone to add or remove logical network interfaces in a running zone.
- *Daemons.* Because the zones can communicate with each other only over the network, they can all run their own server daemons. A specific server daemon, for example, `ftpd`, can run on the same port, say TCP port 21, in each zone without creating any conflict.
- *Command scope.* When you issue a command in a zone, you need to be aware of the command scope, which can be global (i.e., at zone level), or resource

TABLE 15-3 Characteristics of global and non-global zones compared

Characteristic	Global Zone	Non-Global Zone
ID	Assigned ID 0 by the system.	Assigned a zone ID by the system when the zone is booted.
Kernel	Provides the single instance of the Solaris kernel that is bootable and running on the system.	Shares operation under the Solaris kernel booted from the global zone.
Transparency	Aware of all devices, file systems, and the existence of other zones on the machine.	Not aware of physical device paths, and not aware of the existence of other zones.
Management	Other zones can be managed (configured, installed, and uninstalled) from this zone.	No zone (including itself) can be managed from this zone.
Configuration information	Holds the configuration information specific to this zone only such as the global zone host name and the file system table.	Holds the configuration information specific to this zone only such as the non-global zone host name and the file system table
Software	Contains a complete installation of the Solaris system software packages. Can contain additional software packages, and additional software—that is, files and directories not installed through packages—for other data.	Contains a subset of the complete installed Solaris Operating System software. Can contain additional Solaris software packages shared from the global zone, as well as the packages not shared from the global zone. Can contain additional software packages, and additional software: files and directories not installed through packages, for other data.
Product database	Provides a complete and consistent product database that contains information about all software components installed in this zone, the global zone.	Provides a complete and consistent product database that contains information about all the software components installed on this zone—that is, those components present entirely on this non-global zone and those that are shared (read-only) from the global zone.

specific (i.e., specific to a resource). For example, if you are adding a resource type to a zone, the command scope is global; if you are adding a property to a specific resource, the command scope is resource specific.

A natural question to ask at this point is: how are the zones created and managed? The administrator for the global zone, referred to as the global administrator, has superuser privileges for the whole system. The global administrator, who has the primary administrator role, uses the `zonecfg` command to configure the zone and the `zoneadm` command to install software in the zone and to boot the zone. The global administrator can also assign a zone-management profile to a zone administrator whose privileges would be confined to that specific zone.

You can create a zone and delete a zone. At a given moment in its life cycle, a non-global zone can be in one of the following six states:

- *Configured*. The zone in this state has already been configured and the configuration parameters have been committed to permanent storage. The parameters of the zone's application environment that will be specified after the initial boot are not yet present.
- *Incomplete*. The zone is in the middle of state transition by an operation such as install or uninstall.
- *Installed*. The zone's configuration has been instantiated, but the zone's virtual platform is not yet associated with it. Software packages are installed under the root path for the zone. Before installing, you can use the `zoneadm` command to verify that the current configuration can be successfully used on this Solaris system.
- *Ready*. A virtual platform has been associated with the installed zone, and a unique zone ID has been assigned, file systems have been mounted, and devices have been configured. The kernel creates the `zsched` process, but no processes associated with this zone have yet been started.
- *Running*. One or more user processes associated with the zone's application environment are running. When the first user process associated with the zone's application environment (init) is created, the zone enters the running state.
- *Shutting down, and down*. Like the incomplete state, shutting down and down are the transitional states that indicate that the zone is being halted. However, the zone can get stuck in one of these states if it is unable to halt for whatever reason.

The benefits provided by the non-global zones are discussed here in terms of features:

- *Security*. The isolated environments created by the zones provide process security and network security. Once a process has been created in a zone, neither the process nor any of its child processes can change zones. The processes running in one zone are isolated and hence secure from processes running in other zones. By running network services in a zone, you limit the damage that can be caused in the event of a security violation. For example, the actions of an intruder who successfully breaks into the zone by exploiting a security flaw in software running in the zone are confined to that zone. The applications running in different zones on the same system are unable to monitor or intercept each other's network traffic, file system data, or process activity.

- *Virtualization*. In a non-zone world, multiple insolated application environments (including physical devices, IP address, and host name) can be established on different machines, one environment per machine. The zones allow you to create these isolated environments on one machine, one environment per zone. In other words, you virtualize multiple environments on the same machine. You can also split the administrator responsibilities of zones among different zone administrators.
- *Granularity*. You have the flexibility to choose the level of granularity in isolation provided by the zones.
- *Environment*. Think of a zone as a virtual machine that offers the isolated application environment that a computer machine would offer, only with a number of isolated virtual environments on one real machine. Other than that, the zones do not change the environment in which applications execute—for example, they do not introduce a new API to which applications have to be ported. They just provide standard Solaris environments separated from each other on a single system.

Before you can install a zone and use it, it must be configured.

Configuring a Zone

Exam Objective 6.2: *Given a zone configuration scenario, identify zone components and zonecfg resource parameters, allocate file system space, use the zonecfg command, describe the interactive configuration of a zone, and view the zone configuration file.*

You can use the `zonecfg` utility to set up the zone configuration, which includes creating and modifying the zone configuration. Configuring a zone includes configuring zone components—its resources and properties. A property may belong to the zone (a global property) or to a particular resource. The zone configuration consists of resources described here:

- *The file system (fs).* Each zone can have a number of file systems, which are mounted when the zone transitions from the installed state to the ready state. The file systems mounted in a zone can include the following:
  - File systems specified in the zone's `/etc/vfstab` file
  - AutoFS and file systems whose mounts are triggered by AutoFS
  - Other file systems mounted by the zone administrator
- *Net.* The virtual interface name (logical interface). The network interface is plumbed when the zone transitions from the installed state to the ready state.
- *Device.* The `zonecfg` command uses a rule-matching system to determine the devices that should be included in a specific zone; any device that matches one of the rules is included in the zone's `/dev` file system.
- *Resource control (rctl).* The global administrator can set the zone-wide resource controls, which limit the total resource usage of all process entities within the zone.
- *Attribute (attr).* General attributes (defined with name-value pairs) that can be used for user comments, for example.

Once you include a resource in a zone, you also need to assign appropriate properties to the resource. You can also assign properties to the zone, called global properties. The zone configuration contains the following properties:

- *Zone name.* Identifies the zone to the configuration and admin utilities. In naming a zone, obey the following rules:
  - Each zone must have a unique name.
  - A zone name is case sensitive.
  - A zone name must begin with an alphanumeric character.
- *Zone path.* Specifies path to the zone's file system. You must choose a name and path for your zone.
- *Autoboot.* A Boolean whose value indicates whether the zone is booted automatically when the system boots. The default value for this property is false.

- *Pool*. Specifies the name of the resource pool to which this zone must be bound when booted. Multiple zones can share the resources of one pool.
- *Net*. The IP address and the name of the physical network interface. Each zone that needs network connectivity must have one or more IP addresses associated with the logical network interfaces.

The `zonecfg` command can be used in any of the three available modes: interactive mode, command-line mode, or command-file mode.

You can use the `zonecfg` command to get through the following three stages of configurations:

- Creating the zone configuration
- Verifying that all the required information exists
- Committing the zone configuration—that is, saving the configuration parameters to the permanent storage.

You can start the interactive session with the `zonecfg` utility by issuing the following command from the global zone:

```
zonecfg -z <zoneName>
```

The `<zoneName>` argument specifies the name of the zone to be created. Then, on the `zonecfg` command prompt you can issue appropriate subcommands to perform various configuration tasks, as shown in Table 15-4.

exam watch

Note the difference between the `remove` and `delete` subcommands: The `remove` command removes a resource type or properties of a resource type, whereas `delete` destroys the entire zone configuration.

Note the following important points related to the zone configuration:

- A zone name must begin with an alphanumeric character followed by characters that may include alphanumeric characters, an underscore (_), or a hyphen (-). The name global and any name beginning with a prefix `SUNW` are reserved and therefore are not allowed.
- When you change the parameters of a running zone by using the `zonecfg` command, it does not affect the zone immediately. You must reboot the zone for the changes to take effect.

TABLE 15-4 Subcommands that can be used during an interactive session with the `zonecfg` utility

Subcommand	Description
`create`	Create an in-memory configuration for the zone. Without any option, it applies the Sun default settings. Use the `-t` option to use the configuration in a template, the `-F` option to overwrite the existing configuration, and the `-b` option to create a blank configuration with nothing set.
`set`	Set the value of a property, such as: `set autoboot=true.`
`add`	When used in the zone scope (global scope), adds a resource to the zone, and when used in the resource scope, adds a property (name and value) to the resource.
`remove`	When used in the zone scope, removes a resource type from the zone, and when used in the resource scope, removes a property (name and value) from the resource.
`delete`	Delete the configuration from the memory and from the storage. Must be used with the `-F` option.
`info`	Display information about the current configuration. If the resource is specified, only the information about that resource type is displayed.
`verify`	Check the correctness of the current configuration. Make sure all the required properties for a resource type have been set.
`export`	Print the configuration to the standard output, or to the specified file in the form that can be used in a command file.
`revert`	Roll back the configuration to the last committed state.
`commit`	Save the current configuration from memory in permanent storage.
`end`	End the resource specification.
`exit`	Exit the `zonecfg` session.

- The effect of the `delete` subcommand is instantaneous, no `commit` is required in this case, and the deleted zone cannot be reverted.
- Once you use the `exit` subcommand to exit the `zonecfg` utility, the configuration will be automatically committed even if you did not use the `commit` command.

The following exercise demonstrates how to use the `zonecfg` command in its interactive mode.

EXERCISE 15-1

Configuring a Zone

This exercise demonstrates how to use the `zoncefg` command and some of its subcommands to configure a zone.

1. Become superuser in the global zone. If you have not created any zone yet, you are in the global zone.
2. Create a zone named `senate-zone` (as an example) by issuing the following command:

   ```
   # zonecfg -z senate-zone
   ```

   If you are configuring this zone for the first time, the following system message will appear:

   ```
   senate-zone: No such zone configured
   Use 'create' to begin configuring a new zone.
   ```

3. Create the configuration for the `senate-zone` by issuing the `create` command at the zone prompt:

   ```
   zonecfg:senate-zone> create
   ```

4. Set the zone path to, for example, `/export/home/senate-zone`:

   ```
   zonecfg:senate-zone> set zonepath=/export/home/senate-zone
   ```

5. Set the value of the `autoboot` property so that the zone is automatically booted when the global zone is booted.

   ```
   zonecfg:senate-zone> set autoboot=true
   ```

6. Add the virtual network interface to the zone `senate-zone.`
   a. Start setting up the interface with the following command:

      ```
      zonecfg:senate-zone> add net
      ```

b. Assign the IP address 192.168.1.1 to the network interface.

```
zonecfg:senate-zone:net> set address=192.168.1.1
```

c. Set the physical device type for the network interface, such as hme0.

```
zonecfg:senate-zone:net> set physical=hme0
```

7. End this specification for the resource net:

```
zonecfg:senate-zone:net> end
```

The prompt returns back to the zone level:

```
zonecfg:senate-zone>
```

8. Exit the `zonecfg` command:

```
zonecfg:senate-zone> exit
```

Note that once you exit the `zonecfg` command, the configuration will be automatically committed even if you did not use the `commit` command.

After you have configured a non-global zone, you can install it after verifying that the zone can be installed safely on your system's configuration. After that, you can perform other administration tasks on the zone.

Administering a Zone

Exam Objective 6.3: *Given a scenario, use the zoneadm command to view, install, boot, halt, reboot, and delete a zone.*

For each zone that is in the ready, running, or shutting-down state, there is one zone administration daemon, `zoneadmd`, running to manage the zone, which includes booting and shutting down in addition to other tasks. If the daemon is not running for any reason, an invocation of the `zoneadm` command will start it. Although the daemon does the work, you use the `zoneadm` command to administer the zone.

You can use the `zoneadm` command from the global zone to install and administer non-global zones. By using the `zoneadm` command, you can perform the following tasks:

- *Verify a zone.* It's a good idea to verify a zone's configuration before installing it. You can use the `verify` subcommand with the `zoneadm` command for this task. Remember that the verify subcommand is also available in the `zonecfg` utility.
- *Install and uninstall a zone.* The `install` subcommand is used to install a configured zone, and the `uninstall` subcommand to uninstall an installed zone. Uninstalling a zone involves uninstalling all the files under the zone's root file system. If you do not use the `-F` option, the command prompts you for confirmation.
- *Boot or reboot a zone.* The `boot` subcommand is used to boot a zone in installed or ready state and puts the zone into the running state, whereas the `reboot` command is used to boot a zone that is halted.
- *Display information about zones.* Display information about zones in various states by using the `list` subcommand.
- *Halt a zone.* The `halt` subcommand is used with the `zoneadm` command to halt a running zone. Halting a zone removes both the application environment and the virtual platform for the zone. Halting a zone kills all the processes in the zone, unconfigures the devices, unplumbs the network interfaces, unmounts the file systems, and destroys the kernel data structures. The zone is put back into the installed state. If a zone fails to halt, you may need to intervene and perform a few tasks manually. The most common reason for a halt failure is the inability of the system to unmount all the file systems in the zone.

The subcommands used with the `zoneadm` command to perform zone administration tasks are shown in Table 15-5. These subcommands have very trivial names. However, the trick here is to understand the conditions under which each of these commands can be issued. In other words, before issuing any of these subcommands you have to ask two questions:

- Which state is the zone in? You can find that out with the `zoneadm list -v` command.
- Does the subcommand I'm going to use apply on this state?

TABLE 15-5 Subcommands with the `zoneadm` command to perform various tasks (commands are issued from the global zone)

Task	The `zoneadm` Command
Verify a configured zone.	`zoneadm -z <zoneName> verify`
Install a configured zone.	`zoneadm -z <zoneName> install`
Get information about zones.	`zoneadm -z <zoneName> list <option>` Without any option, all running zones are listed. The option `-c` means display all configured zones, `-i` means display all installed zones, `-v` means display verbose information: zone ID, current state, and root directory.
Uninstall a zone.	`zoneadm -z <zoneName> uninstall`
Transition an installed zone to the ready state.	`zoneadm -z <zoneName> ready`
Boot a zone that is in an installed state or a ready state. Booting puts a zone into the running state.	`zoneadm -z <zoneName> boot`
Halt a running zone.	`zoneadm -z <zoneName> halt`

To understand in which zone state a specific subcommand can be applied, you need to understand the states we described previously in this section. The relationships of the states of a zone with each other defined by the transition of states by using the subcommands (with the `zoneadm` command) are shown in Figure 15-3, where the arrows indicate the transitions between states.

After a zone has been installed, you can log into the zone by using the `zlogin` command to complete its application environment. The `zlogin` command can also be used to shut down the zone as shown here:

```
zlogin <zoneName> shutdown
```

If you want to delete a zone, it must be put back into the configured state—that is, if it is running, it must be shut down either by using the `halt` command or by using the `shutdown` command, and then it must be uninstalled. Exercise 15-2 demonstrates how to delete a non-global zone.

FIGURE 15-3 Various zone states in the life cycle of a zone (the `create` and `delete` subcommands are used with the `zonecfg` command, and the other subcommands shown are used with the `zoneadm` command)

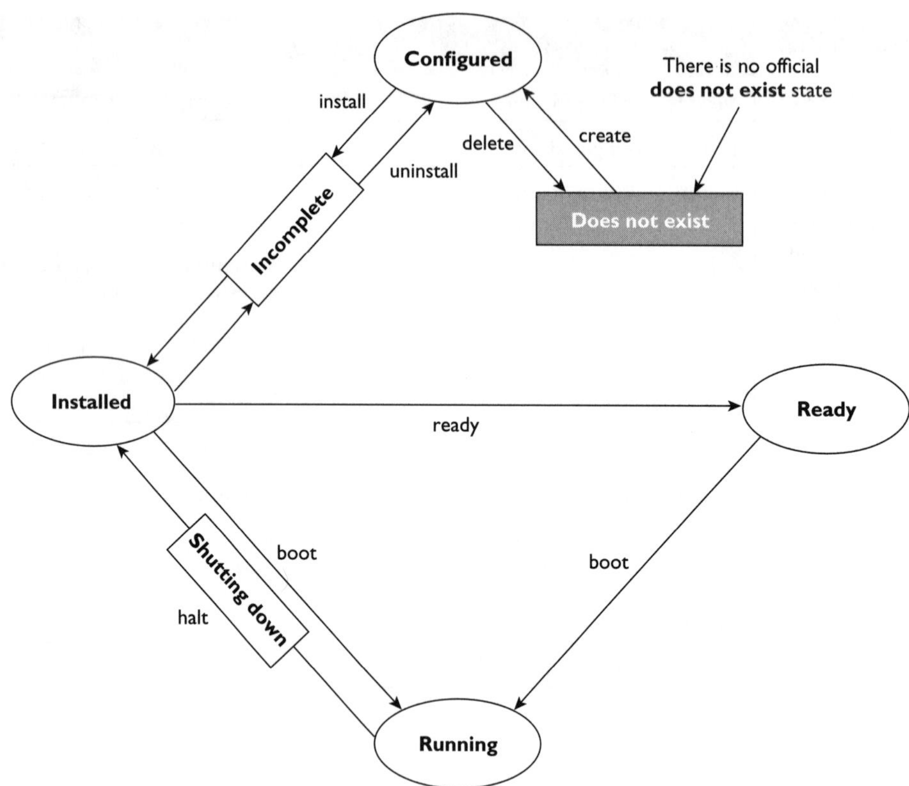

EXERCISE 15-2

Deleting a Non-Global Zone

This exercise shows you how to delete a running zone named senate-zone, as an example. All the commands in this exercise are issued from the global zone.

1. Shut down the zone senate-zone by issuing the following command from the global zone:

```
zlogin senate-zone shutdown
```

2. Uninstall the root file system for `senate-zone` by issuing the following command:

```
zoneadm -z senate-zone uninstall -F
```

3. Delete the configuration for `senate-zone` by issuing the following command:

```
zonecfg -z senate-zone delete -F
```

4. Verify the zone deletion. To verify that senate-zone is not listed, issue the following command:

```
zoneadm list -iv
```

The output of this command will be like the following:

```
ID NAME STATE PATH
0 global running /
```

The three most important takeaways from this chapter are:

- The JumpStart method is used to automate the Solaris installation on a group of machines with identical configuration and software requirements. The automation is achieved by storing the information required for installation in a number of files such as `sysidcfg`, `rules`, and profile files. The flash archive method is used to install the image of an already installed Solaris environment.
- An x86 machine that supports PXE boot can be booted over a network.
- Solaris zones technology allows you to install multiple separated Solaris environments on the same machine instead of on separate machines.

CERTIFICATION SUMMARY

The custom JumpStart installation method enables you to automate the Solaris installation on a group of machines with identical configuration and software requirements. You store the configuration requirements in the `sysidcfg` file, and the software requirements in the profile file. You associate a machine with its profile by combining some system attributes of the machine, such as host name or network address, with the name of the profile file into a rule that is an entry in the `rules` file. The `rules` file, the `sysidcfg` file, and the profile files are all text files that you write. The `rules` file must have the name `rules`, but you can give any meaningful name to a profile file. All these files are stored in the JumpStart directory on a server machine, and the location of the directory is reported to the JumpStart client when it is added to the server with the `add_install_client` command. The images of the Solaris Software are copied from the Solaris Software CDs (or DVD) to the install server by using the `setup_install_server` command.

If you want to make clones of an already installed system, use the flash archive installation method, which involves using a standard installation method to install the image (flash archive) of an already installed system. This is a quick and robust way of performing a large number of identical installations. If your x86 machine supports Intel Preboot Execution Environment (PXE) and it has no local media to boot from, you can boot it over the network by using PXE boot; you can then install Solaris by using a standard Solaris installation method.

Solaris 10 introduces zone technology to set up multiple Solaris environments called zones on one machine, and applications running in one zone are isolated from application running in other zones as if they had a machine of their own. You use the `zonecfg` utility to create and configure a zone, and the `zoneadm` utility to administer the zone after it has been configured.

INSIDE THE EXAM

Comprehend

- You create the `rules` file, but it is the `rules.ok` file (created by the `check` script after verifying the correctness of the `rules` file and the associated profile files) that is actually used by the JumpStart program.
- Before using the Solaris flash archive method, make sure that the planned master and clone systems have the same hardware architecture.
- Solaris flash archive and PXE are not full-fledged independent installation methods. Flash archive refers to using the image of an already installed system, and PXE refers to booting over the network; the installation in both cases is performed by using a standard installation method, such as the Solaris installation program.
- If the `zoneadmd` daemon is not running, it automatically starts when you invoke the `zoneadm` command.

Look Out

- You can give any name to a profile file, but the `rules` file must be named `rules`, and you must verify the correctness of the `rules` file and the associated profile files by running the `check` script.
- If a keyword appears multiple times in the `sysidcfg` file, only the first instance of the keyword is considered valid. The `network_interface` keyword is an exception to this rule.
- When you change the parameters of a running zone by using the `zonecfg` command, it does not affect the zone immediately. You must reboot the zone for the changes to take effect.
- This effect of the `delete` command is instantaneous, no commit is required in this case, and the deleted zone cannot be reverted.
- The `verify` subcommand is available in both the utilities `zonecfg` and `zonadm`.

Memorize

- The `begin` scripts, the `finish` scripts, the `rules` file, and the profile files live in the JumpStart directory on a diskette for a standalone system, and on a server for installation over a network.
- The keywords and values in a profile file are case sensitive, but the keywords in the `sysidcfg` file are not case sensitive.
- The first line in a profile file must specify the keyword `install_type`.
- The zone names are case sensitive.

TWO-MINUTE DRILL

Understanding JumpStart

- For the JumpStart installation to work, you must prepare the `rules` file that contains a rule for each machine or group of machines on which the JumpStart will perform installations.
- Each rule points to a profile file that is used to perform installations on each machine that matches the system attributes in the rule. You create a profile for a machine or a group of machines on which an installation needs to be performed.
- Before the JumpStart program can use the rules and the profiles, you need to run the `check` script to validate the rules and the associated profile files. If the rules and the profiles are verified to be correct, the `rules.ok` file is generated, which is used by the JumpStart program.
- If the installation is to be made over the network, you need to set up the `rules` and profile files on a server in the JumpStart directory.

Implementing JumpStart

- You implement the JumpStart server by setting up an install server, a boot server, and the JumpStart directory.
- You set up the install server by copying the images of the installation software to the local disk of the server machine by using the `setup_install_server` machine.
- You set up the boot server by copying the boot image from the installation CD (or DVD) to the server machine by using the `setup_install_server` machine.
- You use the `add_install_client` command to add clients to the install server.

Understanding and Using the Flash Archive

- The flash archive installation method involves creating a reference image of an already existing Solaris system and then using any basic installation method to install that image on multiple machines, which would be clones.

- The `flar` command combined with subcommands such as `create` and `info` is used to manage the flash archives.

Booting and Installing with PXE

- You can boot an x86-based machine that supports Intel Preboot Execution Environment (PXE) over the network; you can install Solaris on it by using a standard installation method.
- To set up a DHCP server to make a PXE boot work, you can use either the DHCP manager or the command-line utility `dhcpconfig`.

Managing Solaris Zones

- At any time during its life cycle, a zone is in one of its six possible states: configured, incomplete, installed, ready, running, or shutting down.
- The `zonecfg` command is used to create and configure a zone.
- The `zoneadm` command is used to administer a zone after it has been configured, such as installing/uninstalling, booting, running, and halting.

SELF TEST

The following questions will help you measure your understanding of the material presented in this chapter. Read all the choices carefully because there might be more than one correct answer. Choose all correct answers for each question.

1. Which of the following commands can be used to set up a server that an install client can use for Solaris software to be installed on the client?

   A. `add_install_server`

   B. `setup_install_server`

   C. `add_install_client`

   D. `setup_install_client`

   E. `setup_solaris_software`

2. Which of the following files contains the names of `begin` scripts to be used in JumpStart installations?

   A. `rules.ok`

   B. a profile file

   C. `check`

   D. `sysidcfg`

3. Which of the following methods automates the installation of Solaris 10?

   A. Solaris installation program

   B. JumpStart

   C. Flash archive

   D. PXE

4. Which of the following files is read by the JumpStart program to discover where to find the installation software requirements of an installation client?

   A. A profile file

   B. The `rules` file

   C. The `rules.ok` file

   D. The `sysidcfg` file

5. Which of the following scripts is run to validate some of the files to be used in a JumpStart installation?

   A. `check`

   B. `validate`

   C. `preinstall`

   D. `profile`

6. Which of the following are the requirements for a PXE installation?

   A. DHCP server

   B. The installation client machine supports Intel Preboot Execution Environment.

   C. Flash archive

   D. Install server

   E. JumpStart program

7. Which of the following are the states of a Solaris zone?

   A. Sleeping

   B. Waiting

   C. Running

   D. Configured

   E. Incomplete

   F. Halt

8. Which of the following tasks can be performed by using the `zonecfg` utility?

   A. Check the correctness of current zone configuration.

   B. Display information about the current configuration.

   C. Install a zone.

   D. Boot a zone.

9. Which of the following tasks can be performed by using the `zoneadm` utility?

   A. Check the correctness of current zone configuration.

   B. Display information about a zone.

   C. Install a zone.

   D. Boot a zone.

   E. Uninstall a zone.

SELF TEST ANSWERS

1. ☑ **B**. The `setup_install_server` command is used to set up the install server for the JumpStart method.
   ☒ **A** is incorrect because there is no such installation command as `add_install_server`. **C** is incorrect because `add_install_client` is used to add a client to the install server that has already been set up. **D** and **E** are incorrect because there are no such install commands as `setup_install_client` or `setup_solaris_software`.

2. ☑ **A**. An entry in the `rules.ok` file contains the mandatory fields, which are system attributes and the name of a profile file, and optional attributes, which are the names of `begin` and `finish` scripts to be executed at the beginning and end of a JumpStart installation.
   ☒ **B** is incorrect because a profile file contains the installation requirements, not the name of the `begin` or `finish` scripts. **C** is incorrect because the `check` script is used to validate the `rules.ok` and profile files, and **D** is incorrect because the `sysidcfg` file contains the configuration information, not the names of the `begin` or `finish` scripts.

3. ☑ **B**. JumpStart lets you automate the installation by providing the installation information through a set of files such as `rules.ok`, `prfile`, and `sysidcfg` files.
   ☒ **A** is incorrect because Solaris installation program will prompt you for the information; by itself it does not offer an automatic installation. **C** is incorrect because a Solaris flash archive is just an image of an already installed system that can be installed by using any of the available installation methods. **D** is incorrect because PXE is used to boot an x86 machine over the network, after which any installation method can be used to install.

4. ☑ **C**. The JumpStart program reads the installation requirements from the profile file whose name is listed in the `rules.ok` file.
   ☒ **A** is incorrect because the profile file contains the installation requirements, not the name of the file that contains the installation requirements. **B** is incorrect because you create the `rules` file, and the `check` script after validating the rules, the profile files generates the `rules.ok` file from the `rules` file, and it is the `rules.ok` file that is read by the JumpStart program. **D** is incorrect because the `sysidcfg` file contains the configuration information.

5. ☑ **A**. The `check` script is executed to validate the `rules` and profile files; if it finds them accurate, the script generates the `rules.ok` file, which is used by the JumpStart program.
   ☒ **B**, **C**, and **D** are incorrect because there are no such scripts as `validate`, `preinstall`, or `profile` that are used to validate the rules and the profiles.

6. ☑ **A**, **B**, and **D**. Support for the PXE boot, use of the DHCP server to obtain IP address and install parameters, and the presence of an install server to store the installation software are the requirements for PXE installation.
   ☒ **C** and **E** are incorrect because after the PXE boot, the install client can use any standard installation method to install Solaris software. It does not have to use flash archive or JumpStart.

7. ☑ **C**, **D**, and **E**. A zone is in the configured state when it's configured, and the configuration parameters are saved in permanent storage. It is in a running state when at least one process has been started, and in an incomplete state while it's in transition between the configured and the installed state.
   ☒ **A** is incorrect because sleeping is a process state, not a zone state. **B** is incorrect because waiting is not the name of any zone state. **F** is incorrect because halt is not a state—it is a command that can be used to put a running system back into the installed state.

8. ☑ **A** and **B**. You can use the `verify` and `info` subcommands with the `zonecfg` command to check the correctness of current zone configuration and to obtain information about the configuration, respectively.
   ☒ **C** and **D** are incorrect because the zones are installed and booted by using the `zoneadm` command, not the `zonecfg` command.

9. ☑ **A**, **B**, **C**, **D**, and **E**. You can use the `verify` and `list` subcommands with the `zoneadm` command to check the correctness of current zone configuration and to obtain the information about the zones. You can use the `install` and `uninstall` subcommands to install and uninstall a zone, respectively, and you can use the boot subcommand to boot a zone.

A

About the CD

The CD-ROM included with this book comes complete with MasterExam and the electronic version of the book. The software is easy to install on any Windows 98/NT/2000/XP computer and must be installed to access the MasterExam feature. You may, however, browse the electronic book directly from the CD without installation. To register for a second bonus MasterExam, simply click the Online Training link on the Main Page and follow the directions to the free online registration.

System Requirements

Software requires Windows 98 or higher and Internet Explorer 5.0 or above and 20MB of hard disk space for full installation. The electronic book requires Adobe Acrobat Reader.

Installing and Running MasterExam

If your computer CD-ROM drive is configured to auto run, the CD-ROM will automatically start up upon inserting the disk. From the opening screen you may install MasterExam by pressing the *MasterExam* button. This will begin the installation process and create a program group named "LearnKey." To run MasterExam, use START | PROGRAMS | LEARNKEY. If the auto run feature did not launch your CD, browse to the CD and click the "LaunchTraining.exe" icon.

MasterExam

MasterExam provides you with a simulation of the actual exam. The number of questions, the types of questions, and the time allowed are intended to be an accurate representation of the exam environment. You have the option to take an open-book exam, including hints, references, and answers; a closed-book exam; or the timed MasterExam simulation.

When you launch MasterExam, a digital clock display will appear in the upper left-hand corner of your screen. The clock will continue to count down to zero unless you choose to end the exam before the time expires.

Electronic Book

The entire contents of the Study Guide are provided in PDF. Adobe's Acrobat Reader has been included on the CD.

Help

A help file is provided through the help button on the main page in the lower left-hand corner. An individual help feature is also available through MasterExam.

Removing Installation(s)

MasterExam is installed to your hard drive. For *best* results for removal of programs, use the START | PROGRAMS | LEARNKEY | UNINSTALL options to remove MasterExam.

Technical Support

For questions regarding the technical content of the electronic book or MasterExam, please visit www.osborne.com or email customer.service@mcgraw-hill.com. For customers outside the 50 United States, email international_cs@mcgraw-hill.com.

LearnKey Technical Support

For technical problems with the software (installation, operation, removing installations), please visit www.learnkey.com or email techsupport@learnkey.com.

Glossary

`add_install_client` A command used with the JumpStart automatic installation method to inform the server about the clients that can use network installation.

address resolution protocol (ARP) A TCP/IP protocol and a utility based on the protocol that is used by a machine to resolve layer-3 (Network layer) addresses such as IP addresses to layer-2 (Data Link layer) MAC addresses such as Ethernet addresses.

ARP *See* address resolution protocol.

AutoFS A kernel file system that supports automatic mounting and unmounting of remote file systems.

`automount` A command used to update the autofs mount points when necessary, after the system is up and running.

`automountd` An NFS daemon that handles mount and unmount requests from the autofs service.

`banner` A command used at the boot prompt to display the current power-on banner.

block A unit of disk space occupied by a file. The blocks are measured in two sizes: physical block size, which is the size of the smallest block that the disk controller can read or write; and logical block size, which is the size of the block that UNIX (Solaris in our case) uses to read or write files. The physical block size is usually 512 bytes, and the logical block size is set (by default) to the page size of the system, which is 8 Kbytes for a UFS file system, the default file system for Solaris.

block size *See* block.

boot The process, also called *bootstrapping*, that takes the machine from the point where the machine is turned on to the point where the operating system takes over the machine.

bootblk A primary program loaded by PROM that finds the secondary boot program ufsboot located in the UFS file system on the default boot device, and loads it into the memory, which in turn loads the kernel into the memory.

boot block The area (sectors 1 to 15) on the hard disk or other bootable device such as a CD-ROM that stores the boot program, bootblk.

boot server The server that provides information that a JumpStart client (the machine on which JumpStart will install Solaris) needs to boot over the network.

bootstrap *See* boot.

Bourne shell A UNIX shell introduced by S. R. Bourne of Bell Laboratories in New Jersey.

byte The smallest group of binary digits (bits) that the computer works with. The most common byte size is 8 bits, also called octal.

CacheFS Cache File System; uses the local disk drives to cache the data from the slow file systems such as CD-ROM drives or network file systems (NFS). This helps improve system performance.

CDE Common Desktop Environment; a windowing environment that offers some GUI tools such as the CDE process manager to view and manage system processes.

chmod A command used to modify permissions of existing files and directories.

CLI A console or terminal session in which commands are issued at the command prompt.

client A host machine (or an application) that can make a request for a service provided by another application running most probably on another machine on the network called a server. An example is a web browser making a request to a web server for a web page.

client/server networking A networking model in which some machines are clients and other machines are servers. The client makes a request for a service and the server host responds to that request. Most of the existing networks are based on the client/server model.

cluster A logical collection of multiple packages (software modules) that are related to each other by their functionality.

command line interface *See* CLI.

Common Desktop Environment *See* CDE.

concatenation volume A volume that writes data on multiple components sequentially; that is, it writes the data to the first available component until it is full and then moves to write to the next component; no parallel access.

configuration server A server that contains the customized configuration files used to install Solaris in the JumpStart installation method.

core files Files that are created when a process or an application crashes. They contain the crash information used for debugging the problem.

Core System Support Software Group The software group that contains the packages that provide the minimum support required to boot and run a networked Solaris system.

`cp` A command used to copy a file to a file, a file (or files) to a directory, or a directory to a directory.

`cpio` A command used to copy file archives in and out: "copy in" means extract files from the standard input, and "copy out" means read a list of file path names from the standard input and copy those files to the standard output. You can use this command to transfer individual files or groups of files from one file system to another file system.

crash dump files Files that are created when the system crashes. They contain the crash information used for debugging the problem.

C shell A UNIX shell that was written to resemble the C programming language.

cylinder The space on a disk that consists of a set of tracks with the same radius, one from each platter from the stack.

daemons Processes that run in the background to manage various system- and utility-related functions.

dd A command used to make a literal block-level (raw) copy of a complete UFS file system to another file system or to a tape.

devalias An OpenBoot command used to display or create device aliases. The devalias command creates a temporary alias that is lost when the system is reset or power-cycled. Use the nvalias command to create permanent aliases.

Developer Software Group Contains the packages for the End User Solaris Software Group plus additional support for software development, which includes libraries, manpages, and programming tools. Compilers are not included.

df A command used to display disk space usage at the file system level.

dfshares A command used to display information about the resources available to a host from local and remote systems.

differential backup A type of backup that backs up all the changed files since the last full backup.

directory A binary file containing a list of other files; may include other directories as well.

disk controller A chip and its circuitry that instructs the read/write head to move across the platter to read/write data.

disk label The first disk sector that contains information about disk geometry and partitions.

DNS Domain Name System; the name of a TCP/IP-based protocol and the server based on this protocol used to resolve IP addresses to host names and vice versa. It is the standard name service used on the Internet.

domain An administrative entity that consists of several computers on a network that can share some administrative files.

Domain Name System *See* DNS.

du A command used to obtain a report on disk usage at the directory and file levels.

eeprom The utility that Solaris offers to change the values of the OpenBoot configuration variables.

encapsulation The process of pre-pending a header to a data packet received from the upper layer.

End User Solaris Software Group Solaris installation software group that contains the packages to provide the minimum support required to boot and run a networked Solaris system and the Common Desktop Environment (CDE).

Ethernet A popular physical network technology standard that utilizes the Carrier Sense Multiple Access with Collision Detection (CSMA/CD) mechanism to allow multiple stations to share a single medium of transmission.

Ethernet address A 48-bit MAC address burned on a network adapter in a machine connected to an Ethernet network.

Fault Management Resource Identifier (FMRI) The name for a service instance such as svc:/application/print/server:default for the default instance of a print scheduler.

FDDI Fiber Distributed Data Interface; a physical network technology based on fiber optics.

file The smallest unit of data stored on a medium such as a disk.

file system The way an operating system organizes files on a storage device.

File Transfer Protocol A protocol and a utility (ftp) based on that protocol used to transfer files from one system to another on the network or across the Internet.

flash archive An installation method used to make a number of identical Solaris installations by using an image of an already installed system.

fsck File system check; a command used to find inconsistencies in the file system and repair them.

ftp *See* File Transfer Protocol.

full backup A file system backup that copies a whole file system from the system to a storage device such as a tape.

GID Group ID; an identification number assigned to a group.

`grep` A UNIX command used to search files for a specific pattern.

group A logical collection of users created for the purpose of assigning permissions.

`groupadd` A command used to add a new group to the system.

`groupdel` A command used to delete a group from the system.

`groupmod` A command used to modify some properties of a group in the system.

`halt` A command just like the `poweroff` command that synchronizes the file systems and stops the processor. It's not recommended because it does not shut down all the processes.

hard link A pointer to a file that is indistinguishable from the original file; that is, any changes to a file are effective regardless of the name used to refer to the file: the link name or the original file name. Furthermore, a hard link can only point to a file and not a directory. Also, a hard link cannot span file systems, that is, the link and the file have to be on the same file system because both have the same inode number.

High Sierra file system The first file system for CD-ROMs. It's official standard version is ISO 9660 with the Rock Ridge extensions, which provide all the UFS features and file types except the write and the hard links features. It is a read-only file system

host Any computer connected to a network.

host name The name of a computer connected to a network.

hot spare A disk slice that is reserved for automatic substitution in case the corresponding data slice fails.

hot spare pool A collection (an ordered list) of hot spares that SVM uses to provide increased data availability and fault tolerance for a RAID1 (mirrored) volume and a RAID 5 (striped data with striped parity) volume.

HSFS *See* High Sierra file system.

HTTP *See* HyperText Transfer Protocol.

hub The central device in a network based on the star topology. Each computer is connected to a different port on the hub. A hub receives a signal on one port and repeats it on all other ports, and is not aware of the MAC addresses. If it simply provides the electrical connection between ports, it is called a passive hub, and it is typically un-powered. If it amplifies the signal it receives while repeating it on multiple ports, it is called an active port, and it is powered.

HyperText Transfer Protocol The protocol, commonly known as HTTP, on which web browsers and web servers (which make the World Wide Web) are based.

incremental backup A type of backup that backs up only those files from a file system or directory that have changed since the previous backup.

`init` A command that kills all active processes and synchronizes the file systems before changing to the target run level (0 or 5).

`inittab` A file with the path /etc/inittab used to describe the run levels and set the default run level for the system. This file contains two important pieces of information for the init process: what processes to start, monitor, and restart if they terminate; and what to do if the system enters a new run level.

inode A data structure that stores the information about a file such as the file type, the permissions on the file, and the number of hard links to the file.

install server A server that contains the Solaris installation files (an image of the Solaris operating environment from the installation CDs or DVD) used for installation over a network in the JumpStart method.

IP address A 4-octet (32-bit) number used to uniquely identify a host connected to a network.

IP datagram A data packet in the Network layer.

IPv6 The latest version of the Internet Protocol (IP) that allows for better security and increased available addresses. An IP address in IPv6 is 128 bits long.

JumpStart A method to automate the Solaris installation by storing the installation information in a set of files (that is, pre-configuring) so that the install process requires little or no input.

kernel The core of an operating system that communicates with the computer hardware, schedules and executes the system commands, and manages all of the daemons and file systems.

`kill` A command used to send a signal to one or more processes. For example, `kill -9` will terminate (kill) a process promptly, and `kill -25` will start a stopped process.

Korn shell A UNIX shell developed by David G. Korn at Bell Laboratories in New Jersey.

LAN *See* local area network.

LDAP *See* Lightweight Directory Access Protocol.

Lightweight Directory Access Protocol An Internet protocol on which the directory service popularly knows as LDAP is based. It is a lighter version of the original directory protocol called X.500, which is a very complex protocol, and its closest implementation is the original Novell Directory Service (NDS), which offers more features than LDAP and was made LDAP compatible due to the popularity of LDAP.

local area network A computer network that is confined to a local area such as a room, a building, or a group of local buildings.

`lpadmin` A command used to add a new printer or to change the configuration of an existing printer.

LP print service A set of software utilities that automate the process of sharing printers to print files.

`lpsched` A daemon that manages the print requests on a system on which the print server is running. When it is stopped, print requests are neither accepted nor printed.

`ls` A command used to list the contents of a directory, that is, the names and other information about the files and subdirectories.

MAC address A media access control address of a networked machine used in the second layer (Data Link layer) to identify the network connection. It's also called physical address or hardware address. A MAC address on an Ethernet network is called an Ethernet address.

`man` A command, an abbreviation for "manual," used to access information about the UNIX commands on your system. You can use this command to learn more about other commands.

manpages The information database accessed by the `man` command is popularly called manpages.

metadevice An SVM term used to refer to a set of physical disk slices that appears to the system as a single logical device; also called virtual device.

mount point The location (directory) on a partition on the hard drive where a mounted file system's directory hierarchy starts. You can access the file system by using the mount point.

mirroring The process of designating a disk drive as a duplicate (mirror) of another disk drive; both disks are attached to the same disk controller. When the OS writes data to one disk drive, the same data also gets written to the mirror disk.

`mkdir` A command used to create a directory.

`mount` A command used to mount a file system as well as remote resources.

`mountall` A command used to mount all file systems that are specified in the `/etc/vfstab` file. This command runs automatically when the system enters the multiuser mode.

mounting The process of attaching a file system to the directory tree of the system to make it available to users.

`mv` A command used to move files or directories from one location to another.

network A group of computers connected together to share resources such as printers and data.

Network File System A file system that makes the location of the machine on which the file system exists transparent to the users and the applications. Using NFS, a user can mount a file system that exists on a remote NFS server, and use it as if it exists on the local machine.

Network Information Service A service that manages the information specific to a network such as information about machine names, user names, network services, and so forth. The focus of NIS is to make network administration easier by providing central management for distributed information.

Network Information Service Plus A service used to manage network information about machine addresses, mail, network interfaces, network service, and security. It is similar to NIS in terms of what it manages and how it manages such as central management for distributed information. However, it is not an extension to NIS. Unlike NIS, it is hierarchical, more dynamic (can conform to the requirements of an organization), and offers more features such as security.

`newfs` A command used to create a UFS file system.

NFS *See* Network File System.

NIS *See* Network Information Service.

NIS maps The databases used to store the NIS namespace information. These maps were designed to replace the `/etc` files and other configuration files.

NIS+ *See* Network Information Service Plus.

Non-Volatile Random Access Memory A term that refers to the chip on which OpenBoot system configuration variables are stored.

NVRAM *See* Non-Volatile Random Access Memory.

OpenBoot Short for OpenBoot PROM (Programmable Read Only Memory) monitor; refers to firmware that controls the boot process of a Sun workstation, which includes checking the hardware devices connected to the system and loading the operating system.

OpenBoot configuration variables The variables that govern the boot process; also called NVRAM configuration variables.

operating system The set of programs that manages all system operations and provides a means of communication between the user and the resources available to that user.

package The smallest installable modular unit of Solaris software. In other words, a package is a collection of software, that is, a set of files and directories, grouped into a single entity for modular installation and functionality.

packet The basic unit of information that travels over the network or the Internet.

`passwd` The `/etc/passwd` file that contains the user account information. It is also the command used to change a user's password.

patch A software component that offers a small upgrade to an existing system such as an additional feature, a bug fix, a driver for a hardware device, or a solution to address issues such as security or stability problems.

`patchadd` A command used to install a patch or patches on the system.

`patchrm` A command used to remove, or back out, a patch from a system.

path A reference to a file's location.

pcfs *See* personal computer file system.

personal computer file system A file system used to gain read and write access to disks formatted for the disk operating system (DOS) running on the PCs.

`pkgadd` A command used to install software package on the system.

`pkgchk` A command used to check the accuracy of installed files, including the integrity of directory structures and files in a package. You can also use this command to display information about the package files.

`pkginfo` A command used to display information about a package.

`pkgrm` A command used to remove a previously installed package.

POST A part of the boot process that scans the system to verify the installed hardware and memory. POST runs diagnostics on hardware devices and builds a device tree, which is a data structure describing the devices attached to the system.

`poweroff` A command just like the `halt` command that synchronizes the file systems and stops the processor. It's not recommended because it does not shut down all the processes.

power on self test *See* POST.

print server A server that manages print services.

profile A set of specific software installation requirements defined in a file called a profile file. It specifies the elements of installation that you would otherwise determine interactively in a manual installation, such as the software group to install.

programmable read only memory *See* OpenBoot PROM.

PROM *See* programmable read only memory.

`prstat` A command used to display information about selective processes that will be refreshed periodically.

`ps` A command used to display a listing of processes running on the system.

RAID Redundant Arrays of Inexpensive Disks; a term that refers to the method of writing the same data to several disks at the same time to offer fault tolerance in case of data loss.

RARP A protocol to resolve the hardware address of a machine to its IP address; opposite of ARP.

RBAC Role-based access control; a security model for controlling user access to tasks that will normally be restricted to the superuser. The RBAC model offers a more secure and flexible alternative to the superuser model by assigning security rights to what is called a role and then assigning the role to a user.

`reboot` A command that synchronizes the file systems and initiates a multiuser reboot.

Redundant Arrays of Inexpensive Disks *See* RAID.

repeater A device that can be used to amplify or to repeat an existing signal.

Reverse Address Resolution Protocol *See* RARP.

`rlogin` A command used to establish a remote login session from a local console.

`rm` A command used to delete files and directories.

`rmdir` A command used to delete a directory.

role-based access control *See* RBAC.

router An Internet device that receives a frame from a computer (or another router), retrieves the datagram from the frame, figures out (possibly with the help of the routing table) the next recipient, which may be a local host or the next hop router, puts it into a new frame, and sends it.

rule A statement that uses a set of system attributes to identify a group of machines and links it to a profile file. You define the rules in a text file whose name must be `rules`. Before JumpStart can use the `rules` file and the profiles, you need to perform a validation by running the `check` script. This script verifies that the rules in the `rules` file and the associated profiles are set up correctly, and if they are, the script creates the `rules.ok` file, the file that is actually used by the JumpStart program.

`rules.ok` file *See* rule.

run level The state of a system denoted by a digit or a letter. The Solaris system always runs in one of a set of well-defined run levels.

Scalable Processor Architecture (SPARC) A term that refers to Sun Microsystems' proprietary processor design.

server A host and an application running on the host that accepts a request from a client and serves the request.

service instance A service running with a specific configuration. A service may have more than one instance, and a service is managed by SMF by its instance name: FMRI.

service management facility An infrastructure that augments the traditional UNIX startup scripts, init run levels, and configuration files to make the service management more robust.

shell The interface between the user (or an application) and the kernel. The shell interprets the commands from the user for the kernel.

`shutdown` A command that calls the `init` program to shut down the system; the default target run level is S.

signal A message sent to a process in order to affect its operation. Solaris supports the concept of communicating with a process by sending it a signal.

Simple Mail Transfer Protocol A TCP/IP protocol used by mail servers to exchange messages over the Internet.

SMC *See* Solaris Management Console.

SMTP *See* Simple Mail Transfer Protocol.

software group A grouping of software packages and clusters. During initial installation of Solaris, you select a software group to install based on the functions you want your system to perform.

Solaris Management Console A graphical user interface (GUI) utility to access a set of administrative tools.

Solaris Volume Manager A software product used to manage huge amounts of data spread over a large number of disks.

Solaris zone A virtual operating system environment created by one instance of the Solaris operating system. There may be more than one zone on the same machine, and processes running in one zone cannot monitor or affect processes running in other zones. Processes running in different zones can only interact with each other through network APIs.

SPARC *See* Scalable Processor Architecture.

state database A database that contains the configuration and status information about the disk sets, volumes, and hot spares in a disk set managed by the SVM.

sticky bit A permission set used to ensure that a file can only be deleted by its owner.

Stop-A The keyboard combination used to bring a system to the PROM console: the `ok` prompt.

striping A process that breaks the data into small pieces called *stripes*, which are written to multiple disks simultaneously. Because the read/write heads are working simultaneously, striping improves read/write performance.

superblock The area of a disk that contains the file system information.

SVM *See* Solaris Volume Manager.

`swap` A command used to monitor the swap space.

swapfs (SWAPFS) A virtual file system that manages the swap space.

swap space The disk slices, also called swap slices, used for storing virtual memory.

switch A network device such as a hub, but unlike a hub, a switch is aware of the MAC addresses of the computers connected to it and repeats a received signal only on a port to which the intended recipient of the data is connected.

symbolic link An indirect pointer to a file; that is, its directory entry contains the name of the file to which it points. Furthermore, it may span file systems and may point to either a directory or a file.

syslog The system message logging that automatically saves (logs) various system errors and warnings in the message files.

`tar` A command, short for *T*ape *AR*chive, used to archive all the files together into a single file.

TCP One of the two standard protocols at the Transport layer of the TCP/IP protocol stack. The other is User Datagram Protocol (UDP). TCP provides connection-oriented, reliable data delivery service.

TCP/IP A suite of network communications protocols that consists of five layers: Application, Transport, Internet, Network Interface, and Physical. These layers can be mapped to the seven layers of the OSI model.

tmpfs A memory-based file system that maps the `/tmp` directory on the hard disk to the memory. As a result, the applications (such as compiler and database management system products) that use the `/tmp` directory for storing and retrieving their data improve performance.

`touch` A command used to create an empty file.

track Concentric circles on a disk platter to store data.

Transmission Control Protocol *See* TCP.

udf Universal disk format; a format file system used to store information on digital versatile disk or digital video disk (DVD).

UDP User Datagram Protocol; one of the two standard protocols at the Transport layer of the TCP/IP protocol stack used to provide connectionless, unreliable data delivery service. The other protocol is TCP, which provides connection-oriented, reliable data delivery service.

UFS UNIX file system; a file system based on the traditional UNIX file system known as the BSD fast file system, the default for Solaris.

ufsboot The secondary boot program located in the UFS file system on the default boot device. This program, loaded by the primary boot program `bootblk`, loads the kernel into the memory.

`ufsdump` A utility used to back up files.

`ufsrestore` A utility used to restore file systems that are backed up using the `ufsdump` command.

UID User ID; the required unique integer associated with a user name. The numbers from 0 to 99 are reserved for system accounts. Regular users should be assigned UIDs from 100 to 60,000, but they can go as high as the largest 32-bit signed positive number: 2147483647.

`umask` Defines the permissions on newly created files.

`umount` A command used to unmount a mounted file system or a remote resource.

`umountall` A command used to unmount all file systems specified in the `/etc/vfstab` file.

universal disk format *See* udf.

UNIX file system *See* UFS.

`useradd` A command used to create a new user account.

User Datagram Protocol *See* UDP.

`userdel` A command used to delete a user account from the system.

user ID *See* UID.

`usermod` A command used to modify existing user accounts.

`volcheck` A command used to check the accessibility of removable hard media such as a diskette and a removable hard disk.

volume A named chunk of disk space that can occupy a part of a disk or the whole disk; alternatively, it can span across multiple disks, which are called a disk set.

volume manager *See* SVM.

`who` A command used to display the users currently logged into a system.

`whoami` A command used to display the user name of the user on the current terminal.

World Wide Web An application on the Internet that involves web browsers and web servers and is based on HTTP. It is so popular that it has become synonymous with the Internet.

zone *See* Solaris zone.

`zoneadm` A command that can be used from the global zone to install and administer non-global zones.

`zoneadmd` The daemon that manages a zone, which includes booting and shutting down in addition to other tasks. If the daemon is not running for any reason, an invocation of the `zoneadm` command will start it.

`zonecfg` A utility used to set up the zone configuration, which includes creating and modifying the zone configuration.

INDEX

Page numbers for figures and tables are in italics.

A

B

E

F

G

K

L

M

O

Q

R

S

LICENSE AGREEMENT

THIS PRODUCT (THE "PRODUCT") CONTAINS PROPRIETARY SOFTWARE, DATA AND INFORMATION (INCLUDING DOCUMENTATION) OWNED BY THE McGRAW-HILL COMPANIES, INC. ("McGRAW-HILL") AND ITS LICENSORS. YOUR RIGHT TO USE THE PRODUCT IS GOVERNED BY THE TERMS AND CONDITIONS OF THIS AGREEMENT.

LICENSE: Throughout this License Agreement, "you" shall mean either the individual or the entity whose agent opens this package. You are granted a non-exclusive and non-transferable license to use the Product subject to the following terms:
(i) If you have licensed a single user version of the Product, the Product may only be used on a single computer (i.e., a single CPU). If you licensed and paid the fee applicable to a local area network or wide area network version of the Product, you are subject to the terms of the following subparagraph (ii).
(ii) If you have licensed a local area network version, you may use the Product on unlimited workstations located in one single building selected by you that is served by such local area network. If you have licensed a wide area network version, you may use the Product on unlimited workstations located in multiple buildings on the same site selected by you that is served by such wide area network; provided, however, that any building will not be considered located in the same site if it is more than five (5) miles away from any building included in such site. In addition, you may only use a local area or wide area network version of the Product on one single server. If you wish to use the Product on more than one server, you must obtain written authorization from McGraw-Hill and pay additional fees.
(iii) You may make one copy of the Product for back-up purposes only and you must maintain an accurate record as to the location of the back-up at all times.

COPYRIGHT; RESTRICTIONS ON USE AND TRANSFER: All rights (including copyright) in and to the Product are owned by McGraw-Hill and its licensors. You are the owner of the enclosed disc on which the Product is recorded. You may not use, copy, decompile, disassemble, reverse engineer, modify, reproduce, create derivative works, transmit, distribute, sublicense, store in a database or retrieval system of any kind, rent or transfer the Product, or any portion thereof, in any form or by any means (including electronically or otherwise) except as expressly provided for in this License Agreement. You must reproduce the copyright notices, trademark notices, legends and logos of McGraw-Hill and its licensors that appear on the Product on the back-up copy of the Product which you are permitted to make hereunder. All rights in the Product not expressly granted herein are reserved by McGraw-Hill and its licensors.

TERM: This License Agreement is effective until terminated. It will terminate if you fail to comply with any term or condition of this License Agreement. Upon termination, you are obligated to return to McGraw-Hill the Product together with all copies thereof and to purge all copies of the Product included in any and all servers and computer facilities.

DISCLAIMER OF WARRANTY: THE PRODUCT AND THE BACK-UP COPY ARE LICENSED "AS IS." McGRAW-HILL, ITS LICENSORS AND THE AUTHORS MAKE NO WARRANTIES, EXPRESS OR IMPLIED, AS TO THE RESULTS TO BE OBTAINED BY ANY PERSON OR ENTITY FROM USE OF THE PRODUCT, ANY INFORMATION OR DATA INCLUDED THEREIN AND/OR ANY TECHNICAL SUPPORT SERVICES PROVIDED HEREUNDER, IF ANY ("TECHNICAL SUPPORT SERVICES"). McGRAW-HILL, ITS LICENSORS AND THE AUTHORS MAKE NO EXPRESS OR IMPLIED WARRANTIES OF MERCHANTABILITY OR FITNESS FOR A PARTICULAR PURPOSE OR USE WITH RESPECT TO THE PRODUCT. McGRAW-HILL, ITS LICENSORS, AND THE AUTHORS MAKE NO GUARANTEE THAT YOU WILL PASS ANY CERTIFICATION EXAM WHATSOEVER BY USING THIS PRODUCT. NEITHER McGRAW-HILL, ANY OF ITS LICENSORS NOR THE AUTHORS WARRANT THAT THE FUNCTIONS CONTAINED IN THE PRODUCT WILL MEET YOUR REQUIREMENTS OR THAT THE OPERATION OF THE PRODUCT WILL BE UNINTERRUPTED OR ERROR FREE. YOU ASSUME THE ENTIRE RISK WITH RESPECT TO THE QUALITY AND PERFORMANCE OF THE PRODUCT.

LIMITED WARRANTY FOR DISC: To the original licensee only, McGraw-Hill warrants that the enclosed disc on which the Product is recorded is free from defects in materials and workmanship under normal use and service for a period of ninety (90) days from the date of purchase. In the event of a defect in the disc covered by the foregoing warranty, McGraw-Hill will replace the disc.

LIMITATION OF LIABILITY: NEITHER McGRAW-HILL, ITS LICENSORS NOR THE AUTHORS SHALL BE LIABLE FOR ANY INDIRECT, SPECIAL OR CONSEQUENTIAL DAMAGES, SUCH AS BUT NOT LIMITED TO, LOSS OF ANTICIPATED PROFITS OR BENEFITS, RESULTING FROM THE USE OR INABILITY TO USE THE PRODUCT EVEN IF ANY OF THEM HAS BEEN ADVISED OF THE POSSIBILITY OF SUCH DAMAGES. THIS LIMITATION OF LIABILITY SHALL APPLY TO ANY CLAIM OR CAUSE WHATSOEVER WHETHER SUCH CLAIM OR CAUSE ARISES IN CONTRACT, TORT, OR OTHERWISE. Some states do not allow the exclusion or limitation of indirect, special or consequential damages, so the above limitation may not apply to you.

U.S. GOVERNMENT RESTRICTED RIGHTS: Any software included in the Product is provided with restricted rights subject to subparagraphs (c), (1) and (2) of the Commercial Computer Software-Restricted Rights clause at 48 C.F.R. 52.227-19. The terms of this Agreement applicable to the use of the data in the Product are those under which the data are generally made available to the general public by McGraw-Hill. Except as provided herein, no reproduction, use, or disclosure rights are granted with respect to the data included in the Product and no right to modify or create derivative works from any such data is hereby granted.

GENERAL: This License Agreement constitutes the entire agreement between the parties relating to the Product. The terms of any Purchase Order shall have no effect on the terms of this License Agreement. Failure of McGraw-Hill to insist at any time on strict compliance with this License Agreement shall not constitute a waiver of any rights under this License Agreement. This License Agreement shall be construed and governed in accordance with the laws of the State of New York. If any provision of this License Agreement is held to be contrary to law, that provision will be enforced to the maximum extent permissible and the remaining provisions will remain in full force and effect.